John Austin Williams

Newark and Its Leading Business Men,

Embracing Also, Those of Harrison, Kearny, Belleville and Roseville

John Austin Williams

Newark and Its Leading Business Men,
Embracing Also, Those of Harrison, Kearny, Belleville and Roseville

ISBN/EAN: 9783337114503

Printed in Europe, USA, Canada, Australia, Japan

Cover: Foto ©Suzi / pixelio.de

More available books at **www.hansebooks.com**

NEWARK

AND ITS

LEADING

BUSINESS

MEN

NEWARK AND ITS POINTS OF INTEREST

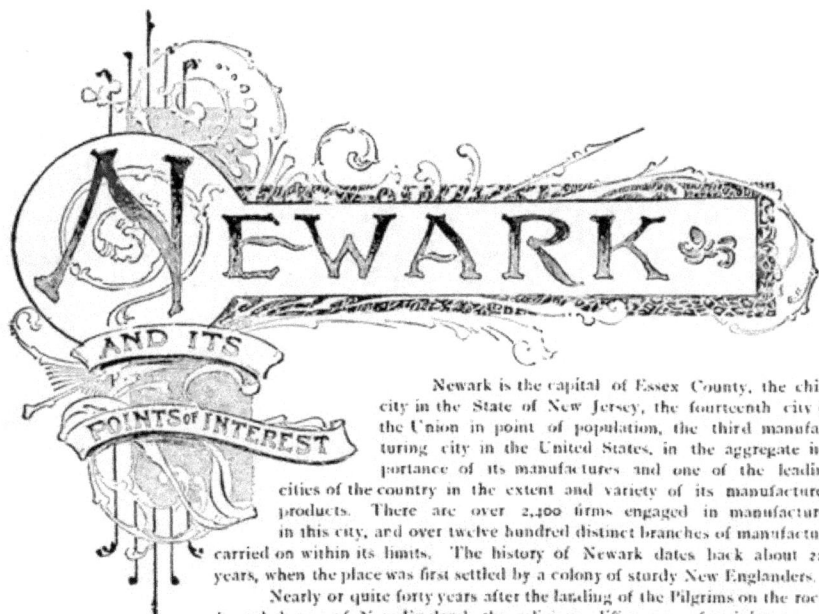

Newark is the capital of Essex County, the chief city in the State of New Jersey, the fourteenth city of the Union in point of population, the third manufacturing city in the United States, in the aggregate importance of its manufactures and one of the leading cities of the country in the extent and variety of its manufactured products. There are over 2,400 firms engaged in manufacture, in this city, and over twelve hundred distinct branches of manufacture carried on within its limits. The history of Newark dates back about 225 years, when the place was first settled by a colony of sturdy New Englanders.

Nearly or quite forty years after the landing of the Pilgrims on the rock-bound shores of New England, the religious differences of opinion among the colonists of Plymouth and adjacent settlements, had increased to such an extent, that it was thought best by some of the leading spirits of two of the towns of the colonies, that new fields should be occupied, and fuller opportunities given for the cultivation of religious thought and action. The New Netherlands, now known as New York, that had been discovered and occupied by the Dutch in the early part of the century, appeared in the judgment of the Puritans of New England, who were seeking for fresh fields and pasture new, to be best adapted for the planting and culture of that form of ecclesiastical polity known as the Congregational form of Church Government. The fame of the goodly land of the "Achter Kull," as the country that lay beyond the "Noordt River," as the Hudson river was then styled, had reached New England, and the settlers at Branford and Milford in Connecticut, appointed a committee to investigate the possibilities of founding a colony in this region of the "Achter Kull," beyond "Noordt River." A correspondence was opened between this committee and Petrus Stuyvesant, the then Governor General of the New Netherlands, which finally resulted in the settlement of "Our Towne on the Passayak." The committee made the following proposition to the Governor-General of the New Netherlands:

That if a church or churches of English shall be planted in the place propounded, they may be allowed by the Authoritie of the high and mighty Lords & States-General of the United Prvinces in the Netherlands, in Europe and with the approbation of the Bewindhebbers of the West India Companie to enjoy all such powers, priviledges and liberties in the Congregation allway as they have enjoyed them in New England, above twentie yeares paste without any disturbance Impedin't or Impositions of any other forms, orders or customs to be observed by them:

2nd That if the English Churches planted under the Dutch Government, shall consent to consociate for mutuall helpfullnes: They may be allowed by the Authorety & with the approbation aforesaid soe to doe, and to call a synod and then to establish by comon concent such orders according to scriptue as may be requisite for the suppressing of haeresies, schismes and false worships, and for the establshm't of

THE CENTRE MARKET ENTRANCE.

Truth wth peace in those English Churches. And that the Governor & Courts at New-Amsterdam shall protect the said English Churches and Synods from any that oppose them or be Injurious to them.

3d—The English planters doe desire that they may have Libertie and power by ye Authority & with ye approbation afoesaid to have the ordering of all Judicatore and of all their civell affaires within themselves, to chuse their owne magestrates and all other officers and constitute and keep Courts and make all such lawes and orders as they shall find most suitable to their condition and welfare in that place And that all persons, planters and others, for the time they are amongst them wthin their prcincts, shall be bound to acquiesce in all their laws, orders, sentences and appointmts of any of their owne Court or Courts and officers determinaltely according to such orders and lawss as are or shall be from time to time agreed upon & ennacted by them and unto their sentencess made & verdicts declared without appeales to Any Other Authority or jurisdiction. This power the English in America within New England have had and exercised in all cauces by the grannt of the late King of England, Charles the First, as is to be seen in his majestie's letters pattent about twentie years to-gether. And it is much more necessary that they have it under the Dutch (whose lawes they know not nor understand their language, and the way and manner of their exercising this their sole power.) We purpose according to the fundamentalls received in New Haven Collonie wch are in print to be seen (or the most of them) so far as we shall find it will alike suite Christs' ends and oru conditions there.

4—That all the lands agreed for be clearly and undeniably purchassed of the Indians by an Athentik Instrum't or Instrum'ts, and that wee may have one of them in our custody, and that the hands

NORTHWEST CORNER BROAD AND MARKET STREET.

of those Indians that have ye naturall and civill sight be subscribed and soe owned by them in the pres-ence of English, Dutch and Indians, as lawfully bought and sould, and that then these lands shall be made ye prpr Inheritance of the English Planters, and their posteritie for ever by the Authoritie and pow'r with the approbation afoesaid according to all prsent and future orders, graunts and agreem'ts or devisions of all soch lands so bought as shall be made by the English alone amongst them themselves by pr'sons Intrusted and empowerd by them for such affaires.

5—That noe Inhabitants be put upon by the Dutch, but that we have the sole power of disposeing our lands and entertaineing or rejecting all Inhabitants according to agreemts that shall from time to time amongst ourselves.

6—That the English Planters in the aforesaid places by Authoritie, and with approbation aforesaid, may have equal liberties of tradeing with the Duch in all respects, they paying all lawfull dues and customs as the Duch do, or wth any other whomsoever.

7—Our humble desire is the pr'mies being granted by those in Holland or to whom the Pattent and power of such grants appertaineth may be declared and ratified by an Authenticall Instrum't signed and sealed by the Pattentees in Europe, if it remaines with them.   And that a coppie of it so signed and

NORTHEAST CORNER BROAD AND MARKET STREET.

sealed and Authentically Attested may be procured for the English Planted under the Duch, to be by them kept among their publique Records for ye benefit of Posteritie.

The Director-General and Council of the New Netherlands, agreed to the first two propositions and also to the third, with certain modifications.   The fourth and sixth propositions were granted, and it was stated in regard to the fifth proposition, that none of the towns in the New Netherlands are "troubled with Inhabitance, the which doe not Lyke her or her Magistrates.

The outcome of these negotiations was that in the Spring of 1666, two diminutive vessels after carefully passing from the harbor of New York, through the Kill von Cull, and into Newark bay, ascended the Pasaic river and landed their passengers on the shore of that river, where the city of Newark now stands.   On the 23d and 24th of June, 1664, the Duke of York had transferred what now constitutes New

Jersey to Lords Berkley and Carteret. Philip Carteret, a nephew of Lord Carteret, was appointed Governor, and on arriving in New Jersey, took up his residence in Elizabeth. The Governor dispatched messengers to New England, who made known to the colonists there the fact that they would be welcome to New Jersey, and would receive civil and religious privileges no where excelled. Tradition has it that the colony which came from Milford numbered about thirty persons, male and female. A treaty was made on the 21st of May 1666 with the Indians by which the land on which Newark stands was purchased. The Indian bill of sale sets forth that Wapamuck and Wanvesene, Peter Captamni, Weeaprokikan, Napsann, Pesawae, Lessom, Mamustome, Cacanakque and Harish, Indians belonging now to Hakinsae the proprietors of a certain tract of land lying on the west of Pesayak river, sell to Obadiah Buen, Samuel Ketchell, Michael Tompkins, John Browne and Robert Denison, "a certain tract of Land, Upland and Meadows of all sorts, Wether Swamps, Rivers, Brooks, Springs, Fishings, Trees of all sorts Quaries and Mines, or meatals of what sort soever, With full liberty of hunting and fishing upon the same, excepting Liberty of hunting for the above said proprietors that were upon the upper common, and of fishing in the above said Pesayak River, which said tract of Land is bounded and Limited with the bay Eastward and the great River Pesayak, Northward, the great Creke or River, in the meadow running to the head of the Cove, and from thence bareing a West line for the South bounds, wh said Great Creek is commonly called, and known by the name Weequachick, on the West Line backwards in the Country to the foot of the great mountaine called Watchung, being as is Judged about seven or eight miles from Pesayak towne, the said Mountaine as Wee are Informed, hath one branch of Elizabeth towne River running near the above said foot of the Mountaine; the bunds Northerly, viz: Pesayak river reaches to the Third River above the towne, ye river is called Yauntakah, and from thence upon a North West line to the aforesaid Mountaine." The deed also sets forth that "these lands are thus sold and delivered for and in consideration of fifty double hands of powder, one hundred barres of lead, twenty axes, twenty Cates, ten Guns, twenty Pistolls, ten Kettles, ten Swords, four blankets, four barrels of beere, ten paire of breeches, fifty knives, twenty howes, eight hundred and fifty fathem of wampen, two Ankors of Licquers, or something Equivolent, and three troopers Coates."

An extract from the original towne records of Newark sets forth that on the 21st day of May, 1666, at a meeting of persons from Milford, Guilford and Branford it is agreed to make one township according to fundamentals mutually agreed upon, and that they desire to be of one heart, and concent that through God's blessing, they may endeavor the carrying on of spiritual concernments as also civil and town affairs, according to God and a godly government. The settlers chose Captain Robert Treatt, Lieut. Samuel Swain, Mr. Samuel Kitchell, Michael Tompkins, Mr. Morris, Sergt. Richard Beekly Richard Harrison, Thomas Blatchly, Edward Riggs, Stephen Freeman and Thomas Johnson, a committee to manage their affairs. It was noted "That none shall be admitted freemen or free Burgesses within our Towne upon Passaick River in the province of New Jersey, but such planters as are members of some or other of the Congregational Churches, nor shall any but such be chosen to Magistracy or Carry on any part of Civil Judicature or as deputies or assistants to have power to Vote in establishing Laws and making or repealing them, or to any chief Military Trust or Office. Nor shall any but such Church Members have any Vote in any such elections; Tho' all others admitted to Be planters shall have Right to their proper Inheritance, and do and shall enjoy all other Civil Liberties and Privileges, According to all Laws, Orders, Grants, which are or hereafter shall be made for this Towne."

"The towne on the Passaick" as at first laid out was planned with but little reference to regularity or symmetry, and the courses of the principal streets were probably made to conform to the surface of the land, and frequently Indian trails were followed. The early settlers made most liberal provision for future public needs. They builded even better than they knew. Broad street, Market street, Washington street, Military, Washington, and South (now Lincoln Park) were all laid out by the early fathers or their descendants. What is now known as Military Park was then known as the training ground. What is now Washington Park was then known as the Market Place, and where Market street now is was once the public watering place. The settlers acquired from the Indians by various purchases a tract of land which included all the territory now embraced in the limits of Newark, Belleville, Bloomfield, Montclair, Caldwell and the Oranges.

The community was emphatically a Christian one ; the original proprietors of the soil brought with them from Connecticut a politico-religious system of government then common in New England, and for more than a century the town and church were one.   The regulation of the material affairs of the church planted by the early settlers, now known as the First Presbyterian Church, was the business of the towns-people, even to the calling of the Minister, the fixing of his compensation and the raising of means for his support.   For years the history of the town and the church were one, and, therefore, much of that early history will be omitted here and reference will be made to it later on in speaking of the First Presby-terian Church.

SOUTHWEST CORNER BROAD AND MARKET STREET.

During the Revolutionary War the people of Newark were noted for the vigor and the patriotism with which they espoused the cause of the colonies against the crown.   The town contributed a liberal quota of its citizens to the the patriot army, and bore its share in the struggles of Princeton, Trenton, Monmouth and Springfield.   Newark was frequently overrun during the war by the contending armies, and there are houses standing in Newark and its vicinity to-day in which the traces of British bullets can be plainly seen.   It is impossible within the limits of a work of this kind to do justice to the early days of Newark, and we have simply undertaken to give a brief outline of that period, in order to show on what a solid and substantial basis "the towne on the Passaick," which has now grown to the great city of Newark with its 200,000 inhabitants, its vast business enterprises and varied industries was established.

A map of the "Towne of New-Ark in the State of New Jersey," published in 1806, shows the population of the city to be confined principally to Broad, Washington, Market, Mulberry and High streets, and a birds-eye view of the city east of Mulberry street published in 1820 shows only a few straggling farmhouses, while now this part of the city is built up solidly with large factories employing thousands of hands and with neat and comfortable homes of well to do mechanics, clerks and others.

By an act of the State Legislature passed February 6, 1833, the township of Newark was divided into four wards known as the North, South, East and West wards. The first annual meeting in each ward was held in the lecture room of a church in the ward, and the influence of church methods of government was still apparent from the fact that the principal officer of each ward was known by the title of Moderator. The first Moderators elected were: East Ward, Joseph C Hornblower, afterwards Chief Justice of New Jersey; West Ward, William Pennington, afterwards Governor of New Jersey; South Ward, Asa Whitehead, one of New Jersey's most eminent lawyers; North Ward, Thomas Ward, a man prominent in affairs of church and State. Newark was chartered as a city in 1836, its first Mayor being William Halsey and its second Theodore Frelinghuysen, who was once a candidate for Vice-President of the United States, on the same ticket with Henry Clay. Among others who have held the office of Mayor of Newark may be mentioned, Oliver L. Halstead, afterwards Chancellor of New Jersey; William Wright, subsequently a United States Senator, Beach Vanderpool, James M. Quimby, Horace J. Ponier, Moses Bigelow, Thomas B. Peddie, Nehemiah Perry, Henry J. Yates and Henry Lang, all of whom were men occupying important positions in the business community. Another Mayor was Theodore Runyon, afterwards Chancellor of New Jersey and one of the most distinguished lawyers of the State of New Jersey.

During the Revolutionary War, Newark and its vicinity suffered severely from the ravages of war. When the struggle broke out, both Newark and Elizabeth were flourishing places, and the homes of thrifty, and even wealthy people. The well-stocked farms of this vicinity were a tempting foraging ground for the troops of King George, who were stationed in New York, and that they appreciated the advantages of this section is evident from the early records of the town, and from the traditions of the old families. The outrages to which the inhabitants were subjected during the war have never been fully described. One very memorable instance is frequently alluded to by the descendants of one of the principal actors even to this day. On the evening of January 25, 1780, a series of outrages were perpetrated, when a regiment of 500 red-coats, under the command of Major Lum, crossed over the Hudson river on the ice, from Newark to Paulus Hook, now Jersey City, and marched out to Newark. At the same time a smaller body of men crossed from Staten Island to Elizabethtown. Lum's men, on reaching Newark, committed a series of outrages, among which were the robbery of private houses, and the pillaging of stores and barns, and the wanton destruction of much property. They burned the Academy, a fine two-story stone building, situated on the Upper Green, now Washington Park. Meanwhile their colleagues in Elizabethtown, who had been conducting themselves in a similar manner, set fire to the First Presbyterian Church there, and the light of the burning building, which could be plainly seen in Newark, was mistaken by Lum and his men for a demonstration of the Americans, and they beat a hasty retreat from Newark. Before leaving, however, they visited the home of Colonel Joseph Hedden, Jr., one of the most prominent patriots of the city, and a Commissioner for the County of Essex of the State Council of Public Safety, with the intention of capturing him, and taking him a prisoner to New York. Mr. Hedden's house stood on Broad street, near Lombardy, and when the British soldiers visited it Colonel Hedden was sick in bed. He was dragged from his bed by the soldiers, who tried to take him into the street in his night clothes, although the night was intensely cold. Mrs. Hedden tried to prevent this, and essayed to get her husband decently clothed. In doing so she was severely cut by the bayonets of the British soldiers. Meanwhile the soldiers carried Colonel Hedden off with little or no clothing on, and marched him at the point of the bayonet down what is now Centre street, and along the river to the Plank Road, and thence to Paulus Hook, and across the ice to New York. Colonel Hedden was thrown into the Sugar House Prison, where, in consequence of the terrible exposure and the rough treatment he had received, he became ill, his legs froze and mortified, and when it became evident that he could not possibly recover, his brothers were allowed to bring him back to Newark. He died on the 27th of September. His remains were interred in the Old Burying Ground. The British did not restrict their plundering to the patriots, but they robbed the houses of Tories also.

One dark wintry night toward the close of the war, Captain John Kidney, Captain Henry Joralemon, Jacob Garland and Halmach Joralemon, started from their homes in Bloomfield, which was then a part of Newark, with the bold project of capturing a British garrison that was stationed at Bergen Heights. A pair of swift horses and an old-fashioned farm sledge furnished them with means of transportation. On arriving in the vicinity of the garrison they learned that the officers and men were having a frolic in the school house. They surrounded the place, Captain Kidney making a great noise as he did so, as though he were manœuvering a large body of men. He then sprang to the door, forced it open and shouted, "You are all my prisoners, surrender or die." His comrades crowded around the door with their bayonets, and the British, supposing they were surrounded by a large body of patriots, promptly surrendered. They were directed to come out of the school house one by one, and as each stepped out he was bound and gagged, and huddled upon the sled. When the party had been secured, Captain Kidney and

MARKET STREET, FROM MINER'S THEATRE, LOOKING WEST.

his associates mounted their sled and drove their prisoners to the Irvington jail, where they were locked up.

Among the patriot families of Newark were the Allings, Balls, Baldwins, Beaches, Bruens, Burnets, Camps, Condits, Cranes, Coes, Heddens, MacWhorters, Meekers, Penningtons and Wheelers. All of these families had members who distinguished themselves in the patriot army, and in the councils of the Federalists. Newark, at the breaking out of the Revolutionary War, had a population of about 1,000, but the war crippled the place and kept back its growth considerably for years ; in fact, Newark grew very slowly for a long time.

THE NEWARK OF TO-DAY.

It is with the Newark of to-day, that this book is chiefly concerned, and the preceding brief review of the early history of the city has been given to enable the reader the better to understand and appreciate, not only the broad and far-sighted policy of the thrifty and God-fearing men who laid the foundations of the town, but, also, to realize into what mighty proportions has grown the structure they began to build. "Our towne on ye Passaick" has grown to be the great city of Newark, with its 200,000 population, its miles of streets stretching out in all directions towards its suburbs, and built up so solidly with houses, stores and factories, that, standing on the Orange Mountain and looking down upon the surrounding country, Newark seems to be one great city, stretching out from the Passaic River on the east to the Orange Mountains on the West, and from the fertile valleys of Waverly on the south to the

THE MARKET STREET STATION, PENN. R. R.

heights of the surrounding townships on the north, and it is hard to tell where Newark ends, and the townships begin. It is only of late years, however, that the Newarkers themselves have begun to awake to a realization of what their city really is, and of its magnificent possibilities for the future. For years there was an impression prevailing not only in the minds of men of other cities, but of Newarkers themselves, that Newark was simply a sort of workshop for New York, and that there were but little advantages in the place to make it an attractive residence. Indeed, twenty years ago, Newark was anything but an attractive place. Providence, it is true, had done much for the place in the way of scenery, giving it a beautiful river along its entire eastern and south-eastern front, a river which such writers as Irving, Poe, Frank Forrester, and Halleck delighted to praise, a rolling country composed of hill and valley, that suggested to the lover of nature grand possibilities for laying out a beautiful city, and to the sanitary engineer superb opportunities for drainage and sewerage. The early settlers had laid out the town in a manner that afforded great possibilities for its future development, but their descendants had grown careless of their glorious heritage.

Along about 1870 a few active and progressive men arose in the community and tried to make Newarkers realize that their city was something more than an overgrown country village, and that laying

out of streets, building of sewers, and other city improvements were needed. The community was awakened and improvements were begun, but as in the case of many other municipalities, improvements ran mad for want of proper men to control them. Streets were laid out in pasture lands where they would not be needed for

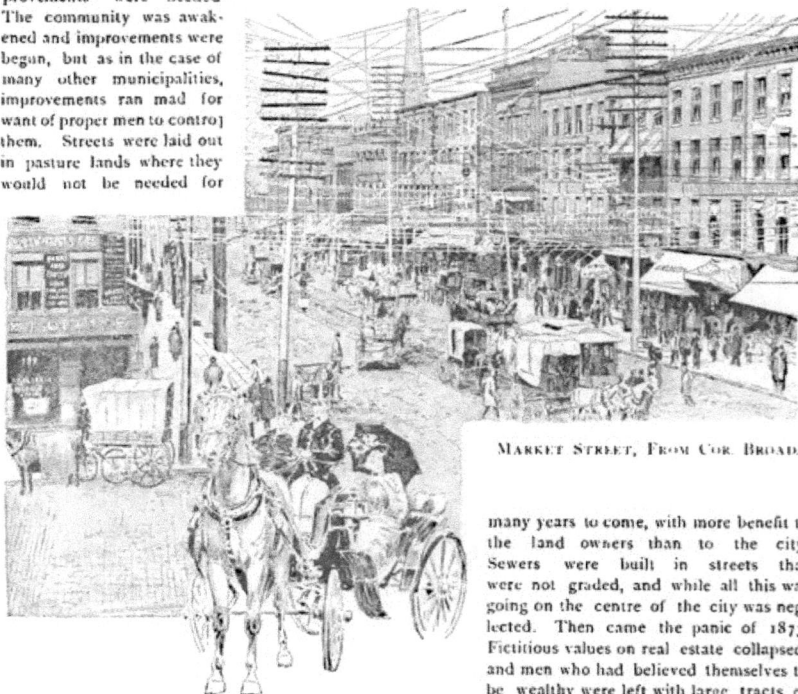

MARKET STREET, FROM COR. BROAD.

many years to come, with more benefit to the land owners than to the city. Sewers were built in streets that were not graded, and while all this was going on the centre of the city was neglected. Then came the panic of 1873. Fictitious values on real estate collapsed, and men who had believed themselves to be wealthy were left with large tracts of land on their hands which they could hardly give away, if the gift carried with it the assumption of the taxes and assessments on the land. So great was this burden that only a few years ago a law had to be passed for the adjustment of these taxes and assessments, and many people are only now out of the troubles into which this wild speculation plunged them. These circumstances put a stop to street improvements for many years, and is one of the main reasons why the streets of the city are not better paved. The growth of the city, however, continued slowly but surely, notwithstanding all these drawbacks.

It was the great Industrial Exposition of 1872, '73 and '74 that really aroused, not only the country at large, but the people of Newark themselves to a sense of what Newark really was. Messrs. George A.

Halsey, A. M. Holbrook and a few other enterprising citizens conceived the idea of giving an exposition of the manufactured products of Newark. They formed a corporation known as the Newark Industrial Institute, secured a building which was formerly an old skating rink, erected an addition to it, and assembled in it the products of Newark's work shops. There was machinery of every description, tools, hardware, cutlery, leather and all its products, trunks, bags, boots and shoes, elegant jewelry, saddlery and harness, celluloid, gems from the lapidary's hands, and in short, almost every article which is in daily use. Thousands flocked to the exposition each year, and this exhibit did more to advertise Newark abroad, and to arouse the local pride of its citizens than anything that was ever done before or since. Soon after this the Board of Trade began to bestir itself in the matter of improvements, and a few spasmodic efforts were made to stimulate a spirit of progress. But it is only within the past few years that Newark has really begun to develop.

The growth of Newark within the last five years has been most remarkable. Property on Broad street, near Market, now sells for $3,000 a foot, and all along that street it brings thousands, where it

THE COURT HOUSE.

brought hundreds a few years ago. Old rookeries are being torn down, and are giving place to new and elegant structures of massive proportions and imposing architecture. The new buildings of the post office and the Prudential Insurance Company, which are in course of construction, together with the buildings of Heath & Drake, the Fidelity Title and Deposit Company, the Liverpool and London and Globe Insurance Company, Wilkinson, Gaddis & Company on Broad street, the new station of the Pennsylvania Railroad Company on Market street, the many handsome structures on Market, Mulberry and Mechanic streets, Railroad, Springfield, Belmont and Central avenues, the handsome residences along South Broad and High streets, at Military and Washington parks, Mount Prospect and Mount Pleasant avenues, are all combining to give Newark a metropolitan appearance. A new water supply is about to be introduced at a cost of $6,000,000, a new court house to cost $1,000,000 is projected, a public park is under consideration, and an extensive tract of land has already been set apart for that purpose. Active

measures are in progress by the Board of Trade to build a hotel large enough to accommodate the pros-
pective increase of Newark. Handsome bridges span the river. Four fine hospitals and a large number of
charitable institutions and churches attest the philanthropic and religious character of its people. On
Military Park stands the statue of New Jersey's greatest soldier, the gallant Major-General Philip
Kearny, who fell at the head of his troops in the late war. On Washington Park is the statue of an
humble son of toil, Seth Boyden, the inventor, who did more for Newark's industries than any man who
has ever lived in the place, and who yet lived and died a poor man. On Lincoln Park is to be reared a
statue of Frederick T. Frelinghuysen, New Jersey's most distinguished statesman. A free public library
with thousands of volumes and a noble building has been established on West Park street. A large

BROAD STREET NEAR SOUTH PARK.

technical school where young men are prepared for active life in Newark's factories as skilled mechanics
has been in successful operation for several years, and the school is soon to have a large and well appointed building on High street. The public school system of Newark is the best in the State. Its fire
department is admittedly one of the best in the Union. The city has an excellent police department. The
financial institutions are sound and prosperous, and her business men, wise, conservative and prudent.
The health of the city is good, the death rate low, and the various branches of the city government are
well and economically administered.

    The city has fourteen banks, Savings and National, of excellent character and stability, with a bank-
ing capital of about $18,000,000. It has one hundred wholesale jewelry manufacturing firms, the products of

whose factories are unrivalled as to quality.   There are eighty-five wholesale manufacturers of leather, in its various forms, whose products are distributed over the United States, Europe, Canada and other countries.   There are fifteen wholesale manufacturers of novelties of various kinds, whose products are widely known and distributed.   There are 100 machinists, tool manufacturers and mechanical engineers ; fifty wholesale hardware manufacturing firms ; sixty wholesale harness and harness trimming manufacturers, eighteen wholesale grocers, one of them selling over $5,000,000 annually ; sixty carriage makers, wholesale manufacturers of carriage hardware and kindred articles ; eighteen large button manufacturers ; twenty-three brass goods makers and founders ; twenty-four wholesale boot and shoe manufacturers ; twenty-one manufacturers of varnish, one of whom conducts the largest business of the kind in the country ; thirty-four saddlery hardware manufacturing concerns ; forty tool makers ; twenty manufacturers of trunks, travelling bags, etc.; twenty-four brewing establishments, with very large capital, which bear favorable comparison with any in the United States.

In the City, and directly across the river in Hudson County, are located the famous Clark Thread Works, and near them in Hudson County, the Mile End Works, the Marshall Thread Works and the Linoleum Works, all comprising a vast body of capital, and employing labor to an enormous extent.   The Domestic Sewing Machine Company's works are also located in the city, with its extensive factory and business.   Within the city limits, on the Passaic River are the Great Lister Agricultural Works, already one of the most important in its field of business, and just now in process of consolidation and enlargement.   The Atha and the Illingworth Steel Works, Babcock's Smelting and Refining Works, surpassed by none in the United States.

Newark also maintains fine theatres, many large wholesale and retail houses, and all the establishments suited to a large city.   Newarkers no longer admit that their city is in any sense a mere appendage of New York or simply its workshop.   They have discovered that near as they are to the great metropolis they still have a great and prosperous city of their own, which is a credit and honor to the great State of New Jersey, a prosperous and vigorous community, with an intelligent, orderly and thrifty population, engaged in wide and varied industries, and whose business men and financial institutions have a credit that is unsurpassed by that of any city of the Union.

The principal streets of the city are already lighted with electricity, and a spirit of progress is manifesting itself throughout the entire community.

For convenience of description, Newark may be said to be divided into six sections, each having a distinctive character of its own.   One is the heart of the city, which is composed of the central or inner wards, and is the older portion of the town.   This contains all the financial institutions, the leading business houses and the majority of the fashionable residences.   Another is the section east of the Pennsylvania Railroad, the more eastern portion of which is frequently called "the neck."   The entire section east of the Pennsylvania Railroad is also known as the "Iron Bound District."   Here are situated some of the largest of Newark's factories, as well as the homes of thousands of her operatives and laboring classes. A few years ago a very large section of "the neck" was almost entirely devoted to truck farms, and indeed, there are several flourishing truck farms yet, but land is fast getting to be too valuable to be used for this purpose and these farms are rapidly disappearing.

The opening of the Newark and New York Railroad, now a branch of the Central, and of the Manufacturers' Railroad, a branch of the same system, did much to develop this section, and to convert truck farms into closely built up streets and sites of vast manufacturing establishments.   The new branches that are being built by the Pennsylvania and Lehigh Valley Railroads will tend to develop this section still further.   The three wards embraced within this territory have a population of 40,961, with a taxable valuation of $16,509,455.00, though the actual value of property there is probably twice as much.

"The Hill," by which name is designated those portions of the Sixth and Thirteenth wards, occupying the elevated ground west of High street, is distinctively the German section of the city.   The evidence of the thrift, industry and intelligence of the population are apparent on every side.   This is notably a settlement of small homes.   In this section are also some large business establishments, including several tanneries, and six large breweries, one of which was recently sold to an English syndicate for $3,000,000.

Here are the principal parks, where the Germans of the city are wont to have their Summer festivities, and the halls in which they hold their meetings and Winter festivities. There are a number of large and handsome churches of all denominations here and several orphanages and charitable institutions.

The Eighth ward, which comprises the northern end of the city, beginning at Eighth avenue, and running north to the Second river, which is the dividing line between Newark and Belleville, is one of the most rapidly developing sections of the city. In point of size of territory it is the largest ward in Newark, and in population and wealth it is also one of the chief wards of the city. Its eastern boundary is the Passaic river, and its western and north-western, the canal, East Orange and Bloomfield. No part of Newark has had such a remarkable growth as has the Eighth ward within the last few years. Whole tracts, that five or six years ago were farm lands, are to-day laid out in broad avenues, built up with tasteful homes, and property is increasing in value, at a ratio far beyond that of any other portion of the city. The ward in itself would make a very respectable city, with its fine streets, the majority of which are well lighted and sewered, and arrangements have been made for paving the principal streets with Belgian block, asphalt or Telford. This ward embraces the flourishing settlement of Woodside, which was once a township by itself, but about twenty years ago was annexed to Newark. It also includes Forest Hill, which is a large and rapidly developing portion of the ward. Within the limits of the ward are four large and well appointed public schools, two of them having buildings that are regarded as among the fines educational structures in the city. There are also twelve churches, of which the Presbyterians have four-the Episcopalians two, the Roman Catholics two, the Methodists one, the Baptists one, the Reformed one and the Congregationalists one. In this ward are situated the extensive works of the Clark Thread Co., large stone works and quarries, and an extensive watch case factory. The manufacturing business, however, is principally confined to that section of the city along the river front, and the ward is pre-eminently a place of residence. Here are the homes of some of Newark's most wealthy and influential citizens. Mount Prospect and Clifton avenues, which occupy the loftiest ground in the ward, running, as they do, along the summit of a commanding hill, afford a superb view of the surrounding country for miles in every direction. On the former avenue is the residence of William Clark, one of the hand, somest and most costly in Essex county. On Clifton avenue a large tract of land has been secured by the Roman Catholic Church, for the erection of a superb cathedral in future years. Among the notable buildings in the ward are the North End Club House, an imposing three story brick structure, on the corner of Broad street and Third avenue, the building of Marcus L. Ward Post, G. A. R., on Belleville avenue, the Park Presbyterian, Centenary M. E., Belleville Avenue Congregational, and Mount Pleasant Baptist churches, and the Franklin Public School. Here also is the Low Service Reservoir, from which the greater part of Newark is supplied with water, and around which is to be formed the new public park The ward is admirably supplied with facilities for reaching the heart of the city, and also with communi-cation with New York. Two lines of horse cars already traverse the ward, and another is in course of construction, while three steam railroads connect this section with the metropolis. In this ward is located the building and extensive grounds of the Riverside Athletic Club, one of the leading clubs of the kind in New Jersey. Here, too, is situated Mount Pleasant Cemetery, the most beautiful place of sepulture in the country. In this ward are located two of Newark's leading charitable institutions, the Protestant Foster Home and the Home for Respectable Aged Women. The former is a massive four-story brick building, on the corner of Belleville avenue and Van Wagenen street. It gives shelter to about 100 chil-dren who otherwise would be homeless, and is undenominational in its work. Its Board of Managers is composed of the leading society ladies of the city, and it is the favorite charity of the town. The other institution, which is usually known as the "Old Ladies' Home," is a handsome brick building on Broad street, near Gouverneur street. It has ample grounds, and among its managers are some of the most prominent ladies of the city. St. Michael's Roman Catholic Church also has a large and flourish-ing parochial school, which is situated in a large brick building on Belleville avenue.

NEWARK'S AVENUES AND STREETS.

The date of the laying out of the first roads in Newark is involved in considerable obscurity, but certain it is, that Broad, Market and Washington streets were among the first laid out by the early settlers. The oldest map of the town on record shows Broad street from Mill Brook (near where Clay street now is), to Lincoln Park, Mulberry street, Washington street from Washington Park (then the public market place), to Clinton avenue, High street about as it now is, Market street from the public dock to the hill back of where the Court House now stands, three or four cross streets south of Market street, from roads leading from the town in a westerly direction, one of which is now Orange street, another following the line of Warren street, and the old Crane road at Roseville. Another short street followed the line of Centre street to the river. The first record of a road laid out by the Commissioners of Highways, to be found in the Essex County Road Book, is dated December 3, 1698, and relates to a

road in Elizabethtown, which was then a part of Essex county. The first legally laid road from Elizabeth to Newark, was laid out in August, 1705. High street was laid out as a legal road in 1709, although it had been in

HIGH STREET.

CORNER CLINTON AVENUE AND HIGH STREET.

existence years before. About 1717, several roads were laid out on the "Neck," and to the meadows, to enable farmers to get in their salt hay. There are now streets built up with large and important factories. The Newark and Pompton Turnpike Company was incorporated on February 24, 1806. Its road ran from North Broad street, now Belleville avenue, in a northwesterly direction to Bloomfield and Cranstown, now Montclair, thence over the First Mountain, through Caldwell to Pompton Plains. This road is now Bloomfield avenue, and is under the care of the Essex County Road Board, within the limits of the county. The Newark and Morristown turnpike followed the line of South Orange avenue, and was laid out as a turnpike in 1811, although the greater part of the road had been in existence many years before.

The streets of Newark were in a wretched condition for many years, and, in fact, many of them are now sadly in need of decent pavements. There are people living in Newark to-day who can remember the time when Broad street was such a slough that a mud scow was run upon it to carry people to and fro. Within the last few years, however, there has been an awakening in Newark on the subject of paving, and the Common Council now puts into the tax levy $50,000 a year for this purpose. In addition to this, the Legislature of 1890 passed a law, authorizing the Common Council to issue bonds for street paving, and in a short time the principal streets of Newark will all be well paved.

SOUTHWEST CORNER HIGH AND SPRUCE STREETS.

The principal roads leading out from Newark to its suburbs are all fine, broad avenues, paved with Telford pavement, and are in charge of the Essex County Road Board. This board had its origin in the far-sighted public spirit of Llewellyn S. Haskell, the founder of Llewellyn Park, West Orange Some years after he had completed that beautiful park, Mr. Haskell conceived the idea of making all Essex county one grand park, with Newark as a centre. His idea was to take the principal thoroughfares leading out from Newark, grade and pave them so as to make easy and pleasant drives, and then connect them by lateral roads. In pursuance of this plan, Mr. Haskell procured from the Legislature of 1868, a law incorporating the Essex Public Road Board. The first members of the board were Llewellyn S. Haskell, William H. Murphy and Francis McGrath. The law was found to be defective, and a supplement was passed in 1869, increasing the number of Commissioners to five. The first Commissioners so appointed were A. Bishop Baldwin, of South Orange, William H. Murphy, of Newark, Jesse Williams, of Orange, George Peters, of Newark, and Robert M. Henning, of Montclair. Mr. Murphy soon resigned, and Mr. Timothy W. Lord, of Newark, was appointed in his place. To these five gentlemen is really due the credit of having laid out and paved the magnificent system of county roads in charge of the Road Board, which, with the many fine streets laid out in the Oranges, Bloomfield and Montclair, form

HIGH STREET, CORNER COLLEGE PLACE, LOOKING NORTH.

in Essex county a system of drives that is unequalled anywhere in the vicinity of New York. The avenues in charge of the Road Board are, Frelinghuysen avenue, extending from Astor street, Newark, to Elizabeth; Springfield avenue, from the Court House in Newark, through Irvington, South Orange and Milburn, to the Morris county line; South Orange avenue, from Springfield avenue, Newark, through South Orange, and up to the county line; Central avenue, from Broad street, Newark, to the Valley road, West Orange; Park avenue, running from Bloomfield avenue, Newark, to Llewellyn Park, West Orange; Bloomfield avenue, from Belleville avenue, Newark, to the county line in Caldwell and Washington avenue, from Belleville avenue, Newark, through Belleville and Franklin to Passaic county. The cost of these avenues to the county was $1,600,000, for which bonds were issued of which $220,000 are still outstanding. These avenues cover a total distance of thirty-five miles and the cost of their maintenance in the year ending May, 1890, was as follows: Frelinghuysen avenue, $1,390.72; Springfield avenue, $3,116.55; South Orange avenue, $6,147.82; Central avenue, $3,313.90; Park avenue, $759.45; Bloomfield avenue, $6,761.17; Washington avenue, $2,404. The Road Board is now under the control of the Board of Freeholders of the county, its members being appointed by the Director of that board from among the members of the latter Board. The present members of that board are: President, Francis McGuinness; James Peck, of East Orange; Cornelius Learey, Owen Cahill, and Thomas W. Kinsey.

MILITARY PARK AND PARK PLACE.

Skirting the northern and eastern side of Military Park is Park place, for many years one of the most fashionable places of residence in Newark. At the extreme northern end is the residence of Mr. H. W. Symington, the treasurer of the Marshall Linen Thread Company, formerly the Dodd mansion. Next to it is Trinity church rectory, looking out on the memorable old mother church of the Episcopalians of Newark, and the park opposite. Adjoining this is the elegant mansion of the late Thomas B. Peddie, twice mayor of Newark, twice a member of the State Legislature and twice a member of Congress, to whose munificence the superb structure of the Peddie Memorial Baptist Church is due. East of this stands the residence of Mr. A. Pennington Whitehead, one of Newark's leading citizens; beyond this in that large, square frame house with its ample grounds, center a score of memories precious to Newarkers proud of Newark's famous sons. There lived the venerable and beloved Theodore Frelinghuysen, one of New Jersey's greatest men, who was ever foremost in her councils and who ran for Vice-President of the United States on the ticket that was honored by the name of Henry Clay for President. Where in later years lived his illustrious nephew, Frederick T. Frelinghuysen, for several years a United States Senator from New Jersey, and afterwards Secretary of State. Through its portals was carried to its last resting place the form of that silver-tongued orator, followed

BROAD STREET, OPPOSITE MILITARY PARK.

by an ex-President and a President of the United States and a host of noted and famous dignitaries, who vied with each other in paying the last tributes of respect to New Jersey's noblest statesman. The house is now occupied by the Senator's oldest son, Frederick Frelinghuysen, who is the president of the Howard Savings Institution, and one of the most deservedly popular young men in Newark. Beyond the Frelinghuysen mansion is the Wright mansion, formerly tenanted by William Wright, United States Senator from New Jersey, and now in the possession of his son, Col. Edward H. Wright. On the corner of Park Place and Centre street is the home of the late James M. Quinby, a former mayor of Newark, and one of her most celebrated citizens, now occupied by his son-in-law Counsellor Charles Borcherling. Beyond this is the Peter Duryee mansion, then the Joel W. Condit manor house, then

the old Benedict homestead, the house of ex-Mayor Yates, every one of which houses calls up a train of
memories that Newarkers love to bring to mind.   Further on the west are the buildings of John Illingworth, one of the leading steel manufacturers of the nation, Stephen H. Condit, a leading business
man, then the old Halsey mansion, and next the residence of Mr. James C. McDonald.

Broad street is the principal street of Newark, and is one of the finest thoroughfares in the country, in respect to its great width and magnificent trees which line it on either side.   It also contains many
handsome residences of the wealthiest men in Newark, the principal stores, the banks, insurance offices

EAST SIDE BROAD STREET, AND FIRST PRESBYTERIAN CHURCH.

and other financial institutions, the two leading newspaper offices, and the principal churches.   It
runs north and south through the greater length of the city, beginning at Mount Pleasant Cemetery in
the Eighth ward, and ending at the Lehigh Valley Coal Company's coal dumps, at the beginning of the
salt meadow land at the extreme southern end of the city.   The upper portion of Broad street from the
Cemetery to Belleville avenue, is given up almost entirely to residences.   From Belleville avenue to Grace
Church, it is principally a business street, although even in this space there are interspersed some handsome residences, being the homes of some of the older families of the place.   The bulk of the business
on Broad Street is done between the Delaware, Lackawanna and Western Railroad, and the City Hall on

the corner of William Street, a distance of about a mile. The banks and insurance offices on this street are all located between Millitary Park and the corner of Broad and Market streets, with but two exceptions, these being the State Bank and the Prudential Insurance Company. In fact the majority of the financial institutions are centered on both sides of the street, in the short space between Commerce and Market streets on one side and Academy and Market on the other. This part of Broad street is frequently called Finance Row. On the east side of the row are the offices of the American, the Merchants' and the Fireman's Insurance companies, the Newark agencies of the Citizens', Germania, Niagara

West Side Broad Street and City Hall.

and other leading New York insurance companies. Here, too, is the handsome building of the Mutual Benefit Life Insurance Company, of Newark, an imposing three-story brown stone structure, on the corner of Broad and Clinton streets. On the same side of the street are the buildings of the Newark City, National, German National, Manufacturers' National, Second National, and Merchants' National banks and that of the Howard Savings Institution. On the western side of the street are the Newark Fire Insurance Company, the Essex County National Bank, National Newark Banking Company, the Fidelity

Title and Deposit Company, the building of Heath & Drake, and within this distance are in process of erection, the superb building of the Prudential Insurance Company, which is to cost over $500,000, and is to stand on the corner of Broad and Bank streets, and the new post office, which is to occupy the block bounded by Academy street and the canal, and will cost nearly as much more. Farther down Broad street stands the building of the Liverpool and London and Globe Insurance Company, a massive brown stone structure seven stories high. The clothing stores are nearly all located on the west side of the street, in the block bounded by Market street on the north and the entrance to the Old Burying Ground on the

CORNER BROAD STREET AND CLINTON AVENUE, OPPOSITE LINCOLN PARK.

south. This block is usually known as Clothing Row. With one exception, all the large retail clothing establishments are centred in this one block. Below Mechanic street, and down as far as Court street, the thoroughfare is given up to miscellaneous business, with here and there a residence sandwiched in between. From Court street down to the coal dumps, the street is almost entirely devoted to residences. The most beautiful portion of Broad street, is what is frequently known as South Broad street, which is that section of the street between Clinton avenue and Emmett street. The fashionable portion of South Broad street is that part opposite Lincoln Park. Here are the residences of Thomas N. McCarter, Jerome Taylor, John H. Kase, Thomas T. Kinney, Oscar Keen and others. Farther north on

Broad street, are the residences of George A. Halsey, Franklin Murphy, Mrs. C. S. Macknet, Dr. F. B. Mandeville, Dr. Edward Ill, Dr. H. W. Gedicke, John F. Dryden, William A. Righter, Mrs. C. Bradley, William Campbell Clark, Mrs. Lathrop and John P. Jube. On Broad street are also seven of the leading churches of the town, namely, the House of Prayer (Episcopal), North Reformed, Trinity (Episcopal), First Presbyterian, Third Presbyterian, Church of the Redeemer (Universalist), and Grace, (Episcopal); all of them are fine structures. On Broad street are also the only three parks of which the city boasts, Washington, Military and Lincoln. The public market faces on this street. On that portion oppo-

WASHINGTON STREET, OPPOSITE WASHINGTON PARK.

site to Washington Park, are also some very handsome residences, among them those of Cortlandt Parker, Mrs. Theodore P. Howell, Mrs. George Farmer and L. Spencer Goble. Broad street is paved with Belgian block from the coal dumps on the south to Belleville avenue on the north, and from thence to its extreme northern terminus it will be paved with Belgian block or asphalt, within the present year. Another attractive feature of the city are the two thoroughfares on the west and south of Washington Park, which are lined with elegant residences. Here are the homes of the most prominent business men, as Warren N. Trusdell, Samuel Howell, George G. Frelinghuysen, Dr. Archibald Mercer, Robert F. Ballantine, John H. Ballantine, Marcus L. Ward, Lewis C. Grover and P. F. Mulligan on Washington street, and Herbert Ballantine, Eugene F. Vanderpool and James D. Orton, on Washington Place. On the northwest corner of Washington place and James street, stands the beautiful structure of the Second Presbyterian Church with its tall spire, and a little above it is the parsonage

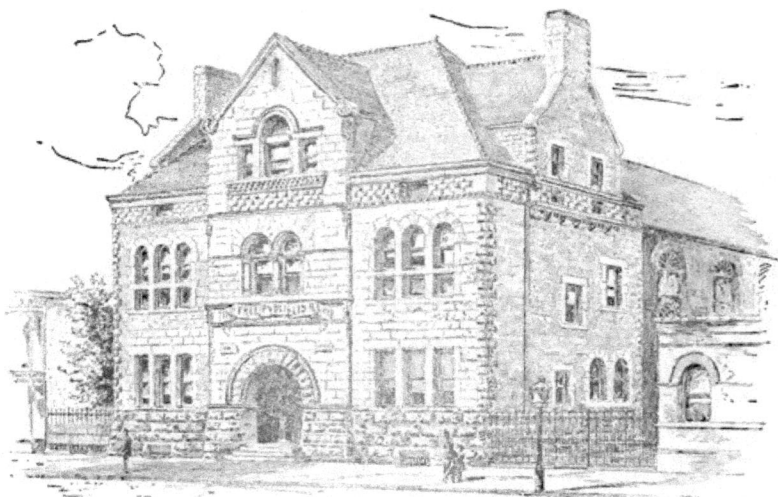

THE FREE PUBLIC LIBRARY.

The Free Public Library of the city of Newark was organized by authority of the Legislature of New Jersey, and will be maintained by an annual tax which has been voted by the citizens, for the use of the people, for whose benefit it is designed.

In January, 1889, the Board of Trustees leased for a term of five years, with privilege of purchase, the new edifice of the Newark Library Association in West Park, near Broad street, which is now opened to the public.

ARCHITECTURAL DESCRIPTION.

The site.—The building is located on an eligible and central site, 101 feet front by 109 feet in depth, adjoining the property of the New Jersey Historical Society.

The front of the edifice and to the depth of forty-six feet is new, the rear portion of the old church building being utilized for the Library Room.

Exterior.—The design is Romanesque, freely treated, built of Belleville stone, with base of rock-faced ashlar to the first-story sills. The entrance-arch is relieved by a carved molding, and the jambs have tooled surfaces. Above the base the walls are faced with pointed ashlar from the old church building, with molding, cornice, etc., so disposed as to maintain the quiet, restful and solid characteristics appropriate to the purpose of the structure. The roof is of slate, with terra-cotta ridging and hip-rolls. The entrance has large wrought-iron grilles or gates.

Entrance Hall
& Stairway

THE ENTRANCE HALL.

The Vestibule and Entrance Hall are faced with Pompeiian brick, used as a base and frieze, also the arches over the several entrances; the dado being of old gold, and the filling above the dado of cream-color brick. The floors of the vestibule and hall, and the wainscoting of the broad slate stairway leading to second and third story rooms are of Georgia marble.

The entrance-doors and those leading to Library and Catalogue Room are of paneled, quartered oak, and the upper panels and semi-circular sashes above the transoms are glazed with polished plate glass.

THE LIBRARY.

The Library is 64x64 feet, with ceiling forty-two feet high, coved on all sides, having a large central skylight filled with rich stained-glass in geometric patterns, and four large windows on either side, five feet wide and twenty-four feet high, giving ample light. The books are arranged in alcoves of quartered oak and wall cases, on the main floor and in the spacious galleries, which are reached by spiral oaken stairways. A lift will carry books to the Library from the basement, where the unpacking and repairing will be done. The present capacity of the shelving is 60,000 volumes, which can be increased to 200,000 volumes. It is lighted by a large central electrolier and numerous incandescent lights on the sides and in the alcoves.

Main Room.

Wide semi-circular arched doors, with plate-glass transoms above, deeply recessed, afford access to the Hall, Catalogue Room, and Women's Reading Room at one end. At the opposite end is the Librarian's desk, and an oak railing on either side of it, following the lines of the case, incloses the space required by the attendants, the centre of the room being left for the use of the public.

The oak settles forming part of the railings are resting places for visitors. The book-cases, wainscoting, and all other wood-work are of quartered oak, paneled, molded, carved and polished. The shelving of the cases is made of uniform length, adjustable and interchangeable. The walls and ceilings are finished with plaster made of yellow sand, harmonizing in tone with the oak.

Women's Reading Room

WOMEN'S READING ROOM

The Women's Reading Room, accessible only from the Library proper, is 20x23 feet, with a chimney-piece, extending across the room, built of light buff brick, with grey-stone shelf and trimmings extending to the ceiling, richly molded and carved. The room is lighted by two stained glass windows over the mantel-shelf, the walls and ceiling being decorated in harmony with the oak trimmings and furniture. On either side of the wide fireplace and tiled hearth are oak settles, with carved ends, panel backs, and upholstered in Spanish leather. An oak sofa and chairs with the same upholstering, with a large round-top table with carved base, complete the furnishing. The floors are covered with Oriental rugs of harmonious coloring, and handsome wrought-iron andirons give an air of inviting comfort.

THE GENERAL READING ROOM.

The General Reading Room, in the second story, with a high ceiling and lighted on two sides by several windows, is fitted with newspaper racks and files on the side walls, and tables for current magazines and periodical literature. There are comfortable chairs to accommodate about 150 persons. A generous fireplace at the west end will provide warmth and cheer, in addition to the steam heat, in

THE READING ROOM.

the Winter evenings. At the east end of the room is the Custodian's desk, and connecting with that, a small coat and hat room.

The basement is used for the steam-heating apparatus, storage, workrooms and janitor's room. The third story is occupied by a large room for the use of the pupils of the public schools, under the direction of their teachers.

The accompanying sketches render further description unnecessary.

THE CATALOGUE ROOM.

On the left of the Hall is the spacious Catalogue Room, with a large stone chimney-piece and carved oak over mantel as a central feature of the wall space opposite the entrance.

Ample light is provided through windows on two sides of the room. The available wall space is occupied by oak cases with divisions for the card catalogues. Two oak tables, in harmony with the other wood-work, are provided for the convenience of those using the general catalogue.

The Librarian's office is located on the right of the entrance hall near the front of the building.

In the Catalogue Room

NEWARK'S RAILROAD FACILITIES.

The position of Newark in regard to railway communication with other cities is unsurpassed. There are five important railways passing through the city, viz: The Pennsylvania, the Central Railroad of New Jersey, the Delaware, Lackawanna and Western, the New York and Greenwood Lake, and the New York, Lake Erie and Western. There are within the city limits eleven different railway stations belonging to the several companies.

Between Newark and New York the five companies are running the following number of trains for local travel, viz: Pennsylvania R. R., arriving, 50; departing, 58; total, 108. Central R. R., arriving, 43; departing, 44; total, 87. D., L. & W. R. R , arriving, 48; departing, 52; total, 100. N. Y., L. E. & W. R. R., arriving, 15; departing, 16; total, 31. N. Y. & G. L. R. R., arriving, 14; departing, 15; total, 29. Totals arriving, 170; totals departing, 185; grand total, 355.

Between Newark and Elizabeth the following trains are run: Pennsylvania R. R., arriving, 43; departing, 40; total, 87. Central R. R., arriving, 27; departing, 27; total, 54. Totals arriving, 74; totals departing, 67; grand total, 141.

Between Newark and Trenton, Philadelphia, the West and South: Pennsylvania R. R., arriving, 23; departing, 21; total, 44. Central, arriving, 12; departing, 12; total, 24. Totals arriving, 35; totals departing, 33; grand total, 68.

Between Newark and Perth Amboy, Sea Shore and South Jersey points, the following trains are run: Pennsylvania R. R., arriving, 11; departing, 11; total, 22. Central R. R., arriving, 11; departing 10; total, 21. Totals arriving, 22; totals departing, 21; grand total, 43.

Between Newark and points not named above, the following trains are run: Pennsylvania & L. V. R Rds., arriving, 9; departing, 9; total, 18. Central R. R., arriving, 8; departing, 8; total, 16. D., L. & W. R. R., arriving, 10; departing, 10; total, 20. N. Y., L. E. & W. R. R., arriving, 16; departing, 15; total, 31. N. Y., & G. L. R. R., arriving, 15; departing, 15; total, 30. Totals arriving, 58; totals departing, 57; grand total, 155.

There are in the city ten lines of street cars, three of which are already equipped with electric motive power, and still other roads are in process of construction, both through the city and to its suburbs. The Newark Passenger Railway Company, which controls the majority of the street railways in Newark, and the Rapid Transit Street Railway Company, are both under contract with the Common Council to run all their roads with electric motors, and the Newark and South Orange Railroad Company, who control the other line, will also probably adopt the electric system. The street railways of Newark carry over 20,000,000 of passengers annually. These lines connect the city with Elizabeth, Irvington and all the Oranges, Bloomfield, Belleville, and Harrison, in Hudson county.

The pioneers in street car traffic were the Orange and Newark Horse Car Railroad Company, who obtained a charter from the Legislature in 1859. This road had its origin in the dissatisfaction which was felt among the people of the Oranges at the wretched management of the old Morris and Essex Railroad, and the projectors of the new horse car company decided to construct a line from Orange to the Market street depot, which would enable the residents of Orange to avail themselves of the facilities offered by the New Jersey Railroad and Transportation Company, now the Pennsylvania Railroad. The projected railroad was vigorously opposed by several property owners in Market street, who imagined that the running of cars through the street would interfere with their business, and one of them, Owen McFarland, brought a suit against the company to obtain an injunction to restrain them from laying the track past his place This suit was carried to the Court of Errors and Appeals, the court of last resort in New Jersey, and was decided in favor of the company. In this suit some important questions of law were raised, and this case is continually cited in railroad suits, not only in New Jersey, but all over the United States. The decision of the Court of Errors and Appeals was rendered in December, 1860, but the excitement in consequence of the unsettled condition of the country preceeding the breaking out of the Civil War, and the breaking out of the war itself, in 1861, delayed the actual building of the road until the Spring of 1862.

The officers of the company were: William Pierson, Senior, M. D. of Orange, President; John C. Denman, Vice-President, of Newark; Martin R. Dennis, of Newark, Secretary and Treasurer: Directors: Nehemiah Perry, Henry R. Remson, David A. Hayes, Anthony F. Keasby and William A. Ripley, of Newark, and Jessie Starr, of Camden.

The first track laid was through Market, Bank and Warren streets to Roseville, which was laid in the early Spring of 1862. Immediately after this road was begun, the road from Orange to the Market street depot was also commenced, and it began to run its cars to Newark on July 4, 1862. Other roads were laid by this company in future years as follows: The Newark and Belleville line, an extension of the Roseville line through Market and Ferry streets. The roads owned by the Orange and Newark Horse Car Railroad Company passed largely into the hands of the United Railroad Companies of New

ENTRANCE TO MOUNT PLEASANT CEMETERY

Jersey, who for years held a majority of the stock. In 1865 Martin R. Dennis was made president of the road, and held this position until his death. In November, 1883, a number of capitalists who were interested in the Newark and Irvington, and Newark and Bloomfield street railroad lines, purchased a controlling interest in the lines controlled by the Orange company, and Mr. S. S. Battin, the President of the Newark and Bloomfield Street Railway Company was made President of the Orange company. This arrangement continued until the Spring of 1890, when a Philadelphia syndicate, headed by Mr. Thomas C. Barr, secured control of all the street car lines in Newark with the exception of the South Orange line, and the system was reorganized, and all the companies consolidated under the title of the Newark Passenger Railway Company, Mr. Barr being its President. Since Mr. Barr has assumed control of the street railway system of Newark, there has been a marked improvement in the service. New cars have been added, more frequent trips made, and several of the lines have been extended, electric cars have been put on two of the lines, and arrangements are being made to equip all the roads with electric motors, and new roads are projected.

The Newark and Bloomfield Street Railway Company bought at a foreclosure sale on January 17, 1876, the property of the old Newark, Bloomfield and Montclair Horse Car Company. The road, as originally laid out, ran up Broad street from Emmett street to State, through State and High street and Summer avenue to Bloomfield avenue, thence through Mount Prospect avenue and the Old Bloomfield road to Bloomfield.

During the Winter of 1875, the old route to Bloomfield was abandoned, and in 1876 the new management laid the track up Bloomfield avenue to Bloomfield, as it at present is. Mr. S. S. Battin was president of this road from 1876 until its transfer to the Newark Passenger Railway Company.

The Newark, Harrison and Kearny Railroad Company opened its road for travel in 1884, Mr. S. S. Battin being its president. Later on its line was extended from the Market street depot, down Market, Union, Elm and Pacific streets to Pennington street.

The Newark and Irvington Street Railway Company opened its road for public traffic in June, 1868. It passed through a series of financial troubles, and finally got into the hands of Messrs. Battin, Keasby and Ballantine, and was by them sold out to the Newark Passenger Railway Company in 1890.

The Newark and South Orange Horse Railroad was started in the Spring of 1868, and also passed through a series of financial disasters. The road was sold at sheriff's sale, and was bought by a company of which Mr. John Radel is president, he and his sons holding almost all the stock. Since Mr. Radel has controlled the road he has made many improvements in it, has several times extended its lines, and has made it one of the best paying, as well as one of the most efficient street railroads in the country.

The Elizabeth Railway Company was started several years ago, its line running from the Erie depot, at Fourth avenue, Newark, through Ogden, Front, Mulberry and Thomas streets, Pennsylvania avenue, Miller street and Elizabeth avenue to Elizabeth. This road has also passed into the hands of the Newark Passenger Railway Company.

The first of the steam railroads to enter Newark, was the New Jersey Railroad and Transportation Company, which was chartered March 7, 1832. The route of the road was required to be through the town of Newark. Dr. John S. Darcy was the first President of the road, and John P. Jackson, Secretary. The first trip over the road was made on September 1, 1834, in the passenger car Washington. Regular trips were commenced on the 15th of September, and the cars were operated by horse power, making eight trips each way. The fare each way was 37 1-2 cents, and the trip was made to Jersey City in half an hour. It was at first thought unsafe to use locomotives, because the embankments across the meadows had not thoroughly settled. The first locomotive was run over the road December 2, 1835. It was known as the Newark, and was a very crude and primitive affair. The cars were drawn over the Bergen Hill by horse power up to January 1, 1838, when the Bergen cut was completed. The road was extended to Elizabeth in 1835, and to Rahway in 1836, and to Philadelphia in 1839. In 1862 the company built a more direct route between Jersey City and Newark, straightening the road at the meadows at Harrison, and crossing the Passaic river at Market street. In 1867 the New Jersey Railroad and Transportation Company was consolidated with the Camden and Amboy Railroad, under the name of the United Railroads of New Jersey. In 1871 the United Railroads of New Jersey were leased to the Pennsylvania Railroad Company for 999 years, and the Pennsylvania Railroad now control over 550 miles of railroads in New Jersey. They are building a new branch, which will cross the Passaic river near the Lister Agricultural Chemical Works in the Twelfth ward, extend through the Twelfth, Tenth and Fourteenth wards, and joins the main line again near Waverly. This will make a short cut for fast freight and through passenger traffic. The company will probably build a spur to reach the western section of the city. The Lehigh Valley Railroad use the Pennsylvania Railroad tracks as far as Metuchen. They are also building a short cut through the lower part of Newark, and the two roads are constructing an immense freight yard in the lower portion of the Fourteenth ward.

The Morris and Essex Railroad, which is one of the principal railroads entering the city of Newark, was constructed in 1855, and originally extended only from Morristown to the Meadows, in Harrison, where it connected with the New Jersey Railroad Company, over which road passengers were carried to New York. In subsequent years the road was extended beyond Morristown to Easton, and in 1860 it was extended from Newark to Hoboken, and the tunnel through Bergen Hill was built. The road has been leased for many years to the Delaware, Lackawanna and Western Railroad Company, who are now operating it, as well as the Bloomfield branch, and have made many improvements.

The Erie railroad reaches Newark by way of the Newark and Paterson Railroad, which it practically owns. Its depots are at the foot of Fourth avenue, at Chester avenue, and in Woodside. This road affords accommodation to a large number of people in the northern part of the city, as does the New York and Greenwood Lake Railroad, which extends from Greenwood Lake to Jersey City, a distance of over fifty miles. This road and its Orange branch, enter the city at its extreeme northern boundry.

The Newark and New York Railroad is a branch of the Central Railroad, and affords communication with New York to a very large number of people residing in the heart of the city. It also has branches extending to Elizabeth, and to all the sea shore resorts along the Jersey coast, and in the Summer season is patronized by hundreds of Newark business men, who go backwards and forwards between the city and their Summer homes.

NEWARK BRIDGES.

The Passaic River is spanned at Newark by eight bridges, five of which belong to the railroads, the others being exclusively for vehicles and pedestrians. Two of the five railroad bridges have accommodations for pedestrians also, so that there are really five bridges that can be used for foot travel. With two exceptions, all these bridges are handsome and substantial iron structures, on which large sums of money have been expended. Of the three bridges devoted to public travel, two are the joint property of the counties of Essex and Hudson, and one is the property of a private corporation, which still exacts a toll for crossing it. Of the railroad bridges, the Pennsylvania Railroad Company has two, and the Delaware, Lackawanna and Western, Erie and New York and Greenwood Lake companies, one each.

The oldest of the inter-county bridges is what is called the Newark Free Bridge. It crosses the river at the foot of Bridge street, Newark, and connects that city with the town of Harrison, in Hudson county. It is the oldest bridge over the Passaic, and has been in existence from the time when "the memory of man runneth not to the contrary." It was formerly the property of a turnpike company, which maintained a wretched road between Newark and Jersey City, and had bridges over both the Passaic and Hackensack rivers, exacting a toll at each. In 1872 the bridge over the Passaic was purchased of the turnpike company by the counties of Essex and Hudson, for $70,000, under an act passed by the Legislature for that purpose. Each county paid one half, or $35,000, and the bridge has been in the care of a joint committee of the Boards of Chosen Freeholders of the two counties ever since. In 1880 the bridge was rebuilt, and a handsome and substantial structure of stone and iron was erected at a cost of $125,000, each county paying one half.

Another bridge used for public travel is the Plank Road bridge, and is situated in the southeastern end of the city, on the old Plank Road, between Newark and Jersey City. It is on the route most frequented by teamsters travelling between the two places, and a toll is exacted for crossing it. The bridge is a miserable and unsightly affair, although the company receives a large revenue from their tolls.

The Clay Street Free Bridge is a substantial iron and stone structure, at the foot of Clay street, and connects the two municipalities of Newark and Kearny. It was built at an expense of $75,000, Essex and Hudson counties each bearing one half of the cost. This bridge was the result of long years of persistent effort and agitation, and was mainly due to the labors of Freeholders Kinsey, of Essex, and Tierney, of Hudson, who carried the scheme through in their respective Board of Freeholders in the face of considerable difficulty. The building of this bridge affords accommodation to a number of large manufacturing establishments on either side of the river, which before the bridge was completed were compelled to send their teams a long distance out of their way in order to make their crossings. An electric railroad is about to be constructed between Newark and Arlington, and this bridge will afford them means to cross the river. The bridge has an ample draw, which is opened and closed by a steam engine.

The Pennsylvania Railroad has two fine iron bridges over the river, one at Market street and one at Centre street. Both are massive structures with draws operated by steam, and the Centre street bridge has a sidewalk for pedestrians. It is used by thousands of persons daily. The Delaware, Lackawanna and Western Railroad Company has also a fine iron bridge across the Passaic, with a draw operated by steam. Foot passengers are not allowed on this bridge. The Erie Railroad Company has an iron and frame bridge at the foot of Fourth avenue, and there is a foot path on it over which thousands of people cross daily on their way to and fro between their homes in Newark and the large mills on the opposite bank.

NEWARK AS THE COUNTY SEAT

Newark has been the County Seat of Essex County for over two hundred years. The House of Assembly of the Province of New Jersey, in 1675 passed a law making provision for the establishment of courts in the State, and enacted that Newark and Elizabethtown should form a county, but no name was given to the county, nor were its boundaries very definitely settled. The name of Essex was first applied to the county in the year 1682, in an "act to erect County Courts," in which it was provided that the services of the courts should be held in Newark and Elizabethtown. The boundaries of Essex County were definitely established in an act passed by the House of Assembly January 21, 1710, in which it was enacted : "That the County of Essex shall begin at the mouth of the Raway River, where it falls into the sound, and so to run up the said Raway River to Robeson's Branch, thence west to the division line between the eastern and western division, and so to follow the said division line to Pequaneck River, where it meets Passaick River, thence down Pessaick River to the Bay and Sound, thence down the Sound to where it began." These limits were altered on November 4, 1741, when a part of Essex County was annexed to Somerset. In 1837 Passaic County was formed from the northern part of Essex, and in 1687 Union County was set off from the southern portion. In 1692 Essex County was divided into three townships, known as Newark, Elizabethtown and Aquackanock. The first building used as a court house in Essex County was the church or meeting house of the Presbyterian congregation, which was built in 1668 and 1669. The site of this building was on Broad street, near where No. 1 Engine Company's house now is. In 1686 and 1687, mention is made in some of the records of the county prison, but exactly where that prison stood is not known, but it is believed to have stood near the meeting house. About the year 1700, a brick jail was built on Broad street south of the church. The upper story was used for years as a court room. The courts after 1791 were held in the old building on Broad street, which was abandoned by the Presbyterians for their present church structure. In the beginning of the present century there was a bitter contest between Newark and Elizabeth, as to which was to have the court house in its limits, as it was evident that a new court house must be built. The election lasted three days, and in these elections women were allowed to vote. This permission, however, was confined only to single women and widows, the law expressly excluding "married women, idiots, infants, lunatics, paupers, Indians and slaves." In 1810 a new court house was erected on the corner of Broad and Walnut streets where Grace Church now stands. It was a large three-story brick building and also contained the jail. This building was burned August 15, 1835. The present court house, which stands at the junction of Market street and Springfield avenue, was built in 1837. It is a two-story brown stone building and resembles an Egyptian tomb in appearance. It is a very uncomfortable and ill-ventilated structure and is very unsuitable for the present needs of the county. It has several patch-work additions, notably the County Clerk's office, Prosecutor's and Grand Jury rooms. The County Register's office adjoins the court house on the south and is a handsome three-story brown stone structure. The upper story is used by the Board of Chosen Freeholders, and the other two stories are used by the Register of Deeds and Mortgages for the keeping of records of these important instruments. In the court house are to be found the offices of the Sheriff, Surrogate, County Clerk, County Auditor, and County Collector. The County Clerk is also the clerk of all the courts of the county, with the exception of the Orphans' court, of which the Surrogate is clerk. In the County Clerk's office are to be found all the ancient records of the courts as well as those of later date, and the records of the roads of the county, as well as many other important documents of great value to the public. On the second story of the court house are two large court rooms, the one on the south side being known as the Circuit Court room and the one on the north as the Common Pleas and Sessions Court Room.

New Jersey follows the ancient English practice of having separate courts for law and equity practice. It is only the law courts that are held in the court house. The Equity courts, or as they are termed in New Jersey, the Chancery Courts, have their headquarters in Trenton, and are presided over by the Honorable Alexander McGill, Chancellor of New Jersey. There are, however, two large Chancery Court Rooms in the Liverpool and London and Globe building, where the Chancellor frequently holds court, and where Vice Chancellor and Advisory Masters are almost daily in attendance, hearing motions and trying causes. The Vice Chancellors are Abram V. Van Fleet, J. V. Bird, Henry C. Pitney and Robert S. Green. The Advisory Masters are: Washington B. Williams and John R. Emory. Vice Chancellor Van Fleet is a resident of Newark, as are the two advisory masters. The law courts are divided into the Circuit Court, where the more important civil suits are tried, the Court of Common Pleas, where minor civil cases are disposed of, the Court of Oyer and Terminer, where cases of murder and very grevious criminal offenses are tried; the Court of Quarter Sessions and Court of Special Sessions, in both of which the bulk of the criminal business of the county is done. The Circuit Court is presided over by Judge David A. Depue, who is one of the Justices of the Supreme Court of the State. Judge Depue also presides over the court of Oyer and Terminer, and when sitting in that court has one of the

THE NORTH END CLUB HOUSE

Common Pleas judges associated with him. Judge Depue has held his present position since 1866. He is regarded as one of the ablest jurists that has ever adorned the Supreme Court bench, and is one of the most influential members of the Supreme Court. He is beloved and respected by the entire community. The court of Common Pleas is composed of a President Judge, who is a lawyer, and two Associate Judges, who are laymen. The present judges are: President Judge, Andrew Kirkpatrick; Lay Judges, Michael J. Ledwith and Dr. Carl F. Buttner. These judges are also the judges of the Court of Quarter Sessions and of the Court of Special Sessions. The latter court sits every Monday and tries the cases of persons accused of crime who, for the purpose of having a speedy trial, are willing to waive the right of trial by jury. These same judges are also the judges of the Orphans' Court, where matters relating to wills, the settlement of estates, the guardianship of children, etc., are disposed of.

The present county officers are: Dr. Edward DeL. Bradin, Dr. Charles Schwartz and Dr. Michael J.

Phelin; Sheriff, Jacob Haussling; County Clerk, Samuel A. Smith; Surrogate, John B. Dusenbery; Register, Richard F. Cogan; Prosecutor of the Pleas, Elvin W. Crane; Assistant Prosecutor of the Pleas, Louis Hood, County Auditor, Hugo Geissele; Assistant County Auditor, Harry Housel; County Collector, Thomas J. Regan; Clerk of the Grand Jury, Walter J. Knight. The judges of the court and the prosecutor of the pleas are appointed by the Governor of the State. The assistant prosecutor is appointed by the prosecutor, the Coroners, Sheriff, Clerk, Surrogate and Register, are elected by the people The Auditor, Assistant Auditor and Collector are appointed by the Board of Chosen Freeholders. The Clerk of the Grand Jury is appointed by the judges of the court.

The present county jail was built in 1837. It occupies the entire block bounded by the Morris canal on the north, New street on the south, Wilsey street on the east and Newark street on the west. There are about two hundred prisoners confined there on the average all the year round. A very large and substantial addition is being constructed to the jail, which will give about ninety more cells. The jail is in charge of Roger Marshall, Warden. In addition to the jail the county maintains a large penitentiary at Caldwell, some eight miles from Newark. This building was erected about fifteen years ago. It stands in the midst of a large farm, on which there is a valuable stone quarry. The convicts in the penitentiary are employed in getting stone out of the quarry, and breaking it up for the making of the county roads. Others of them work upon the farm. The penitentiary is in charge of Warden John Murray, and it is justly regarded as one of the best managed penal institutions in the country.

The affairs of the County of Essex are administered by the Board of Chosen Freeholders, which is composed of eleven members, one from each assembly district of the county, and a Director, who is the presiding officer of the Board, and is elected by the people of the county at large. This Board has charge of all the financial affairs of the county, the care and maintenance of the bridges in various portions of the county, the jail, penitentiary and lunatic asylum. The present members of the Board are: Director, Dr. Eugene F. Tiessler, of Orange; James Peck, of East Orange; Owen Cahill, Cornelius Leary, Frank McGuinness, John Scanlan, Peter Mullin, Soloman DeJonge, Thomas W. Kinsey, Ellis R. Carhuff, of Newark; Charles W. Winckler, of Orange. Of this Board Messrs. Peck, Kinsey, Carhuff and Winckler are Republicans, the others are Democrats. Mr. Peck has been a member of the Board for about thirty years. The officers of the Board are: Director, Dr. Eugene F. Tiessler; Clerk, Joseph Atkinson; County Counsel, Frederick W. Stevens; County Collector, Thomas J. Regan; County Auditor, Hugo Geissele; Assistant Auditor, Harry Housel; County Physician, Dr. James T. Wrightson; Warden of County Jail, Roger Marshall; Warden of Penitentiary, John Murray; Superintendent of County Lunatic Asylum, Dr. Livingston S. Hinckley; County Engineer, James Owen; Superintendent of Public Works, Michael Conroy.

The County Lunatic Asylum is an institution of which the people of Essex County are especially proud. It was started some seventeen or eighteen years ago in a small frame building on Camden street, on a lot which was owned by the City of Newark, and which had been purchased by the city for hospital purposes. The building was erected on what was known as the pavilion plan and was placed in charge of Major John Leonard as warden and Dr. J. A. Cross at physician. The asylum had its origin in the dissatisfaction which the members of the Board of Freeholders felt at the treatment the patients of Essex County were receiving at the State Lunatic Asylums at Trenton and Morris Plains. The county asylum proved itself a success from the outset and grew continually. New buildings were added at frequent intervals, until the asylum occupied an immense series of buildings. These, however, were but miserable frame structures, totally unsuited to the needs of a great institution such as the Essex County asylum had grown to be, and several years ago the Board of Freeholders purchased a large tract of land on South Orange avenue, near the city line, and began the erection thereon of an imposing and substantial brick structure, four stories high. Just before the building was finished and ready for occupation, Major Leonard, the Warden, to whose wise, humane and judicious management the success of the asylum was largely due, resigned, and Dr. L. S. Hinckley was appointed Superintendent to succeed him. Dr. Hinckley opened the new asylum and has been in charge several years. He brought about many improvements in the management, and has introduced many novel features in the care and treatment of the insane. He has made the Essex County Lunatic Asylum one of the model institutions in the Union for the care of the insane. The percentage of cures here is larger than in any institution in the country. The original asylum building has been added to several times until now there is a vast system of massively constructed, well ventilated, well lighted and cheerful buildings. These buildings were all erected with the greatest care and attention to sanitary matters. They were constructed under the personal supervision of Messrs. Staehlin & Steiger, who are among the leading architects of New Jersey, and have given a great deal of attention to the erection of public buildings. There are at present nearly four hundred and fifty patients in the asylum. The institution is under the immediate care of the Committee on Lunacy of the Board of Freeholders. It costs the County of Essex about $75,000 to maintain the institution.

MANUFACTURING INDUSTRIES

Newark is frequently called the Birmingham of America, and it well deserves the title, for within its limits are over 1,200 firms engaged in manufacturing, turning out millions of dollars worth of goods annually, giving employment to tens of thousands of working people and having a capital of over $40,000,000 invested in its manufactures. Newark is the third city in the Union in the extent and variety of its manufactures and one of its establishments alone does a business of over $10,000,000 a year. Another gives employment to fully 4,000 hands, and its works cover acres of ground on both sides of the river. In several branches of manufacture Newark is acknowledged to lead all other cities in the country and any article that bears the stamp of a Newark manufacturer finds a ready sale in any market, for the reason that it is universally acknowledged that Newark Artisans turn out only the best of goods.

During the first century the growth of the manufacturing industries of the town was steady but slow, always thrifty, owing to the industry and frugality of the settlers and their descendants. The apple was planted quite extensively soon after the settlement, for in 1682 Governor Carteret, writing to the Proprietors in England, said: "At Newark is made great quantities of cider exceeding any that we can have from New England, Rhode Island or Long Island." The reputation for making a superior quality of cider has been maintained ever since. This is the first mention that I find in searching the early history of Newark of manufactured goods. The first shoe maker came here about the year 1676, and the first tannery was started in the "swamp," now part of Market street, in 1698.

The progress of manufacturing goods in the town of Newark, during the eighteenth century, was not very rapid, beyond what was needed for home consumption. Toward the close of the century shoemaking was the most prominent industry, and many who attended their farms during the growing season, turned their attention to shoe-making in Winter. About the same time the manufacturing of carriages and leather was begun on a larger scale. In a description of the town written in the year 1806, it is represented as one of the most flourishing and prosperous in the United States, noted for its fine cider, carriages, coach-lace and quarries.

From the year 1806 until 1830 the town grew rapidly both in population and wealth, with a very noticeable increase in the variety of articles manufactured for other than home markets. In 1830 a committee, of whom Charles H. Halsey was Chairman, made a careful canvass of the town to learn the magnitude of the manufactured products. In this report it is stated, among the leading industries carried on in Newark, are carriages, shoes, hats, and saddlery hardware.

The decade between 1860 and 1870 was an eventful one, bringing about many and important changes in the industries of Newark. The breaking out of the civil war suddenly cut off a market for many articles of manufactured goods which were made up expressly for the South. The check upon the sales, with the total loss of the outstanding debts, cramped and strained many of our then stanchest houses, who were forced from these causes to curtail, retire from business, or turn their capital and machinery from their legitimate channels to that of producing a different class of goods. Fortunately for many the Government soon became a large, reliable and steady customer for all kinds of articles needed to supply the wants of a large army. Newark manufacturers were not slow in adapting their factories to furnish these articles in unlimited quantities, and they reaped a harvest of prosperity, at the same time adding new laurels to this city as a place where large quantities of goods were manufactured; and these goods were seldom if ever condemned by Government inspectors. Every factory was run to its utmost capacity, and there is no doubt that manufacturers made money faster than during any previous period in our history.

The manufacturing of jewelry was started in this city in the early part of the present century by Epaphras Hinsdale, with a small capital and only half a dozen of hands employed This firm was afterwards Hinsdale & Taylor. Then came Downing & Phelps, and Carington & Baldwin, and later still, Taylor & Baldwin. In 1836 there were four jewelry establishments in Newark, employing 100 men and having an annual product of $225,060. This branch of industry has from the start improved steadily, and now in 1880, three-quarters of a century since Mr. Hinsdale began business here, there have grown up among us seventy-two establishments, with a capital of $2,501,899, employing 2,535 hands, paying in wages $1,094,016, giving an annual product of $4,632,827, and if we add to this the product of gold and silver refining and smelting, we have the enormous amount of annual productions of $13,427,427. One of the chief advantages which Newark possesses over other cities is its proximity to New York, where it is said *twenty-five per cent.* of the jewelry trade of America is transacted, and the manufacturers of Newark can thus enjoy the advantages of meeting leading wholesalers from all parts of the United States and Canada on their visits to that city twice a year. In the matter of rents the advantages enjoyed by the Newark manufacturers over those of New York are readily seen, not to mention that of labor, which averages less in this city (owing to cost of living). Newark enjoys another advantage from the fact that it is known far and wide as a jewelry center, thus attracting skilled workmen from all parts of Europe. To be successful in this business new designs must be constantly added, and many of the best and most attractive designs are furnished by foreigners, although they frequently have to be modified for the American trade. Thus it will be seen Newark offers to the manufacturers many advantages not possessed by other cities.

The leather business—that is, tanning and currying of hides and skins—has a history similar to jewelry, and is now the largest single interest that is carried on in Newark.

ARTHUR W. MOORE, OF MOORE & CO., M'F'G JEWELERS.

The manufacturing of hats is one of the industries started at an early period in Newark, and one that has maintained its position in the foremost ranks of our profitable industries.

The manufacturing of boots and shoes, that was the first and leading industry of Newark, at which two-thirds of the inhabitants of the town were employed in the beginning of the present century, has not kept pace with, nor has it held its position with some of the branches started.

The manufacturing of trunks was begun here early in the present century, but made slow progress until 1850. It is now among the leading industries of Newark, and it was made so by the men who are now actively engaged in the business.

Saddlery hardware is another important and large interest in this city.

The manufacture of malt liquors is a large and growing interest in Newark. In 1830 there were only two breweries in the town, either of which would be considered very small concerns when compared with the mammoth establishments now in successful operation in Newark. There are at present twenty-six breweries and one malt-house in this city, with a capital of $2,592,300, employing 536 men, paying them in wages $329,800, and manufacturing 601,161 barrels of beer and ale, these, with other salable products, making a gross annual total of $4,508,707.

All of Newark's factories and workshops are busy and prosperous. Four large thread works, a linoleum factory, licorice factory, mammoth chemical, zinc and smelting works (one of the latter doing a business of $13,000,000 a year), are all to be found in the limits of this city or its suburbs on the opposite banks of the Passaic. There are three large steel works here, and, indeed, it is hard to tell anything that is not made in Newark. The leather industry is an immense one, and is growing all the time. Newark is noted the world over for its fine jewelry. The manufacture of celluloid, which was begun in Newark a few years ago, in a very small way, has now swelled to vast proportions, and extended from this city to various parts of the country. Already there are several large factories in the city employing hundreds of hands. Recently all the celluloid interests in the country have been consolidated under the management of one company, known as the Celluloid Company, with a capital of $6,000,000, and it is probable that in a short time all the celluloid factories in other parts of the country will be closed, and the entire business removed to Newark.

BOARD OF TRADE

The Newark Board of Trade was organized in 1868. Its first president was Thos. W. Dawson and its first secretary, Col. G. N. Abeel. The objects of the Board are:

"The promotion of trade; the giving a proper direction and impetus to all commercial movements; the encouragement of intercourse between business men; the improvement of facilities for transportation; the diffusion of information concerning the trade, manufactures and other interests of the city of Newark; the co-operation of this with similar societies in other cities, and the promotion and development of the commercial, industrial and other interests of said city."

The present officers of the Board are: President, Col. A. L. Bassett; Vice-Presidents, Jas. E. Flemming, Samuel Atwater, John B. Stobaeus; Secretary, P. T. Quinn; Treasurer, E. L. Joy; Directors, Jas. A. Coe, Henry M. Doremus, Geo. S. Duryee, E. Luther Joy, R. G. Salomon, S. S. Sargeant, Wm. A. Ure, Geo. W. Weidenmayer, Geo. A. Williams. The Standing Committees of the Board are: Arbitration—James W. Miller, Benjamin Atha, Joseph Coult, Samuel C. Howell. Manufacturers—C. T. Williamson, Hugh Smith, C. W. Wheeler, Thomas Hagstoz, Theodore E. Beck, Joseph Colyer, W. B. Durand, A. E. Seliger. Railroad Interests—S. J. Meeker, A. Q. Keasbey, Wm. Clark, David T. Campbell, James E. Flemming, B. W. Hopper, H. H. Mundy. Passaic River—A. B. Twitchell, George B. Swain, John H. Ballantine, P. Sandford Ross, James S. Higbie, Edward Balbach, J. W. Hyatt, Walter Tompkins. Legislation—A. F. R. Martin, R. Wayne Parker, Chandler W. Riker, M. T. Barrett, Gottfried Krueger, P. T. Quinn, John V. Diefenthaeler. New Business—Wm. A. Ure, J. Watts Kearny, W. Campbell Clark, Wm. E. Gordon, Cyrus Peck, Elias S. Ward, Lott Southard, M. D. The present membership of the Board is two hundred and thirty.

CHURCHES OF NEWARK

Newark is fairly a rival of Brooklyn in the claim to be called the "City of Churches." There are one hundred and ten churches in the city as well as a large number of mission chapels. Of the churches the Presbyterians have twenty; the United Presbyterians, one; the Reformed, nine; the Congregationalists, two; the Baptists, fifteen; the Episcopalians, eleven; the Reformed Episcopalians, one; the Methodists,

THE PEDDIE MEMORIAL BAPTIST CHURCH.

eighteen; the Methodist Protestants, one; the Lutherans, four; the Swedenborgians, two; the Roman Catholics, nineteen; and the Jews have five Synagogues.

The Presbyterian denomination was the first to gain a foothold in Newark, and, indeed, the history of that denomination is coeval with that of the city. For many years the entire city was run as a branch of the Presbyterian Church. The town meetings were held in the First Presbyterian Church and all the affairs of the town were regulated by that body. The oldest of the Presbyterian churches is the First Church, which stands on Broad street, near Mechanic. The present edifice is one hundred years old, having been dedicated in January, 1791. The centennial of its dedication was observed in the early part of January, 1891, with impressive services, when Rev. David R. Frazer, D. D., the pastor, delivered an interesting historical sketch of the early history of the present church edifice and spoke of some of the eminent men of the State who have been connected with that parish The congregation of the First

INTERIOR OF PEDDIE MEMORIAL CHURCH.

Presbyterian Church numbers among its membership some of the wealthiest and most influential men of Newark. Rev. Dr. MacWhorter, who was its pastor one hundred years ago, was one of the most active and influential of the Revolutionary patriots, and the Rev. Jonathan F. Sterns, D. D., who was its pastor during the Civil War, was also eminent for his patriotism and his devotion to the cause of the Union. On the Monday when the news of Fort Sumter reached Newark, one of the first places from which the National flag was displayed, was the steeple of the First Church. A crowd collected in front of the building and Dr. Sterns addressed them, delivering a stirring Union speech. This church has in connection with its church edifice a large and handsome two-story brown stone build ing, containing lecture and Sunday school rooms, ladies' parlors, and other apartments for church work

The congregation of this church are liberal contributors to benevolent objects of all kinds, as well as to domestic and foreign missions, and have done much towards building up younger and weaker parishes in other parts of the city.

The Second Presbyterian Church, which is situated on Washington street, corner of James, facing on Washington Park, has a beautiful brown stone edifice with a lofty steeple. This structure was erected a few years ago, and is one of the handsomest churches in town. The history of the church dates back to 1810, when the congregation was formed. The first church building was erected in 1811. The church is very strong and maintains one or two flourishing missions in other sections of the city. The present pastor is the Rev. J. Pleasant Hunter.

The Third Presbyterian Church, which stands on Broad street, near Hill, was organized 1824, and is also very strong financially, and socially its members are among the leading men of the city. It present pastor is the Rev. A. Nelson Hollifield, who is one of the ablest preachers in the city.

The Park Presbyterian Church, which occupies a remarkably handsome brown stone edifice on the corner of Belleville avenue and Kearny street, is the largest in membership of any Presbyterian church in New Jersey. Its present pastor, the Rev. J. Clement French, D. D., who has been in charge since October, 1879, is one of the most eloquent, genial and popular preachers in Newark, and is constantly in demand for lectures and public gatherings. The No. Park Church on Aqueduct street is an off-shoot of this church.

The leading churches of the Reformed denomination are the First, on Market street near Beaver, the north on Broad, opposite Washington, Park and the Clinton Avenue on the corner of Clinton avenue and Halsey street. All of these have large and handsome buildings and are in a flourishing condition as regards membership and finances.

The principal Congregational church is the Belleville Avenue Congregational, which is near Fourth avenue, and occupies a very unique brown stone edifice. Its pastor is the Rev. Samuel Loomis.

The Baptists, who have fifteen churches, are very strong in Newark. The leading church of this denomination is the Peddie Memorial, which is situated on the corner of Broad and Fulton streets. This is a unique and beautiful edifice, constructed of Indiana lime stone. The style of architecture is a combination of Romanesque and Byzantine. The interior is remarkably handsome. The church and the ground on which it stands cost $355,000. It was erected mainly through the munificence of the late Thomas B. Peddie, who was twice mayor of Newark, twice a member of Congress and one of Newark's leading business men. The church furnished $107,000 of this amount. Mr. Peddie came to Newark a poor boy from Scotland, and by his own industry, thrift and business ability built up an immense trunk and bag business, amassed a fortune and in the last years of his life built this church as a mark of his gratitude to God for the manner in which He had prospered him. Mr. Peddie died before the completion of the building and his widow generously carried out his intentions and completed the building. On the anniversary of his death in February, 1891, she endowed the church, giving it a building in Chamber street, New York, with $125,000, the income of which is to be devoted to sustaining the church. The First Baptist, as the Peddie Memorial Church was originally called, has always been one of the leading churches of Newark. Its pastor during the Civil War, Rev. Henry Clay Fisk, D. D., was one of a coterie of brilliant and patriotic pastors, who did much toward moulding the public sentiment in favor of the Union cause. The church sent many men to the front. Its present pastor is the Rev. W. W. Boyd, D D., who is one of the most eloquent and original pulpit orators in Newark, a man who takes an active interest in public affairs, and is beloved and esteemed by all who know him.

Trinity Church is the oldest of the Episcopal churches, and its history dates back to a period anterior to the Revolutionary War. The first services of the Episcopal church were held in Newark about 1736, and the first church edifice was built in 1743, on the site now occupied by the present structure. The corner stone of the present church was laid May 22, 1809, and the building was consecrated May 21, 1810. Trinity church has always been a pronouncedly Low or Evangelical church. The congregation are liberal contributors to the cause of domestic and foreign missions.

Grace Church is the second of the Episcopal churches, and had its origin in services that were held over a savings bank on Broad street, and afterwards in a building on Market street, subsequently occupied by a livery stable. The church was organized in 1837, with the Rev. George T. Chapman, D.

D., as its first rector. The present church edifice, on the corner of Broad and Walnut streets, was built in 1848. A new chancel and sanctuary and parish building were added a few years ago at a cost of $50,000. The church is overgrown which ivy brought from England by the late Bishop Doane. Grace Church is one of the most pronouncedly "Ritualistic" churches in Newark. Its music is rendered by a vested choir of men and boys, and it has the credit of having the finest musical service of any church in the State of New Jersey. Its Rector is the Rev. George M. Christian, who is the most eloquent and able preacher in the Episcopal church in New Jersey.

Christ Church is the third of the Episcopal churches in Newark, and was organized in 1849. It has a beautiful altar and Reredos erected to the memory of the late Bishop Odenheimer.

The House of Prayer, which stands on the corner of Broad and State streets, is one of the prettiest of the Episcopal churches in Newark. This church has been one of the pioneers in the Ritualistic or Catholic movement in the Diocese of Newark, and is noted for its elaborate ceremonial and fine music. It has a large and commodious Sunday school and parish building, and there are two sisters of the order of St. Margaret attached to the parish, who work among the sick and poor.

The other Episcopal churches are St. Paul's, on the corner of High and Market streets, St. Phillip's (colored), on High street, St. Matthew's (German) on Kinney street, St. Stephen's, on Clinton avenue, St. Barnabas', on Sussex avenue, St. John's, on Elwood avenue and St. James', on Belleville avenue.

The Methodist denomination is remarkably strong in Newark, and numbers among its membership some of the most prominent and influential citizens of Newark. The leading church of this denomination is St. Paul's, on the corner of Broad and Marshall streets, which has recently been enlarged and improved at a cost of $15,000.

Next in importance to this comes the Central M. E. Church, on Market street. Among the other leading Methodist churches are St. Luke's, on Clinton avenue, the Centenary, on the corner Summer avenue and Kearny street, the Halsey Street Church, on Halsey street, near New, and the Roseville M. E. Church, on the corner of Orange street and Bathgate place. The latter is one of the most beautiful and imposing churches in Newark.

The Roman Catholic Church is growing in numbers and importance faster than any other denomination in Newark. The leading church in Newark is St. Patrick's Cathedral, on the corner of Central avenue and Washington streets. The church has a fine parochial school building on Central avenue, a home under the care of the Christian Brothers, and a young ladies' academy on Washington street, under the care of the Sisters of Charity.

The oldest Catholic church in Newark is St. John's, on Mulberry street. This also has a flourishing parochial school and Sister's home.

Among other prominent churches in Newark are St. James', on Lafayette street, St. Aloysius', on the Bowery, St. Michael's, on Belleville avenue, and St. Joseph's, on Warren street.

NEWARK'S CHARITABLE INSTITUTIONS.

Newark is noted for the number and extent of its charities, and if there are any poor or sick persons in the city who are not properly cared for it is not for a lack of suitable institutions to meet their cases.

The oldest of the charitable institutions of the city is the Female Charitable Society, whose headquarters are located in a handsome three-story brick building on the corner of Halsey and Hill streets. The object of this society is not so much to give alms as it is to help poor women to help themselves. The society conducts a day nursery for children, where women can leave their little ones when they go out to work; a laundry where women are taught washing and ironing, a sewing room and a department where young girls are instructed in general housework. Its Board of Managers is composed of the leading ladies of Newark.

The Orphan Asylum, whose building is on the corner of High and Bleecker streets, and the Protestant Foster Home, whose building is on the corner of Belleville avenue and Van Wagenen streets, are doing a noble work in caring for poor and neglected children, who, otherwise, would be without a home, as is also the Home for the Friendless on South Orange avenue. Each of these institutions numbers among its managers representatives of the leading families of the city.

Newark has six hospitals, all of which are model institutions. The oldest of them is St. Barnabas, which occupies a large and handsome brick structure on the corner of High and Montgomery streets. This hospital is in charge of the Sisters of St. Margaret, and its business affairs are managed by a Board of Trustees composed of the Bishop of the Episcopal diocese of Newark and representatives of all the Episcopal churches of Newark and vicinity.

The largest hospital in the city is St. Michael's, on the corner of High street and Central avenue, which is an institution of the Roman Catholic Church, and is in charge of the Sisters of the Poor of St. Francis. There is also a Woman's Hospital and an Eye and Ear Infirmary in connection with this hospital.

The other hospitals are the City Hospital, on Bank street and Fairmount avenue, the Women and Children's Hospital on South Orange avenue, the German Hospital on Bank and Wallace streets and the Newark Charitable Eye and Ear Infirmary on Sterling street.

Among the other charitable institutions of the city may be mentioned the Bureau of Associated Charities on Market street, the Children's Aid and Society for the Prevention of Cruelty to Children on the same street, the Gottfried Krueger Home for Aged Men at Irvington, the Newark City Home a reformatory institution at Verona, the Old Ladies' Home on Mt. Pleasant avenue, the Women's Christian Association on Court street, the Women's Christian Association on Clinton street, and a number of orphanages and benevolent institutions in charge of the various sisterhoods of the Roman Catholic Church

THE WATER SUPPLY

Newark is supplied with water from the Passaic River, the water being taken from the stream at Belleville, about four miles above the heart of the city. As early as 1800 a company was incorporated under the title of the Newark Aqueduct Company, to supply the citizens of Newark with water. They derived their supply from Branch Brook and distributed the water over the city through wooden pipes. Some of these pipes are yet found in making excavations or sewers and other improvements in the various streets in the older parts of the town. In 1828 iron pipes were substituted for the wooden ones. The Newark Aqueduct Company, however, did but a limited business, and by 1860, the need of a general supply for the entire city had become so apparent that the Newark Aqueduct Board was incorporated. By its act of incorporation the Aqueduct Board succeeded to all the capital stock, rights, franchises, lands and property of the Newark Aqueduct Company, the consideration being $100,000. The Aqueduct Board soon began making inquiries in regard to a new supply of water. Several sources were considered, but it was finally determined to utilize the Passaic river, which at that time was a beautiful, clear stream. A large tract of property was purchased on the bank of the river at Belleville, a short distance above the settled portion of that village, and works were erected thereon. These works were completed in 1869, and have been several times added to. The water is pumped from the river by two 8,000,000 gallon Worthington pumps, two 5,000,000 gallon pumps, and from the river is forced to the distributing reservoir, which is located on the summit of a high hill a mile west of the river. From there it is carried in large distributing mains to two reservoirs in Newark, one known as the Low Service Reservoir, on Clifton avenue, and the other as the High Service Reservoir on South Orange and Fairmount avenues. The former supplies the low lying section of the city, and there is also a special high service system at the Clifton avenue pump house which supplies a section of the city that cannot be conveniently supplied by the High Service Reservoir, so that in point of fact the Clifton avenue reservoir supplies the major portion of the city. At both the Clifton avenue and South Orange avenue pump houses there are large and powerful pumps for the purpose of forcing the water over the city. As early as 1876 the Aqueduct Board and the citizens of Newark generally began considering the subject of a new source of water supply for the city, the consideration being forced upon them by the condition of the Passaic river, which was constantly being more and more polluted by sewage from Paterson and other places. Experiments were made with driven wells on the property of the Board at Belleville, but they proved to be any thing but satisfactory and the idea of utilizing them as a source of supply was abandonded. In 1878 the Aqueduct Board employed Messrs. J. J. R. Croes and Geo. W. Howell, two of the most eminent hydraulic engineers in the United States, to examine and report upon the best source of supply for the city These engineers, after months of patient research, made a most elaborate and carefully written report, in which they advocated abandoning the Passaic altogether as a source of supply, and procuring water from the Pequannock region in Morris County. The cost of this was estimated at $4,000,000. This report has been the basis of everything that has ever since been written on the subject of water supply for Newark, Jersey City and adjacent places. The Aqueduct Board and the people of Newark generally stood aghast at the idea of spending $4,000,000 for anything, and the few people who were bold enough to advocate the adoption of the recommendations of Messrs. Croes and Howell were frowned down upon by almost the entire community, and told that they were trying to bankrupt the city. For years the matter of new water supply was allowed to remain in abeyance, except now and then there would be a sporadic revival of the subject and a rattling of dry bones among the old fossils of the city, who were thrown almost into convulsions at the prospect of being taxed for this new supply. The Aqueduct Board, however, did not altogether abandon the idea of getting a new supply. Indeed, the necessity of one was growing every year more apparent as the pollution of the river increased. The subject began to be discussed frequently at meetings of the Board of Trade and at citizens' meetings. Many sources of supply were considered, such as driven wells, artesian wells, a dual supply, that is one source for drinking and culinary purposes and another for manufacturing and like purposes; another project was to take the water from some of the many small ponds and lakes in the vicinity of Newark or in the adjoining counties of Morris and Sussex. Another project was to purify the Passaic river water by filtration. Nothing, however, was done in the matter until 1888, when a joint committee of the Common Council and the Aqueduct Board, with Mayor Haynes as chairman, was appointed to consider the subject of new water supply. This committee held a large number of meetings, considered all the various projects, and received propositions from owners of water rights in Sussex and Morris Counties. Among the principal parties who offered to sell water to the city were the Lehigh Valley Railroad Company, who had become possessed of valuable water privileges by having secured control of the franchises of the Morris Canal and Banking Company, Julius H. Pratt, who also owned valuable water rights in the northern part of the State and W. A. Bartlett, who also had acquired large water privileges, including several lakes, in this section. All of these parties had availed themselves of the valuable information contained in Messrs. Croes and Howell's report, and had quietly set about acquiring all the water sheds, water rights and lakes which they could purchase, knowing that in time Newark and other cities would be obliged to come to them for a supply, the process of taking these sources of supply by condemnation being far too expensive to be thought of. In the early part of 1889 a report was presented by the joint committee favoring the acceptance of a proposition made by the Lehigh Valley Railroad Company, who were the owners of water rights in the Pequannock, Wynockie and Ramapo water sheds, who offered to sell the city a supply outright for $6,000,000, or to supply it with water by the million gallons for twenty-five years at the rate of $39 for each 1,000,000 gallons up to a consumption of 2,000,000 gallons per day, making a reduction in all water in excess of that amount until it shall reach the sum of $36 per million gallons. After a full discussion of the subject at several meetings of the Aqueduct Board and the Common Council, a contract was finally drawn up, by the terms of which it was stipulated that a corporation to be known as the East Jersey Water Company should be incorporated under the laws of the State of New Jersey, and that the Lehigh Valley Railroad Company should guarantee the faithful performance of the contract on the part of the East Jersey Water Company. The East Jersey Water Company agreed in the contract to supply the city with 27,000,000 gallons of water per day for a term of years, at the rate of $36 per ,000,000 gallons. In the contract it was expressly stipulated that the city was to have the option at any time within eleven years of buying the entire plant, including reservoirs, pipe lines, conduits, etc., for $6,000,000 and issuing bonds running thirty years in payment for the same. The city at once exercised this option, and the East Jersey Water Company are now engaged in constructing an extensive system of reservoirs, conduits, etc., to supply the city of Newark. The supply is to be taken from the Pequannock river region, where the water is of exceptional purity, and which is the very section most strongly recommended by Croes and Howell. Extensive reservoirs are being conducted at Oak Ridge, Macopin and Clinton in Morris County.

These reservoirs are 350 feet above tide water, high enough to carry the water over the top of any building in Newark. The water will be constructed from these reservoirs in large steel or wrought iron pipes across the country down to the distributing reservoir in Belleville, from which place it will be distributed into the mains leading to Newark and forced to all parts of the city by gravity, the pressure gained by the great headway of the water at its source of supply, owing to its extreme elevation being sufficient to carry it all over Newark without pumping. This will be a great saving to the taxpayers of Newark, as the cost of pumping amounts to nearly

ROSEVILLE AVENUE AT RAILROAD CROSSING.

$100,000 a year. The new water works are to be completed and the water delivered to the city by May, 1892. When this is done Newark will have one of the finest water supplies in the Union. The water has been carefully examined by chemists, and found to be about the purest that is to be had east of the Rocky Mountains.

ROSEVILLE.

Roseville, as that cluster of beautiful villa sites that skirt the line of the Delaware, Lackawanna and Western Railroad, along the elevated portion of the western limits of the city is called, was once a separate township by that name, but for many years has been annexed to Newark, forming its Eleventh ward. This is one of the most charming and desirable places of residence in the city. The ground is elevated, and the entire section is free from malarious influences, and the slope of the land is towards the river, affording natural advantages for drainage and sewerage. Rose-

PRESBYTERIAN CHURCH AND ROSEVILLE AVENUE

ville is essentially a settlement of homes, being free from factories and nuisances of every kind. Its people are among the most refined, cultured and progressive in the city. There are three public schools, there are two Presbyterian, one Episcopal, one Roman Catholic, one Baptist and one Methodist church

A ROSEVILLE STREET.

in the ward. Here also are a number of fine stores and a flourishing athletic club with a handsome building and well appointed grounds. In this ward are also some of Newark's most prominent charitable institutions, notably the Home for the Aged, under the care of the Little Sisters of the Poor, the House of the Good Shepherd (an institution for the reformation of fallen women), and the Dominican Convent. The population of Roseville is 12,076, and the taxable value of property, $5,000,880

THE POLICE FORCE

Previous to 1850 there was no organized day police force, and the police duty was performed by constables who were hired for that purpose from time to time, as occasion might require, although there was a night police force earlier than this, composed of a mere handful of men, mostly constables, who were known as the leather-head police. In 1850 the first marshal of police was appointed. His name was Whitbeck, and he used to have his headquarters on the second floor of Centre Market. The lockup about this time and for some years previous, was in the basement under the Court House on Market street. The cells that were used then are still in existence, and are sometimes exhibited to visitors as samples of the tortures inflicted on prisoners in bygone days. They are little, narrow apartments in which a man can hardly stand upright, and when the doors are closed are almost pitch dark. About a quarter of a century ago, one of the Essex county judges ordered a man locked up in one of these cells for contempt of Court. He became interested in a case he was trying and forgot all about the unfortunate prisoner, whom he had only intended to lock up for a few minutes, more for the purpose of frightening him than any thing else, and left him in the cell for three hours. When the man was taken out he was unconscious, and at first it was thought dead, but after working with him some time he recovered, and since that time these cells have never been used. Marshal Whitbeck went to California in 1853 or 1854, and Richard Francisco was elected Chief Marshal and Eliphalet C. Blazier and Robert Lang Assistant Marshals. They also had their headquarters over Centre Market. The city subsequently rented a brick

VIEW FROM ATHLETIC CLUB HOUSE

building on Academy street, where the post office now stands, and established a police station there. Robert Lang was made Chief Marshal in 1856. In 1857 the police force was reorganized, and Henry C. Whitney was made Chief, and the headquarters were moved to the lower end of Centre Market, where a lockup was fitted up. In 1865, the Police Headquarters building was erected on William street in the rear of the City Hall, and for many years this was the only police station in Newark. About fifteen years ago the Second Precinct station house was opened in the City Armory building on Morris and Essex Railroad avenue. There are now four police station houses in Newark, as follows : the First Precinct, or Police Headquarters, on William street; the Second Precinct, on Morris and Essex Railroad avenue; the Third Precinct, on Ferry street; the Fourth Precinct, on Springfield avenue. The police force of Newark for years was entirely under the control of the Common Council, and whenever the political complexion of that body changed there was a general overturning among the officers of the department, and wholesale removals even of patrolmen. For a few years past, however, the control of the department has been taken from the Common Council and placed in the hands of a non-partisan board of four Police Commissioners, two Republicans and two Democrats. Since then there has been a marked improvement in the morale and discipline of the force. The present Board of Police Commissioners are : President John W. Strahan, (Democrat); Osceola Currier, (Republican); Edward Maher, (Democrat); Henry Dilly, (Republican); Joseph M. Cox is the secretary of the Board. The present Chief of Police is Henry Hopper, who has been a member of the force for over ten years, and entered the department as a patrolman. He was promoted to the position of Captain of the Second Precinct in 1887, and was made Chief of Police in 1887. Chief Hopper is a thorough disciplinarian, a man fully conversant with all the requirements of police duty, an agreeable and courteous gentleman and a man of unblemished reputation. He has brought the police force up to a remarkable standard of excellence, and in so doing has been ably seconded by the four captains under him, who are: Michael Corbitt, First Precinct; Andrew J. McManus, Second Precinct; William P. Daly, Third Precinct; Charles Glori, Fourth Precinct. All of these captains are men who have risen from the ranks and have won promotion by their merits. The force at present consists of one Chief of Police, four Captains, ten Lieutenants, ten Sergeants, five Detectives, under the command of Detective Sergeant Stainsby, 170 Patrolmen and six detailed men, one Police Surgeon, one Truant Officer, one Electrician, four Drivers, one Stableman, and one Janitress. The city is now equipped with a police patrol signal system, by which through signal boxes placed at convenient intervals about the streets, the patrolmen can communicate with their respective station houses, and summon patrol wagons to their aid with a reserve force of men when needed, so that in case of riot or disturbance it would be possible to concentrate a large force of policemen at any given point in a few minutes.

The Newark police force to day is a well disciplined body of men; neat and clean in their personal appearance and habits; well drilled in all the military movements and tactics necessary far them to know, so much so, in fact, that when marching through the streets of the city favorable comment from citizens is heard on all sides.

LIVERPOOL LONDON AND GLOBE BUILDING.

THE NEWARK FIRE DEPARTMENT.

The Fire Department of Newark is admitted by all firemen to be one of the best in the United States. The history of the department dates back to nearly a hundred years ago. In January, 1797, the elegant residence of Judge Elisha Boudinot, on Park place, caught fire and was burned down. This led to the organization of Newark's first fire company. A call was issued for a meeting of the inhabitants of Newark, who had subscribed and were willing to subscribe towards the purchase of a fire engine, to meet at the Court House on January 17, 1797, for the purpose of consulting on the purchase of an engine, and the formation of two fire companies. It does not appear, however, that an organization was effected on that evening, but on January 26th a company was formed, composed of the best men in the town. On February 6th, 1797, the Newark Fire Association was formally organized. The members of the association procured leathern fire buckets, and for many years afterwards these buckets were kept hanging in the halls of the leading residents of the city, where they could readily be grasped in case of fire. The first fire engine was a very rude affair, and even the few small fires that occurred in Newark at that time taxed it to its utmost capacity. The first serious fire that occurred in Newark was in 1805, when the largest store in town, which was situated on the corner of Broad and Orange streets, was burned down. About 1815, a second fire company was organized under the name of Relief Engine Co. No. 2. In 1819 Fire Company No. 3, was organized and a new engine, the first ever built in Newark, was brought into use. Somewhere about 1831, fire companies Nos. 4 and 5 were formed. In June, 1854, the Town Council, who had become disgusted at the disorders and insubordination in the various companies, took possession of the engine houses and locked them up, and then began the work of reorganizing the department. The rowdy element was eliminated from the various companies and effective and well disciplined companies were brought into existence. In 1860, there were thirteen fire companies in Newark, and it was urged that there should be steam fire engines purchased. The project was bitterly opposed by many of the firemen. During this year, however, two steamers were procured, the Minnehaha and Washington. The former was operated by members of Exempt Engine Co. No. 1. The Fire Department was again organized in 1888, when the control of the department was taken from the Common Council and placed in the hands of a non-partisan commission, composed of two Republicans and two Democrats, appointed by the Mayor. During the year 1889, the department was made to consist entirely of men paid to devote their whole time to the service, and the call system as it had heretofore existed was abolished. Up to that time there had been a few men attached to each company who were paid to give their whole time to the service of the department, but the bulk of the department consisted of what are known as "call men," who were engaged at other avocations, and who on the sounding of the fire alarm bells dropped their work, ran to the scene of the fire and found their respective companies. Now the entire force is a permanent one, whose members are always on duty. The doing away of the call system has made a marked improvement in the discipline and efficiency of the force, which even prior to that time had a most excellent reputation all over the Union. The department now consists of eleven steam fire engine companies, one chemical engine company and three hook and ladder companies. The present Board of Fire Commissioners are President Edward Schickhaus, (Democrat); Hugh Kinnard, (Democrat); Henry R. Baker, (Republican); Marcus L. DeVoursney, (Republican). The Secretary of the Board is Mr. J. Frank Hewson, who has held that office since the organization of the Board. The Chief Engineer is Robert Kiersted, who has held that office since 1885. Chief Kiersted has been connected with the department since boyhood, and has risen from the ranks by his own merits. He is one of the best firemen in the country, and is noted for his coolness and bravery at fires. He is a strict disciplinarian and at the same time is a genial and courteous gentleman, and is liked and respected by the men under him, while he possesses the confidence and esteem of the insurance underwriters, and of the business community generally. The headquarters of the fire department are on the corner of Halsey and Academy streets, and here the chief engineer has his office. Here also the inspector of buildings is located. Chief Kiersted has a valuable coadjuter in the person of his clerk, Mr. Horace H. Brown, who has been Chief Engineer's clerk under several chiefs. Mr. Brown has been connected with the fire department since boyhood, and knows more about its workings and its history and about fire matters generally than any other man in Newark. The Assistant Chief Engineer is William C. Astley, who has his headquarters at the chemical engine house on Market street. He is also an old fireman, having many years experience in various positions. Next in rank to him comes District Engineer Louis M Price, who looks after the "Hill" section of the city and has his headquarters at No. 3 truck house. The fire department consists of 138 men as follows : one Chief Engineer, eleven Captains of steam engine companies, three Captains of truck companies, one Captain of chemical company, eleven drivers of steamers, eleven drivers of horse wagons, eleven engineers of steamers and eight or nine men attached to each steam engine company, nine men attached to each truck company, four men attached to chemical company, and seven men detailed for other purposes. The city has the Gamewell electric fire alarm system, which is in charge of Superintendent Adam Bosch, who has three linemen under him

LEADING BUSINESS MEN OF NEWARK.

PETERS & CALHOUN CO., Wholesale Manufacturers of Fine Saddlery and Harness, Nos. 906 and 908 Broad street, Newark, N. J. New York Salesroom, 33 Warren street, corner Church street. Boston Salesroom, Nos. 54 and 56 Sudbury street. The Peters & Calhoun Company rank with the largest and most generally known wholesale manufacturers of fine saddlery and harness in the country, their productions having an unsurpassed reputation, and a very extensive sale among the most critical trade in all parts of the Union. The company have a New York salesroom at No. 33 Warren street, corner of Church street, and a Boston salesroom at 54 and 56 Sudbury street, their factory being located at Nos. 906 and 908 Broad street, in this city. This representative enterprise was inaugurated in 1826, by Messrs. Slaugard & Macknet, and passed under the control of Messrs. Peters and Calhoun in

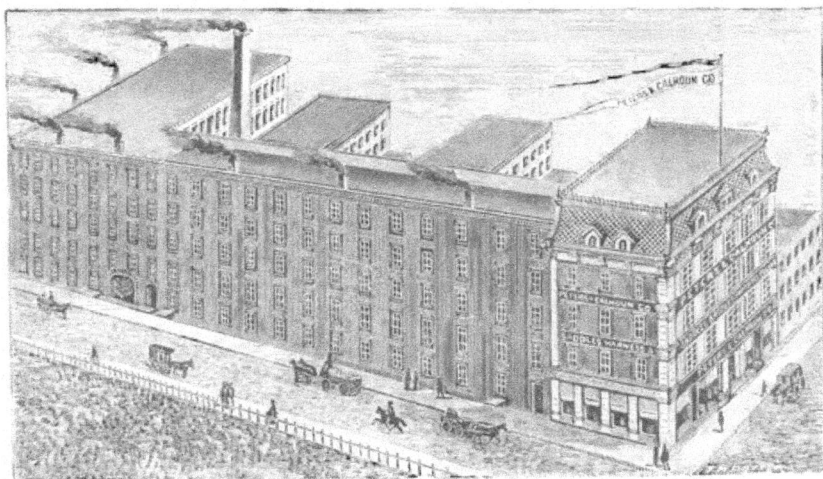

1874, being continued by that firm until it attained a magnitude which caused the incorporation of the existing company, of which Mr. G. Willis Peters is president; Mr. Jno. L. Dodge, Treasurer; Mr. Clarence Peters, Secretary and Assistant Treasurer, and Mr. George Peters, General Manager. The premises utilized, comprise five floors of the dimensions of 44x300 feet, and are equipped with an elaborate plant of improved machinery, including a 50-horse power engine and boiler. Employment is at present given to 250 assistants, but the number varies greatly with the season, and the class of work most in demand, the company having had 1,100 hands on its pay-roll at one time. With such facilities it is almost unnecessary to add that the most extensive orders can be filled at short notice, while it is conceded among the trade, that no house quotes lower prices for equally desirable goods.

The Mutual Life Insurance Company
Of New York.

RICHARD A. McCURDY, President.   ROBERT A. GRANNIS, Vice-President.

IT HAS PAID TO POLICY HOLDERS SINCE ORGANIZATION OVER $304,000,000.

The Twenty-Year Distribution Policy issued by this Company is the Most Liberal in its Terms, and the Cheapest and Best.

This Company issues the Most Approved Forms of Life and Endowment Policies

GEO. B. RAYMOND, General Agent,

745 & 747 Broad Street, Newark, N. J.

STEWART HARTSHORN, Manufacturer of Spring Shade Roller, Branch Offices, New York, 486 Broadway; Chicago, 45 Plymouth Place. Branch Factories, Muskegon, Michigan, Toronto, Ont. Main Office and Factory, East Newark, N. J. The above cut represents the Eastern shade roller factory of Stewart Hartshorn. These buildings were started in 1872 and occupied January 1st, 1873, by removal of business from New York. At that time the east side of the Passaic did not have the various enterprises that now appear so prominent. The ground on which the present thread companies are located was then a farm, and corn stalks were more common than bricks all over that part of Hudson county. Mr. Stewart Hartshorn, anticipating in part at least, the future demand for his goods, and knowing the value of room from previous restricted quarters commenced this factory after purchasing, what was then thought more ground than was necessary. The growth of the business has been such that more than double as much room is now occupied, and still he feels crowded. The factory occupies the space bounded by Grant avenue, President street and Mullock place, and therefore part is in the township of Kearny and part in the township of Harrison. The immense demand for the Hartshorn roller proved that it could not be all handled from the Eastern factory, and, therefore, one that occupies vastly more ground is now running in Muskegon, Michigan, and also one in Toronto, Canada. All adults can remember the troublesome cord and ratchet devices used on shade rollers before. Mr. Hartshorn invented the self acting pawl spring shade roller in 1864, a new departure in mechanical devices, one that is now known all over the civilized globe, and by its use giving satisfaction wherever shades are used. Improvements in manufacture are being continually made. Long experience guides the careful testing of every supposed improvement until proof is had of merit, and when proven, is adopted, regardless of cost. Dealers in this line of goods well know their standard character, and also know the business-like treatment always received at the hands of Stewart Hartshorn.

HARRISON & HOAG, Wholesale Dealers in Heavy Wrapping, Book, News, Manilla and Straw Paper, Card Board, Ruled Blanks, Paper Bags, Twine, etc., Nos. 177-179 Halsey Street, Near Market, Newark, N. J. The gentlemen whose card heads this article inaugurated their business in the year 1884. Since the inception of the enterprise a large trade has been established, and to-day this house does as much business in this line as any we could point out in the city of Newark. Close relations exist between it and the trade, who have learned to appreciate the many advantages to be derived in placing orders with Messrs. Harrison & Hoag. The chief feature of the enterprise, as we have stated above, is in dealing both at wholesale and retail in heavy wrapping, book, news, manilla and straw paper, card board, ruled blanks, paper bags, twine, etc. This line of goods is, of course, used more by factories, stores, printing and publishing establishments than any others, and it is not out of place, in our opinion, to dwell a little at length, in a work of this kind, upon the extensive and varied stock which the house of Harrison & Hoag carry. There are two things which characterize a well appointed printing and publishing establishment, and they are, of course, first, a varied assortment of fonts of type, and second, but no less important, a well furnished stock room. Book paper of all sizes, weight and quality, news or light paper stock suitable for newspaper and hand bill purposes, and manilla and straw paper for purposes in which they are commonly used should also as equally abound upon the shelves of a well appointed printer's stock room. Now the question arises to the printer, "Where can I get what I want at reasonable rates?" If we were to be permitted a suggestion we would say, call on Harrison & Hoag, of Nos. 169 and 171 Halsey street, Newark, N. J. Here you will find the stock complete and the lowest market rates quoted. You will also find that honorable business methods are the only ones made use of by this house, and that no delays will occur in filling your orders. Five courteous assistants are ready to lend cheerful service and advice in your selection, if you need it. Messrs. Harrison & Hoag's premises comprise a large space of flooring and storage rooms. An immense stock is carried, and you are sure to find what you want. A visit of inspection will convince any who may not entertain our opinion that our statements are not even doing quite enough justice to the stock carried by Messrs. Harrison & Hoag. The chief feature of the stock, however, is its light and heavy wrapping paper for offices, stores and manufacturing establishments. In this line a heavy business is done, and Messrs. Harrison & Hoag head the list. Orders for all sorts of wrapping paper are filled at short notice.

RESIDENCE OF S. J. MEEKER 394 BROAD ST.—JOHN E. BAKER, ARCHITECT.

JOHN E. BAKER, Architect, 748 Broad Street, Newark, N. J. Mr. John E. Baker not only has a thorough technical training, but also long practical experience as an architect, for he has practiced his profession for about seventeen years, having begun operations in 1873. He is a native of East Orange, N. J., and came to Newark in 1882, after having been located in New York for two years. The premises utilized are located at 748 Broad st., and comprise three rooms. Employment is given to four assistants, and designs, estimates, plans and specifications can be furnished at very short notice, in cases where haste is desirable. Mr. Baker makes a specialty of country houses, and is one of the most original and successful designers of such in the State. He has erected over two hundred houses in the Oranges and vicinity. Mr. Baker was the architect for Senator McPherson's handsome residence at Washington, D. C. He is now building a large number of residences at Washington, including the Chapel and President's residence of the Howard University. He is also building in Massachusetts, New York, Pennsylvania, New Jersey and at other points, among these structures being some very elaborate and handsome buildings. His facilities, however, are in proportion to the demand upon them, and all commissions are assured prompt and careful attention. Many desirable plans for large and small country houses may be seen at his office, and those contemplating the erection of a structure of this kind, may save time and trouble by communicating with him in person or by mail. Mr. Baker has published several works of architectural designs, which will be of great assistance to those who contemplate building. These books can be sent by mail to any part of the United States. The above cut is of Mr. S. J. Meeker's residence, which was designed by Mr. Baker, which will give you some idea of the class of work he is doing.

G. L. ERB, Furnishing Undertaker, 22 William Street, Newark, N. J. Telephone No. 519. Orders Promptly Attended to. Open Day and Night. First Class Work. Embalming a Specialty. Fine Coaches for Weddings and Receptions. The business which Mr. G. L. Erb carries on at his ware-rooms, No. 22 William street, was inaugurated in 1859 by Mr. A. L. Erb. Subsequent to the latter's decease in 1883, his wife, Mrs. Eva M. Erb, assumed control of the business, with the services of Mr. G. L. Erb as manager. This gentleman came into possession of the business in 1890, and continues to maintain for it the high reputation it enjoys, as being one of the best establishments of this nature to be found in the city of Newark. The duties of an undertaker are difficult and irksome at the best, and the citizens of this city have reason to congratulate themselves on the high character and merit of the gentlemen who carry on this business in their midst. Where the stand-

ard of excellence in this business is as high as it is in Newark, perhaps it is not quite proper to make comparisons, and, indeed, we have no intention of so doing, still, for all that, we cannot forbear calling the attention of our readers to Mr. Erb's establishment at No. 22 William street, for it is one of the best appointed and well managed in the city, and deserves the appreciation it has met with in the more than thirty years it has existed. Mr. G. L. Erb, who has been in the business for a great number of years, has always shown his fitness for the task he has undertaken. He carries on all the branches of his profession, funeral directing, furnishing and embalming, and everything pertaining to the management of funerals, and employs six courteous assistants. Mr. Erb is a native of Cleveland, Ohio, and the premises he occupies are 20x50 feet in dimensions. Orders are received by telephone (519), and the office may be found open day and night. The services of an undertaking establishment should be courteous in the superlative degree, and such a service the public may be sure of receiving in the sad event of their requiring it, if they secure the services of Mr. G. L. Erb.

J. FITZGERALD, Machinist, 276 Halsey Street, Newark, N. J. The establishment conducted at No. 276 Halsey street, by the gentleman whose card we print above, is worthy of special mention in a book of this kind. The nature of the work turned out by Mr. Fitzgerald is that of the general machinist, and no shop of this city in proportion to its size is better prepared to execute machinery work than is Mr. Fitzgerald. His establishment is equipped with all the necessary appliances and machinery to facilitate operations, and as none but first-class workmen are employed, the patrons of this house will testify that the work turned out is of a superior order of workmanship. Lathe and drill work of all descriptions are paid special attention to, and accuracy and promptness in filling orders are characteristics of the house. A large ten horse engine furnishes the motive power for the shop, which is 25x100 feet in dimensions. Mr. Fitzgerald is a native of Newark, and inaugurated his business in 1870. By hard work, patience and economy, this gentleman has succeeded in attaining a reputation for good work, which many other, and more pretentious firms, fairly envy. We earnestly invite the public to send in their orders for machine work to Mr. Fitzgerald's shop at No. 276 Halsey street, Newark, N. J.

DOREMUS BROS., Wholesale and Retail dealers in Fine Groceries, Fruits, Wines, Cigars, etc., 378 Broad Street, and 25 Eighth Avenue, Newark, N. J. New York Office, 187 Church Street. Among those establishments which have combined to make the name of Newark well and favorably known as an enterprising and progressive trade centre, a high rank must be given to that now carried on by Doremus Bros., for whether we judge by the number of years this enterprise has been successfully prosecuted or by the position which it now occupies among similar undertakings in the city, its claim to be regarded as representative in the full sense of the word must be conceded to be a just one. The premises occupied are located at 378 Broad street, and have a representative establishment at 25 Eighth avenue, their office being situated at 187 Church street, New York. An immense stock is carried, and both a wholesale and retail trade is conducted, the commodities dealt in including groceries, liquors, wines, cigars, etc. Mr. H. B. & J. M. Doremus are both natives of Morris county, Mr. H. B. having served as Freeholder for the Eighth ward. The stock of groceries comprises everything in that line, and being made up of goods selected expressly for family use it contains nothing that cannot be guaranteed to prove as represented.

W·T·Rae   V M Wright

WM. T. RAE & CO.,

Jewelers,

707 Broad St.,   Newark.

Nearly all rare and costly things have their cheap imitations in these days. Perhaps this is more the case with jewels than with other articles, for the precious metals and stones are naturally very expensive, and the taste for adornment is born in most people. Therefore, many who cannot afford the real are willing to put up with sham. The market is flooded with these really beautiful imitations, which need the trained eye of an expert and connoisseur to detect from the real. It is not surprising, then, that many people spend large sums on beautiful stones, only to find when too late, that they have been abominably swindled. It is never safe to trust to one's individual judgment in the choice of jewels. There are many establishments that make a speciality of these things, and that have a reputation for strict integrity in their dealings. These are to be found in Newark as elsewhere, and among them we take pleasure in calling attention to Messrs. Wm. T. Rae & Co. This house was founded in 1866 by Mr. Rae, who, four years later, associated himself with Mr. V. M. Wright, his present partner. These gentlemen are both natives of New York State, but from their long residence in Newark and their high standing, are very well known in this city. They make a speciality of diamonds, of which their stock is large and choice. Watches of all kinds and prices will be found here, as well as a fine assortment of jewelry. The premises occupied are at 707 Broad street, at the corner of Cedar street. Five courteous assistants are in constant readiness to show these choice goods to customers, to whom we can only recommend a call upon Messrs. Rae & Co., if they need anything in this line.

THE NEWARK FIRE

INSURANCE COMPANY.

Office: 741 and 743 Broad Street.

JOHN J. HENRY, *President.*
> GEORGE F. REEVE, *Vice-President.*
>> OSCAR O. BREWER, *Secretary.*
>>> JOSEPH WARD, Jr., *Treasurer.*

ALEX. M. LINNETT'S Lincoln Park Pharmacy. Prescriptions a Specialty. Clinton Avenue, corner Washington street, Newark, N. J. An establishment in which the residents of Newark put great confidence, is that of which Mr. Alexander M. Linnett is the proprietor, for during the twenty years that this house has been in existence, it has been invariably managed in a straightforward and painstaking manner, that is worthy of unreserved commendation. Mr. Linnett was born and brought up in Newark, and settled himself in business here in 1876. Two years ago he moved into his present quarters, which are handsomely and conveniently fitted up for the purpose. The store is conveniently situated at the corner of Clinton avenue and Washington street, and covers an area of 50x30 feet. Mr. Linnett lets no element of chance enter into the operation of the prescription department, for he makes a specialty of this, having the most improved facilities for it, and employing only experienced and trustworthy assistants. These average about four. They know their business, and, thus, annoying delays rarely occur. The charges made are always as reasonable as could be expected, where only the best drugs and materials are used.

E. CLAYTON BERNHEIM,

191 Market St., Newark.

GOLD WATCHES AT CLUB RATES.

Should you desire a fine gold watch for a very small amount of money call on E. Clayton Bernheim, successor to New Jersey Keystone Watch Co., No. 191 Market street, Newark, N. J. He sells on an entirely new club plan that is more advantageous to the purchaser than any other club plan. Call and have the new plan explained. Agents make a fine salary by securing members for us.

New York Life Insurance Co.,

781 Broad Street, Newark, N. J.

JAMES S. EDWARDS, Cashier.

An insurance company that has been in existence for nearly half a century, must have made a record sufficiently broad and comprehensive to show conclusively what its methods and resources are, and when we see so old-established a company rapidly increasing its business among the most intelligent classes in the community every year, the natural inference is that its record must be equal to the best. It is unnecessary, therefore, to eulogize the New York Life Insurance Company, for since its incorporation in 1845 it has steadily increased in popularity, and now holds a leading position among similar organizations throughout the country. Mr. James S. Edwards, Cashier, has held the position of cashier for the State agency for New Jersey since 1884, and those wishing detailed information concerning the methods and resources of the company should make application at his office, No. 781 Broad street, for they will be most courteously received, and will be given every facility to become familiar with the facts in the case. Mr. Edwards is a native of Sussex county, N. J., and served nine months in the Army of the Potomac, during one of the most eventful periods of the war. He is a resident of Irvington and is very widely known throughout this section of the State. He was collector of taxes for three years and receiver of taxes for two years, for the township of Clinton. Having made a study of life insurance matters as well as having had practical experience in the business, he is thoroughly well informed in regard to its many details, and is in a position to give valuable counsel to those uncertain as to which form of policy is best adapted to their needs, so that such of our readers as are intending to insure their lives, would best serve their own interests by giving him a call. In the year 1885, Henry W. Baldwin, Esq., was appointed by the company General Manager for the State. Mr. Baldwin has his main office in the Boreel building, 115 Broadway, New York. Under his skillful and energetic management and matchless talent for handling agents, the increase of business of the New York Life has simply been marvelous. Below will be found a summary of the forty-sixth annual report of the company:

SUMMARY OF THE FORTY-SIXTH ANNUAL REPORT OF THE NEW YORK LIFE INSURANCE CO.

BUSINESS OF 1890.

Premiums,	$27,228,309.34
Interests, Rents, etc.,	4,929,890.74
Total Income	$32,158,100.08
Death-claims and Endowments,	$7,078,272.48
Dividends, Annuities, and Purchased Insurances,	6,201,271.54
Total to Policy Holders,	$15,279,544.02
New Policies Issued,	45,754
New Insurance Written,	$153,556,065.00

CONDITION JAN. 1, 1891.

Assets,	$115,942,809.97
Liabilities, Company's Standard	$101,049,359.11
Surplus (4 per cent.)	$14,898,450.86
Policies in Force,	173,469
Insurance in Force	$561,558,726.00

PROGRESS IN 1890.

Increase in Benefits to Policy Holders,	$1,158,422.96
Increase in Premiums,	2,642,288.24
Increase in Income,	2,994,832.84
Increase in Assets,	10,894,209.01
Increase in Insurance Written,	8,456,977.00
Increase in Insurance in Force	73,736,756.00

"DOMESTIC" ART ROOMS. Novelties, and Art Materials for Home Decoration. Order Work, Stamping, Embroidering, etc., a specialty. Lessons in Oil, Lustre and Water-Color Painting, China Decorating, Embroidery, etc. It is safe to say that no business establishment in Newark is more generally or more favorably known among the ladies than the "Domestic" Art Rooms, for the inducements here offered **are** as a whole unequaled in the State, and these rooms may justly be called **the** headquarters for home decorations, so far as this city is concerned. Operations were begun in 1885, and the business has developed from comparatively small beginnings, for originally this was simply the agency of the Domestic Sewing machine, the Art department being subsequently added, and attaining its present importance by years of steady growth. The proprietors, Messrs. Fletcher & Faulkner, are still general agents for the Domestic sewing machines, conceded to be the lightest running sewing machines in the market, and so well and favorably known as to require no description in these columns. They are also agents for the Domestic Paper Fashions, and carry a complete line of them at all times, including the very latest designs. The premises occupied are located at No. 677 Broad street, and comprise two floors measuring 20x80 feet, and an annex of the dimensions of 20x40 feet. An exceptionally complete assortment of novelties and art materials is constantly carried, anything in this line being furnished in quantities to suit at the lowest market rates. Particular attention is given to order work, stamping, embroidering, etc., commissions being executed in a superior manner at short notice. Lessons given in all branches of painting, etching, embroidery, etc., by experienced and competent teachers at moderate rates, and orders by mail will receive immediate and careful attention.

WYMBLE MANUFACTURING COMpany, Silversmiths, Electro-Deposition, with Silver in all its processes. Factory office northwest corner Chestnut and Mulberry street, Newark, N. J. The Wymble Manufacturing Company of Newark, N. J., makers of solid silver goods by **the** electro deposit process in flat and repoussé effects on glass ware. They have at once come in the favor of the trade, and their work is acknowledged to be of the finest in workmanship as well as design and finish. Their line consists of a magnificent and varied assortment, few of which are, viz: Claret pitchers, wine decanters, cologne bottles, pickle jars, sherry pitchers, flasks, pipes, cigar holders, bon bon and butter dishes, porridge and tea sets, cane and umbrella handles etc. One of their new pieces, a claret pitcher, an entirely new shape in glass, part of which is richly cut, has a design called "The Chase," with figures of huntsmen riding in pursuit of the game, interlaced with a fine tracery of scrolls and flowers all handsomely engraved. They also make a specialty is hollow wire, hair pins, book marks and other novelties. Among the patterns worthy of special mention are a number entirely new which must be seen to be appreciated. They also wish to announce that they will move about the first of May to their handsome and commodious new building at Woodside, N. J., where they will have all the facilities for making all kinds of Hollow silverware in addition to the above mentioned goods.

MARTIN R. DENNIS & CO., Bankers and Brokers, Passenger Agents for All Lines of Ocean Steamships, 774 Broad Street, Five Doors above Market Street, Newark, N. J. The business conducted by Messrs. Martin R. Dennis & Co., was founded more than forty years ago, and has developed to such proportions as to justly entitle it to be called the representative enterprise of the kind in this city. The head of the firm is now Alfred L. Dennis, son of the late Martin R. Dennis. That the undertaking has been, and is skillfully and honorably managed, is proved by the leading position it now occupies, for the public have certainly had abundant opportunity to become thoroughly familiar, with the facilities offered since operations were begun in 1848. The premises utilized have an area of 1,200 square feet, and are centrally located at No. 774 Broad street, five doors above Market street. The firm are passenger agents for Cunard line, White Star line, Anchor line, Guion line, National line, State line, Inman line, Allan line, North German Lloyd line, Hamburg line, Red Star line, Rotterdam line, Fabre line, Mallory line, French line, and all other lines of ocean steamers, and can furnish cabin, intermediate and steerage tickets, and one of the most important departments of their extensive banking business is the issuing of drafts, letters of credit and bills of exchange, through Brown Brothers & Co., Drexel, Morgan & Co., Knauth, Nachod & Kühne. Sums of any amount will be sent direct to any address, however remote, by safe and expeditious means, and packages and valuables will be forwarded by the Transatlantic express. A full assortment of foreign money is constantly on hand, including sovereigns, Napoleons, and German, Russian, Italian, Austrian and Swedish paper money, and exchanges will be made at a very reasonable commission. Stocks, bonds, etc., are bought and sold, and an extensive fire insurance business is done, risks being placed in first-class companies, at the lowest market rates. It is evident that such an establishment as this must be a great public convenience, and it certainly deserves the liberal support it receives.

ORRIN E. RUNYON, Real Estate, Insurance and Loan Broker, 800 Broad Street, Newark, N. J. The subject of this sketch occupies fine offices on the ground floor of the Liverpool, London and Globe building, at 800, 802 and 804 Broad street. He is the successor to the old firm of R. Burgess & Co., whose business was conducted at the above place for several years. Mr. Runyon first came to Newark in the year 1881, as a bookkeeper for the firm of J. C. Smith & Co., large grain and flour dealers. He remained with them for two years, and left them in 1883, to take a place in Mr. Burgess' office, where he remained until May, 1884, when he ventured out for himself in New York city. The Summer of 1884 was an unusually dull one, and at Mr. Burgess' solicitation, Mr. Runyon returned to Newark, in September of that year, and acquired a half interest in the business. In October, 1887, Mr. Runyon bought out his partner, and since then has conducted a large and successful business in his own name. He enjoys the confidence and influential patronage of a large class of realty investors, and has successfully carried through some of the largest transactions in the city, among them the recent purchase of some $300,000 worth of property in the Fourth ward, for the Central Railroad of New Jersey for their freight department, the property now occupied by Wilkinson, Gaddis & Co., at Broad and Fair sts., and many others of a like nature. His services are in constant demand, he has three able assistants, and his past record gives assurance of intelligent and faithful service. He is the Newark member of the American Real Estate Association of the United States, and is the agent for the United Security Life Insurance and Trust Co., of Pennsylvania. Any business entrusted to him will receive prompt attention and faithful service.

MISS E. WEHRLE, Ladies Hair Goods, No. 169 Washington Street, Newark, N. J. The lady whose card heads this article carries on an extensive business in the manufacture of ladies' hair goods. She leases the recently enlarged and renovated store at No. 169 Washington street, where all the facilities for working human hair can be found. A full stock of ladies' hair goods, such as Langtry bangs, Saratoga invisible parts, switches, braids, etc., is carried. Dyeing and bleaching in all colors, cutting and curling of hair is also done, and special attention is paid to the "shingling" of bangs. Bang fluffing lotions and hair dressing is kept in abundance, and all that pertains to the hair business. Ladies' hair work is done in all its branches, and hair dressing and bang cutting are specialties. Ladies in need of hair goods should call upon Miss Wehrle's place of business, No. 169 Washington street. The higher classes of trade are especially catered to, and ladies of society have recognized a more than ordinary degree of artistic tonsorial ability in Miss Wehrle's work. The apartments occupied by this lady are delicately suggestive of neatness and order. The walls of the building are neatly finished off and are fire proof. Miss Wehrle's prices are moderate on all work executed and goods sold. A visit of inspection is respectfully solicited.

M. & E. SCHMITT, Dealers in Perfumery, and Barbers' Supplies, Complete Outfits for Barber Shops a Specialty, 332 Plane Street, near Market Street, Newark, N. J. The enterprise conducted by Messrs. M. & E. Schmitt, in this city, is quite of interest to all of us who use a razor, or have one used on our faces, for these gentlemen, as we have said in the caption which heads this article, are dealers in perfumeries and barbers' supplies. They inaugurated their business in 1888, and with close personal attention to the wants of their customers, have succeeded in building up an extensive business. Both gentlemen are natives of this city and have hosts of both business and social friends. The premises they utilize are 20x60 feet in dimensions, and employment is given to two courteous and obliging assistants. A retail and wholesale business is done, and the stock of barbers' supplies which these gentlemen carry is as complete as it is varied. The best shaving soaps on the market are kept by them, and razors, scissors, brushes, clippers, combs and the usual paraphernalia of the business may be had at surprisingly low rates. We wish to call attention to their choice line of cosmetics, wax, hair oil, camphor ice and magnesia also. The purest of these is a feature of the stock, and cups, sponges, perfumeries and other private property of customers, abound in great abundance. A call, or trial order is respectfully solicited.

BREAKENRIDGE & TICHENOR,

Brokers and Dealers in Real Estate,

766 BROAD ST., NEWARK, N. J.

NORTHWESTERN MUTUAL LIFE INsurance Company, C. D. Paul, State Agent for New Jersey, 800 Broad Street, Newark, N. J. The Northwestern Mutual Life Insurance Company does not claim to be the largest insurance company in the world, but it does claim to be in all points of real and substantial benefit to policy-holders unquestionably the most successful life insurance company in the world, and, of course this is the sort of company that those seeking insurance are looking for. But three companies have a larger amount of insurance in force than the Northwestern, and it should be remembered that the latter has always pursued a most conservative policy as regards membership, refusing to establish agencies in foreign countries, and limiting its business to the healthy portions of the United States. The result is that during the ten years ending in 1889, the Northwestern's average death rate was lower than that of either of its twelve leading competitors, and what is yet more remarkable, it was actually lower than any of the twelve companies during each one of the ten years. High interest and low mortality are the most powerful factors in earning surplus for members, and it is interesting to note that while the percentage of losses to mean amount of risk during the five years from 1885 to 1889 inclusive, varied from .82 to 1.01 per cent. in the Northwestern, the average of all the companies reporting to Massachusetts for 1889 was 1.32 per cent. At the beginning of the current year the Northwestern's surplus on a 4 per cent. basis was $6,552,724.18, this being an increase of $891,377.65 over the surplus of a year ago, the assets having increased $5,757,602.15 during the same time. The actual new business written in 1889 was $58,671,744, or, including restorations, etc., as is done in official reports and the advertisements of other companies, the total would be over $62,000,000. The following summary of what the company has accomplished since organization is worthy of careful study by those contemplating the taking out of a life policy:

During the thirty-two years since the company commenced business it has paid to the representatives of its deceased policy holders, for death losses, $21,055,600.05

And to its living policy holders for dividends, matured endowments, surrendered and lapsed policies, 31,299,960.84

Total, $52,299,560.84
Add present assets, 42,575,912.66

Amount paid to policy holders and held for them, $95,135,512.80
Total premiums received, $4,575,800.96

Excess of assets and payments to policy holders over premium receipts, $40,563,711.84
The payments to policy holders added to the present assets amount to nearly ten and a half millions more than the entire premium receipts.

The Newark office is located in the Liverpool and London and Globe building, No. 800 Broad street, and is in charge of Mr. C. D. Paul, State agent for New Jersey, in which section the company is rapidly extending its operations.

MOORE & CO., Ring Manufacturers, 359 Mulberry street. We have not the figures at hand showing the total annual production of rings and other articles of jewelry in Newark, but the sum total must be very large, for a great amount of capital and hundreds of hands are engaged in this branch of production here. One of the most completely equipped and most favorably known of these establishments is that conducted under the firm name of Moore & Co., at No. 359 Mulberry street. This business was founded in 1886 by Mr. Arthur W. Moore, under the existing firm name, and has steadily increased until it now holds a representative position among other enterprises of a kindred nature. Mr. Moore is a native of Birmingham, England, and has had long and varied experience as a manufacturer. He makes a specialty of the production of rings, and has both the mechanical facilities and the skilled assistants necessary to enable him to meet all honorable competition, both as regards the quality of the work turned out and the prices quoted on the same. The factory has an area of 2,200 square feet, and employment is given to thirty or more assistants. All orders are assured prompt and careful attention, no pains being spared to maintain the high reputation thus far held. The growth of the business conducted by Messrs. Moore & Co. is phenomenal. Starting less than five years ago with seat room for but one man, they now employ over thirty, and do a business of from $80,000 to $85,000 per year.

JOSEPH H. MENAGH.

EXCLUSIVE DEALER IN

Black Goods, Silks and Mourning Millinery,

Now at **Nos. 673 & 675 Broad St.,** 2d Floor

WILL REMOVE

On or before May 1 to the elegant new store, No. 19 Academy Street, adjoining W. H. & R. Burnet, Furriers.

DAVID YOUNG.

SURVEYOR,

775 Broad Street, Newark.

BEFORE I WENT.   AFTER.

BOSTON DENTAL ASSOCIATION.

No. 222 Market Street, Newark, N. J. It would be difficult to name a branch of business more important to the welfare of the community than that of the dentist, or one demanding on the part of those engaged in this profession more ability and scientific knowledge. One of the most prominent establishments of this kind in the United States, is that of the Boston Dental Association, located at 222 Market street, with branch offices in the leading cities throughout the country. Here in Newark they are doing the leading business, and their workmanship and materials used are of the finest quality and unsurpassed by any other dentists. Their operations are all modern dentistry and at most reasonable prices. Their crown and bridge work (Sheffield system) which came to our notice, was extraordinarily fine and might cause the envy of any dentist. The great success attained by the Boston Dental Association, not only in this city but at all the many points at which they have offices, proves that the people are quick to appreciate a really superior dental service, and encourages the association to continue their efforts to do work unequalled for neatness, strength and general utility. No expense is spared in providing the very latest improved tools and appliances, and utilizing the most expeditious and thorough processes, and it is worthy of note that the association is not confined to the use of any one system, but are at liberty to employ whatever method may be best adapted to individual cases. In a word, they practice "Painless Dentistry" in the true sense of that much abused phrase, and their facilities are so perfect and their operators so expert that the most timid need feel no fear of placing themselves under treatment; while busy people, whose time is of value, will especially appreciate the promptness and celerity with which work is done, and all classes can join in admiring the permanence and beauty of the results attained. A specialty is made of crown and bridge work, and those who require artificial teeth, but object to the use of a plate, will find the association prepared to satisfy their wants perfectly and at as low a price as can be quoted on really first-class work. Four large rooms are utilized at No. 222 Market street, where Dr. Holt, the Manager, with three competent assistants, will cheerfully attend to all who desire their services.

L. S. PLAUT & CO.'S

New Departures.

In connection with the information relating to the "Bee Hive" stores of L. S. Plaut & Co's, set forth on pages 100 and 101, it will prove of interesting note to state that a department of Millinery as well as that of a shoe department for men have been recently opened. This is but the beginning of extensive additions, alterations and improvements shortly to be made by this firm, in anticipation of their occupancy of adjoining buildings.

ALEXANDER DON & CO., Plumbers, Steam and Gas Fitters, Corner Elwood and Washington Avenues, Woodside, Newark, N. J. Telephone 247. Agents for Furman Steam and Hot Water Boiler. When we say that it is far better that there should be no plumbing at all, in a house than what there is should be improperly done, we may be accused of exaggeration, and yet we have no doubt but that physicians in general will endorse the statement and agree that it is fully justified by facts. Defective plumbing has caused much sickness, and not a few deaths, and those having occasion for the services of a plumber, owe it to themselves, and to their families, to see that an entirely competent man is employed. Few of us are able to judge of the skillfulness of a workman in this line, therefore, the only practical way to do, is to place your order with a house of established and unquestioned reputation, such an one we believe that to be, which is conducted by Mr. Alexander Don & Co. They have been established long enough to gain an enviable reputation for the conscientious filling of orders, and an evident desire to deal honestly by every customer. Orders for plumbing, steam and gas fitting, will be given prompt attention, there being ten assistants employed, and all necessary facilities at hand to attain the best results. Alexander Don & Co., are agents for the Furman Steam and Hot Water Boiler. The store occupied is 40x25 feet in dimensions. The firm consists of Mr. Alexander Don and Mr. John Lever. Both of these gentlemen are natives of Newark, New Jersey. They are well known for their faithful performance of all work entrusted to them.

John Lever,

Real Estate & Insurance Broker,

188 WASHINGTON AVENUE,

Woodside.   Newark. N. J.

Money to Loan on Bond and Mortgage

EMIL F. HOFMANN, Manufacturer of Gas Fixtures, Fine Kerosene Lamps, etc., Brass and Silver Signs, Railing and Office Fixtures. Importer of Decorated Shades, Globes, etc., No. 133 Market Street, Newark, N. J. No finer selection of gas fixtures can be found, than at this house, and he who fails to be satisfied with the goods here displayed, must indeed be difficult to please. Mr. Hofmann is a manufacturer as well as dealer in brass and silver goods, being the only manufacturer of brass and silver signs in the State. He established his present business in Newark in 1885, after having been for a time Assistant Superintendant to J. S. Conover & Co., the well known brass goods house of West 23d Street, New York. In this position Mr. Hofmann gained a wide experience of the business, and for this reason he is eminently fitted to carry on an extensive trade on his own account. He is, himself, an expert designer and mechanic, and he employs none but first-class mechanics to do his work. Mr. Hofmann has the largest assortment of globes and shades in the city. He imports them directly for his own business, and they are of all varieties. Mr. Hofmann also manufacturers brass railings and office fixtures. These goods are all of fine quality, and give the best satisfaction at lowest prices.

THE MASSACHUSETTS MUTUAL LIFE Insurance Co., Springfield, Mass. A. W. Bray, Jr., General Agent, 740 Broad Street, Newark, N. J. The desirability of Life Insurance being no longer a subject for argument, the question to be settled by the ordinary individual having others dependent upon him, or being desirous of taking out an endowment policy narrows itself down to just about this—"In what company can I insure to the best advantage?" Attention is naturally first called to Massachusetts companies, for this State leads the Union in life insurance legislation, and a company chartered under existing laws is not only obliged to make its policies clear and explicit, but is held closely to its obligations even to the most trivial detail. Among Massachusetts companies the Massachusetts Mutual Life Insurance Company of Springfield stands easily first, and whether you want dependable insurance at the lowest possible cost, or are seeking particularly to obtain a policy that one with the poorest head for figures can readily understand, you can possibly do no better than to make application at the office of A. W. Bray, Jr., General Agent, 740 Broad Street, Newark, New Jersey. He will be happy to give you all desired information, and will furnish circulars, etc., which clearly explain the peculiarities of the State laws governing the policies, and also treat in detail of the value of any given policy at any given time. Every policy issued by the Massachusetts Mutual is incontestable after two full annual premiums have been paid, and thereafter has

a cash surrender value which can be demanded and recovered upon any anniversary of the policy date making it in fact a bond given by a company whose assets exceed ten millions. Mr. Bray is widely and favorably known in Newark, where he has been a member of the Board of Education for several years. Since accepting the agency of the company in 1887, he has largely increased its business in this section, and has gained the reputation of being one of the best informed and most reliable insurance men in the State.

The Following Represents the Actual Cash and Paid-up Values of a Twenty-Payment Life Policy for $10,000. Age, 35. Annual Premium, $342.00.

Year.	Paid Up.	Cash.	Year.	Paid Up.	Cash.
2d	$ 663	$ 296	12th	5,807	2,669
3d	1,192	454	13th	6,301	2,868
4th	1,717	620	14th	6,794	3,199
5th	2,240	853	15th	7,285	3,510
6th	2,760	1,076	16th	7,776	3,834
7th	3,277	1,308	17th	8,267	4,170
8th	3,790	1,543	18th	8,761	4,520
9th	4,301	1,799	19th	9,259	4,884
10th	4,807	2,062	20th	10,000	5,261
11th	5,309	2,329			

These values are exclusive of dividends.

HARRISON VAN DUYNE

SURVEYOR,

AND

Dealer in Real Estate,

No. 760 Broad St., Newark, N. J.

A. H. BURKHARDT, Dealer in Fine Groceries, Teas, Coffees, Sugars, Spices, etc., Fruits and Vegetables in Season, Flour, Feed and Grain, 246 Ferry Street, corner Ferguson, Newark, N. J. A representative enterprise in this neighborhood is that conducted by Mr. A. H. Burkhardt, dealer in fine groceries, teas, sugars, spices, etc., fruits and vegetables in season, flour, feed and grain. It was inaugurated in the year 1867, by Mr. Burkhardt in person, and under his skillful management it has thrived since its very inception. Mr. Burkhardt is a native of Germany, but as he has resided here and been in business in our midst so long (twenty-three years), he has made a large circle of both business and social friends. He was for four years one of the Board of School Commissioners, a fact which shows that he is a highly esteemed member of the community. He gives employment to four courteous and competent assistants in his business, and his store is 25x45 feet in dimensions. He also utilizes a store-house 16x37 feet in dimensions, for duplicates, etc., his hay and feed being stored in a spacious shed. Mr. Burkhardt has acquired an enviable run of custom during his business career. His invariably and strictly honest business methods and policy is what told the story of his success, and which tells it in any business. Our readers need but place a trial order with this establishment to be convinced that our favorable mention of it is not out of place. Remember the place, No. 246 Ferry street. A. H. Burkhardt, grocer.

JAS. H. LINDSLEY, Architect, 762 Broad Street, Newark, N. J.

No one at all acquainted with building operations will deny that on the skill of the architect depends in a great measure, not only the convenience and tasteful character, but also the cost of the finished structure, and it may be accepted as an unvarying rule that it always pays to employ the best talent available in the architectural line. Before opening his office in 1876, Mr. Lindsley was a student with the late R. G. Hatfield, of New York, an architect identified with many prominent works in that city, and after several years experience in practical building, has been engaged for fifteen years in the practice of his former profession, fully equipped in all its varied departments for its most successful exercise, as is evinced by many prominent works in this city, notably the Murphy Varnish Works, the Monmouth Street School Building, a large number of private residences and business buildidgs throughout Essex County, and the recent remodeling of St Paul's M. E. Church.

JOSEPH A. SMITH,

(Successor to M. H. Smith.)

⇥ PRACTICAL ✦ PLUMBER. ⇤

Steam and Gas Fitter, Copper, Tin and Sheet Iron Worker, Hardware, Stoves, Ranges, Heaters, &c.

Telephone No. 515   **63 PENNSYLVANIA AVE., COR. PARKHURST ST., NEWARK, N. J.**

The most magnificent mansions quite unfit for occupancy unless its drainage has been carefully and skillfully attended to, and the most healthful location that can be found would soon become a hot-bed of disease unless similar precautions are taken. Plumbing and drainage are now beginning to receive the enlightened attention their importance demand, and the result is to be seen in the diminished death rate of our large cities. Mr. Joseph A. Smith is a practical plumber, steam and gas fitter, copper, tin and sheet-iron worker. He also deals in hardware, stoves, ranges, heaters, etc. This business was founded by Mr. M. H. Smith in 1868, who was succeeded by his brother, Mr. Joseph A. Smith, in 1886. The premises occupied are located at No. 63 Pennsylvania Avenue, and comprise two floors, each 50x50 feet in dimensions, with store-house. Mr. Smith gives employment to eighteen assistants, who are constantly employed, as his experience in this line has made his services in great demand, and he has gained a leading position in this city. Among some of the buildings which he has furnished with plumbing and piping are the City Hospital, Centre Market, Mr. J. Frank Fort's house, Mr. Marshall's house, Newman & Co.'s factory on St. Francis Street, besides the Public Library. He has worked for Mr. E. E. Bond for ten years, and is now at work on forty-eight houses. His amount of work for this year is $40,000, $10,000 more than any previous year, and thinks it will still go beyond that. With the above record it is hardly necessary to add that he gives his personal attention to his business, and guarantees entire satisfaction. Telephone No. 515.

Edward E. Sill,

LIFE INSURANCE,

Office : 780 BROAD STREET.   -   -   -   -   -   NEWARK. N. J.

State Agent National Life Insurance Company of Montpelier, Vermont.

Since the days when "in the name of the great Jehovah and by the authority of the Continental Congress," brave Ethan Allen thundered at the gates of the British fortress of Ticonderoga, the snug little Green Mountain State has been unsurpassed in the heroic qualities of its sons, the womanly virtues of its daughters and the beauty and staying qualities of its horses. The business institutions of a State partake of the character of its people. The granite hills of Vermont, in their massive strength and durability, are an emblem of the State's leading financial institution—the National Life Insurance Company of Montpelier. Incorporated in 1848, its business career practically covers the whole history of life insurance in America. Among its original incorporators were the honored names of Henry Clay, of Kentucky; Amos Abbott, of Massachusetts; Alexander Ramsey, of Pennsylvania, and Paul Dillingham, ex-Governor of Vermont, the last of whom at ninety years of age is still one of the vigorous and active directors of the Company. Its officers have always been men of conservative and economical tastes and habits. Its president, Hon. Charles Dewey, is by common consent, one of the leading financiers of New England. The National is a purely mutual company, every dollar of its earnings being divided exclusively among its policy holders. Beside its large cash dividends annually paid its policy holders, the National has for more than forty years past paid its entire death losses from its interest earnings alone. Only wisdom and rigid economy of management with great care in selection of its risks has enabled the Company to achieve such results. With its business well distributed through only the healthful Northern States of the Union, its mortality has been very low. Another of its crowning glories is in the fact that the National has always been the pioneer in every just and liberal provision known to policy contracts. It indulges in no guess work or deceptive "estimates," which are sure to disappoint the policy holder, but in every form of bond or policy the National writes in plain black and white on the face of every contract *definite guaranteed surrender values* either in CASH, PAID UP INSURANCE, or EXTENSION OF INSURANCE, as the holder may prefer. The National is emphatically "a policy holders' company." It protects their interests and, therefore, has their entire confidence. Being located in Vermont it is not subjected to the heavy expenses incident to business in a large city. Its salary list is the lowest of all the regular companies. Hence its large dividends and its liberal cash surrender values. While issuing all legitimate forms of policies, its endowment bond is in the judgment of insurance men and others, the most unique, satisfying and profitable form of insurance investment ever offered. At the same time its rates are lower than most of the companies. Col. Edward E. Sill is the State agent of the Company for New Jersey, and if you call in person or write him at his office, No. 780 Broad street, Newark, he will courteously give you any information in life insurance desired.

JACKSON AWNING Co., Manufacturers of Awnings, Tents, Flags, Banners, Horse, Truck and Wagon Covers, Decorations for Balls, Parties and Receptions. Floor Crash and Canopies to let. Awnings taken down and stored for the Winter. Orders by Mail will receive prompt attention. 186 Market Street, much time and trouble may be saved in the carrying out of any project, by going directly to headquarters, if possible, and as the establishment of the Jackson Awning Company is the headquarters for awnings, tents, flags, banners, decorations, etc., such of our readers as want anything in this line, would do well to pay the company a visit. The premises made use of are located at No. 186 Market street, and comprises two floors, having an area of 2,400 square feet. This business was founded in 1878, by Messrs. Jackson & Co., the present company having been organized in 1886. Mr. J. Wesley Jackson, president and general manager, is a native of Morris County, and is very generally and favorably known in Newark and vicinity, he having held various local offices, among them that of Superintendent of Wharves, which position he retained six years. The company possesses all necessary facilities to enable operations to be carried on to the best possible advantage, and a sufficiently large force of assistants is employed to ensure the prompt filling of every order. Awnings will be taken down and stored for the Winter, and put up again in the Spring at moderate rates, and any necessary repairing will be neatly and durably done. Horse, truck and wagon covers will be furnished at very short notice, and floor crash and canopies are to let, and will be supplied, together with any desired decorations, for balls, parties, receptions, etc. Orders by mail are assured prompt and careful attention.

and the enviable reputation of the company for affording an efficient and economical service will be fully maintained

THE NONPAREIL Manufacturing Company (Incorporated), Manufacturers of Winkers, Fronts, Housings, etc., Leather Goods and Novelties, Children's Carriage and Shawl Straps, all kinds of Fancy Articles in Leather, 28 Mechanic Street, Newark, N. J. There is an almost endless variety of articles made of leather, and as new uses for this material are constantly being found, the manufacture of leather goods is one of the most progressive as well as one of the most important of all our industries. The Nonpareil Manufacturing Co. occupies a prominent position among the many concerns engaged in this line of work, for its productions are as excellent in quality as they are varied in kind, and the demand for them is steadily and rapidly increasing. This company was regularly incorporated in 1886, Mr. H. F. Lord being president, and Mr. T. W. Lord, secretary and treasurer. Both these gentlemen are natives of Newark, and are widely and favorably known in manufacturing and general business circles. The company operate a very thoroughly equipped factory at No. 28 Mechanic street, and employ a sufficient number of assistants to enable them to fill all orders at short notice. Among their more prominent productions may be mentioned winkers, fronts, housings, etc., leather goods and novelties, children's carriage and shawl straps, and all kinds of fancy articles in leather. The lowest market rates are quoted on these commodities, and no trouble is spared to furnish goods that will give excellent and permanent satisfaction.

J. A. SCARLETT, Notary Public, Stamp

Station of Post Office, Commission, Signature and Seal on File in the Pension Department at Washington, D. C., for the Transaction of Pension Business, Dealer in Choice Cigars and Tobacco, Fine Confectionery, etc. Orders Taken for all publications, No. 386 Washington Street, Newark, New Jersey. One of those places which is both profitable and agreeable to visit, is that conducted by Mr. J. A. Scarlett, at No. 386 Washington street. This opinion is doubtless held by hundreds of others besides the writer, for the patronage accorded the enterprise is very generous indeed, and is steadily increasing. The undertaking in question had its inception in 1888, its founder being the present proprietor. The premises made use of are of the dimensions of 40x15 feet, and are very attractively fitted up, and are well stocked with choice confectionery, etc., and a fine assortment of the best foreign and domestic cigars is always to be found here, and also a complete line of smokers' materials. Mr. Scarlett is prepared to receive orders for all publications, and will fill and deliver same when promised. He gives his business close personal attention, and with the assistance of two competent clerks, can guarantee prompt and courteous service to all callers. He puts his prices at very reasonable figures, and as his goods are always first-class, there is no occasion for surprise at the steadily increasing magnitude of his business. Mr. Scarlett is a Notary Public, and attends to pension claims. Parties interested would do well to consult Mr. Scarlett, as he is in a position to furnish information on this subject, which many pension claim agents envy.

JACOB HERMAN, No. 178 Market, Corner

Broad Street, Newark, N. J. Men's Furnisher, "Advertiser Building." The goods coming under the head of "gents' furnishings" are so varied in character, that were we to attempt even to catalogue all the articles comprised in the stock carried by Mr. Jacob Herman at his establishment, No. 178 Market street, corner of Broad street, we would soon exhaust all our available space, for this gentleman offers one of the most complete assortments of gents' furnishings to be found in this section, and is constantly receiving late and fashionable novelties. The premises occupied by him are 20x30 feet in dimensions, and the stock contained therein is so arranged as to make it easy to choose intelligently from the great variety of goods open to inspection. Mr. Herman is a Connecticut man by birth, and has been identified with his present establishment since 1889. He has built up a large and steadily increasing retail trade, by supplying desirable and reliable articles at the lowest market rates, and the most careful dressers speak very highly of the advantages to be gained by patronizing this establishment. Three competent assistants are employed, and every caller is assured prompt as well as courteous attention.

CHAS. L. FEUERSTEIN, Wholesale and

Retail Dealer in Fine and Staple Groceries, Teas, Coffees, Sugars, Spices, etc. No. 46 William Street, Newark, N. J. It is certain that our account of the representative business enterprises of the city of Newark, New Jersey, would remain incomplete were we to omit the one conducted at No. 46 William street by Mr. Chas. L. Feuerstein, who inaugurated his retail grocery business in the year 1888. This gentleman is a native of Germany, and is widely known in business and social circles. The establishment which we speak of is 20x30 feet in dimensions, and employment is given to two competent and faithful clerks. The retail customers of Mr. Feuerstein are unanimous in their praise of the stock of goods carried, and of the prompt, accurate and courteous attention their orders receive. A full assortment of the choicest flour, teas, coffees, spices, kerosene, molasses, etc., etc., is carried, and delays are seldom. Families trading with this store are sure of receiving pure and fresh goods every time, as the business transacted is so large that the stock is continually in rotation, and does not have time to become unsalable for the want of purchasers, as sometimes happens in other stores. The prices quoted on purchases are as low as they can be quoted, and the terms allowed are satisfactory to all. Orders are called for and delivered to all parts of the city without extra charges. There are a great many establishments of this nature in this city, but the one in question is above the average, and we advise the public to try it.

JAMES DE JIANNE, Choice French and

American Confectionery, Foreign and Domestic Fruits a Specialty, 447 Broad Street, Opposite Continental Hotel, Newark, N. J. It is really no wonder that some people are almost afraid to eat ice cream and confectionery of any description, for the newspapers have devoted considerable space to articles on the subject of ice cream and candy adulterations, and not everybody who reads these articles is in a position to see the many positive absurdities which many of them contain. "Space writers" must have something to write about, that is sure, and if nothing else offers, why they pitch into the confectionery manufacturer. This seems to be about as reasonable an explanation as can be offered, and the readers of the alarming articles alluded to will notice that no names are mentioned, and that no direct statement is made that can be taken up by any individual manufacturer. The confectionery establishment and ice cream parlor, located at No. 447 Broad street, has been under the management of Mr. James de Jianne since 1888, and those who have done business with him, and have personally and repeatedly tested the quality of the goods he handles, need not be told that they are just as represented in every respect. Mr. de Jianne was born in Italy, and has a large circle of friends and patrons in Newark. His premises cover an area of 500 square feet, and contain a fine stock of confectionery, fresh fruits, nuts of all kinds and Kenny & Dixon's ice cream, also cigars, cigarettes and tobacco of the best brands. Mr. de Jianne caters to all classes of trade. Competent assistants are employed, and all orders are promptly and satisfactorily executed.

G. NEWMAN, Dealer in Beef, Veal, Mut-

ton, Lamb, Pork, etc., etc., 292 Plane Street, Newark, N. J. The meat and provision market conducted by Mr. Newman, is very popular among the residents of this vicinity, and one does not have to seek far to find the reason for this state of affairs, as it is evident from very little observation, that the stock carried is an exceptionally complete and desirable one, and the prices quoted on the goods composing it, are of themselves enough to ensure its frequent renewal, while the prompt and polite attention given to every customer, completes the favorable impression made by the goods and the prices. As Mr. Newman carries on a first-class meat and provision market, no detailed description of the stock is possible within our limited space, but speaking generally, it may be said to be made up of a great variety of thoroughly dependable articles, the bulk of which are selected expressly for family use. Fresh meats, poultry, fish, oysters, vegetables, etc., of the best quality, are constantly on hand. The premises occupied are located at No. 292 Plane street, and cover an area of 650 square feet. Three thoroughly reliable and well-informed assistants are employed. All goods sold here are guaranteed to prove as represented, and no trouble is spared to completely satisfy every customer.

E. E. BERGEN & CO., Fruit and Produce

Commission Merchants, No. 28 Commerce Street, Newark, N. J. It is expected in a city of Newark's size, that a great deal of fruit and produce should be handled by commission merchants, and in this article we wish to call the reader's attention to the large commission establishment of E. E. Bergen & Co., at No. 28 Commerce street, in this city. We will preface the mention of the enterprise began in 1872, with Messrs. Van Dyke & Bergen as founders. In 1879 however, Mr. E. E. Bergen began to continue the business alone, and it was in the year 1888 that he admitted Mr. H. K. Gardner into partnership with him, as the Co. of the present firm name. Both these gentlemen are business men of ability, and well known to the citizens of our city as honorable business men, and the usage of none but strictly honorable business methods is what has attained success for the house. Mr. Bergen is a native of Mercer County, N. J., and Mr. Gardner of this State also. Their premises take up three floors, each 28x160 feet in dimensions, so that there is an available space of 8,400 square feet of flooring in which to do a good business. Fruit and produce of all kinds is handled, and it is said with truth, that no house in the city carries as full a stock in these goods at such moderately reasonable market rates as E. E. Bergen & Co., No. 28 Commerce street. The public would do well to place a trial order here.

THE CONTINENTAL HOTEL,

THE CONTINENTAL HOTEL, under the proprietorship of C. H. Bartlett and Louis F. Cooke, is situated at 448 to 454 Broad street, Newark, N. J., directly opposite the D., L. & W. R. R. station, and as will be seen from the topographical illustration, is conveniently reached by every line of railway between Newark and New York city. During the past season the "Continental" has undergone extensive and radical changes, making it one of the very best hotels to be found anywhere, and for the first time in its history, Newark now boasts of having a hotel conducted on first-class principles, which will compare favorably with any hostelry in the Metropolis or elsewhere. Among the extensive alterations and improvements recently inaugurated we find the dining room removed from the second story to the ground floor and enlarged to a capacity of 200 guests at one sitting, while the tables are artistically arranged and laid with whitest linen and new silver which sparkle forth a brilliant welcome beneath the blaze of electric light illumination. The office has also been re-arranged, decorated and fitted up in a most inviting manner. Additional chambers have been created, the billiard room, bar and cigar stand have also received elaborate attention, while the house throughout bespeaks the careful and expensive policy of the new management. Mr. Bartlett is an old hotel man of vast experience, while Mr. Cooke, who is known the world over as the general manager of Barnum and Bailey's "greatest show on earth," says. "It is the policy of this management to avoid and overcome all the unfavorable conditions encountered during twenty years' travel and experience to hotel life throughout the world." Therefore, the "Continental" should prove one of the most satisfactory hotels in all this broad continent, and where the weary traveller, or the tired "Commercial men" exclaim in the language of an unknown poet:

> "Whene'er has traveled life's full round,
> Where'er his stages may have been;
> Must sigh to think he still has found
> His warmest welcome at an inn."

This house is conducted on the American plan exclusively; and the rates are $2.00, $2.50 and $3.00 per day, very reasonable considering the nature of the accommodations provided. Employment is given to forty assistants, and the service is prompt and courteous, both at the table and elsewhere. The proprietors offer their guests a great variety of excellent cooked food to choose from, and those who appreciate good living, a central location, comfortable rooms and beds, and liberal dealing, will most heartily endorse the accommodations given at the Continental.

MORRIS RAPHAEL, Sale and Exchange

MORRIS RAPHAEL, Sale and Exchange Stables. Always on Hand, a well Selected Stock of Working and Driving Horses, No. 624 Springfield Avenue, Newark, N. J. Telephone 986. Though somewhat away from the center of traffic, the above establishment traffics sufficiently in the buying, selling and exchanging of horses and cattle at its location, No. 624 Springfield avenue, to do credit to a busier section of the city. The proprietor, Mr. Morris Raphael, always has on hand from forty to fifty horses, which he offers for sale or exchange. We have personally seen these horses on Mr. Raphael's splendid stables, and pronounce their general appearance and soundness as perfect. After reading this article, those entertaining an idea of buying, selling or exchanging horses, would do well to do as we did, and drive up to Mr. Raphael's stables to see what he has got. We assure our readers that the visit of inspection will prove satisfactory, and will lead to an agreement of some sort. The motto of Mr. Raphael in business is honesty and correct representation. This is what is wanted, and the public may depend upon square dealing every time, at this establishment. Mr. Raphael is a native of Lorraine in France, and came to this country in 1872. He employs three stablemen and two salesmen. Courteous attention is assured to all, and easy terms are quoted. Cattle of all kinds are also bought, sold and exchanged. Previous to locating here Mr. Raphael had for eight years been on Boyden street.

E. TUCKING, Grocer, 357 Plane Street,

E. TUCKING, Grocer, 357 Plane Street, Newark, N. J. Although there are doubtless many people who believe that no special degree of ability is required to carry on a retail grocery store successfully, as a matter of fact, it would be difficult to find a branch of trade which requires more careful and skillful management. Of course, there are some men in the business who let their stores run themselves, but the condition of their trade is not such as would encourage any good business man to adopt similar methods. A fine example of what may be done in the grocery line by intelligence and industry, is that afforded by the establishment conducted by Mr. Tucking, at No. 357 Plane street. This gentleman founded his present business in Newark in 1885. He is a native of N. J., and well known throughout Newark and vicinity. The premises utilized comprise one floor 20x22 feet in size, which contains a fine line of choice staple and fancy groceries, and a specialty is made of milk, cream, butter and eggs. It will thus be seen that Mr. Tucking is prepared to supply housekeepers with many things needed in the food line, and the manner of families dealing with this house shows how the inducements offered are appreciated. Three assistants are employed, and prompt attention is given to all, and prices are as low as the goods are reliable.

A. LYONS, Manufacturer of Fine Havana

A. LYONS, Manufacturer of Fine Havana Cigars, 565 Broad Street, Newark, N. J. Smoke the club cigar! Every year the consumption of cigars increases, and so far as can be seen at the present time, this increase is liable to go on for an indefinite period, for more people smoke every year, and the richer the country grows the higher is the grade of cigars generally called for. Of late years, many special brands of cigars have been put on the market, and some of these have gained so firm a hold on the favor of the public that thousands of boxes are consumed annually. For advertising purposes alone it pays a merchant to have his name identified with a uniformly good grade of cigars, known by some "catchy" name, and when once a large trade has been built up, the enterprise is directly as well as indirectly profitable. Mr. A. Lyons is a successful, skillful and progressive manufacturer of fine Havana cigars, and he is prepared to make special brands to order for any party, and to guarantee uniformity of excellence in workmanship and material. He is a native of Newark, and has carried on his present business since 1888, during which time he has built up an extensive and steadily increasing trade. Mr. Lyons is located at No. 565 Broad street, and is in a position to fill all orders promptly, and to quote the lowest market rates.

J. MORELAND, Dealer in Fine Groceries, Teas, Coffees, Sugars, Spices, etc., Fruits and Vegetables in Season, No. 25 Belleville Avenue, Newark, N. J. Mr. John Moreland began business here in 1869, and that he is well known throughout this vicinity, goes without saying, for his establishment is one of the most popular to be found hereabouts, and the manner in which he uses his customers makes friends, as well as draws trade. A store at No. 25 Belleville avenue, 20x50 feet in dimensions, is occupied, and a large stock is carried, consisting of teas, coffees, sugars, spices, etc., also, fruits and vegetables in season, the quality of all being guaranteed. Employment is given to three active and intelligent assistants, and customers are assured prompt and willing service. Mr. Moreland quotes prices in all lines of his business, which will not suffer at all by comparison with those named, by concerns handling the same line of goods. Every article in stock is guaranteed to prove just as represented, and the inducements extended will be found to be strictly genuine in every respect. Mr. Moreland is a native of Ireland, and has resided here for a great many years.

GEORGE TEAGUE, Successor to Thomas Wolfe, Practical Horseshoer, Blacksmithing in all its Branches, No. 13 and 15 Belleville Avenue, Corner Broad Street, Newark, N. J. There are penalties as well as pleasures connected with the ownership of a carriage, and one of them is, that even the best made vehicles have a way of breaking down at times, or of becoming so injured by accident or long continued use, as to render repairing necessary. The old proverb tells us that "a stitch in time saves nine," and the principle holds good in the care of carriages also, for five dollars expended on repairs to-day may be the means of saving several times that sum a few weeks from now. Therefore, see that your vehicle is kept in good condition, and when it needs "tinkering up" a little, don't put it off, but go at once to a thoroughly competent blacksmith, as, for instance, Mr. George Teague, doing business at 13 and 15 Belleville avenue, corner Broad street. He is a native of this town, and has been connected with this business for many years, and is a practical horseshoer and blacksmith in all its branches. He employs four competent men, and pays particular attention to all work entrusted to his care, while his charges are uniformly moderate, and will compare favorably with others in the same trade.

MRS. R. SAMUELS, News Dealer, Cigars and Confectionery, No. 84 William Street, Newark, N. J. Mrs. Rosa Samuels inaugurated her business in 1886. She keeps a news stand, of all local and foreign daily, weekly and monthly papers, magazines and periodicals. We should all of us read the papers, for after leaving school and engaging in the various pursuits in life, we have but two modes of education left us, and they are observation and newspaper reading. We can observe what is going on in our own little circle, but what transpires in the "far, far away" can come to us only by reading. We owe ourselves and our children a good education, and we should leave no stone unturned to enlighten ourselves about our country, and foreign ones, too. We are fortunate to be able to purchase this knowledge so cheap, and the writer has often meditated that we often pay a great deal more for some things that are not half so valuable to us. Mrs. Samuels also keeps choice brands of cigars and confectionery. She is an estimable lady and deserves the encouragement she solicits.

WILLIAM T. NEIMAN, Employment Bureau, No. 22 Cedar Street, Newark, N. J. Mr. William T. Neiman, proprietor of the German-American Employment and Real Estate Agency, of No. 22 Cedar street, in this city, enjoys the distinction of having built up the largest and most successful business of this character in town. He successfully introduced that which had heretofore not existed in the city, viz: the supplying of male help for any capacity, and that, too, in the face of so many insurmountable obstacles. He also makes a specialty of negotiating sales on business places of all kinds, procuring partners with capital, buying and selling of patents, and a general real estate business. He is an energetic young man of a social disposition, and well known throughout the city.

F. HERDER, Boots and Shoes, No. 259 Springfield Avenue, Newark, N. J. The boot and shoe store which Mr. Herder conducts at the above address is not unknown to the residents of this section of the city. We do not stretch the truth any either when we say that even though it may not boast of the proportions which other shoe stores do in the city, that it would pay the resident who lives in the extreme opposite end of the same to come and make their purchases at this establishment. In substantiation of this assertion we can give the "whys" and the "wherefores." Some of these are as follows: In the first place we will preface that Mr. Herder established his business in the year 1874, and that the public has had the opportunity of seeing this store tested for the past sixteen years. This is not a bad starter, but this is also not all. We can state that in ninety-nine cases out of a hundred the people who have ever made a purchase at this establishment have returned to make a second. This is not a bad recommendation for a store, either. What can we infer from the existence of such circumstances, but the fact that good goods are sold by Mr. Herder, and that satisfaction is assured every purchaser. None will contradict us, surely, for the conclusion is too plainly evident. Mr. Herder is a native of Germany, and has hosts of both business and social friends in Newark. He employs a courteous assistant, and his premises are 22x75 feet in dimensions. To families who buy in large quantities we wish to say that they can economize by trading with Mr. Herder in boots and shoes. Remember the place and give him a call, No. 259 Springfield avenue, Newark, N. J.

CHARLES S. WELDON, Carriage Trimming, 30 Lawrence Street, Newark, N. J. Considering what small sum it costs to have a carriage retrimmed and made as good as new so far as this line of repairing is concerned, it seems strange that any owner of an otherwise handsome and stylish vehicle should be satisfied to allow it to remain worn and shabby looking, and we believe that if the facilities afforded by Mr. Charles S. Weldon were more generally known there would be fewer carriages in Newark and vicinity unable to bear close inspection. Mr. Weldon makes a specialty of carriage trimming, and turns out work that will compare favorably with the best in the trade. He uses carefully selected materials, employs six skilled workmen, and puts his prices down to the lowest figures consistent with a fair profit. He was born in Newark, and is well known throughout the community. He began operations as a carriage trimmer in 1858, and now occupies premises located at No. 30 Lawrence street, covering an area of some 2,625 square feet, which are very thoroughly equipped for carriage trimming in all its branches, and we have no hesitation in assuring satisfaction to those who may take advantage of the inducements offered. Orders can be filled at short notice, and we repeat that the charges made are very low for first-class and reliable work.

BALDWIN & MUNN, Retail Grocers, West Kinney, Corner Halsey Street, Newark, N. J. The most of us have to work pretty hard for what money we get, so it is perfectly natural that when we come to spend it, we should desire to receive as much in return as circumstances will allow. There is really as much art in knowing how to spend, as in knowing how to earn, and one of the first principles of this art is to deal with a firm of high reputation. Such a concern is that conducted by Baldwin & Munn, for since these gentlemen began operations here in Newark, they have followed such a liberal and honorable policy in their management of affairs as to have gained the entire confidence of such of the public as are acquainted with their methods. Both the gentlemen are natives of New Jersey, and are personally well known in Newark. The premises occupied are located on West Kinney street, corner Halsey and are of the dimensions of 25x60 feet. The stock consists of staple and fancy groceries of all kinds, and is complete in every detail. For competent assistants are employed, and every caller is given immediate and polite attention. Fair dealing and bottom prices are the causes of this establishment's popularity, and we are happy to note success so honestly deserved.

HENRY LISSA & CO., Manufacturers of Trunks, Traveling Bags and Satchels, No. 505 Broadway, opposite Metropolitan Hotel, New York. Factory, Newark, N. J. The leather trade is unusually well represented in Newark, more so than in most cities of its size. Manufacturers and wholesale and retail dealers abound, but among them all, none takes a higher stand, or reaches a greater degree of prosperity than the firm of Henry Lissa & Co. This house was founded in January, 1881, and it is surprising to note to what magnitude the business has grown within ten years. When we think to what universal use leather is put in these days, and what beautiful and serviceable articles are made of it, it is not astonishing that so many of the foremost firms in the country should be engaged in this manufacture. The house in question does an enormous business in the manufacture of trunks, traveling bags and satchels, which are made of the finest materials, the best, of course, being of leather, and the workmanship of all is guaranteed. The salesrooms are situated at 505 Broadway, New York, opposite the Metropolitan Hotel, where a large and choice stock of these articles may be seen. The factory, located in Newark, comprises eight large buildings, most of them being of four stories height. Employment is given to seventy skilled operatives, and the buildings are fitted with the most approved machinery, and every appliance and convenience for carrying on this business. Mr. Lissa is a native of New York. His superintendent, Mr. Max Sachs, has had many years experience in this branch of industry, and is eminently well fitted to attend to every detail of this far famed establishment.

CHAS. E. BOND, Practical Plumber and Metal Worker, Steam Heating and Gas Fitting, 49 William Street, Near Washington Street, Newark, N. J. In a large city of Newark's size, there is always a great deal to do in the plumbing line, and we suppose that it is owing to this fact that there are so many engaged in the business. Not every one engaged in it are competent men, however, and this is noticeable in many trades where plenty of work can be had. Now it is known to many that a great progress has been made of late years in the mode of plumbing houses and buildings, and that improved devices of all sorts have been introduced, which tend to make our buildings more sanitary, yet many also ignore the fact, and in building or repairing their premises, engage the services of incompetent plumbers or "job-botchers" as they are termed. The public should wake up to the fact, that the plumbing of their dwellings is a very important one, and that when they have work of this kind to be done, to procure the service of men who have kept up to the times and know their business. A gentleman of this stamp is Mr. Charles E. Bond, doing business at 49 William street, in this city. He has had a long and varied experience as a practical, theoretical and sanitary plumber, and if he cannot do a good job, why the public need look nowhere else. He began business in 1888, with a Mr. Baumann, who was in partnership with him, but he now runs the business alone. He employs nine men, and also attends to steam heating and gas fitting and works metals. His premises are 20x25 feet in dimensions, and orders are dispatched in a thorough, workmanlike manner, at low prices.

A H. LINNEMANN, Boot and Shoe Store, Custom Work a Specialty, No. 531 Halsey street, Newark, N. J. Mr. A. H. Linnemann has had sole control of his present enterprise since 1870, and the best proof that could be wished that his methods are honorable as well as energetic, is that afforded by the fact that a large proportion of his sales is to regular customers. Any man is apt to be imposed upon once, some of us will submit to imposition several times in succession, but there is no one so easy-going, that he will make a practice of trading where he is liable not to get the full value of his money, so we say the existence of a regular patronage is the best proof that Mr. Linnemann is both able and anxious to deal fairly by all. His store is located at 531 Halsey street, and measures 20x50 feet, there thus being room enough to accommodate a stock of foot wear of all kinds. The goods are in every instance guaranteed to prove exactly as represented, and the prices rule low enough to satisfy the most close and careful buyers. Mr. Linnemann employs two assistants, and insist upon equally prompt and polite attention being shown every caller, a rule that has much to do with the general popularity of the store. He also does the custom work at as low rates as can be found in the city.

CHARLES W. MENK, Dealer in Drugs, Medicines, Chemicals, Fancy and Toilet Articles, Soaps, Brushes, Sponges, Combs, Perfumery, Stationery, etc., 105 Market Street, Newark, N. J. While it may be accepted as an indisputable fact that it is not at all pleasant to be sick, still there is no reason that any man should grumble and growl because he is so, for the only sensible course for him to pursue is to straightway set to work to get well again as soon as possible. Now this is not to be accomplished by unmanly repining by any means, and as the poet sings "there is a balm for every ill," why not go in person, or send to some reliable drug store and try to get something to "suit your complaint." We won't say that Dr. Charles W. Menk has actually a "balm for every ill," as with all due consideration for the poet, we don't believe that such has ever been discovered, but we will say that at his finely equipped store, at No. 105 Market street, he has about as fine a stock of drugs, medicines, chemicals, etc., as is to be found in Newark. Dr. Menk is and old established druggist, and has so increased and managed his business as to gain the confidence of the public. Five assistants are employed, and prompt and polite service is assured to all. Dr. Menk is well fitted for the position he has assumed, and carries one of the largest stocks in the city, which includes not only drugs and medicines of all kinds, but also fancy and toilet articles, soaps, brushes, sponges, combs, perfumery, stationery, etc. He maintains a close supervision over his establishment, which includes a store 20x50 feet in dimensions, where special and most painstaking attention is paid the compounding of prescriptions, which are made up of the best material, and furnished at the most reasonable prices.

EVERETT & COLE (Successors to Bedford & Everett), Dealers in Groceries and Provisions, 379 Washington Street, Corner Court Street, Newark, N. J. The above firm is an old established house in Newark. Its inception took place forty years ago, with Mr. David Bedford as inaugurator. Mr. Bedford was a native of Madison, N. J. He had with him for twenty years, Mr. Wm. H. Everett, who acted in the capacity of clerk. In 1880, Mr. Bedford admitted his clerk into partnership with him, and at the death of the former, Mr. Everett associated with him in 1888, Mr. Franklin A. Cole, so that the firm name is now "Everett & Cole." Mr. Cole had in turn, been clerk for Bedford & Everett for several years. Mr. Everett is a native of Newton, N. J., and Mr. Cole of this city. Thus we see that the present proprietors of the old stand, have grown with the business itself, and have for a long period been identified with the grocery business. They know from experience the needs of their customers, and meet them with accuracy and dispatch. The premises utilized comprise one floor and cellar, each 30x70 feet in dimensions. Both a wholesale and retail business is done, and the public may depend that none but first-class goods are kept in stock. The use of three teams is necessary to fill regular customers' orders, and an able body of assistants furnishes an accurate and courteous service. Everything choice in flour, tea, coffee, spices, sugar, molasses, kerosene, etc., etc., is sold at bottom prices. A specialty is made of fine fruits and vegetables in season. These are bought direct of the growers, and supplied to customers fresh from mother earth. A trial order convinces everybody that at Everett & Cole's satisfaction is given.

E. C. DUELLY, Fine Confections, Ice Cream and Soda Water, Flavored with Pure Fruit Extracts, No. 489 Broad Street, Newark, N. J. The establishment conducted by Mr. E. C. Duelly, is well worthy of prominent and favorable mention, for the entire community are interested in an enterprise which has for its object the furnishing of fine confections, ice cream and soda water to the public, at moderate rates, and this is just what Mr. Duelly is prepared to do, as a visit to his store, and a trial of his productions will prove to the satisfaction of the most skeptical. Mr. Duelly is a native of Germany, and is very well known throughout Newark. He opened the establishment to which we have reference, in 1867, and has built up a large wholesale and retail trade. The premises utilized comprise one floor and a basement, each 25x75 feet in dimensions, and are equipped with all necessary facilites to carry on operations to the best advantage. Employment is given to seven competent and careful assistants, and no pains are spared to produce confections that will suit the most fastidious. Ice cream is manufactured in the basement, the materials used being carefully selected, the flavors being pure fruit extracts, and the various details are given close personal supervision by Mr. Duelly, who is thus enabled to guarantee that his products shall prove just as represented. Prompt and courteous attention is assured to every caller, and the stock is so frequently renewed, as always to be fresh and tempting, while the prices quoted are as low as can possibly be named on articles of equal excellence.

J. W. KATZ, Embroidery and Braiding works, 353 Mulberry Street, Newark, N. J. One of the most interesting manufacturing establishments in Newark is that conducted by Mr J. W. Katz at No. 353 Mulberry street, corner of Chestnut, for the spacious premises are very thoroughly fitted up as embroidery and braiding works, and the work turned out is large in amount, varied in kind, and excellent in quality. This business was founded in 1887, and has already reached large proportions, Mr. Katz selling to the trade only, and employing twenty-four experienced assistants. He is a native of Hartford, Conn., and is exceptionally familiar with every detail of his business, to which he gives close personal supervision, allowing no imperfect work to leave the establishment. Among the articles worked may be mentioned mantel lambrequins, window lambrequins, table and piano covers, bureau covers, plush covers, carriage robes, scarfs, tidies, etc., the variety of designs being practically unlimited, and comprising the very latest novelties. Mr Katz has every facility for doing braiding and cording on cloaks and suits for the trade. The machinery is driven by steam power, and Mr. Katz is prepared to execute the most extensive commissions at short notice and at the lowest market rates.

CONRAD BRANDT. Manufacturer of all kinds of Mineral Waters, 39 William Street, Newark, N. J. Telephone No. 602. Mr. Conrad Brandt started in the business in which he is yet engaged, in 1879. Thus we see that his establishment is in its twelfth year of existence, and that fortune has favored Mr. Brandt in his undertakings. The house, in fact, enjoys a reputation for manufacturing mineral water of superior quality, and has kept the same customers for years. This is the best advertisement which could be given the waters which Mr. Conrad Brandt manufactures. He supplies the trade and families both. Drug stores and refreshment saloons rank his mineral waters high in the ranks which the best concerns manufacture. This is a no mean recommendation, and we are pleased to inform the fact to those who may not be aware of it. Many prefer mineral water to the thousand and one drugs prescribed by physicians, and in some cases we must admit that we cannot differ with them, as very strong medicinal properties are to be found in mineral waters, as every one knows. Mr. Brandt is a native of Germany, and has many acquaintances in the city, both business and social. He affords employment to five pleasant and courteous assistants, who deliver orders with dispatch. Two floors, each 30x50 feet in dimensions, are utilized, so that plenty of room, plenty of help and the best machinery and other general appointments enable Mr. Conrad Brandt to serve the trade in its mineral water wants as well and as at low figures as any one else in the city. Orders received by telephone 602.

JOHN V. DIEFENTHAELER, Clothing Manufacturer, Maple Place, Rear, 44 Green Street, Newark, N. J. It is not surprising to note, in a city of Newark's size, the many different kinds of business carried on, for it is said that every thing is manufactured here from a needle to an anchor. A business which is a representative one of this city's many industries, is that of the manufacturing of clothing. There are many engaged in it, too, but not all of them are as worthy of our attention in a work of this kind, as the establishment which is carried on by Mr. John V. Diefenthaeler in the rear of 44 Green street, on Maple place. We will preface that Mr. Diefenthaeler inaugurated his establishment in 1862, and that he is a native of Germany, employing one hundred hands and occupying three floors of 32x50 feet each. He is prepared to manufacture clothing with every facility, in the respect of plenty of help and machinery to do the work in which he is engaged. There are manufacturing clothiers who do good work, and who employ good materials only, and there are some who neither do good work or employ good materials, so it lies with the trade to ascertain which are the reputable houses, and the unreputable. We need not attempt to tell the trade that Mr. Diefenthaeler's establishment is placed among the foremost ranks of wholesale manufacturing clothing establishments, however, for this fact has been recognized by it long since the inauguration of the house in question, in 1862. In twenty-eight years a firm's reputation has had time to leak out, and had Mr. Diefenthaler's house not been of the highest order, it would long since have dwindled into insignificance, but, on the contrary, its reputation for turning out work and goods of a higher grade and superior order has been pre-eminently illustrated to the market, and we should not wonder at the great success it has attained.

A. C. HAZEN, Dealer in Fine Groceries, Milk, Butter and Cheese, Corner Cedar and Halsey Streets, Newark, N. J. The enterprise established and carried on by Mr. A. C. Hazen was started in 1872, and being an experienced and discriminating buyer, he enjoys such relations with producers and wholesalers as to enable him to purchase at bottom rates, an advantage, the profit of which is fully shared with patrons. Choice teas and coffees, pure spices are always in stock, also a full supply of milk, butter and cheese. All such goods are to be had of Mr. Hazen, at prices as low as the lowest, and more staple articles are also offered in proper variety and at the very lowest market rates. The premises occupied by this enterprise are 50x25 feet in dimensions, and a large retail business is done giving employment to three assistants. Callers may safely depend upon receiving immediate and courteous attention, and orders will be accurately delivered at short notice.

CHARLES B. SMITH, Deal-
er in Acids, Chemicals, Dyes, White
Lead, Oils and Photographic Chemicals.
Manufacturers' Supplies a Specialty, 881
Broad Street, Newark, N. J. Very few
persons, aside from those whose business keeps them informed on the subject,
have any adequate idea of the enormous
consumption of drugs, chemicals, dye-
stuffs, etc., in this country, for, leaving
what are used for medical purposes entirely out of the question, there would
still remain a tremendous demand on
the part of manufacturers, photographers, dyers, etc. One of the leading
wholesale druggists of New Jersey is
Mr. Charles B. Smith, who is a native
of Lackawanna, Penn., and has been
identified with his present enterprise
since 1885. It was inaugurated in 1855,
by Mr. C. W. Badger, and in 1875 came
under the control of Messrs. C. W. Badger & Co., who were succeeded by the
present proprietor fifteen years later.
Mr. Smith is a dealer in acids, chemicals,
dyes, white lead, oils, and photographic
chemicals, and makes a leading specialty of manufacturers' supplies. Very
commodious premises are utilized, located at Nos. 881, 883 and 885 Broad street,
and containing an exceptionally heavy
and complete stock, for Mr. Smith stands
ready to furnish anything and everything in his line of business, in quantities
to suit and at very short notice. Employment is given to thirty assistants,
and the business is so thoroughly systematized that the maximum of speed and
accuracy is attained, mistakes in the delivery of orders being of a very rare occurrence. Orders by mail or telephone
are assured immediate and painstaking
attention, goods being delivered free,
and the lowest market rates being quoted on all of the many commodities
handled.

L. S. YOUNG,

WHOLESALE AND RETAIL DEALER IN

Flour, Feed, Hay and Grain.

Cider, Vinegar, Country Produce, Etc.,

399 BROAD STREET, - - NEWARK, N. J.

TELEPHONE, 84.   Orders by Mail Promptly Delivered.

MRS. MARY WARREN & SON,

DEALERS IN

Fruit, Poultry, Game and Country Produce,

Stands Nos. 20 and 21 Centre Market,

NEWARK, NEW JERSEY.

Goods delivered to any part of the City Free of Charge.

C. WEIGAND, Wholesale and Retail Dealer in Beef, Veal, Mutton, Lamb, Pork, Smoked Meats, Canned Goods of all Kinds, Poultry, Vegetables, Fruit and Game in Season, Fish and Oysters a Specialty. Branch of Washington Market, No. 5 Ferry Street, Newark, N. J. All Orders Promptly Attended to. The meat market conducted by Mr. Weigand, at No. 5 Ferry street, in this city, is as nice a one as could be picked out, among the many hundreds to be found in Newark. There are many in the city, consequently our assertion becomes quite a strong one; however, we are able to prove our statements. In the first place, Mr. Weigand's meat establishment at this stand is a spacious one, of the dimensions of 20x70 feet. It is one of the most finely lighted, well ventilated and free from flies, to be found anywhere. An atmosphere of cleanliness, purity and freshness greets the nostrils as one enters. This is an agreeable feature in a meat market, and tends to increase the liking the public has for it. The fixtures are admirably adapted for the purposes for which they are intended, and, in a word, the general appointments of the market are A-1 in quality and style. So much for the store, now a word for the stock. It is selected with great care, by Mr. Weigand in person, who knows the wants of his patrons. All his meats are obtained from the most dependable sources. Besides the butcher's regular stock of beef, veal, mutton, lamb, pork, etc., smoked meats, canned goods, poultry, vegetables, fruit and game, and fish and oysters are carried. Mr. Weigand established his business in the year 1879. He is a native of New York city. Employment is afforded to three competent and courteous assistants, and all orders and patrons receive immediate and painstaking attention.

A. W. LODKEY'S Merchants' Lunch and Dining Parlors, Meals at All Hours, Special rates to Churches, Societies and Clubs, Furnished Rooms with First-Class Board for Gentlemen only, 27 Bank Street, Newark, N. J. It would surprise many of our readers to learn the number of residents of this city who make a regular practice of eating all their meals in public restaurants, for this habit is rapidly gaining in popularity, and bids fair to continue to do so for a long time to come. The expense is much smaller than would naturally be supposed, and the service is so much superior to that afforded at the average boarding house, that comparison is hardly possible. Of course there are restaurants of which this cannot truthfully be said, but there are others which deserve the highest praise which can be given them, and among this class must be ranked Mr. A. W. Lodkey's Merchants' Lunch and Dining Parlors, at 27 Bank street. The bill of fare is varied and abundant, the cooking strictly first-class, and the service intelligent, obliging and prompt. Mr. Lodkey will cheerfully give any desired information concerning prices, etc., on application, and such of our readers as may decide to avail themselves of the accommodations afforded will thank us for calling their attention to this liberally managed establishment. He also has furnished rooms with board for gentlemen only, at low rates.

WILLIAM KRAFT, Clothing Manufacturer, Franklin Court, Newark, N. J. The manufacturing clothing establishment carried on by Mr. William Kraft, in this city, is worthy of our especial mention. The inauguration of the enterprise took place in 1865, with Mr. Kraft as founder. This gentleman is a native of Germany, but has lived here so long that he has hosts of both business and social friends. Mr. Kraft has associated with him as partner, Mr. Chas. Becker, who is also a gentleman well known in this city and abroad. These gentlemen afford employment to 250 hands in the busy season, so that we can see that a large business is done. They enjoy close relations with the trade, and manufacture exclusively for it. Three large floors are occupied by the help and machinery, both being of a high grade. Possessing these superior facilities the firm turns out clothing which is all that can be desired. The best of material is invariably used, considering the relative value of the garments made, and the work turned out is pronounced as good as custom made. An electric motor furnishes the motive power. We need dwell no longer upon the high standing this firm enjoys, for the trade are well aware of the fact. Honorable business methods will win such a reputation every time.

N. BLANK & SON, Painters, Paper Hangers, Decorators, Dealers in Paints, Oils, Glass, Decorations, Fine Wall Paper, Ornamental and Sign Painting, 265 Springfield Avenue, one Door from Boyd Street, Newark, N. J. Jobbing of all Kinds a Specialty. Estimates Furnished. The firm at whose head we find Messrs. N. Blank & Son, was inaugurated by them in the year 1893. Though yet comparatively fresh from its inception, this firm has met with a patronage worthy of a house of much longer standing. The gentlemen who conduct the enterprise, are both natives of Europe, but have resided in America, and in this city, especially, for some time. They give employment to a force of four men, who are skilled workmen, each in their respective branches. The premises utilized are 15x50 feet in dimensions, and are well fitted up for the purposes for which they were intended to serve. A large and varied stock of paints, oils, glass, decorations and fine artistic wall paper may be found in them, and the proprietors make it a point to carry none but the best in each of these several lines. The question of painting a house, whether it be for the first time or a matter of repainting, is an important one to the real estate owner, and we should be cautious whom we employ to do this work, as it takes men who know their business from actual experience, to do a good job. The material is also to be considered, and should be of the best. In this connection we take pleasure in recommending to our readers the superior abilities and facilities which this house have to execute such work. Messrs. Blank & Son are no less proficient in the art of paper hanging, for they also have had a long experience in this line, and the help which they employ are also competent men. Their stock of wall paper is as varied as it is fresh, and contains some elegant and very desirable designs. The firm also execute some very artistic work in ornamental and sign painting. In this line they may have equals, but no superiors, for we have had our attention called to some of their work, and we pronounce it artistic in the superlative degree. Jobbing of all kinds in the above lines are undertaken, and estimates are cheerfully given. Give this deserving firm a trial.

MRS. CROSSLEY, Dealer in New and Second Hand Furniture, Goods Bought, Sold and Exchanged, 39 and 41 Belleville Avenue, Newark, N. J. Everybody must have furniture, everybody must have carpets, and everybody should have spring beds, mattresses or feather beds; for these are very powerful aids in resting a tired body, and the body that works to earn the money to buy them, should be made as comfortable as possible. The average individual spends one-third of his life in bed, and, therefore it is important that the latter be made as healthful and easy as is consistent with circumstances. When any of our readers have occasion to purchase any of the articles, such as furniture, carpets, etc., etc., to say nothing of baby carriages, oil cloths, straw matting, feathers, or, in fact, anything from a "tea pot to a parlor suit," we recommend them before purchasing, to call and examine the stock of goods to be found at Nos. 39 and 41 Belleville avenue, for this establishment is conducted by Mrs. M. Crossley, a native of England, but who, for the past five years has conducted this enterprise very successfully, until now the business occupies three floors 20x50 feet in size. Three competent assistants are employed, her prices are very moderate, and her representations can be confidently relied upon.

ALBERT BALDWIN, Wood Turning, Rear of 256 Market Street, Newark, N. J. The enterprise conducted by Mr. Albert Baldwin, at the rear of 256 Market street, is very popular with those who are conversant with the methods employed therein, for the proprietor spares no pains to satisfy every customer, and turns out work which will compare very favorably with that done at establishments making much greater pretentions. Mr. Baldwin is a native of New York, and he started his present enterprise here in Newark, in 1879. He has gained the reputation of being a skillful man, who makes a study of his business, and is always improving every method of working. The premises are 24x64 feet in dimensions, and are fitted up with every facility necessary. Wood turning in general is carried on in accordance with the most approved methods. Mr. Baldwin employs ten experienced assistants constantly and all orders are filled promptly, and at the lowest market rates.

SCOTT & VEHSLAGE (Successors to C. C.

Scott), Pattern and Model Makers, 25 Railroad Place, Wheaton's Block, opposite Market Street R. R. Depot. Residence, 65 Monmouth Street, Newark, N. J. Among those engaged in this line of business, none stand higher than this firm. Although recently established in Newark, they have rapidly come to the fore, and are now well known among the trade, as skillful makers of patterns and models, and for their reasonable prices and fair dealing in all matters of business. Particular attention is given by this firm to the designing of machinery and mechanical drawing, also to the making of working models. The premises occupied by them are conveniently situated, at No. 25 Railroad place, in Wheaton's block, directly opposite the Market Street depot of the Pennsylvania Railroad. The shop is as well equipped as any, and gives employment to more hands than any other in this city. This industry is an important one in connection with many lines of manufacture, but not understood by most people outside of such lines. Patterns, after drawings are made, are the first things that enter into the making of cast iron columns, girders, beams, plates and washers and an almost endless variety of ornamental work in architecture, and castings for almost every kind of machinery, from the largest to the smallest. No steam engine, either locomotive, marine or stationery, can be made without first making patterns for the castings. They enter into the manufacture of valves, cocks and faucets for steam, gas or water, coach, saddlery and harness hardware, toys, and a thousand and one articles that we think indispensable at the present day. These patterns are made of hard or soft wood, brass or soft metal, according to the requirements of the case. This business was established by Mr. C. C. Scott, since which it has become a firm through the association of Mr. Henry D. Vehslage. Mr. Scott is a native of Wisconsin, but a resident of this State for many years. Mr. Vehslage is a native and resident of Irvington, and a son of the well known Irvington preacher of that name.

NESLER & CO., Manufacturing Jewelers,

38 and 40 Crawford Street, Newark, N. J. The manufacturing jewelry industry is extensively carried on in Newark, and many of the leading firms in the country are among those engaged in the business in our midst. Foremost in the ranks of these establishments extended mention should be made of the house of Nesler & Co., composed of Messrs C. F. Nesler and W. G. Nerpel, both of whom are natives of this city and State. These gentlemen both had had a long experience in their trade before the inauguration of their establishment, the inception of which took place in 1885. These gentlemen employ twenty competent men, and utilize an entire floor of a large building located at Nos. 38 and 40 Crawford street. The trade pronounces the work turned out by these gentlemen as of a much superior order than that found in other shops, and the reason is that the members of the firm are more than exceptionally good workmen in their trade. They make a specialty of hoop earrings, and in these goods alone an extensive business is done annually. General jewelry manufacturing is also done. We invite that portion of the trade not yet having had the pleasure of visiting Messrs. Nesler & Co.'s samples to do so at their earliest convenience, and be convinced of the truth of our statements.

HENRY DISCH, Staple and Fancy Grocer-

ies, 499 Washington Street, Newark, N. J. There are grocery stores, but not all of them are model grocery stores. It makes a great deal of difference in the satisfaction we experience, where we buy our groceries, and of whom we buy them. It is a good idea, then, to adopt your regular grocer, but first be sure that you adopt a reliable one, one who in taking your interest, takes his own. This is important, for a careless grocer never gives entire satisfaction, if he gives any at all. In an establishment of energy and push, should be kept a stock as varied as it should be abundant, that the patrons may have something to select from. Also should the greatest inclination be prevalent to suit patrons, for an ounce as for a pound. When small quantities are bought, it is a sign that no more is needed, and when people buy all they need at any place of business, it is within the bounds of propriety and courtesy to do all that can be done to give satis-

faction. This, all grocers do not seem to understand, and when they see their customers drop off, they wish they had paid more attention to ounces, for they know pounds might have resulted. No unpleasantness of this kind happens at Mr. Disch's store, however, for the paying of strict and undivided attention to small orders is exactly what has brought him the success he enjoys in business to-day. The inception of Mr. Henry Disch's business took place in 1889, and the encouragement he has received is the result of his hard work and faithfulness to his patrons. Two competent assistants are employed, and promptness in filling orders is a feature of the establishment, which measures 20x35 feet in dimensions.

FR. W. BUERCK, Bakery, 83 William

Street, Corner Plane Street, Newark, N. J. The establishment conducted by Mr. F. W. Buerck, at the corner of Plane and William streets, is worthy of extended comment in a work of this kind, for this gentleman has been at the location we have signified for the past twelve years, and his long experience and close personal application to the business with which he is identified, enables him to cater to the most fastidious customers. Mr. F. W. Buerck is a native of Germany, and has hosts of both business and social friends in this section of the city and elsewhere. A select stock of fresh goods is a feature of this establishment, and the immediate neighborhood may well patronize the store in question, as the prices quoted are bound to suit the most judicious purchaser. The premises utilized comprise an area of 20x50 feet, so that the available space furnishes ample accommodations for the extensive business done and the large stock carried. Two courteous assistants furnish prompt and polite service to all callers. We know of no better place in which to make our bakery and grocery purchases than at Mr. Buerck's store. Call and leave a trial order with him, and satisfaction is sure to follow.

J. D. PIERSON & BRO., Dealers in all

Kinds of Fresh Meat, Poultry, Fish, Oysters, Fruits and Vegetables in their Season, No. 35 Court Street, Newark, N. J. Messrs. J. D. Pierson & Bro., are probably about as busy men as even the busy city of Newark can show, for they are identified with the retail meat and vegetable business, and produce of all kinds. Messrs. Piersons are both natives of Newark, and established their meat market in 1883. The premises now in use have an area of 25x23 feet, and a cellar of the same dimensions. They are located at 35 Court street, and contain a well selected stock of fresh and salt meats, beef, pork, mutton, lamb, veal, poultry, fish, oysters, and fruit and vegetables in their season. The prices quoted are always in accordance with the lowest market rates, and as the goods are of excellent quality, and customers are promptly and politely attended to by four efficient assistants constantly employed, it is perfectly natural that a large and growing business should be done.

GEORGE K. SCHMIDT, Manufacturer of

Clothing and Custom Work, No. 324 Plane Street, Newark, N. J. The manufacturing clothing establishment conducted in this city by Mr. George K. Schmidt, at No. 324 Plane street, is one of Newark's representative business enterprises. Mr. Schmidt is a native of Germany, but has resided in the United States for many years, and enjoys a large circle of both business and social friends. The house enjoys close and extensive business relations with the trade for whom they manufacture exclusively. Employment is afforded to a large force of tailors, who are all experienced men and women in the business. The ready made clothing manufactured by Mr. Schmidt approaches the nearest to perfection of any made in the State, as it has always been the aim of the house to supply the trade and the market with thoroughly reliable and reputable goods. The material used is the best consistent with the relative value of the garments made. The house is extremely busy in the seasons when such establishments are running full blast. The premises utilized are 25x50 feet in dimensions, and the machinery used is of the highest and most approved order. The trade would do well to have Mr. Schmidt fill a trial order.

HENRY KIRCHNER, Dealer in Choice
Beef, Veal, Mutton and Lamb, Poultry and Game in Season.
197 Mulberry Street, Between Fair and Green Streets, Newark, N. J.   Mr. Henry Kirchner has had considerable experience in his present line of business, and since opening the establishment now conducted by him, in 1895, has built up a large retail trade by the simple process of dealing honorably by his customers, and working hard to furnish unsurpassed accommodations.   The premises are located at No. 197 Mulberry street, between Fair and Green streets, and are of the dimensions of of 20x50 feet.   Among the articles dealt in may be mentioned all kinds of fresh and salt meats, also, poultry and game in their season.   Most of us are rather particular about what we eat, and, therefore, it is no wonder that Mr. Kirchner's store is steadily gaining in popularity, for the articles there furnished are carefully selected, and are bound to prove satisfactory to the most fastidious.   Some very choice cuts of meats are always carried in stock, and those who appreciate a tender and well flavored steak, and have had some difficulty in procuring anything of the kind, will find that they may purchase here with the full assurance, that whatever representations are made in regard to the meats, etc., dealt in, are always warranted by the facts.   The prices are uniformly satisfactory, for, although Mr. Kirchner does not claim to sell "below cost," he does claim to give patrons the worth of their money, and surely no reasonable man should expect more than that.

FIRTH & BAILEY, Dealers in Household
Necessities, on Weekly or Monthly Payments, No. 63 Bank Street, Newark, N. J. Some people boast that they never buy goods on the installment plan, but we have known many such, who, in order to do so, would have to break a tooth-pick in two, to economize.   This is not necessary.   We fail to see why people who are in need of certain articles in their homes, and cannot afford to pay in full on purchasing, should not wish to avail themselves of such advantages as Messrs. Firth & Bailey offer the public.   O, they say, they charge exorbitant prices when you do this! This is all flim-a, installment dealers do business in this way only to accommodate the public and make customers for themselves, as other dealers have their modes of doing business, hiring advertisements, in the newspapers, and all that.   They have to pay heavily for their "luring advertisements," and it is our candid opinion, that the surplus you have to pay on the goods to help meet these expenses, and the difference between spot cash and installment prices are balanced unequally in your disfavor.   Just reason with common sense a minute.   See the enormous rents these furniture houses pay on our best streets, and again we say, see the "busting" they have to do in order to meet their heavy advertising bills!   Do our readers think they do not have to pay handsomely for all this superfluity?   Well, we rather guess they do!   On the other hand, take such men as Messrs. Firth & Bailey, who have just as large stocks, just as handsome stores, and all that, but are content to invite their patrons to take a walk down there on Bank street, just a step from Broad (No. 63), and are not at all scrupulous about saying that their rent is reasonable, and not exorbitant, and that the *merits* of their goods are their only advertisements.   It makes no difference in the quality or durability of the goods, whether they are for sale on Bank or Broad street, but it *does* most emphatically make a difference in the price asked, though, and let us not be foolish enough to doubt the point, for the argument is too strong in its favor.   Buy on the installment plan by all means, if you are not able to pay the cash down.   It is no disgrace; why, we would be willing to proclaim it from the house tops, if we were the interested parties, for is it policy to go hungry to have the satisfaction of saying that "that rug, or that chamber set cost me so much and so much, on Broad or Market streets, at this one or that one's handsome furniture store?"   Ridiculousness and fiddlesticks we say.   Buy your goods where you can buy them cheapest.   Let fools pay for a "name," and not intelligent people like you and I.   Messrs. Firth & Bailey, then, we say, sell cheaper in every way than those would-be "big guns" who often "hust up," (as the expression goes), to get square with their creditors.   At the establishment in question are courteous and willing salesmen, who will spare no pains to impress upon you the fact that household necessities can be bought a great deal cheaper on Bank street than on Broad.   Call on a visit of inspection and be convinced of the truth of our statement; it will cost you nothing.

WINKLER'S Confectionery and Ice Cream
Parlor.   Home Made Candies a Specialty, 235 Market St., cor. Mulberry St., Newark, N. J.   Purity is very desirable in anything that is to be eaten, and the experiments of men of science have proved this to be particularly the case where confectionery and ice cream were concerned.   Now we by no means agree with those who assert that the bulk of the confectionery in the market is adulterated, on the contrary, we are certain that this is far from being the case, but still undoubtedly some impure confectionery is sold and the only way to be sure you are not the purchaser, is to buy exclusively of reputable firms.   There, for instance, is Mr. Peter Winkler, proprietor of Winkler's Confectionery and Ice Cream Parlors.   This gentleman has carried on his present line of business as manufacturer and retail dealer in pure confectionery since 1886, and there can be no question but that his productions are pure in fact as well as in name.   The premises occupied comprise a store located at No. 235 Market street, covering an area of 1,500 square feet, and a shop rear of Spaeth's furniture store, on Market street.   Mr. Winkler claims to carry one of the best assortments of confectionery to be found in the city, and certainly it would be hard to find a more extensive and tempting stock.   Home made candies are made a specialty, and all the articles dealt in are quoted at the lowest rates consistent with the use of first-class materials, and the employment of skilled assistants.

CHAS. OPPEL'S SONS, Steam Cigar Box
Manufactory.   Cigar Manufacturers' Supplies, 54 and 56 West Street, Newark, N. J.   The millions of cigars which are annually made in the United States, require the manufacturing of boxes in which to ship them, and this part of the business alone affords employment to thousands of workingmen and women.   Mr. Chas. Oppel's Sons have one of these large steam cigar box factories, and they employ on an average thirty men and women to do their work.   Their establishment takes up three floors, each 50x56 feet in dimensions, so that an area of 5,000 square feet is utilized.   The power is furnished by a large fifteen horse-power engine, and the machinery and general appointments of the factory are all of the latest and most improved order.   This state of things greatly facilitates operations, and large orders are filled at short notice.   Mr. Chas. Oppel inaugurated the business in 1867, and in 1886 his sons began to continue the enterprise, and have maintained its high reputation.   Messrs. August and Berthold Oppel are both natives of Newark, and are widely known, both by the citizens of this city and the trade at large, as energetic men of business.   The Messrs. Oppel both served terms in the late Civil War.   Mr. Berthold Oppel enlisted in company B of the 39th N. J. Regiment, and Mr. August Oppel in the 35th N. Y., Co. I.

M. COHEN, Manufacturer of and Dealer in
Havana and Domestic Cigars.   Also, a Fine Assortment of Meerschaum Goods, Smokers' Articles, etc., 355 Mulberry Street, Newark, N. J.   When a stranger arrives in a city or town, his first questions are generally affected in a great measure by his personal habits.   Of course he will want a good hotel, but after that point is provided for, if he be a smoker, the chances are he will want to know where he can get a good cigar.   Well, if in Newark, no better place can be found than the establishment of which Mr. M. Cohen is the proprietor, located at No. 355 Mulberry street.   This enterprise has been carried on here since 1864 and a large manufacturing and retail business has been built up.   Mr. Cohen is a manufacturer of as well as dealer in Havana and domestic cigars, and recognized the fact that he must furnish a good article if he wished to establish a permanent business, and from the very beginning he has taken pains to manufacture and sell cigars that were uniform and excellent in flavor, as well as low in price.   The premises occupied cover an area of 1,400 square feet, and employment is given to seven assistants.   The business is not confined to the manufacture of cigars, but includes the sale of foreign cigars, tobacco, and smokers' articles in general, and a fine assortment of meerschaum goods, cigars by the box being made a specialty.   Mr. Moses Cohen is a native of New York, and is very well known throughout Newark.   He warrants his goods to prove just as represented, while the prices quoted on the same will be found very low.

C. V. BAUMANN, Plumbing and Heat-

ing, Steam and Gas Fitting, Copper, Tin and Sheet Iron-Worker, 43 William Street, Between Halsey and Washington Streets, Newark, N. J. One of the chief features in a well built building should be its job of plumbing. More stress is laid now-a-days in this matter, than formerly, for medical men have found out that in buildings poorly piped in plumbing, lay secretly hidden the poisonous source of many diseases contracted by the inmates. We can see the possibility of this statement's truth when we stop to reflect on the filth and grease which is so liable to accumulate along the course of the piping, if it is not properly done. Great care should be exercised, therefore, to have our plumbing done by thoroughly practical and experienced men, who know their business. It is better to put a little more money in a good job of plumbing to start with, than to be obliged to keep repairing every now and then. Great importance should be attached to this matter, we repeat, for it really is a serious one. All over the country an edict has been proclaimed to the school committees of our various cities, to look to the plumbing of school houses. We mention this to illustrate the necessity of our waking up to the fact that for our own health and that of those who are dear to us, we should, in furnishing our homes, look to such matters ever so much more than we have in the past. Have your plumbing done by competent men, such as Mr. Baumann, of No. 43 William street, Newark, N. J., and you may rest in peace as to its being done as well as it can possibly be done. This gentleman also does tin work, steam and gas fitting, and similar work. We know of no house in the city having better facilities at hand to execute work of this nature, and besides good equipments, good mechanics and good work, Mr. Baumann has a fine assortment of stoves, ranges and tin ware constantly on hand, at the lowest prices which can be quoted on such articles. He is a native of Newark, and gives employment to five hands. His premises are 20x30 feet in dimensions. Orders entrusted to his care are promptly attended to.

DURAND & CO., Manufacturing Jewelers

and Importers of Precious Stones. Factory, 49 to 51 Franklin Street. Office and Salesroom, 44 East Fourteenth Street, New York. Promoting the industrial thrift of Newark by the employment of numerous skilled workmen, and fostering a trade which extends far beyond the ordinary range of our surrounding dependent territory, the house of Messrs. Durand & Co. is entitled to more than passing mention is this work. The house was established forty-two years ago by Mr. James M. Durand, and to-day the factory of the firm is one of the most complete in the United States, being supplied with every facility and appliance known to the trade. The plant of the firm, located as above, comprises a large three-story building, 60x40 feet in dimensions, with an extension 40x85 feet, also three stories high. Here are employed one hundred and twenty-five operatives, in the various departments of the business. The aid of a steam engine is required to give motive power to the machinery in use, which is, however, of limited quantity, owing to the fact that the major portion of the work, being of a highly artistic character, is made by hand. The products of this house consist of the finest quality of gold jewelry and watch cases. The trade of the house extends to all parts of the United States, and their goods are distributed throughout the world. The individual members of the firm are Messrs. W. R. and Wallace Durand, and Joseph G. Ward, all of whom have had an active practical experience in the business, of many years. Their productions are made with great care and nicety, and for beauty and originality of design and perfection of finish, are unexcelled by any other house in the world. It is with pleasure that we draw attention to this house, convinced, as we are, that whoever may have trade dealings with it, will receive ample satisfaction, not only in the character of the goods, but in manifest advantages in terms and prices.

GEORGE B. BERGEN, Provision Market,

Meats and Vegetables, Poultry and Game, No. 50 Marshall Street, corner Halsey, Newark, N. J. There is not a more popular establishment in this immediate neighborhood than Mr. Bergen's meat market. The stock of meats, vegetables and poultry which is carried is as complete as could be desired, and the stock is always fresh. Mr. Bergen believes that in treating his customers fairly, he adopts the best means to arrive at success, and we coincide with his views,

for "honesty is the best policy," especially in business. People who give their hard-earned money to store keepers year in and year out, should not be trifled with by unscrupulous dealers, but receive a fair equivalent for their money. Mr. Bergen is a square dealer, and uses everybody rightly. The large patronage which favors him, tends to show that the establishment which Mr. Bergen conducts is worthy of encouragement. This is a no mean recommendation, and the people of this vicinity would do well to leave their meat orders at Mr. Bergen's.

TELEPHONE NO. 128.

Briant & Logan.

UNDERTAKERS.

No. 830 Broad Street,

NEWARK, N. J.

An historical account of Newark's representative business enterprises, would certainly be considered incomplete were not extended mention made of the firm whose card heads this article. The individual members of the house to which we have reference, are Messrs. J. A. Briant and J. A. Logan. The inception of the enterprise in question took place in the year 1862, with Messrs. Lum & Briant as inaugurators. In 1872, however, the firm of Briant and Woodruff succeeded this firm. The house was known by this name for eight years, when Mr. Woodruff withdrew from the business. This was in 1880, and Mr. Briant then associated his son with him. The latter died about five years after, however, and Mr. Briant having arrived at an age when heavy business responsibilities, and cares better fit the strength of younger men, associated Mr. Logan with him, in the year 1885. The combined experience of these gentlemen has tended much to increase the already high standing the house has enjoyed since its first inception, for they are thoroughly practical in their business methods, and the atmosphere of refinement and sympathy which characterize them in the sad moments when their services are called into requirement, have made for them hosts of friends, who recognize that they perform their duties with an appreciative sense of the feelings of their patrons. There is much in this, for the truly first-class undertaking establishment in any community, is characterized by such men. We have seen men in this necessary line of business, whose hearts were as of stone, so mechanically and unsympathetically did they perform their duties. In moments of bereavement, therefore, when sympathy softens the pangs of sorrow, it is well for every family and the community in general, to know of a reliable undertaking house. The senior member of the well-known establishment of Briant & Logan, is a venerable old gentleman, who has seen sixty years experience in the undertaking business, without a doubt, according to the latest statistics. Mr. Briant is the oldest undertaker in the union to-day, he having been the longest in actual continued business. Mr. Briant in his experience has buried about 11,000 persons. What proof have we that speaks for itself more than this? This statement proves that others besides us, have in the past shared our favorable opinion of his services. The firm do their own cloth work at Nos. 8 and 10 Pearl street, in this city, where their stables are also located. Their office and parlors at No. 830 Broad street, are elegantly fitted up, and comprise two floors, each 25x75 feet in dimensions. Employment is afforded to ten skilled and courteous assistants, who render painstaking attention at all times. We can recommend this house to our readers, as highly as any in the city. There are others worthy of praiseworthy mention, no doubt, but none more so than the oldest in the city—that of Briant & Logan, who have been at No. 830 Broad street for twenty eight years. Telephone call, No. 128. Embalming, funeral directing and all departments of the business are paid attention to by this house.

T. P. FOWLER, Dealer in Honey Brook, Sugar Loaf, Sugar Creek, Jeddo and Other Best Qualities of Coal. Also, Wood at the Lowest Market Rates, No. 379 Plane Street, Newark, N. J. There is not a household in which the question of coal and wood is not of greater or less importance, and we are sure that our readers will give their attention while we point out how to purchase fuel to the best advantage. First of all, patronize a liberal and reliable house. This is a good rule to follow in making purchases of any kind, but particularly so when coal or wood is to be bought, and for obvious reasons. Poor coal is dear at any price, for it spoils stoves, tries tempers, and makes it practically impossible to keep up a fire without constant attention. The question of weight is also to be considered, as is also that of prompt delivery, so that we repeat, patronize a reliable house. There is more than one to be found in this city, but there is not one more trustworthy in every respect, than that carried on by Mr. T. P. Fowler, whose office and yard are located at No. 379 Plane street, in this city. This enterprise was inaugurated in 1858 by Messrs. C. R. Fowler & Bro., but Mr. T. P. Fowler, the present proprietor, came into sole possession in 1865. He is a native of Union county, N. J. Employment is given to four assistants, who deliver the orders received at short notice. Mr. Fowler has acquired a reputation for fair dealing, and handles all the best grades of coal, wood and kindlings, and is in a position to supply anything in this line at bottom prices, as he buys in large quantities and enjoys favorable relations with producers. Orders are respectfully solicited.

JOHN WAFERLING, Wholesale Grocer, and Salt Dealer, Nos. 325 and 327 Halsey Street, Newark, N. J. Wholesale groceries abound in large numbers in Newark, that is, many small concerns make a pretention of being engaged in a wholesale business, who really do not deserve being classed with such reputable wholesale grocery houses as exist in the city. We *have* many fine ones, and foremost in the ranks, is that conducted by Mr. John Waferling, at Nos. 325 and 327 Halsey street. This house has stood before the purchasing trade and public for twenty two years, and we think this is sufficient guarantee that its business methods have always been strictly honorable. This is what tells the story, and it is useless to look for a firm's source of success elsewhere than in honest, upright and square dealing with all its patrons. Mr. Waferling inaugurated his business in 1868. He was Justice of the Peace for five years under Governor McClellan. The store which he occupies is 20x50 feet in dimensions, and an able corps of assistants is employed to furnish the excellent service, which is a characteristic feature of the house. None but those goods usually found in a first-class wholesale grocery house are kept in stock, and the best and choicest brands of goods are to be had at the lowest market rates. A retail business is also done, and the public may find in this establishment, goods not usually kept in any but wholesale houses, as it stands to reason, that doing both a wholesale and retail business, the stock must be as varied as complete.

GEO. H. SWEASY, 318 Mulberry Street, Newark, N. J. Retail Stationery, Cigars and Confectionery. Newark has its full share of cigar stores, and no doubt each of the various establishments of this kind in town has something to recommend it, but we are sure that at not one of them is the purchaser more sure of getting the full worth of his money than at that conducted by Mr. Geo. H. Sweasy, at No. 318 Mulberry street. Mr. Sweasy was born in Newark, and began business in 1871. He has already built up a very desirable trade, and has made a very favorable impression upon the purchasing public, for he makes it a rule to handle goods that will give the best of satisfaction, and his prices are certainly low enough to suit even the most economically disposed. Dispute all that has been said to the contrary, it is now conceded that pure tobacco is perfectly harmless when used in reasonable moderation, and the cigars, tobacco, etc., offered at this well managed store may be relied upon for purity as well as for delicacy of flavor. Cigars, stationery and confectionery of all kinds are offered by Mr. Sweasy, at very reasonable prices. Callers are assured immediate and polite attention, and lovers of the "weed" should make trial of some of the cigars which Mr. Sweasy offers at so low a figure.

WM. WIGGINS, Proprietor, Excelsior Shoe Stores, 21 and 197 Mulberry Street, Newark, N. J. Ladies', Gents', Boys' and Misses' Boots, Shoes, Slippers and Rubbers. Custom Made Shoes, $2.50 and up. In order to offer really attractive inducements to the public, it is necessary to thoroughly understand the goods in which you deal, and, therefore, when we say that Mr. Wm. Wiggins, has been identified with the shoe business for the past eight years, it is equivalent to saying that he is in a position to give exceptional value to purchasers of boots, shoes and foot wear in general. Mr. Wiggins established his business here in Newark in 1882, and now occupies two stores, one located at No. 21, the other No. 197 Mulberry street, each being fitted up throughout in accordance with the most approved modern methods, and the stock carried is correspondingly extensive comprising as it does, a full line of ladies', gents', boys' and misses' boots, shoes, slippers and rubbers. Mr. Wiggins is the proprietor of the Excelsior Shoe Store, and makes a leading specialty of fine footwear, but he caters to no one class of trade to the disadvantage of others, striving, on the contrary, to offer genuine and strong inducements to the purchasing public in general. He is in a position to quote bottom prices, to guarantee that every article shall prove just as represented, and to assure immediate and intelligent service to all, for, besides giving personal attention to the wants of customers, he employs always four, and sometimes more, experienced and efficient assistants. Particular attention is also paid to custom work, and repairing of all kinds, a guarantee being given that the work shall give satisfaction in both quality and price. Mr. Wiggins is a native of Belfast, Ireland, and has built himself up a prosperous business by hard work and honest dealing.

WM. J. ASCHENBACH, Maker of Hand Made Harness, and Horse Furnishing Goods, 70 Market Street, Newark, N. J. Orders and Repairing Solicited. It is both safer and cheaper to use a good harness than a poor one, and there need be no difficulty about getting a good harness if you go to the right kind of a place. We have no hesitation in recommending that carried on by Mr. Wm. J. Aschenbach, at No. 70 Market street, for the gentleman has carried on operations for thirty three years, having started his present business in 1867, and is both able and willing to produce good harness at prices as low as the lowest for similar work. His establishment covers an area of 2,400 square feet, and is completely fitted up for the making of hand made harness of every description, and the doing of repairing in general. A well selected stock of horse furnishing goods is constantly carried, these articles being offered at moderate prices, and being guaranteed to prove as represented. Mr. Aschenbach was born in Germany. He is very well known throughout Newark, having held the office of Alderman for '67-'68, Road Commissioner for one year and was a member of the School Board for four years, from '70 to '74. He has a large number of friends in Newark and vicinity, and numbers among his customers some who have traded with him for many years. His reputation for turning out uniformly reliable work, is as high as it is deserved, and applies to repairing as well as to the making of harness to order. Selected material is used in the filling of every order, and as ten skilled workmen are employed, work can be done at very short notice.

JACOB HOEFER, Grocer, 41 Montgomery Street, Newark, N. J. Many a house-keeper is looking for just such an establishment as that conducted by Mr. Jacob Hoefer, at 41 Montgomery street, and we take great pleasure in commending this enterprise to such inquirers, for we know that Mr. Hoefer's methods are bound to please, and we know that those who have done business with him are out-spoken in their approval of the accommodations offered. Operations were begun here in 1885, and the trade has since been steadily increasing. The premises utilized are of the dimensions of 20x39 feet, and the stock on hand is an unusually fine one. It includes staple and fancy groceries of all kinds, and the prices quoted are all that can be reasonably desired, and it is well worth while giving this store a call. The goods offered comprise the best the market affords, and are received direct from the producers, and are sold at figures as low as the lowest. A competent assistant is employed by Mr. Hoefer, and all customers are assured courteous and prompt attention at all times.

F. X. AMMANN, Bread Cake and Pie

Baker, 60 William Street, Newark, N. J. There are bakeries enough in Newark to supply the wants of the people as far as quantity goes, but the trouble is in supplying the wants of the people in the right *quality* of bread, cake and pie. Many bakeries in this city use inferior flour and other materials used in baking, and the consequence is, that they charge market rates for inferior goods, and the public suffer and pay for it. Others, who really use goods that *are good*, do not know how to use them to turn out nice bread, cake and pie. In other cases, some bakers' ovens are not good and do not bake well. Now, the establishment which was inaugurated by Mr. John Whitlin in 1887, and which is at present conducted at No. 60 William street, by Mr. F. X. Ammann, a native of Germany, uses none but the best brands of flour and groceries in its baking. The proprietor has had a long experience and knows his business, and the oven used in baking is all right in every way, shape and manner, so that we are pleased to inform our readers that at Mr. Ammann's place of business the people of this vicinity will find nothing but " A1." bread, cake and pies, and prices are as low, if not lower, than anywhere else in this neighborhood. The store premises utilized by Mr. Ammann are 15x30 feet in dimensions, and the shop itself is 20x55 feet in dimensions, so that we see there is lots of room in which to do a good business. Orders are respectfully solicited.

JACOB L. SCHLOSS (Successor to Jos.

Schloss), Dealer in Choice Groceries, Beef, Veal, Lamb, Pork, Mutton, etc., Corned and Smoked Meats, Poultry, Fruits, Vegetables, Fish, Oysters, Clams and Canned Goods, No. 75 William Street, near Plane Street, Newark, N. J. As we have said in the card at the head of this article the enterprise of which Mr. Jacob L. Schloss is at present the proprietor, was formerly that of Mr. Jos. Schloss, who inaugurated it in 1870, Mr. Jacob Schloss having come into possession in 1890. This gentleman is a native of Newark, and consequently widely known. His experience in the grocery and meat business dates back many years, and he probably knows how to handle these goods as well as the next one. His shop is well rigged with all the conveniences which facilitate work in the business, and as he employs three competent assistants, the wants of his patrons, both regular and transient, are provided for with a service worthy of commendation. His premises measure 20x75 feet in dimensions, and contain an elegant ice box, in which the meat is preserved as pure and fresh as it is possible for meat to be preserved. Besides his regular stock of fresh meats, Mr. Schloss always has on hand corned and smoked meats, poultry, fruits, vegetables, fish, oysters, clams and canned goods. Thus we see by this enumeration of the goods carried, that Mr. Schloss must do quite a business, and he does in reality. Mr. Schloss invariably endeavors to give a fair equivalent for every dollar he receives, and this has been the key to his success. The people of this neighborhood would do well to patronize this house if they want the best, at the lowest prices. A choice line of groceries has recently been added, and hereafter will be a feature of the establishment. Patronize a house furnishing pure and fresh goods, at low rates, at all times.

MRS. S. A. VAN RIPER, Manufacturer of

Vests, 322 Washington Street, Corner William Street, Newark, N. J. The enterprise now conducted by Mrs. S. A. Van Riper, was founded by Mr. Wm. H. Van Riper in 1874, and came under the control of Mrs. Van Riper in 1878, who has shown great enterprise and ability in carrying on the business. The premises now are located at No. 322 Washington street and are very spacious and well equipped, being of the dimensions of 40x75 feet, and when we say that every inch of available space is made use of, it becomes almost unnecessary to add that a very large trade is done. Vests of all descriptions are manufactured, and in the best manner. Mrs. Van Riper employs seventy-five assistants, who are competent and experienced in every detail of their business, and as a result all work turned out by this establishment is strictly as represented to be in every instance. The proprietress is thoroughly conversant with the requirements of her customers, and she gives close personal attention to the task of catering to those wants. All orders are given equal consideration, and as for prices, no manufacturer in the State can quote lower for equally good work.

THE NEWARK NEWS COMPANY,

Wholesale Newsdealers, Booksellers and Stationers, Blank Book Manufacturers and Law Blank Publishers, Jobbers in Pipes, Cigars and Tobacco, No. 251 Washington Street, Newark, N. J. Telephone 179. The Newark News Company was inaugurated in 1870, and Mr. M. Chandler is its manager. This gentleman is a native of Newark, and the spirit of enterprise which characterizes his business adaptabilities is well known and duly appreciated by all who have the pleasure of knowing or doing business with him. The nature of the enterprise is that of wholesale news dealers, book sellers, stationers, blank book manufacturers and law blank publishers. We notice at a glance, the wide scope of the work and business which is transacted by this house, for the nature of the business itself embraces so much detail which requires the attention of *education* that we wonder so much is undertaken in one business. The assistance of thirteen regularly employed persons who possess practical experience, explains matters somewhat, however, and we can see how each department may be perfected to the degree found in those of the establishment in question. Great care, accuracy and neatness must be exhibited in the manufacture of blank books, and especially law blanks, but this firm is equal to the occasion, and furnish the market with the best in this line. The firm also carry on a business quite of a different nature from the one we have already mentioned, for they are "jobbers" in pipes, cigars and tobacco. Dealers in these articles know the reputation of this house too well to have us repeat it to them, so we will but say to those who may not yet have given the firm a trial order, that it would be to their advantage to do so. Three floors and a basement, each 25x100 feet, furnish 10,000 square feet of available space, and all of it is utilized to the fullest.

LUDOLPH KIESEWETTER, Plumber and

Gas Fitter, Tin Roofer, Manufacturer of Tin, Copper and Sheet Iron Ware. Also, Dealer in Stoves, Ranges, etc., 357 Washington Street, opposite Hill Street, Newark, N. J. Mr. Kiesewetter, who is engaged in the plumbing and gas fitting business, at No. 357 Washington street, in this city, went into business in 1868, and has consequently had a practical experience in all branches of the business for twenty-two years. Plumbing has taken an important step in the trades of late years, and at the present time the greatest attention is paid to the manner in which it is done. To be a good plumber, a man must have a good experience and have kept time with the progress which has been made in the trade. Many new devices have been introduced which have completely revolutionized the art, and a man must not only be a plumber as well as the same used to imply, but he must also be a *sanitary* plumber. By this we mean that a man must understand how to do a job in plumbing which will tend to do away with all that is unhealthy. So many diseases are contracted in buildings where a poor job of plumbing was put in, that in most large cities to-day, a plumbing inspector is paid a high salary to examine work of this kind when reported as unhealthy. Thus we see the importance of having our plumbing done by men who know their business, and who do their work as Mr. Kiesewetter does, in a thoroughly workmanlike manner. So well is this gentleman known to do good work in this respect, that building contractors seek him to do their work. This is no mean recommendation to a man's abilities, so those who have plumbing jobs to have executed, would do well to try Mr. Kiesewetter. He also pays special attention to gas fitting, and has all the facilities at hand to execute work of this nature as in plumbing. Heaters are placed into position when orders are received, and ranges and furnaces in great variety may be found at Mr. Kiesewetter's store. Copper, tin and sheet iron ware are manufactured extensively, and everything new in the line of the latest improvements in plumbing, such as water closet and sink bowls, etc., are kept in stock for the inspection of customers. Mr. Kiesewetter employs six skilled workmen, and is prepared to fill orders at short notice, in the most satisfactory manner. The store has lately been completely renovated and enlarged to do justice to the large increase of business with which Mr. Kiesewetter has been favored. We invite the public to remember this gentleman's place of business, at No. 357 Washington street, when anything in his line is needed. Satisfaction is guaranteed, as all who have thus far had occasion to deal with Mr. Kiesewetter will testify.

F. H. WISMER, Wholesale Clothing Manufacturer, 14 and 16 Green Street, Newark, N. J. We all know what millions and millions of dollars are expended yearly in clothing, and what a great factor the manufacturing of clothing is in commerce. We know also, and perhaps only too well, by actual experience, how much of the ready made clothing which comes from some manufacturing establishments, is deficient, either in the quality of the goods with which the garments are made, or in the manner in which they are made. It is undeniably a fact, that some manufacturers of these goods, urged in the desire of accumulating large fortunes in small spaces of time, do not scruple in using material, which, to the eye, when newly made, are to all intents and purposes, good goods for the money, but which eventually prove to be worthless, or comparatively so. On the other hand, also, it is well known to the trade, if not to the general public, that some manufacturers do an honest and conscientious business in this line, and that generally, their goods may be relied upon as being just as represented. A firm enjoying this more favorable reputation is that of Mr. F. H. Wismer, at No. 14 and 16 Green street, in this city. Mr. Wismer has been engaged in the manufacture of clothing for the past thirty-five years, and we need not say, that, in all this time the standing of his house among others engaged in the same business has reached a level as high as any among the more reputable manufacturing clothiers in this country. This is no mean recommendation for the standing of a house, but "honor to whom honor is due," and we are pleased to characterize Mr. Wismer's establishment in this manner. To correctly form an idea of the large proportions of this establishment, it is but necessary to be told that employment is given to two hundred hands the year round, and that two floors of vast area are utilized. Mr. Wismer's establishment is well appointed with every facility for carrying on the manufacturing clothing business, and the trade can find here all sorts of goods made up into fine savings. Mr. Wismer's goods are noted for their excellence in style and durability. The immense amount of business done yearly is ample corroboration of our statements. The trade would do well to bear this house in mind.

PFROMMER & LAYER, Dealers in Fancy Groceries, No. 133 Spruce Street, Corner Somerset Street, Newark, N. J. The store located at No. 133 Spruce street, corner Somerset street, and occupied by Messrs. Pfrommer & Layer, is most admirably adapted for the purposes for which it is used, as well as being an ornament to the thoroughfare on which it stands. It affords excellent accommodations for the heavy and varied stock carried by Messrs. Pfrommer & Layer, consisting of choice teas, pure coffees and spices, and everything in fact usually to be found in a first-class establishment of this kind. The firm is composed of Mr. John G. Pfrommer, who is a native of Germany, and Mr. Frank P. Layer, who was born in this city. Their present enterprise was founded in 1889. The premises comprise one floor 50x48 feet in size, and a large basement for storage. Four competent assistants are employed, and customers are served with courtesy and promptness, that go far to explain the popularity this enterprise has attained, while the prices quoted afford the best possible evidence that the firm enjoys the most favorable relations with producers and wholesalers, and are in a position to supply first-class goods at the very lowest market rates. It would be simply impossible to give a detailed description of the articles comprising the large stock within reasonable limits, and therefore we will simply say it is exceptionally complete in every department, and is made up of goods selected from reliable sources. Special attention is given to the handling the best butter, which is supplied at bottom prices.

WOERTENDYKE, Newsdealer, Confectionery, Ice Cream, Thompson's Celebrated Soda Water and Root Beer. Full line of Cigars, Tobacco, etc., No. 119 Washington Street, Newark, N. J. This establishment, which ranks among the first of its kind in this section of the city, is one of the most popular dealing in daily, weekly and periodical papers, confectionery, ice cream, soda, root beer, cigars and tobacco. Mr. David Woertendyke, the present proprietor, established his business in 1887, and to his skill, able management and untiring industry, is due, in a great measure, the progress and success which has been attained during its career. Mr. Woertendyke possesses every facility

for giving his patrons and friends extra inducements, both in low prices and excellent quality of goods sold. The store occupied is located at No. 119 Washington street, and covers an area of 25x85 feet. It is eligibly located, and is filled with as large and reliable a stock as can be found in any similar establishment. A splendidly furnished reception room is a feature, and ice cream, soda and other refreshments are served, popular prices predominating. It is a first rate place to drop in of an evening with your friends to enjoy a cool and refreshing drink of root beer. Cigars and tobacco are also kept; as good five and ten cent cigars are sold here as can be found in the city. The man who does not read the newspapers, deprives himself of one of the best means of education, and there is no doubt in our minds that the man who does not read the newspapers is seriously handicapped in the race for wealth. By wealth we do not mean money alone. There is a wealth of information, a wealth of many other things, without which money is of but little value, and a man who takes interest in general affairs, outside his own little circle, has an unlimited source of enjoyment to draw upon.

ALBERT W. FAY, Wholesale and Retail Dealer in Beef, Veal, Mutton, Lamb, Poultry and Game in Season, Fresh Fish, Oysters and Clams, Butter, Cheese, Eggs and Lard a Specialty, 433 Broad Street, Newark, N. J. In 1887, Mr. G. W. Clayton inaugurated the above business, which, in 1880, Mr. A. W. Fay, the present proprietor, purchased. Mr. Fay was born in Eatontown, N. J., and has long been known to the Newark public as an enterprising business man of integrity and push. Upon entering his establishment, an air of "systematic business" is instantly felt, and the purchaser has the inward satisfaction of knowing that in dealing with Mr. Fay, he will invariably receive new and fresh meats and fish every time he orders. The meat and fish business is not like others, for unless a house of this nature is favored with a large patronage such as Mr. Fay enjoys, it is almost certain to carry over goods, which, when finally sold, are almost unfit to cook. Mr. Fay's large store, occupying a space of 18x60 feet, is constantly stocked with beef, veal, mutton, lamb, fresh fish, oysters and clams, butter, cheese, eggs and lard. Neatness seems to be the motto, for in all departments of the establishment, the observer notes the extreme care taken to preserve the goods in the purest state possible. A specialty is made of the prompt and accurate delivery of goods without extra charge, and all orders receive immediate and painstaking attention. Mr. Fay enjoys the trade of some of the most careful buyers of meat and fish, butter, cheese and lard, in the city of Newark. Of course there are plenty of meat and fish markets in the city, so that no one need go hungry, but it is undeniable, that more or less difficulty is experienced in obtaining really first-class goods in this line, and the object of this article is to acquaint those who do not already know, it that at No. 433 Broad street, Mr. Fay keeps a first-class meat and fish market.

C. A. SLACK, Carriage, Coach and Wagon Trimming, The Manufacture of Buggy and Extension Tops a Specialty; also, Dealer in Wagon and Carriage Wheels, Spokes, Rims, Bows, etc., No. 324 Plane Street, Newark, N. J. Mr. C. A. Slack inaugurated the business in which he is engaged, in the year 1883. The nature of his enterprise is that of carriage, coach and wagon trimming. This business is of interest to those who own vehicles needing either repairing or brand new trimmings, and we wish to call special attention to the workmanlike manner in which Mr. Slack executes his work. Those who have once given Mr. Slack a piece of work to do invariably return when they have more, and all praise the neatness and durability of work done at this establishment. This gentleman also pays special attention to buggy and extension tops. Parties owning carriages whose tops are worn out, should have them retopped at Mr. Slack's. He will make the hardest looking carriage look brand new before he leaves it. Mr. Slack's charges are very moderate considering the superiority of the work done and the material used. He carries a large and select stock of wagon and carriage wheels, spokes, rims, bows, etc., at all times. Employment is afforded to three competent hands, and all orders are dispatched with a promptitude worthy of commendation. The premises occupied are at No. 324 Plane street, and measure 20x85 feet, three floors being utilized.

78

LEADING BUSINESS MEN OF NEWARK.

WM. H. O'DONNELL, Dealer in Produce, Butter, Eggs, Cheese, etc., First-Class Fish and Oyster Market. Canned Goods a Specialty, 267 Mulberry street, Corner Walnut, Newark, N. J. Mr. Wm. H. O'Donnell has "got on the right side" of many of our most experienced householders, for the inducements offered to customers at his establishment are hard to resist, and the quality of the goods handled is always first-class. One thing that strikes a stranger doing business with this house for the first time, is the cheerfulness and alacrity with which he is waited upon. Nothing is more exasperating than to go into a store and have to wait around until some one sees fit to attend to you, and yet this experience is the rule rather than the exception in some establishments that could be named. The proprietor of the market under question, Mr. Wm. H. O'Donnell does not do business that way, and callers at his store may feel assured of being served at the earliest possible moment. The result of this and other popular features of the management, is to be seen in the large retail business built up since Mr. O'Donnell assumed entire control of affairs in 1888. The premises occupied are located at No. 267 Mulberry street, corner of Walnut street, covering an area of 1,000 square feet. The assortment of goods on hand comprise produce, butter, eggs, cheese, etc., as well as everything to be found in a first-class fish and oyster market, canned goods being made a specialty. Employment is given to four efficient and polite assistants, and no pains are spared to facilitate operations as much as possible. A good deal of business is done with very little fuss and trouble. Mr. O'Donnell is a native of Pennsylvania, and served as Corporal in Company B, 1924 Regiment Penn. Volunteers during our late war. A wagon is kept soliciting and delivering orders to all parts of the city at all times.

F. PFAUS, Merchant Tailor, Market Street. Corner Mulberry Street, Newark, N. J. While economy is doubtless a virtue of no small importance, and extravagant expenditure is to be deplored and discouraged as much as possible, still care should be taken that economy does not degenerate into parsimony, and it should always be borne in mind that it is necessary to spend money if you want to make money. For instance, applying this principle to the purchase of wearing apparel, is it not evident that the advantage gained by reason of a neat and stylish personal appearance much more than counterbalances the expense of the necessary articles to attain such, and especially every young man should dress as well as possible, and if judgment and good sense be used, there is no need of spending any exorbitant sums of money to do so. Mr. F. Pfaus, located at the corner of Market and Mulberry streets, has been identified with his present business since 1873, and has mastered it so thoroughly that he is in a position to produce the best results, at the smallest possible cost. The premises now occupied at the above named address, are 15x30 feet in dimensions. The clothing made by Mr. Pfaus is extremely low in price, when the quality and work is considered, and his facilities are such that satisfaction can be guaranteed in every particular. Experienced assistants are employed, and the assortment of goods carried comprises staple as well as the latest fashionable novelties.

ANDREW READY, Custom Shoe Store, No. 457 Washington Street, Newark, N. J. Mr. Ready, who keeps a shoe store at the above address, was for seven years located on Clinton avenue. The premises he now has are conveniently located, and are of the dimensions of 15x20 feet. The general run of the public like to wear well made, soft and good fitting shoes, but unless we place our orders for shoes at a good custom shoe maker's establishment, such as Mr. Ready keeps, at No. 457 Washington street, we are not likely to receive the satisfaction we would, did we do so. Mr. Ready has been in business several years, and is known throughout the city as an exceptionally fine workman. No work leaves his store or shop but what is executed in an A1 manner. Mr. Ready has hosts of regular customers who have traded with him for years. This is ample proof that he does good work, and we advise those who wear custom made shoes to leave their orders in the future with this gentleman. Repairing is also neatly done and with dispatch. Remember the number, 457 Washington street, Newark, N. J.

FRANK TRENSCH, Choice Staple and Fancy Groceries, No. 67 South Orange Avenue, Newark, N. J. Did amount of space permit, we would deem it a pleasure to describe in detail the large and varied stock of groceries carried by Mr. Frank Trensch, for it is carefully selected, and deserves special mention in the columns of the "History of Newark and its Leading Business Men." We must confine ourselves to the statement that it is made up of a variety of goods in demand in every family, and that it is well worthy of the liberal patronage it receives. Our readers would do well to place a trial order with the establishment in question. It is a model grocery store of high merit, and its proprietor, Mr. Trensch, is a man known to employ honest business methods; a man who does not misrepresent his goods, and a man whose reputation for integrity is irreproachable. To get an adequate idea of the variety, purity and freshness of the stock carried by Mr. Trensch, one must visit the store, for seeing leads to belief. The enterprise was inaugurated in the year 1884, by a Mrs. Weis, and fell to the possession of Mr. B. Albers, in the year 1886. Since Mr. Trensch has had it (1889), business has redoubled, and success seems to be in store for the proprietor. The store is admirably adapted for the purposes for which it was intended, and the fixtures tend to the better displaying of the goods. Mr. Trensch is a native of Germany. He employs two courteous clerks, and the store is 20x55 feet in dimensions. We invite all our readers in this neighborhood to patronize Mr. Trensch's grocery store. Satisfaction is guaranteed.

WILLIAM ECKER, Bread, Cake and Pie Bakery, 153 Mulberry Street, Newark, N. J. The bakery conducted by Mr. William Ecker, is entitled to rank among the most popular of the many excellent business establishments of this kind carried on this city, and those who argue that there can be "no effect without a cause" will find evidence to support their views in the history of this meritorious enterprise, for the causes which have brought about the popularity referred to, are too obvious to be overlooked, consisting as they do, of prompt and reliable service, equal courtesy to all patrons, and the furnishing of unsurpassed commodities at the lowest market rates. Mr. Wm. Ecker, the proprietor of the bakery in question, is a native of Troy, N. Y. He began business operations here in 1886, and now occupies premises at No. 153 Mulberry street. Employment is afforded to two assistants, and bread, cake and pie of the finest quality, are always in stock, as well as a full assortment of goods usually found in a first-class bakery. Special attention is given to family trade, all orders being given immediate and painstaking attention, and entire satisfaction being guaranteed, both as regards the quality of the goods furnished, and the reasonableness of the charges made. The best materials are used, and the results attained are pleasing to the most fastidious.

J. EBLE, Butcher and Dealer in Fish, Oysters and Clams. Also Fruits Vegetables, Poultry, Provisions, etc., 421 Mulberry street, Newark, N. J. In analyzing the popularity that the enterprise carried on by Mr. Jacob Eble unquestionably enjoys, we find that it does not seem to be due to any one thing, but rather to the impression made by his methods of doing business, when considered altogether. For instance Mr. Eble does not claim to sell cheaper than everybody else, although he does offer his goods at the lowest market rates. Neither does he claim to carry the largest stock in this section of the city, but nevertheless the variety on hand is such that all tastes can be suited. He strives to fully satisfy every customer, and give a dollar's worth of value for every dollar he receives, and it may be said that this is probably one of the chief causes of the popularity referred to. Mr. Eble is a native of Germany, and has had considerable experience in his present business. He is a butcher and dealer in fish, oysters and clams, also fruits, vegetables, poultry, provisions, etc. He founded his establishment in 1889, and is now located at No. 421 Mulberry street. All classes of trade are catered to, the prices are placed at the lowest figures consistent with the handling of dependable goods. An extensive retail business is done, requiring the services of five well-informed and reliable assistants, and every caller is assured prompt and courteous attention. Mr. Eble also has a store on South Orange avenue, and two teams attend to orders.

JOHN BREUNIG, Ph. D., Druggist and
Pharmacist, 250 Springfield Avenue, Opposite Boyd Street,
Newark, N. J. Telephone No. 273. There is no establishment
so thoroughly American as the modern drug store. There
is no more popular and deserving member of society of the
present day than the enterprising druggist. When one con-
siders the variety of wants that the pharmacist is called
upon to satisfy, the thousand and one calls upon his patience
in and out of his ordinary line of business, one ceases to
wonder at the unique position that he holds in the affections
of the American public. The child learns early the path to
the store, with the request, "please, mister, give me a picture card." The young miss comes regularly for her two
cent stamp, preferring the politeness of the drug clerk, to
the morose curtness of the stamp clerk at the post office.
The school boy comes for a nickel's worth of battery fluid, and
the adult citizen is fain to linger among the magic phials and
chat with the intelligent dispenser of chemicals. Thus the
drug store has become an essential feature of our modern
home life. All of these demands are made upon one of the
busiest and most responsible of professions. Newark is especially fortunate in the possession of well-equipped pharmacies. One of the most popular of these, is that conducted
by John Breunig, at No. 250 Springfield avenue. Mr. Breunig
was born in this city in 1859, where he received his education in public schools, and private schools. After being
graduated with honor at the college of Pharmacy, of New
York, in 1879 he took charge of Dr. Ill's drug store on Springfield avenue. In 1885 Mr. Breunig entered business on his
own account, and now has one of the handsomest drug stores
in the city. It is fitted up in the most improved style. That
his services are appreciated, is shown in the fact that Mr.
Breunig has been called upon for two terms in succession to
represent the Sixth ward in the Board of Education of Newark. He is now Chairman of the High School Committee,
one of the most important committees of the board. There is
no better drug store in the city. Both as to quality, price
and promptness in service, his pharmacy ranks A No. 1.

JOHN MERZ, JR., Grocer, 87 Waverly
Place, Corner Broome, Newark, N. J. Among the establishments which merit mention in this book, that conducted
by Mr. John Merz should be given a place, for, although this
store makes no great pretentions, still it is worthy of the
most liberal patronage, for the simple reason that no goods
are sold under false pretences, every article being guaranteed to prove just as represented in every respect. Mr.
Merz is a native of New York city, and began business here
in Newark in 1888. He has built up quite a large business,
for the public are not slow to appreciate fair dealing and
enterprise, and are pretty sure to support any undertaking
in the management of which these are combined. The
premises are located at No. 87 Waverly place, and contains
a choice supply of staple and fancy groceries. This gentleman does not claim to sell lower than every body else, nor to
be constantly offering goods "below cost," he is content
with a small margin of profit, and a dollar will go about as
far in his store as at any similar establishment in this city.
A competent assistant is employed, and all orders are
promptly filled, while every caller is sure of polite attention.

G. TOBELMANN, Baker, 264 Mulberry
Street, Newark, N. J. In calling attention to the establishment conducted by Mr. Gustav Tobelmann, we feel sure
that we are but giving expression to the sentiment of many
people in this vicinity when we say that it is one of the
most reliable enterprises of the kind in the entire city, and
those who have made a practice of dealing with this establishment speak of the even excellence of the goods offered,
and the uniform courtesy and consideration extended to
every customer. Business was begun in 1880, and has grown
without a pause until it has reached its present large proportions, which now require the services of seven competent
assistants. The premises are located at No. 264 Mulberry
street, and always contain a desirable and varied stock of
bread, cake and pastry, which is offered for sale at the very
lowest rates. The goods sold here enjoy an enviable reputation in the neighborhood, and it is only natural that they
should, for they are made from carefully selected materials
by skilled and experienced assistants. Fresh bread and
pastry are to be had here daily, and is offered to the public
in great variety. Mr. Tobelmann is a native of Germany,
and highly respected throughout Newark.

H. D. BALDWIN, Practical Plumber, Steam
and Gas Fitter, Copper, Tin and Sheet Iron Worker, Stove,
Furnace and Heater Work. Sewer Connections Made, 317
Mulberry Street, Newark, N. J. In placing an order for
plumbing work, it should be borne in mind that although
theoretical or "book-knowledge," is an excellent thing in its
way, still it by no means takes the place of that other kind
of knowledge that can only be gained by practical experience. Every intelligent person has some idea of the importance of proper drainage, etc., and every intelligent person
should know that it is worth while to take some trouble to
see that whoever is entrusted with such work, is a competent
and responsible party. Mr. H. D. Baldwin has been identified with the plumbing, steam, gas fitting, copper, tin and
sheet iron work of this city for several years, and has been
in business for himself since 1877, having thus had a wide experience in all branches of his business. We believe he has
few equals, and no superiors, and as he gives close personal
attention to his business to all its details, no better man can
be found with whom to place any orders of that kind. His
business premises are located at No. 317 Mulberry street,
and are of the dimensions of 20x50 feet. Employment is
given to five thoroughly competent workmen, and anything
in the line of stove, furnace and heater work, sewer connections, roofing, gutter and leader repairing or putting up,
will be done at short notice, and in a thoroughly satisfactory
manner. Mr. Baldwin is a native of Plainfield, N. J., and is
very well known throughout Newark, as a thoroughly practical plumber, steam and gas fitter, and one who is competent to undertake the most intricate jobs, and to guarantee
that they will give entire satisfaction when completed.

F. W. KRALERT & CO., Manufacturers of
Decorated Shades and Lamp Bodies, 37 Ward Street, Newark, N. J. N. Y. Office, 38 Park Place. As it takes all kinds
of men to make up the world, so it takes all kinds of business to form the industries of a city, and in Newark, the industries are as varied as they are numerous. The enterprise conducted by Messrs. F. W. Kralert & Co., was inaugurated in 1888 by Messrs. Kralert & Chipman, but on the
first of January, 1889, the firm became known under its
present name, with Mr. E. H. Fessenden as the company.
Two kilns for firing which are used in the process of manufacturing the goods handled are features of the establishment, and six floors, each of the dimensions of 20x75 feet, are
utilized. This affords 9,000 square feet of available space.
Employment is afforded to fifteen to twenty-five skilled
workmen the year round, and the goods chiefly dealt in are
decorated lamp shades and lamp bodies. In the estimation
of the trade this house ranks high, for its prices on a superior line of these articles are reasonably quoted at all times.
Considerable art must be displayed in the manufacture of
these goods, which are as delicate as useful. The company
are equal to the occasion, however, and are able to fill the
largest orders with commendable promptness. Mr. Kralert
is a native of Austria, but has resided in this country many
years. The trade's attention is respectfully solicited to the
company's goods.

CARL F. SEITZ & SON, Manufacturers of
Fur Crush Hats, Nos. 27 to 37 Ward Street, Newark, N. J.
Salesroom, 159 to 161 Greene Street, New York. The house
of Carl F. Seitz & Son, manufacturers of fur crush hats, is
well known to our citizens, and the trade at large. Mr. Seitz
founded his business in 1857, so that for thirty three years
this house has stood the several test of time. In 1878 Mr.
Seitz, who is a native of Germany, admitted his son, Mr.
Julius Seitz, into partnership with him. The great experience of these gentlemen in the hat manufacturing business,
and the facilities which they have at hand in their establishment for doing this work, enables them to fill out the largest
orders. They employ a force of 150 men, so that we see a
considerable business is done. The premises which the establishment occupies comprises an area of three floors, each
75x100 feet in dimensions. This affords 22,500 square feet of
available space, and it is all utilized. None but a wholesale
jobbing trade is done, and the line of goods dealt in is that
of fur crush hats. Messrs. Seitz & Son have an office and
salesroom at Nos. 159 and 161 Greene street, New York, and
the manufactory is located at Nos. 27, 29, 31 and 35 Ward
street, Newark, N. J.

GEO. O. TOTTEN, Grocer, 500 Orange Street, Corner Roseville Avenue, Newark, N. J. It is true, that often what is of great interest to one man may have no attraction for another, but there are some subjects in which all are interested to a greater or less degree, and among these may be placed those relating to where reliable goods may be bought to the best advantage. Therefore, we feel sure that our readers will not begrudge the time spent in learning a little concerning the establishment conducted by Mr. George O. Totten, at No. 500 Orange street, corner of Roseville avenue, Newark, for this is certainly a store where a large stock is carried, a varied assortment offered, and low prices quoted. Here is a combination of advantages worthy of careful consideration, and we are convinced that the more thoroughly the inducements here offered are investigated, the more solid and substantial they will be proved. Mr. Totten handles a large variety of goods, dealing in line groceries of all kinds. His assortment is made up of both staple and fancy articles, and is selected expressly for family use, being obtained from the most reliable sources. The fact that our prices will bear comparison with those of any other dealer in this section, has a great deal to do with the large retail business done. Four competent assistants are constantly employed, and ensure prompt and civil attention to every customer, and it should be especially noted, that Mr. Totten's motto is "finest goods at lowest prices." He is a native of Tottenville, Staten Island. He was Justice of the Peace and P. M. in Cranford for four years, and is very favorably known throughout Newark, where he has been identified with the retail grocery business since 1875.

W. LEVERATT, Dealer in all kinds of Fresh, Salted and Smoked Meats. Also, Butter and Cheese, Fruits and Vegetables in their Season. Eggs Received Fresh from the Country twice a week, Corner Boyden and Orange Streets, Newark, N. J. That there are many meat and provision markets to be found in Newark, our readers need not be told, for the fact is plainly evident to any one who has even a slight acquaintance with that section, but it requires something more than a slight acquaintance to become posted as to the relative merits of these establishments, and, therefore, whatever information we can give in that line is quite sure to be acceptable. In this connection we should like to call attention to the enterprise of which Mr. Wm. Leveratt is the proprietor, located at the corner of Boyden and Orange streets, for we believe that no better goods are to be found in the city than are obtainable at this market, and we are sure that no more honorable business methods can be practiced anywhere. The establishment occupied covers an area of 814 square feet, and employment is given to four obliging and well informed assistants. An extremely large and varied stock of fresh, salted and smoked meats is constantly carried, as well as choice butter and cheese from the most popular dairies, also, fruits and vegetables of all kinds in their season, while eggs are received fresh from the country twice a week, and the prices quoted are very reasonable, especially when the superior quality of the goods is remembered. Mr. Leveratt is a native of England, and started his business in this city in 1856, and in 1887 purchased the property at the corner of Boyden and Orange streets, and erected there a building well equipped for all the purposes of his growing trade. This establishment he has carried on long enough to make it evident that success is assured under a continuance of the present liberal and enterprising management.

WILLIAM HENRY SAYRE, Druggist, 588 and 590 Orange Street, Newark, N. J. The establishment conducted by Mr. William Henry Sayre is entitled to prominent mention among the best known, most reliable and most popular of Newark's pharmacies, for it was opened nearly a score of years ago by the present proprietor, and has made a record which fully explains its present leading position, and fully justifies the implicit confidence reposed in it by the public. Mr. Sayre was born in this city, and served during the rebellion as First Lieutenant in the 13th N. Y. Volunteers. He founded his present business in 1874. The premises utilized comprise one double store and two basements, and are located at Nos. 588 and 590 Orange street. They contain a heavy and complete stock of drugs, medicines and chemicals, besides a full assortment of such other goods as are usually to be found in a first-class city drug store. Some wholesale business is done, but the great bulk of the trade is retail, and it is to this class of customers that Mr. Sayre especially caters, particular attention being paid to the compounding of prescriptions, and no trouble being spared to ensure the very nicest accuracy in the filling of all orders of this kind, while the drugs used are obtained from the most reliable sources, and are as fresh and pure as can be found in the market. Moderate charges are made in all cases, and as the store is conducted by three licensed pharmacists, prompt and careful attention is assured to every caller.

JOHN SANDERS, Practical Plumber, 262 South Orange Avenue, Newark, N. J. The gentleman carrying on the business located at the above address, inaugurated the enterprise in the year 1887. He is a native of Newark, and has been engaged in business here for a number of years. He affords employment to five experienced and practical plumbers the year round, and frequently employs more in busy moments. His establishment is of the spacious dimensions of 25x60 feet. In it is to be found a complete outfit of plumbers' and roofers' tools and materials. The most modern sanitary appliances are carried in great variety, and patrons select according to their liking. Water closet cabinets, bowls, sinks, piping, tin, etc., abound, and the prices which Mr. Sanders quotes on these articles are as low as can be named on goods of relative value. It is a well-known fact that a great revolution has taken place of late years in the plumbing trade. The old style way of plumbing has given way to the more modern, and better way. Mr. Sanders has kept pace with the times, and is prepared to execute all jobs he undertakes in the most workmanlike manner. It is better to lay out a little more money on a good job of plumbing at the start, than to be obliged to continually lay out money for repairatives on a poor job. This is the principal which real estate owners work on, and if parties who have such work to be executed place their orders with men who know their business thoroughly, as Mr. Sanders does, no difficulty will arise in the future. We take particular pains to recommend the gentleman in question to the favorable consideration of the readers of the "History of Newark and its Leading Business Men," for we believe him to be thoroughly competent to execute the most difficult jobs. Satisfaction is guaranteed in all cases by Mr. Sanders. His establishment, as we have said, is located at No. 262 South Orange avenue. Orders left here, or mailed, will receive immediate and painstaking attention.

WM. DIXON, DEALER IN ICE CREAM.

Manufactory 675 Broad Street, Newark, N. J. There are certain wiseacres who delight in alarming the public, and their favorite means of doing so is to make grave insinuations and sometimes positive statements concerning the harmful effects of articles of food and drink. There is not a food, from roast beef to raw oysters, that has not been declared "dangerous under certain conditions;" there is not a beverage, from French brandy to well water, that has not had a similar experience, and were we to believe the doleful statements so frequently published, each of us would have to have a private chemist to analyze whatever we proposed to eat or drink, the alternative being to die of fear, starvation or thirst, neither of which is an especially agreeable death. But, happily, we don't believe these assertions. They sometimes have some truth in them, and they make us uncomfortable at times, but common sense exposes their exaggerations, and the American people have a large fund of common sense. The rapidly increasing demand for ice cream shows that the foolish attacks made upon it have had no effect, for experience proves that ice cream, properly made of suitable materials, is healthful as well as refreshing and delicious. There is ice cream in the market that is injurious, perhaps, but those who buy of reputable dealers run no risk whatever, and there are enough such to fully satisfy the demand. The estate of Wm. Dixon is one of the most extensive and best known ice cream manufacturers in this section of the country, having begun operations in New York in 1864, and removing to Newark in 1876, utilizes premises, spacious and well equipped, at No. 675 Broad street, employs eighteen assistants and does an immense wholesale and retail business throughout this vicinity. Using the best of ingredients and having exceptionally complete facilities, they are in a position to satisfy the most fastidious tastes, to fill the largest orders without delay and to quote as low prices as can be named on a strictly first-class article. A specialty is made of the restaurant department of the business, as meals can be served at all hours from 9 a. m. till 12 p. m. One hundred people can be seated at a time and promptly served with the best the market affords. In the manufacture of ice cream and ices of all kinds a fifteen horse-power engine is used, and facilities are at hand for the manufacture of 600 quarts per hour. A Tonstill ice crusher, with all modern improvements, was added in March, and triplet freezers also put in. Ices of all flavors are made a specialty.

COOGAN, NUGENT & CO., WHOLE-

sale and Retail Manufacturers and Dealers in Parlor Suits, Furniture, Carpets and Oil Cloths, No. 128 Market Street, Newark, N. J. When a firm occupies a building comprising five floors, each measuring 25x100 feet, it is to be conjectured that they are not only doing a flourishing business, but that their stock is large and they have something worth showing to customers. This is most emphatically the case with Messrs. Coogan, Nugent & Co., who have an establishment of this magnitude, for the manufacture and sale of furniture at 128 Market street, Newark. Notwithstanding the size of the premises, they are none too large to accommodate the great variety of furniture always kept in stock by Messrs. Coogan, Nugent & Co. The enterprise inaugurated by these gentlemen only dates back five years, and it is truly surprising that they should have been able to build up so large a trade in a comparatively short time. It certainly speaks well for the class of work done by them as well as for their honest and upright dealing. They make all grades of furniture, and they enjoy the reputation of making the best. A specialty is made of elegant parlor furniture, either in sets or odd pieces, and this will be found to comprise all the latest styles in fancy wood and upholstered work. This firm caters to all classes of trade, and for those who cannot afford the finest grade of furniture there are pretty and durable sets to be had for an extremely moderate price, equal consideration being shown to all buyers, whether they wish to expend much or little. The business is both wholesale and retail, and employment is given to fifteen assistants. We thoroughly recommend a visit to this house to any one in search of a large or small quantity of furniture, or other house fittings, such as carpets, oil cloths, etc., a choice variety of which is always on view. A special feature is their credit or instalment, which enables parties to pay either by weekly or monthly payments. The firm is formed of Messrs. D. Coogan, C. Nugent, Jr., and D. Moriarty, all well known in the business world of Newark.

A. R. BERRY, REAL ESTATE AND

Insurance, No. 749 Broad Street, Newark, N. J. Among the many real estate and insurance agencies to be found in this city, we know of none offering more prompt, efficient and reliable service than is obtained at the establishment conducted by Mr. A. R. Berry, at 749 Broad st. Operations were begun in 1887 by Mr. Berry. He also has a branch office at Woodbridge, N. J., where he conducts an extensive insurance business, representing some of the strongest companies in the world, and makes a specialty of the handling of property located in that section. A general real estate business is done, including buying, selling, exchanging, renting and leasing, and as Mr. Berry always has some desirable city and suburban property on his books, intending investors would best serve their own interests by giving him a call. He is always prepared to place insurance in standard companies on the most favorable terms, making a specialty of writing policies on dwelling houses and household furniture, and protecting the interests of his customers in every legitimate way. Orders are promptly and carefully filled, communications by mail receiving immediate and painstaking attention.

J. WILBUR SMITH, Manufacturer of

the "Welcome" Shirt, 154 Market St., Newark, N. J. Shirts Made to Order. Fit Guaranteed. It probably seems strange to some that careful dressers should be so fastidious as regards the fitting of shirts—garments which are scarcely seen excepting when worn in connection with evening dress—but the truth of the matter is, that, quite aside from the discomfort of wearing an ill-fitting shirt it is practically impossible to get outer garments that will fit as they should when worn over such an article. The great popularity of the "Welcome" shirt is due in a great measure to the shapeliness of its design, and to the fact that it is made in so great a variety of sizes that an excellent fit is assured in almost every instance. This famous shirt is manufactured by Mr. J. Wilbur Smith, who succeeded in 1885, Messrs. Kirkpatrick & Smith, who had carried on operations since 1878. Mr. Smith is a native of Massachusetts, and is widely and favorably known in business and social circles in Newark and vicinity. He is constantly striving to improve his products, and the material and workmanship put into the "Welcome," make it as durable and handsome a shirt as the market can show. Shirts will be made to order at short notice, a perfect fit being guaranteed and uniformly moderate prices quoted.

YALE BROS., PAINTERS AND DEC-

orators, Fine Wall Papers, Signs of every description, Manufacturers of Art Novelties, 556 Broad Street, Newark, N. J. Opposite Post-office. With the growth of our country and the increasing artistic development of the people, interior decoration has ceased to be looked upon as a luxury unattainable and unappreciated except by the comparatively few. Year by year the demand is greater for tasteful adornments for our homes, which all are eager to beautify as far as their means will permit. Nothing furnishes a house better or makes it look more homelike than well chosen wall papers. Such beautiful designs and colorings are now shown for a trifling cost that there are few persons who cannot indulge their taste in this line. To persons contemplating improvement in their household interior, we strongly recommend a visit to 556 Broad street, where Messrs. Yale Bros. have recently established a house which deals largely in this business. The position is most desirable and central. Messrs. Yale Bros. are natives of Erie, Pa. Though established in their present quarters so recently, they are doing an extensive retail trade. The stock is valued at $10,000, and no less than twenty assistants are in constant employment. The business is by no means restricted to wall papering. Besides the exceptionally fine selection here found, Messrs. Yale Bros. undertake to do all manner of painting and decoration in the most approved and artistic manner, including the painting of signs of every description. They are also successful manufacturers of a great variety of art novelties. We heartily recommend a call at 556 Broad street to any one in search of something to please the eye. Such a visit will most surely prove one of interest and pleasure.

E. & W. DIXON, BRUSH MANUFAC-
turers, 50 Market Street, Newark, N. J. It is fair
to suppose that nearly every man, woman and child
in the land makes use of one or more brushes, yet
how few who use them think of their great utility, what
they would do if deprived of them—how and of what
they are made. A brush is an instrument for removing dirt from various surfaces by friction, for arranging the
hair, for polishing and applying paints, varnishes, etc., etc.
A large portion of brushes used for friction are made from
hogs' bristles, but for delicate work camels', badgers',
sables' and rabbits' hair is used. Wire brushes are also extensively used in various departments of manufacturing industry. Broom-corn and twigs of trees are often employed
for stiff brushes, and even split whalebone is sometimes used
as a substitute for bristles. Most brushes are made by join-
ing so me of the above materials to a stock of wood, leather,
bone or metal by various methods, which industry gives employment to many thousands of workmen, both in this country and in Europe. Many ingenious machines have been invented for facilitating this work, and these have greatly reduced the labor and cost of making some kinds of brushes,
still there are some which must be made by hand. The
beautiful brushes seen in the dressing tables of many fashionable ladies are really works of art, and would seem too
handsome for use. The backs are made of delicately
wrought silver or flawless ivory, with finely carved crest
or monogram, and each year seems to bring something newer
and more beautiful. We would mention as prominent manufacturers of these indispensable articles the firm of E. &
W. Dixon. They have a large establishment at 50 Market
street, Newark, where they occupy three floors of 30x70 feet
dimensions. The size of the premises and the number of employees, amounting to sixty, show that the business done is
very extensive. The house was established in 1855, and has
thirty-five years of prosperity to look back upon. A specialty is made of machine brushes, jewelers' brushes and
patent leather brushes.

HANCOCK & CO., SHIPPERS OF WEST-
ern Grain, Bran, Middlings, etc., 755 Broad Street, Newark, N. J. Represented by Frank A. Champlin. Messrs.
Hancock & Co. hold a leading position among the great
wholesale houses engaged in the handling of Western grain, bran, middlings, etc., for they began business about a score of years ago and have built up a
very extensive and still increasing trade. They have a
Newark office at No. 755 Broad street, this being under the direct management of Mr. Frank A. Champlin, a native of this city, and so well and favorably known hereabouts as to render extended personal mention quite unnecessary. Messrs. Hancock & Co. carry on operations on a
very extensive scale, and are prepared to furnish Western
grain and mill feed in car-load lots, at short notice and at
positively the lowest market rates. Their principal offices
are at No. 131 South Second street, Philadelphia; No. 422
Produce Exchange, New York, and Nos. 11 and 13 Chamber
of Commerce, Peoria, Illinois, interior offices being located at
Wilkesbarre, Pa., Newark, N. J., Lancaster, Pa., Boston,
Mass., and Portland, Me. With such facilities it is not surprising that the concern should have a national reputation,
and should hold an enviable record in connection with the
prompt, accurate and generally satisfactory filling of orders and in the settlement of claims.

C. E. FREDERICKS & CO., Gentlemen's
Fine Furnishings, 835 Broad Street, Newark, N.
J. Full Dress Shirts and Neck wear. This business
was founded by Mr. C. E. Fredericks, in 1884. The
store occupied for the carrying on of this concern
is 30x70 feet in dimensions. It is finely arranged for
displaying the choice and carefully selected assortment of
gentlemen's fine furnishings, which embraces all the small
and necessary articles, so essential to the comfort of one who
knows how to dress. Those who want the latest fashionable
novelties in these goods are sure to obtain them here at
reasonable prices. A specialty is made of full dress shirts
and neckwear. Employment is given to three capable assistants. Our readers will find it difficult to learn of any establishment offering greater advantages to its customers
than this one, for Mr. Fredericks is liberal in his prices, and
makes it a point to give a generous equivalent for all that he
receives. He believes also, in supplying the wants of those
who think ready-made articles are good enough to wear,
hence his counters are filled with goods of every variety.

R. DOMBEY WADSWORTH, Practi-
cal Optician, Diamonds, Watches, Jewelry and Silverware,
837 Broad Street, Newark, N. J. Mr. Wadsworth,
who is a native of England, has conducted this business since 1868. He is a practical optician. The public should know that only a scientific optician can
select spectacles and eye glasses, which, by relieving the
eyes of all strain, bring about a condition highly favorable to
regaining their original power, and in many cases the impair-
ment of the vision can be entirely or partially arrested by
proper treatment. Suitable glasses are powerful aids towards regaining perfect sight. Mr. Wadsworth has had
many years experience in this business, consequently there
is no one in this vicinity better qualified to give advice
when in need of glasses, as he deals extensively in optical
goods. He also carries a large and fine assortment of diamonds, watches, jewelry and silverware. The goods displayed here are first-class in every respect, and embrace
many new and desirable articles in each department. The
premises occupied are 20x70 feet in dimensions.

FIDELITY TITLE & DEPOSIT CO.,
of Newark, No. 781 Broad Street. The Fidelity Title
and Deposit Company was organized February 14, 1887;
commenced business May 1, 1887, at No. 754 Broad
street, and removed to the elegant new granite fire-
proof building, No. 781 Broad street, May 1, 1889. The
company has a capital of a quarter of a million and is
admirably equipped in every way, the main features
of its business being the providing of a safe place of deposit
for silverware, jewelry, securities and valuables of every description; the examination and guaranty of titles; the transaction of a general real estate business, and the discharge of
all duties devolving upon a trustee, guardian, executor,
administrator, assignee, receiver, committee, attorney, etc.,
the company being legally authorized to receive and execute
trusts of every description under the appointment of
courts, corporations and individuals. The safe deposit
vaults were built in 1888 by Herring & Co., of New York,
and that firm certify that these vaults combine all their latest improvements, and that no safe deposit company in the
country offers greater security than the Fidelity Title and
Deposit Company. The vaults are guarded night and day
by armed watchmen; the regularity of the night service
being assured by a detector system which compels regis-
tration at stated intervals. The interior of the vault is
divided into small compartments for the use of safe renters;
the renter holding the only key to his box, while the company holds the master key which throws off the spring, so
that every box must be opened in the presence of an officer
of the company, thus insuring to the renter that he alone
can get at the contents of his own box. The rental varies from
$10 to $30 per annum, which includes the use of private
rooms, desks and other conveniences. Special facilities are
offered for the safe keeping of bonds, boxes, trunks and
packages of all kinds containing valuables, the vaults being
open from 9 A. M. to 7 P. M. The company examines and
guarantees the titles to all real estate in Newark and Essex
county at fixed rates, no extra charge being made for search
or examination fees. The guarantee is absolute protection
against loss by anything that renders the title unmarketable;
the company's capital stock being pledged as a guaranty
fund to secure the holder of one of its policies, and the company defending at its own expense any action which may be
brought against a policy holder by reason of alleged defects
in the title guaranteed. These policies are assignable to
mortgagees at the nominal cost of $1, thus making real estate
so protected a readily convertible security. In connection
with its real estate business the company acts as agent for
buying, selling, holding and leasing property in Newark and
vicinity; negotiates mortgages, assignments of mortgages and
places ground rents. The entire charge of property, including the collection of rents, the payment of taxes, making
of needful repairs, etc., will be assumed at moderate
charge; this service being especially valuable to ladies,
invalids and non-residents, as they are relieved from
all care in the matter, and are assured prompt remit-
tances. The following well known gentlemen are identified with its management: *Officers*—President, Thomas T.
Kinney; Secretary and Manager, U. H. McCarter; Directors, Thomas T. Kinney, Charles W. Henry, William E. Pue,
J. Levering Jones, Schuyler B. Jackson, John D. Harrison,
John F. Dryden, William H. Stanke, Jerome Taylor, Ber-
nard M. Shanley, Julius Stapff, Charles A. Feick, James
Ferry; Counsel, Hon. Theodore Runyon.

D. OSBORN & CO., Successors to Camp & Osborn, Importers and Wholesale Liquor and Cigar Dealers; Fine Imported, Domestic and Key West Cigars; 619 and 621 Broad Street, Newark, N. J. The enterprise conducted by Messrs. D. Osborn & Co., at Nos. 619 and 621 Broad street, is one of the most truly representative, and one of the oldest established of the kind in the State, it having been inaugurated more than eighty years ago, and having long held its present leading position. Operations were begun in 1806 by Mr. John H. Stephens, and in 1853 Messrs. Camp & Osborn assumed control, being succeeded by the existing firm in 1882. Since the decease of Mr. Osborn in 1880 the business has been conducted by Mr. E. V. B. Dodd, under the old firm name, and are too well known throughout this vicinity to require extended personal mention. The premises utilized comprise three floors of the dimensions of 40x100 feet, and contain an immense stock of imported and domestic wines, liquors and cordials, together with a full assortment of fine imported, domestic and Key West cigars. Both a wholesale and retail business is done, and every facility is at hand to enable orders to be filled accurately and promptly, there being employment given to twenty assistants. The firm are prepared to quote the lowest market rates on pure wines and liquors, and can furnish goods that will satisfy the most fastidious, they being direct importers of many of the articles they handle, and making a specialty of catering to the most critical trade. Cigars are also dealt in at wholesale and retail, Messrs. Osborn & Co. being agents for such celebrated brands as El Telegrapho, Solace and El Tratado, all of which are pure Havana Key West cigars. Special prices are quoted on box lots, and those looking for a uniformly good cigar at a moderate price would do well to take advantage of the facilities here offered.

EUGENE J. BECK, SELECT BAKERY,

Fine Cakes, Pastry and Confectionery. Wedding Cakes a Specialty. No 900 Broad Street, Corner Green Street, Newark, N. J. There are some who say that the day is rapidly approaching when cooking at home will be a thing of the past, as in that happy age the cooking for an entire city will be done in a few mammoth establishments, at which better results can be obtained at less cost than would be possible at home. That this would be a desirable change from the present order of things is undeniable, and some idea of the advantages it would bring about, may be obtained from the great amount of work and trouble saved to housekeepers nowadays by the maintenance of public bakeries. These vary greatly in efficiency, but those in Newark average well, and among them not one is more worthy of favorable mention and liberal patronage than that conducted by Mr. Eugene J. Beck, at No. 900 Broad street, corner of Green street. This gentleman began operations in 1883, and has already built up an extensive retail trade, increasing every year over the preceeding one, for his productions are unsurpassed, and his prices are uniformly moderate, while his facilities are such that all orders can be promptly and carefully filled, employment being given to four competent assistants. Fine cake, pastry and confectionery can always be had at this "Select Bakery." Wedding cakes are made a specialty, and all goods are carefully and skilfully made from selected materials.

J. JACOB HOCKENJOS, PAINT, OIL,

Glass and Lamp Store, 349 Broad Street, Newark, N. J. This is one of the old established enterprises of this city, but its claim to prominent mention in a review of the representative business houses of Newark does not rest so much upon its long standing as upon its present high position among the wholesale and retail houses in this line of trade. For twenty-six years the business has been carried on by Mr. J. J. Hockenjos, who is a native of Germany, and was in the store with the former proprietor for nine years previous. He deals very heavily in paint, oil, glass and lamps. The magnitude of the stock carried may be judged from the size of the premises utilized, these comprising two floors 50x70 feet in dimensions. Both wholesale and retail business is done in paints and oils. Employment is given to five competent assistants, so that all orders, large or small, are assured prompt and careful attention. Mr. Hockenjos enjoys most favorable relations with manufacturers, and is prepared to quote the lowest prices on all materials dealt in. He has a long list of regular customers, and his trade is constantly increasing.

ZEBINA D. TAYLOR, Successor to

Chas. Garrabrant, Ladies' and Gents' Fine Footwear. Ordered Shoes a Specialty. 885 Broad Street, Newark, N. J. The demand for footwear that combines style, comfort and durability is steadily increasing, or it is becoming generally known that style and comfort are by no means inconsistent; that a neatly-fitting boot or shoe is more easy, and with proper usage, more durable than the broad, ill-shaped productions which were once thought to be indispensable to solid comfort, so far as the feet were concerned. In the purchase of boots and shoes, as in that of clothing, there are some who prefer custom work, while others find the ready made articles perfectly satisfactory. The magnitude of the trade secured by Mr. Taylor, doing business at 885 Broad street, is in a great measure due to the enterprise he shows in catering to both classes of patrons. The premises occupied are 20x70 feet in dimensions. They are conveniently fitted for the business, while the employment of efficient assistants assures prompt attention to customers. Mr. Taylor carries a large and varied stock of fine boots and shoes, the latest fashionable novelties being well represented in his assortment. He has every facility for doing custom work in a superior manner, as he makes ordered shoes a specialty.

A. PATTERSON, UMBRELLA MAKER,

910 Broad Street, Newark, N. J. Canes, Fans, etc., on Hand and Repaired. A thoroughly well-made umbrella will last for years, and it pays to get a first-class article, for the best is the cheapest, every time, so far as umbrellas are concerned. Everybody is not able to tell the difference between an umbrella honestly made and one made only to sell, but everybody can at least patronize an experienced and reputable manufacturer, as for instance, Mr. A. Patterson, of No. 910 Broad street, and thus be sure of getting an honest article at an honest price. Mr. Patterson is a native of Sweden, and founded his present business in 1880. He is a first-class workman himself, and as he employs two assistants, and has all necessary tools and other facilities, he is prepared to fill orders promptly and to confidently guarantee satisfaction. A fine assortment of umbrellas, canes, fans, etc., is constantly on hand to choose from, and the prices quoted will compare very favorably with those named by other dealers in articles of equal merit Mr. Patterson gives particular attention to the repairing of anything in his line of business, and does the work so neatly, strongly and durably, as to have built up a large and growing patronage.

WESTERVELT, SIGN PAINTER, SILK

Banners, Wood Wire, Glass and Brass Signs, 791 Broad Street, Third and Fourth Floors, Newark, N. J. This is the age of advertising, and, other things being equal, the man who advertises most judiciously does the largest business. A handsome and tasty sign is one of the most efficient means of advertising, and also one of the cheapest, for although its first cost may be considerable, it lasts for an indefinite number of years and there is no question but that the money invested in it pays big dividends. Sign painting is not only a business by itself, but it may be said to have been elevated to a fine art of late years, and the practice of having elaborate and striking signs has become so universal among the more progressive business men that not to be provided with one argues old fogyism or an incorrect idea of economy. Of course the nature of the sign should vary with the business; a professional man doesn't want a sign thirty feet long, and a dry goods merchant has no use for a modest brass plate, but in any case the design and workmanship should be first-class, and in any case Mr. John A. Westervelt is in a position to furnish a sign that will give entire satisfaction, for he has had long and varied experience, and turns out work equal to the best in every respect, including silk banners, wood, wire, glass and brass signs, and in short everything in that line. Mr. Westervelt was born in Paterson, N. J., and has carried on his present enterprise since 1880. He is widely known hereabouts, and enjoys a high reputation for promptness in the filling of orders and the quoting of uniformly moderate prices. He occupies the third and fourth floors at No 791 Broad street, and has every facility at hand to enable him to carry on operations to the best possible advantage. Orders are assured immediate and painstaking attention, and all work is fully guaranteed to prove as represented in every respect, while designs will cheerfully be shown and prices quoted on application.

F. S. TAYLOR, MANUFACTURER AND

Dealer in Bedding, Mattresses, Feathers, Spring Beds, Cots, etc., No. 96 Market Street, Newark, N. J. Notwithstanding the state of health, the average person necessarily spends so much time in bed that it is naturally of great importance to have mattresses and bedding of good quality, and when we have the choosing of it, to select not only what looks good, but an article made of good material and warranted to wear well. Many people not accustomed to consider the matter of house furnishings are apt to consider the choice of bedding a slight matter and of small or moderate expense. They are soon undeceived, however, when they go to price these articles, and they find to their surprise and consternation that good hair mattresses and fine feather pillows cannot be bought cheap. That they are, on the contrary, more expensive than the furniture, and that the greater part of the money set aside to be expended on the bedroom furniture, must go for what is not seen. For those who cannot afford hair mattresses, very good and cheap ones can be made of moss, excelsior, husks, tow, etc. One of the large manufacturing establishments of bedding in this section of the country, is the one carried on by Mr. F. S. Taylor, of 96 Market street, Newark. He is a native of New Jersey, and has been engaged in his present business in this city since 1876. His trade as manufacturer of and dealer in all sorts of mattresses, pillows, etc., is very large and constantly increasing, besides which he keeps a full stock of spring beds, cots, etc., of the most approved makes and newest styles. The premises used comprise four floors of 25x75 feet dimensions, well stocked with the many materials and machinery used in this industry, and constant employment is given to seven assistants. The most extensive orders are filled at the shortest possible notice, and full satisfaction is guaranteed. Mr. Taylor served in the late rebellion as an officer in the 35th N. J. Vols., and is a member of Lincoln Post, No. 11, G. A. R.

MRS. E. WEICK, ART STAMPING,

Embroidery Materials, etc., Agent Butterick's Patterns and Staten Island Dyeing establishment, 804 Broad Street, Newark, N. J. No person can visit this store, inspect the attractions offered, and note the courteous attention paid to customers without being convinced that the establishment fully deserves its popularity, and when the prices quoted are learned, this conviction will be strengthened and confirmed. The premises utilized are of the dimensions of 15x50 feet, and located at No. 804 Broad street, employment being given to five competent assistants. Embroidery materials of all descriptions are carried in stock, and no surer way of learning what are the latest novelties in these goods can be found than to examine the assortment here presented. Mrs E. Weick is a native of New York city, and considering her long experience, it is hardly necessary to state, understands her business thoroughly in every detail. Mrs. Weick is agent for the Butterick Patterns, also for the old Staten Island Dyeing Establishment. She gives close personal attention to the supervision of the various departments conducted by her, and is ever seeking to improve the efficiency of the service. Art stamping and order work is done at short notice, and in a neat and tasteful manner, and a full line of embroidery materials is also carried. All goods dealt in are offered at the lowest market rates. Mrs Weick invites all to inspect her stock and prices.

J. BRINTZINGHOFFER, WHOLESALE

and Retail Dealer in Cigars and Tobacco, No. 873 Broad Street, Newark, N. J. This business was originally founded by Mr. John Brintzinghoffer, who died in 1888. Mr. W. Brintzinghoffer, a native of this city, is now manager. The premises are 12x100 feet in dimensions. Both a wholesale and retail business in cigars and tobacco is carried on here. It is a fact that every smoker appreciates choice tobacco of a natural and delicate flavor, and therefore, it is not at all surprising that the cigars and tobacco dealt in by Mr. Brintzinghoffer should prove entirely satisfactory to the most fastidious purchasers. He is thoroughly conversant with every detail of the business, and is in a position to offer a sufficient variety to suit all tastes and all purses. He advertises to sell the best five and ten cent cigars to be found in the city. Those who have tested their quality can testify to the truth of this assertion. This store is located at No. 873 Broad street, and every caller is assured prompt and courteous attention.

G. SHEPLEY, MANUFACTURER AND

Repairer of Musical Instruments, No. 65 Market Street, Newark, N. J. Strings of all kinds, of the Finest Quality. It sometimes seems as though the more we prize a thing and the more careful we are of it, the more liable it is to be injured by some unlooked for accident, and this is especially the case with musical instruments, for the majority of these are of necessity quite delicate in construction. No one but a musician appreciates the feelings of a man who has badly injured his pet violin, for instance, and no one but a musician can appreciate his delight when he finds a repairer capable of making the instrument as good as before. There are many repairers of musical instruments, but few artists in this line, and we therefore feel that we are doing our readers a service by calling their attention to the facilities offered by Mr. G. Shepley, at No. 65 Market Street, for he is prepared to do work fully equal to the best, and his charges are never exorbitant under any circumstances. He was born in Manchester, England, and has had exceptional experience, having carried on his present enterprise for forty years. The premises utilized comprise a salesroom measuring 15x60 feet, and a well appointed shop in the rear, and a carefully chosen stock is carried, including strings of all kinds, of the very finest quality. Mr. Shepley is a manufacturer as well as a repairer of musical instruments, and offers them for sale at very reasonable prices.

INSURANCE COMPANY OF NORTH

America, W. F. Ryerson, Agent, Newark. Very nearly a century has elapsed since the formation of the Insurance Company of North America, for it was organized in 1792, incorporated in 1794, and has steadily increased in wealth, usefulness and influence, now being one of the largest, best known, best managed and most absolutely reliable insurance companies in the world. The scope of its business is as exceptional as its magnitude, for the company furnishes fire, marine and inland insurance, and is represented in every city and in every town of any importance in the country. The constant and rapid growth of its business is due to a variety of causes, but chiefly to its policy of prompt and equitable adjustment and payment of losses and the avoidance of those legal quibbles which sometimes stand in the way of the collection of insurance money. Unjust and fraudulent claims will of course be resisted, but mere technicalities are never made the excuse for refusal to discharge obligations incurred. The company has a capital of $3,000,000, and a surplus over all liabilities approximating the same sum. Insurance is written at the very lowest market rates, and the policies are so plainly and explicitly worded that their provisions can be easily and fully understood. The home office is at No. 232 Walnut street, Philadelphia, Pa., and the principal officers are as follows: Charles Platt, President; T. Charlton Henry, Vice-President; William A. Platt, Second Vice-President; Greville E. Fryer, Secretary; Eugene L. Ellison, Assistant Secretary. Mr. W. F. Ryerson is agent in this city, and all applications are assured immediate attention, losses being promptly adjusted.

LIVERPOOL, LONDON & GLOBE DIN-

ing Rooms, No. 800 Broad Street, Newark, N. J. Thomas Scheel, Proprietor. Take Elevator at Broad or Mechanic Street Entrances. These dining rooms have a reputation by no means confined to this city, and as the enterprise is a representative one in the best sense of the word, it should be given prominent mention in reviewing the leading undertakings carried on here. The "Liverpool, London and Globe dining rooms," were established by the present proprietor, Mr. Thomas Scheel. These rooms are located at No. 800 Broad street. The premises, which are 20x60 feet in dimensions are very conveniently arranged for the purpose, and have two entrances, one on Broad street, and the other on Mechanic street. There is an elevator at each door, for the use of patrons. Employment is given to seven courteous assistants, that all customers may be promptly served. The food provided here is of the best quality, and as the cooking is first-class also, it is not surprising that the most fastidious should express themselves as perfectly satisfied. That Mr. Scheel thoroughly understands his business, needs no further proof than that offered by the increasing number of customers

NORTH BRITISH & MERCANTILE IN-

surance Co, of London and Edinburgh, U. S. Branch 54 William Street, New York City; Capital $10,000,000; Organized 1804; Branch Office No. 812 Broad Street, Newark, N. J., Griffith H. Teller, Special Agent. The city of Newark has long been known as a very important insurance centre, and the standing as well as the number of companies doing business here is remarkable, and in fact exceptional, but despite this the opening of a branch of the North British and Mercantile Insurance Company, of London and Edinburgh, in this city in 1889 may properly be regarded as an event in the commercial history of Newark, for this is one of the great insurance companies of the world, and does business on a scale of tremendous magnitude. It was organized in 1809, and has a capital of $10,000,000, but what gives even a more comprehensive idea of its resources than the immensity of its capital, is its record in connection with three of the greatest conflagrations of modern times—the "Chicago," the "Boston" and the "St. John" fires. It met and promptly paid losses amounting to $2,750,000 at the "Chicago" fire, to $750,000 at the "Boston" fire, and to $800,000 at the "St. John" fire, while since organization it has paid losses aggregating more than $97,500,000, and by the latest statement now at hand, has a net fire surplus (excluding paid up capital) of $7,550,623.40, this being among the largest of any company doing business in any country. Let figures be twisted as they may, and the fact remains that it is the net fire surplus that constitutes the real strength of any fire company, and consequently further remark concerning the nature of the protection afforded by the North British and Mercantile would be quite superfluous. The United States home office of the company is at No. 54 William street, New York city, and the Newark branch is located at No. 812 Broad street, and is in charge of Mr. Griffith H. Teller, special agent, who is a native of New York State, and is well and favorably known in insurance circles. Applications made at this branch are assured prompt and careful attention, and the company's high reputation for prompt and equitable adjustment of losses will be fully maintained.

HERMAN SCHULZ, DECORATOR and

Painter, Fine Wall Papers, Shades, etc., No. 863 Broad Street, Next to City Hall, Newark, N. J. It is necessary to dwell upon the importance of the exercise of taste and skill in the painting, decorating and papering of a house, for every intelligent person knows that the effect of the most handsomely and elaborately designed structure may easily be ruined by carelessness in this respect. That the residents of Newark and vicinity appreciate this fact, is proved by the liberal patronage accorded to Mr. Herman Schulz, for he is conceded to be one of the most skillful decorators and painters in the State, and an idea of his facilities may be gained from the fact that employment is given to sixty assistants. Mr. Schulz is a native of Germany, and founded his present business in 1875. His establishment is located at No. 863 Broad street, next to City Hall, and comprises three floors of the dimensions of 22x80 feet. An exceptionally large and complete stock of fine wall papers, window shades, etc., is constantly carried, embracing the very latest novelties in these goods, and including many of the more popular productions of foreign manufacturers. No finer assortment of artistic paper hangings is to be found in the State, and the range of prices is such that all purses as well as all tastes, can be suited, while every order, large or small, is assured prompt and painstaking attention.

MILTON H. GRUET, PIANO TUNER

and Regulator, Dealer in Musical Instruments, Strings, Second-hand Pianos, etc., No. 693 Broad Street, Upstairs, Next to Lauter's Piano Rooms, Newark, N. J. Special Attention Given to Repairing of all Kinds. A great deal of nonsense has been written concerning the purchase of pianos, for one would think to read some of the articles on the subject that imposition was almost impossible to avoid, and that manufacturers and dealers were leagued together to defraud the public in every possible way. Now of course this is absurd, for it as true in buying a piano as in buying a sofa or a bed, if you deal with a reputable person you will be used honorably and satisfactorily. To be sure there are pianos "made to sell" and of no real value as musical instruments, but they are not handled by men doing a legitimate business, and therefore are easily avoided. Such of our readers as wish to buy a piano, or a

musical instrument of any kind would do well to call upon Mr. Milton H. Gruet, doing business at No. 693 Broad street, upstairs, for he deals largely in new and second-hand pianos, etc., and not only quotes low prices, but guarantees every instrument to prove as represented. He is a native of this city and inaugurated his present enterprise in 1885, having previously been with Hazelton Brothers of New York, where he learned his trade as a tuner and regulator of grand, square and upright pianos. Mr. Gruet makes a specialty of repairing of all kinds, and can fill orders at short notice, as he employs two experienced assistants and has all necessary facilities at his command. A full line of imported violin, guitar and banjo strings is carried in stock, together with musical merchandise in general, and the prices quoted are always in strict accordance with the lowest market rates.

NEW YORK LIFE INSURANCE CO.,

No. 781 Broad Street, Newark, N. J. James S. Edwards, Cashier. An insurance company that has been in existence for nearly half a century, must have made a record sufficiently broad and comprehensive to show conclusively what its methods and deserts are, and when we see so old-established a company rapidly increasing its business among the most intelligent classes in the community every year, the natural inference is that its record must be equal to the best. It is unnecessary, therefore, to eulogize the New York Life Insurance Company, for since its incorporation in 1841 has steadily increased in popularity, and now holds a leading position among similar organizations throughout the country. Mr. James S. Edwards, Cashier, has held the State agency for New Jersey since 1884, and those wishing detailed information concerning the methods and resources of the company should make application at his office, No. 781 Broad street, for they will be most courteously received, and will be given every facility to become familiar with the facts in the case. Mr. Edwards is a native of Sussex county, N. J., and served nine months in the Army of the Potomac, during one of the most eventful periods of the war. He is a resident of Irvington and is very widely known throughout this section of the State. He was collector of taxes for three years and receiver of taxes for two years, for the township of Clinton. Having made a study of life insurance matters as well as having had practical experience in the business, he is thoroughly well-informed in regard to its many details, and is in a position to give valuable counsel to those uncertain as to which form of policy is best adapted to their needs, so that such of our readers as are intending to insure their lives, would best serve their own interests by giving him a call.

SUMMARY OF THE FORTY-FIFTH ANNUAL REPORT OF THE NEW YORK LIFE INSURANCE CO.

BUSINESS OF 1889.

Premiums,	$24,585,921.10
Interest, Rents, etc.,	4,577,315.14
Total Income,	$29,163,236.24
Death Claims and Endowments,	$6,252,025.50
Dividends, Annuities and Purchased Insurances,	5,869,095.16
Total to Policy Holders,	$12,121,121.66
New Policies Issued,	59,499
New Insurance Written,	$151,119,088.00

CONDITION JAN. 1, 1890.

Assets,	$105,033,680.96
*Divisible Surplus, Co.'s New Standard,	$7,517,854.28
†Tontine,	7,765,052.11
Liabilities, New York State Standard,	$88,761,058.57
Surplus by State Standard (4 per cent.),	$15,603,003.60
Policies in Force,	159,581
Insurance in Force,	$495,601,920.00

PROGRESS IN 1889.

Increase in Interest,	$203,053.00
Increase in Benefits to Policy-holders,	1,148,051.61
Increase in Surplus for Dividends,	1,716,840.01
Increase in Premiums,	3,458,533.35
Increase in Total Income,	3,761,985.11
Increase in Assets,	11,575,414.41
Increase in Insurance Written,	26,079,517.60
Increase in Insurance in Force,	73,715,065.00

*Exclusive of the amount especially reserved as a contingent liability to Tontine Dividend Fund.

†Over and above a 4 per cent reserve on existing policies of that class.

JOSEPH H. MENAGH, SPECIALTIES

in Black Goods, Silks, etc., 673 and 675 Broad Street, Newark, N. J. There is such an immense variety of textile fabrics now produced in this and other countries, and modern facilities for transportation have so broadened the field from which supplies may be taken, that it is a practical impossibility for any merchant, however great his resources or extensive his trade, to offer his customers a full line of such fabrics in a general stock. In commerce, as in the professions and in manufacturing, the various branches are best carried on by specialists, and a striking example of this may be seen in the establishment conducted by Mr. Joseph H. Menagh, who devotes himself exclusively to the handling of specialties in black dress goods, silks, etc., and carries on business at Nos. 673 and 675 Broad street. He is a native of this State, having been born at Schooley's Mountain, Morris County, from whence he came to Newark when quite a young man, and entered the store of Mr. Thomas C. Davis, then the leading merchant of Newark, where, by his fidelity to the interests of the house, he earned promotion rapidly, and for many years was at the head of the black goods and silk departments of Morris & Doty, the successors of Mr. Davis, which position he resigned to take charge of same departments of Messrs. Heath & Drake, which position he held about six years, resigning it to enter the firm of John P. Davis & Co. early in 1886, in which firm he sold his interest two and a half years later and has since been identified with his present enterprise, having already built up a large trade and gained the reputation of offering exceptional inducements in the various lines he handles. Mr. Menagh caters to the very best and most discriminating trade, dealing exclusively in the *very best makes of black dress goods, dress silks, etc.* His stock is at all times complete in its various departments, and no fabric is sold that cannot confidently be guaranteed to prove as represented, while the light scale of expense under which they are handled admits of prices ruling *lower* than corresponding qualities are usually sold.

JOHN LEONARD, WHOLESALE DEAL-

er in Wrought, Cast and Scrap Iron, Metals, etc., Horse Shoe Iron and Refined Bar Iron, 75, 77 and 79 Clinton Street, Between Mulberry and Lawrence Streets, Newark, N. J. Telephone 199. Newton Smith, Manager. The business carried on by Mr. John Leonard at Nos. 75, 77 and 79 Clinton streets, between Mulberry and Lawrence streets, was inaugurated in 1886, but properly speaking should be credited with a much earlier origin, for it is really a branch of an enterprise started by Mr. Leonard in New York city in 1865. The "Manhattan Rolling Mill," as this New York establishment is called, is located at Nos. 415 to 451 West street, and Nos. 177 and 179 Bank street, and is devoted to the manufacture of horse shoe iron, toe calks, steel and refined bar iron. Mr. Leonard's productions are very widely and favorably known among iron and steel workers, and particularly among blacksmiths, they being celebrated for their excellent and remarkably uniform quality. The Newark establishment is under the direct management of Mr. Newton Smith, and affords employment to five assistants. An extensive wholesale trade is carried on in wrought, cast and scrap iron, metals, etc., particular attention being given to orders for horse shoe iron and refined bar iron. Mr. Leonard is in a position to quote positively the lowest market rates at all times, and to fill the most extensive orders at short notice. Communications may be sent by mail or telephone, No. 199.

A. BERNHARDT, FANCY CABINET

Furniture, Upholsterer and Decorator, Hair Mattresses, Curtains, Lambrequins, etc., 922 Broad Street, Opposite Hill Street, Newark, N. J. This concern was established in 1886 by Mr. A. Bernhardt, who is a native of Germany. The premises, which are located on Broad street, comprise three floors 25x110 feet in dimensions. He conducts an extensive retail business in fancy cabinet furniture, parlor, bed room, library and office furniture, hair mattresses, etc. He is also an upholsterer and decorator, and is prepared to receive orders for making and hanging curtains, lambrequins, etc. He is sole proprietor, manufacturer and wholesale dealer in the "Eclipse Rocking Chair," the only rocking chair that does not squeak or get out of order. Employment is given to six efficient assistants, that all customers may receive prompt and polite attention.

It is not our purpose in compiling this work to assume a partisan attitude in advocating the claims of any dealer, but it is a fact with which many are acquainted that certain houses excel in special lines of trade, and we feel that we are justified in calling attention to this establishment. Mr. Bernhardt believes in selling goods on their merit, and those purchasing of him may depend upon getting just what they pay for. Orders for decorating or upholstery will be properly executed in the most thorough and artistic manner.

SAMUEL MEEKER, MANAGER Niagara

Fire Insurance Company, of New York; Branch Office 766 Broad Street, Newark, N. J. The "Niagara" is an especially appropriate name for a fire insurance company, for the association between a "Niagara of Water" and the prompt extinguishing of the largest fire, and a Niagara Fire Insurance Company capable of averting the severe pecuniary loss attending such a conflagration cannot but be felt by the least fanciful. But figures and not fancies are what practical men demand, particularly in connection with insurance matters, so we hasten to present the following condensed statement of the condition of the Niagara Fire Insurance Company, of New York, January 1, 1890:

ASSETS.

Stocks and bonds (market value),	$1,438,620.00
Cash in bank and cash items,	188,815.98
Real estate (unincumbered),	521,812.59
Loans on bond and mortgage,	46,058.00
Loans on collateral security,	19,600.00
Interest due and accrued and other assets,	15,675.78
Rents due and accrued,	6,058.75
Cash in hands of agents and in course of collection,	253,911.92
Total assets,	$2,490,654.02

LIABILITIES.

Cash capital,	$ 500,000.00
Reserve for re-insurance,	1,298,622.04
Reserve for unpaid losses,	228,435.18
Contingent reserve,	20,000.00
Other liabilities,	44,096.73
Surplus,	389,502.07
Total,	$2,490,654.02

It is pleasant to be able to say that this, the seventy-sixth semi-annual statement of the company, shows substantial gains in every item, as for instance:

To the surplus account,	$ 9,961.81
To the reserve account,	30,151.35
To the gross assets,	130,518.65

A yet more convincing proof of steady, good management is that afforded by the remarkable increase in cash assets during the past decade:

Cash assets, January 1, 1880,		$1,351,777.10
"	1882,	1,587,486.15
"	1883,	1,725,502.32
"	1884,	1,760,486.35
"	1885,	1,874,054.97
"	1886,	1,881,892.39
"	1886,	2,080,160.14
"	1887,	2,236,470.96
"	1888,	2,237,491.50
"	1889,	2,360,135.37
"	1890,	2,490,654.02

All policies of this company are now issued under the New York Safety Fund Law, and it is not too much to say that in no company in the world are the interests of policy holders more fully protected. The Newark branch office is located at No. 766 Broad street, and is under the management of Mr. Samuel Meeker. Employment is given to six assistants at this office, and applications and other business are assured immediate and painstaking attention. The officers of the company are as follows: Peter Notman, President; Thos. F. Goodrich, Vice-President; West Pollock, Secretary; Geo. C. Howe, Assistant Secretary; C. H. Post, Agency Manager. Directors—David Stewart, J. Taylor Johnston, William H. Wisner, Edward L. Hedden, James R. Taylor, Peter Notman; James W. Elwell, Thomas G. Ritch, Thos. F. Goodrich, William E. Tefft, Austin Corbin, J. Herbert Johnston, George A. Hussey, Charles R. Farwell, Dumont Clarke. The buildings, 764 and 766 Broad, valued at $130,000, are owned by the company.

R. F. JOLLEY & CO., SHIRT MAKERS

and Men's Furnishings, 829-831 Broad Street, Newark. R. F. Jolley & Co., is the oldest house in this city, devoted exclusively to the men's furnishing goods business, or, in other words, to the business of furnishing gentlemen with the various articles necessary to make them comfortable, presentable and happy. Their principal trade is in shirts, both custom and ready made, for which they have gained a very high reputation in Newark, and, in fact, throughout the entire State of New Jersey. In the many other lines of goods for men's wear, such as collars, cuffs, suspenders, underwear, hosiery, gloves, bath robes, dressing gowns, smoking jackets, etc., etc., they make it a rule to keep every reputable line of goods manufactured. Their long experience, and a constant desire to please, has made their store the centre of trade for gentlemen of taste and fashion. Adjoining, and connected by an archway, is their hat department, where a complete line of fine goods can always be seen. They are the agents in this city for "Youmans" hats, and other superior makes. This department, although comparatively new, has become very popular, and is very largely patronized by the best trade in town.

GEO. MILLER, DEALER in Groceries

and provisions, Canned Goods and Vegetables. Fine Fresh Meats. 79 Thomas street, Newark, N. J. A well known business man of Newark, is Mr. Geo. W. Miller, whose establishment is located at No. 79 Thomas street, and this gentleman is as popular as he is well known, for his honorable and enterprising business methods have combined with his other qualities, to give him the prominence he now enjoys. Mr. Miller is a native of New Jersey. The premises occupied are of the dimensions of 25x50 feet, and a large stock is carried, comprising choice staple and fancy groceries, provisions, canned goods and vegetables, also, fresh meats of all kinds, while employment is afforded to two competent and polite assistants. The goods handled by Mr. Miller will be found uniformly reliable and desirable in every respect, and are offered at prices that no one can reasonably object to. Operations were began in 1875, by Mr. George W. Miller, and the rapid growth of the business since that date, would seem to indicate that the public appreciate the advantages to be gained by patronizing this establishment. Orders are very promptly delivered, and every caller may depend upon receiving the uniform courtesy and consideration that Mr. Miller believes to be the due of all customers.

GEORGE MINGUS, DEALER IN COAL,

Wood and Charcoal, Feed, Grain, Hay and Straw, cor. Astor and Austin Streets, one Block east of Broad St., Newark. Among the representative business enterprises of Newark, that conducted by Mr. George Mingus, should be given a prominent position, for during the twelve years that this undertaking has been carried on it has developed largely, and has become widely and favorably known among wholesale and retail consumers, throughout this section of the State. Mr. Mingus is a New Jersey man by birth, and has been prominently identified with the coal and wood business in Newark since 1878. He carries a very large stock, and is prepared to fill all orders at very short notice and at the very lowest market rates. Coal, wood, and charcoal, also feed, grain, hay, oats and straw are extensively handled. The premises occupied are located at the corner of Astor and Austin streets, and cover an area of 10,000 square feet, including extensive storage facilities. Employment is given to three competent assistants, and every order is assured immediate and careful attention. We would, therefore, advise all our interested readers to inspect Mr. Mingus' stock and prices before placing orders elsewhere for any of the above.

JOHN RUCK, DEALER IN BEEF,

Veal, Mutton, Lamb, Pork, Poultry, Sausage, Lard, etc., 33 East Kinney Street, Newark, N. J. It is by catering especially to family trade, that Mr. John Ruck, who is engaged in the sale of meats, vegetables, etc., at No. 33 East Kinney street, has worked up the very liberal patronage he now enjoys, and no one who has observed the methods by which his establishment has been advanced to its present prominence, can begrudge him the success attained, for it has been won, not by belittling competitors, and seeking to injure any man, but by conscientious, intelligent, and untiring work, of the hardest kind. Mr. Ruck was born in Germany,

and founded his present business in 1870. He now occupies a store of the dimensions of 15x30 feet, and employs sufficient help to enable him to fill all orders with celerity and accuracy. The stock on hand is a very full and varied one, including, as it does, beef, veal, lamb, mutton, pork, poultry, sausage and lard, also, hams and tongues, both salt and smoked, as well as vegetables of all kinds in their season. Mr. Ruck has reason to take special pride in the goods furnished to patrons, for it is often remarked among those who have tested them, that their equal is very hard to find elsewhere for the money. The prices are reasonable in every department, and customers of this house can depend on getting a fair equivalent for their money every time.

IRA P. SMITH, Manufacturer of Sash,

Blinds and Doors, 335 Orange Street, Newark, N. J. Estimates cheerfully given. All orders promptly attended to. It is generally known that wood-working machinery has been brought to a greater perfection in this country than anywhere else in the world, and the result of this perfection is to be seen in the cheapness and accuracy with which such articles as sash, blinds and doors can be produced. Mr. Ira P. Smith is a well known manufacturer of these goods, and his facilities for furnishing them in any desired quantity are first-class. For the convenience of customers, a salesroom is maintained at No. 335 Orange street, where all orders may be left with a certainty of their receiving immediate and careful attention. Mr. Smith carries an assortment of sash, blinds and doors of standard dimensions, but can furnish any dimensions desired at short notice, and at the lowest market rate. He is a native of Morristown, N. J., and began operations here in 1876, having built up his present business by keeping faith with his customers, and being satisfied with a small margin of profit. Mr. Smith has many friends and patrons in Newark and vicinity. He will cheerfully furnish estimates, and attend promptly to orders, executing the same in a thorough and workmanlike manner.

J. H. ESELGROTH, Successor to A. Froe-

lich, Dealer in Repairs for Stoves, Ranges and Heaters, 22 Mechanic street, Newark, N. J. The busy, thriving city of Newark is continually growing, and the business houses here form one of the most important branches of the commercial interest in the State of New Jersey. Manufactories and wholesale and retail establishments of almost every kind flourish in this city, and the trades are divided and subdivided. One of these divisions is the making of repairs for stoves, ranges and heaters of every variety. This forms an active business in itself, and as an example of a house dealing in this line of industry, one cannot quote a better one than that of which Mr. J. H. Eselgroth is the proprietor. In his establishment, which is situated at 22 Mechanic street, and of 25x75 feet dimensions, every description of article needed for the repair of stoves, ranges, etc., may be found. This business was started by Mr. A. Froelich, who carried it on in an energetic and successful manner for a number of years, when he retired, and was succeeded by Mr. J. H. Eselgroth, the present proprietor. The house is known to be among the foremost in this line of trade, Mr. Eselgroth being a competent business man, dealing in only the best and most durable goods. He employs two efficient assistants, who attend to orders in the most prompt manner.

WILLIAM HAHN, PAINTING AND

Graining, Kalsomining and Paper Hanging, No. 47 Frelinghuysen avenue, Newark, N. J. All Orders Promptly Attended to. It is wonderful what a change may be worked in the appearance of a house by the judicious use of a few rolls of wall-paper and a few gallons of paint; and a little money will go a great ways if invested to the best advantage in articles of this kind. We know of no establishment where it can be better invested than at that conducted by Mr. William Hahn, at No. 47 Frelinghuysen avenue, for here orders are received for all kinds of painting and paperhanging, and the prices quoted are in every instance as low as the lowest for first-class work. The proprietor is a native of Newark, and has carried on his present business since 1882. He is widely known, and respected, both in business and social circles, of this city. Mr. Hahn is prepared to do anything in the line of painting, graining, kalsomining and paper-hanging, in first-class style at moderate rates; and as he employs some fifteen assistants he is in a position to fill the most extensive orders at very short notice.

NEW BUILDING OF THE PRUDENTIAL INSURANCE COMPANY.
(NOW IN PROCESS OF ERECTION.)

THE PRUDENTIAL INSURANCE COM-

pany, whose new building, at the corner of Broad and Bank streets, we show on the opposite page, is perhaps the most thoroughly known of any financial institution in the city. It is so because, in the first place, it has been so phenomenally successful as to attract the attention of business men all over the country. In the next place, its system of insurance necessitates the agents of the company visiting the house of each policy holder every week, and in this way the company has come not only to be well known, but its methods of operation are kept before the minds of the people so continually that they come to feel a personal interest in its working. More than half of the population of the city are policy holders in this company. While its growth has been remarkable, it has nevertheless been gradual and healthy, its directors exercising the truest kind of conservatism, being cautious when caution was necessary, and enlarging their field of operations just as rapidly as their resources made it safe to do so. The consequence is, that while it is doing such an enormous business, having written about 700,000 policies during the last year, it has a surplus for the protection of policy holders of over a million of dollars. The company has gained an enviable reputation for fairness and liberality, especially in the matter of paying death claims, and every family where they have been paid, is made by this means a strong advocate of the Prudential. It pays its claims within twenty-four hours after proof of death has reached the home office, and it does away entirely with all unnecessary technicalities, so that there is no necessity for such proof being delayed. Its specialty is issuing small policies, from ten to a thousand dollars in value, the premiums upon which are paid weekly, in amounts ranging from five cents to one dollar and ninety cents. It has departed from the ordinary methods, by insuring women at the same rate as men. It also issues policies upon the lives of children over one year of age, so that it is possible in this company, to secure a life insurance policy for every member of a family between the ages of one and seventy, provided they are in good health. It gives the most liberal policy of any industrial insurance company. It is termed "Special Adult," and is issued for even amounts of five hundred and a thousand dollars, but the premiums are paid weekly, as in the case of the regular industrial payments mentioned above. It gives not only immediate benefit, but several other features are introduced, making it of great advantage to the policy holder. At the end of each five years, if the premiums have been regularly paid, a dividend in the form of an addition to the original policy will be declared, which will be based on the profits arising from these policies, thus making the insured a sharer in the profits of the company. Another decided advantage is, that after five years' premiums have been paid, it may be surrendered to the company for a paid-up policy of a like amount, which will be continued in force for a term of weeks, as shown in the table printed on the back. Industrial insurance, which was introduced by the Prudential into America, possesses all the benefits offered by ordinary life companies, with the additional advantage that the premiums may be paid in small amounts weekly, as persons among the industrial classes receive their money, instead of calling for a large amount annually, semi-annually or quarterly. As the collection of premiums is made by the agents of the company at the house of the policy holder, they are relieved of all care in the matter, simply having to provide the small amount of five cents per week, or more, as they may choose, by the time that the agent makes his regular call. Experience shows that when persons have insured in the Prudential they become more and more thoroughly convinced of the benefits arising from its system, and they add one policy after another to those already in their possession, until they require something of a larger denomination than the industrial branch furnishes. To accommodate such persons, and all others who desire and can pay for a large policy, the premiums of which are payable annually, semi-annually or quarterly, the Ordinary Branch has been opened. This branch issues policies of amounts ranging from a thousand to ten thousand dollars, upon as liberal terms as those given by any company in America, and carrying with them advantages which are not offered by other companies. One of the most popular is the Twenty Payment Life Accumulative Dividend Policy. By its terms the amount of the policy is payable to the beneficiary at the death of the insured, provided the premiums have been regularly paid. Or if the policy holder has paid premiums for the twenty years, at the expiration of that time, he is offered various options: He may surrender his policy and receive in exchange a guaranteed cash value, and in addition thereto

dividends which will in all probability make the total cash value more than the total premiums paid in twenty years; or he may use those dividends for additional paid-up insurance, and this will increase his policy more than fifty per cent. of its face value; again, he may draw his dividends in cash; or he can purchase with the cash value, annuities either for life or a term of years. Each policy contains a schedule showing the amount of cash that may be borrowed upon the policy, after three years premiums have been paid, and also the paid up values that are guaranteed in exchange. In addition to this form of policy, others embracing attractive features are also issued by this branch. The officers of this company are: John F. Dryden, President; Leslie D. Ward, Vice-President; Edgar B. Ward, Counsel; Forrest F. Dryden, Secretary.

A. STIVERS & SON, BRASS FOUND-

ers, Established 1835, 58 Mechanic Street, Newark, N. J. There are many brass foundries in Newark and vicinity, but it is safe to assert that not one of them is more widely and favorably known than that of which Messrs. A. Stivers & Son are proprietors, for this business was established more than half a century ago, having been founded in 1835, and successfully carried on ever since. The premises made use of are located at No. 58 Mechanic street, and have an area of about 4,000 square feet. They are fitted up with every facility to enable orders to be filled in first-class style, at short notice, and employment is given to six experienced assistants, every detail of the work being carefully and skillfully carried out. The most difficult commissions can be executed in a thoroughly workmanlike and satisfactory manner, and the charges made are uniformly moderate. Under these circumstances it is not surprising that an extensive business should be done, and that this old established and representative enterprise should be one of the most popular undertakings of the kind to be found in the State.

G. W. TICE, DEALER IN BEEF, VEAL,

Mutton, Lamb, Poultry, Game, Vegetables and Canned Fruit, 61 Frelinghuysen Avenue. The importance of the quality of meat which is brought to the city market for the daily consumption of its inhabitants, cannot be over estimated. It is truly one of the most prominent industries, engaging the attention of a large number of firms and individuals, and employing labor and capital to a marked degree. Though thousands of tons of meat and vegetables are sold each year, there is still a great demand for first-class goods. Mr. G. W. Tice is a dealer in Beef, Veal, Mutton, Lamb, Poultry, Game, Vegetables and Canned Fruit. Among the many houses devoted to the above named business he occupies an honorable position, which he has gained by his honest dealings and by selling only such goods as could be depended upon as fresh and fit for family use. He established this business in 1878, and has secured a good number of regular customers, who have found him to be reliable and accommodating at all times. His store is 21x40 feet in dimensions. He requires the services of two assistants to attend to customers and the careful filling of orders.

J. E. HELLANDER, DEALER IN STA-

ple and Fancy Groceries, Fruits and Vegetables in their Season, Corner Frelinghuysen Avenue and Astor Street, Newark, N. J. Much or little can be meant by the term "Fancy Groceries," according to the way in which it is used, but in its legitimate sense, it includes an immense variety of commodities, for new articles have been added to the list, until now it has reached formidable proportions. Probably as fine a stock of staple and fancy groceries as is to be found in this vicinity, is that carried by Mr. J. E. Hellander, at his establishment at the corner of Frelinghuysen Avenue and Astor street. The premises are 50x40 feet in size. Employment is given to three assistants, as an extensive retail trade is carried on in these articles. He has a fine collection to choose from, and has also a large variety of fruits and vegetables in their season. These goods will be found fresh, and of the best, and cannot fail to please the most fastidious. Low prices rule, and customers are served promptly, and goods sent as promised. Mr. Hellander is a native of Dover, N. J. He has by his strict attention to the demands of customers, succeeded in building up a good business, which is steadily increasing, as the advantages to be gained by trading here become known.

BRUNO, LUNDENE & STONE, MANU-

facturing Jewelers and Art Novelties, Depositing on Wood, Glass, etc., our Specialty. Factory 555 Mulberry Street, Newark, N. J. Among the enterprising firms recently established in Newark, is that of Messrs. Bruno, Lundene & Stone. They were formerly engaged in business in Providence, R. I., where they carried on a successful manufacturing trade for a number of years. They made their reputation in that city, for producing first-class work in the precious metals and various kinds of art novelties, so that when they settled in this city in 1890, they immediately took a high stand among the numerous houses engaged here as manufacturing jewelers. The factory, situated at 555 Mulberry street, is of 25x75 feet dimensions. Here are employed fifteen workmen. They have all been brought up in the trade, have had years of experience, and are fully fitted to make and finish these artistic articles in the most careful manner. The specialty of this firm is the depositing of gold and silver upon wood, glass and other surfaces. This is done in a particularly fine manner, and the articles coming from this establishment, are not only beautiful but exceedingly durable. Art novelties of many kinds are also made by Messrs. Bruno, Lundene & Stone, which are exceedingly popular, and are in great demand by the retail firms, both here and in New York. The members of the firm are already well known in Newark, where they are recognized as able business men.

A. M. HAZEN, Agent, WHOLESALE

and Retail Dealer in Cream and Milk, Also, Retail Dealer in Groceries and Produce, 141 Pennsylvania Avenue, Corner Wright Street, Newark, N. J. Everybody is interested in obtaining first-class creamery supplies at moderate rates, and as the enterprise recently established by Mr. A. M. Hazen is capable of doing much to bring about this very desirable result, a brief account of its origin, and of the facilities of those having it in charge, can hardly fail to be acceptable to our readers. Mr. Hazen is a native of Newark, and began business operations in 1890. He is a wholesale and retail dealer in cream and milk, and also does an extensive retail trade in groceries and produce. The premises occupied cover an area of 720 square feet, and are located at No. 141 Pennsylvania avenue, corner Wright street. The public have already learned that the quantities of the supplies furnished here is thoroughly dependable, and as Mr. Hazen quotes the lowest market rates, it is but natural that he should have built up an extensive and rapidly growing business. Cream, milk, reliable groceries, and fresh produce are appreciated all the more on account of their comparative rarity in the market, and as this enterprising gentleman makes a specialty of supplying just such goods, he deserves all the liberal patronage which he receives.

H. T. WOOD, PHOTOGRAPHER, 615

Broad Street, Newark, N. J. Amongst the large number of photographers doing business in and around Newark, a stranger in the city may well be excused for not knowing whom to patronize, and even those residing here are often at a loss to decide where they shall place their orders. Now of course, it is not in our province to draw invidious comparisons, and to declare that A produces a good article while B produces a bad one, but we are at least free to call attention to true merit wherever found, and take advantage of this liberty to advise such of our readers as are interested in really artistic photography to call on Mr. H. T. Wood, located at No. 615 Broad street, and see what this gentleman has to offer in that line. Mr. Wood is not what may perhaps be called a "newspaper photographer." He does not announce himself in startling type as "the leading photographer," but, nevertheless, he does a large business, and one that is rapidly increasing. The enterprise was established by Mr. Wood in 1867, the premises occupied comprising one floor 23x80 feet in dimensions. Two competent assistants are employed, and an important and controlling reason of the excellence of Mr. Wood's work is explained by the fact of his giving every order careful personal attention. Mr. Wood is a native of New York, and is well known throughout Newark, being an old resident of that community. Considering the uniform excellence of the work done at this studio, the prices asked are very low indeed, and no one will regret favoring him with an order.

JAMES F. CAFFREY, UNDERTAKER,

Ware Rooms 18 1-2 Thomas street, Residence, 134 Thomas street. Personal Attention Day and Night. The establishment carried on by Mr. James F. Caffrey, may justly be called representative in every sense of the word, for the character and magnitude of the patronage received and the reliability and efficiency of the service rendered, combine to give it a leading position in the special field it occupies. Mr. Caffrey is a thoroughly competent and experienced funeral director. He is widely and favorably known in business and social circles of this city, having the tact so essential to success in his profession. Mr. Caffrey has been in business for himself since 1890. His warerooms are located at No. 18 1-2 Thomas street, and his residence at No. 134 Thomas street. Orders left at either of these establishments are assured prompt and careful attention. He gives personal attention to his profession day and night, and is prepared to assume entire direction of funerals, furnishing everything that may be required, and making uniformly moderate charges. A full line of caskets, coffins, robes and other funeral supplies is constantly carried in stock, and the most improved facilities are provided for embalming, and other duties incidental to the profession. Employment is given to a sufficient force of experienced assistants, undue delay being thus entirely avoided.

HASBROUCK'S TROY LAUNDRY, W.

R. Hasbrouck, Prop., No. 19 Clinton Street, Newark, N. J. There are many people who object to the inconvenience of having their washing done at home, and yet who are afraid to trust their clothes to the public laundries. It is undoubtedly the case that in many of these establishments, the methods employed are the ruination of linen in a very short time, and for this reason a decided prejudice has sprung up against them. There is no necessity for this ill treatment if the work is entrusted to persons who know how to conduct such an establishment and who value their reputation. The Hasbrouck Troy Laundry, of which Mr. W. R. Hasbrouck is proprietor, is the one which has borne a good name from the beginning, and is known to turn out none but excellent work. It was started in 1876 by Mr. Hasbrouck, who came here from Troy, N. Y. The laundry is situated at 19 Clinton street, and is of 20x100 feet dimensions. Mr. Hasbrouck has introduced the latest improved machinery for laundry work into the premises, and he employs fifteen competent and skilled assistants. All goods are delivered promptly and free of charge. Mr. Hasbrouck has in connection with his laundry business a department which furnishes and keeps clean a supply of towels for the use of offices and stores, a plan which many avail themselves of, it insuring a constant and reliable supply of towels at a trifling cost. It is conducted under the same reliable management as his laundry.

J. F. WADDINGTON, NEWS DEPOT.

Dealer in First-class Groceries, Teas, Coffees, Butter and Eggs, Cigars, Tobacco, Candy and Stationery, No. 108 Emmett Street, Newark, N. J. People living on Emmett Street, and in the vicinity of the Emmett Street Station, have long since discovered the advisability of going to No. 108 on that street, for many household commodities and every day necessities. The shop here located is presided over by Mr. J. F. Waddington, who has been engaged in business in this place since June, 1888. The popularity of this house is attested by the rapid growth of business, which has increased surely and steadily since its beginning. This is due, not less to the skilful management of the proprietor, than to the excellent class of goods which are always to be had at his establishment. These consist of the finest groceries of all kinds, comprising everything pertaining to the family grocery trade, and a full line of the best canned goods. Fresh country butter and eggs from neighboring farms, are to be had here at all times, as well as choice fruits in their season. Mr. Waddington makes a specialty of keeping fine grades of cigars and tobacco, and a choice assortment of delicate confectionery. With this business he unites that of a news depot, where all the daily and weekly papers, periodicals and magazines may be had. Mr. Waddington employs an efficient assistant. His store is attractively fitted up, and his business is in a thriving condition.

O. J. VALENTINE & CO., Manufacturers

of Fine Gold Jewelry, 13 and 15 Franklin Street, Newark, N. J. The manufacture of fine jewelry is one of the most widespread of all the industrial interests in Newark. The aggregate amount of the products of these factories reaches a most enormous sum. The offices of the establishments are all in New York, and it is curious to think that a large part of the jewelry sold in New York, is made in Newark. One of the prominent firms engaged in this business, is that of Messrs. O. J. Valentine & Co. These gentlemen do a large manufacturing business in fine gold jewelry of every kind. They have a commodious factory, 40x125 feet dimensions, fitted up with the best machinery, and with every appliance and convenience for the production of beautiful ornaments made of this precious metal. The work done here is unsurpassed for quality and finish, the employees numbering twenty, being all picked men, brought up to the trade, and unusually skillful in its practice. A powerful steam engine is in use, and the amount of work done is very great. The firm consists of Messrs. O. J. Valentine, D. N. Crane, and E. F. C. Theurer, all natives of Newark. The office is at 13 & 15 Franklin Street, Newark, N. J. Orders sent here are assured prompt and careful attention.

W. A. & T. V. AGENS, Successors to Johns

Agens, Boots and Shoes, 493 Broad Street, Newark, N. J. It would be difficult to find an establishment that can compete with the one conducted by Messrs. W. A. & T. V. Agens. This house was established in 1820, by Mr. Jonas Agens, who was succeeded by the present proprietors. They are manufacturers and dealers in boots and shoes of all sizes and a variety of styles. A house that has successfully carried on the wholesale and retail trade that this has, for seventy years, should certainly be thoroughly familiar with its every detail, and should have a very accurate conception of what is wanted by the purchasing public, so that the inducements offered by Messrs. Agens are what might naturally have been expected. Their store is 25x88 feet in dimensions, and contains a fine stock of ladies', misses and children's, men's, boy's and youth's boots and shoes. All goods are represented, and all tastes and purses can be suited. Their extensive business requires the employment of a number of assistants, who are competent to attend to customers, and give all necessary information in regard to the quality and fit of shoes and boots. They are prepared to fill orders without delay, while the prices quoted in every department of the business, are as low as the lowest, quality being duly considered. These gentlemen are both natives of this city, and of course, they are very generally known in business and social circles throughout this vicinity.

GRAHAM & CO., BANKERS AND BROK-

ers, and Steam Ship Agents, 810 Broad Street, Newark, N. J. Dealers in Passage Tickets, Drafts on England, Ireland, Scotland and all parts of the Continent. Also, agents for Cook's Tours. Telephone 709. Prominent among the firms in the banking and brokerage business in this city, is the well known one of Messrs. Graham & Co. These gentlemen are natives of Newark, and have been engaged for a number of years in their present business, the firm having been established in 1876. Those who have had any experience with this firm will be glad to testify to their integrity, and strictly fair dealings in every instance, in the many branches which they pursue. Besides the usual banking and brokerage, they are dealers in commercial papers, government securities, stocks, bonds and foreign exchange. They will furnish without delay, drafts on England, Ireland, Scotland and all parts of the Continent. They are agents for nearly all the principal lines of ocean steamships, as well as for the Charleston, Savannah and other Southern lines, and are prepared to furnish passage tickets to or from all parts of Europe. They are also agents for the celebrated English firm of Thomas Cook & Son, who carry the wondering tourist in the most comfortable modern manner, through the ancient and now semi-civilized lands. Such a firm as Messrs. Graham & Co. is of the very greatest benefit to any community, and should be patronized as much as possible, as they can furnish steamship tickets at the same prices asked at the head steamship offices, and secure state rooms for their customers without extra charge. Information relative to the sailing or arrival of all steamships will be cheerfully furnished. Their office is at 810 Broad street, State Bank Building, centrally located for the convenience of their patrons.

J. POTZTROFF. & CO., UPHOLSTERERS.

Furniture of all kinds Repaired and Varnished. Parlor Suits made to order, Carpets fitted and retail, Hair Mattresses made over, Slip Covers made to order, 52 Sherman avenue, corner Murray street, Newark, N. J. While there is much work about a house that a careful housekeeper can do herself or have done under her own directions in the way of cleaning and renovation, there is also considerable that requires special facilities and experience to do successfully, and here is where the services of a competent upholsterer becomes of value. We are aware that there are some claiming to be practical upholsterers who are utterly unworthy of the name, but there are others who may be entrusted to perform all the work allotted to them with fidelity and discretion, and prominent among such in Newark are Messrs. J. Potztroff & Co., at No. 52 Sherman avenue, corner of Murray street. They established their business here in 1862. Their business premises cover an area of 800 square feet, and every facility is at hand to perform all the work which may be received, at short notice and in the same thoroughly first-class manner that has ever characterized the operations of this enterprise. Furniture will be made to order, or repaired, and varnished. Curtains, mattress, and carpet work of every description, carefully attended to at very lowest rates consistent with satisfactory results. Three skilled assistants are employed, and we can assure our readers that they will find it to their advantage to avail themselves of the inducements presented by Messrs. J. Potztroff & Co. in the line of upholsterers and furniture makers.

P. J. MOORE, DEALER IN BEEF, LAMB,

Mutton, Pork, Poultry, Fruit and Vegetables in Season, 56 Astor Street, Newark, N. J. There are many things about the establishment carried on by Mr. P. J. Moore that makes it worthy of special consideration in these pages, and not the least important of these is the liberal spirit which characterizes its management. Mr. Moore is evidently a believer in the "Live and let Live" principle, and has no desire to set up a monopoly of any kind, only asking for "a fair field and no favor." He welcomes legitimate and honorable competition, and has no fear but that he will be able to compete with such at all times. The public has long since discovered that the proprietor of the establishment in question, was wide-a-wake and progressive, and as this spirit is just what the people admire, Mr. Moore has no reason to complain of the patronage accorded him. Business was begun in 1889, by Mr. Moore, who is a native of New Brunswick, N. J., and is personally well known in Newark. Premises measuring 25x30 feet, are occupied, and beef, lamb, pork, and poultry are extensively handled, also fruits and vegetables of all kinds in their seasons. This establishment is located at No. 56 Astor street, and orders are promptly and carefully delivered, employment being given to four competent assistants. The stock is constantly being renewed, and thereby kept fresh and seasonable, and those searching for reliable goods at fair prices, will find just what they seek in Mr. P. J. Moore's, at No. 56 Astor street, Newark.

J. W. FELIX, FANCY CAKE AND PIE

Bakery, 91 Sherman Avenue, Newark, N. J. It is difficult to make a perfectly satisfactory meal without good bread, and plenty of it, and while even the most elaborate repast seems lacking in something, if bread be wanting, it as possible to be content with but little meat provided the supply of bread be unstinted. Certainly bread is a very economical article of food, and there is really no excuse for going to the trouble of making it at home, for it can now be bought in this city of as good quality, and fine flavor, as could be desired by the most fastidious. The bakery run by Mr. J. W. Felix, at No. 91 Sherman avenue, Newark, has gained a most surprising hold on the public favor since operations were begun in 1888, although, after all, it is not so surprising as it might be, for the uniform and superior excellence of the articles sold here has had its natural effect in creating a brisk and increasing trade. A store is occupied measuring 20x50 feet in dimensions, and a full assortment of bread, cake, and pies is manufactured, and constantly on hand to choose from. The extensive retail trade transacted at this establishment, requires the services of three reliable and competent assistants. Mr. Felix is a native of Germany, and his efforts to faithfully serve the public with first-class food supplies, have been fully recognized and appreciated by the residents of this city.

THE STATE MUTUAL LIFE ASSUR-

ance Company of Worcester, Massachusetts, Samuel Wright, General Agent, 802 Broad street, Newark. Massachusetts is conceded to lead the Union in insurance legislation, the interests of policy holders in companies chartered under the laws of that State, having been fully protected since April, 1864, while the present nonforfeiture law secures to every policy holder who pays his premiums for two or more years, either a definite cash value payable on demand, or a definite amount of paid-up insurance without the surrender of the original policy, or any other action on his part. Policy holders in the State Mutual Assurance Company, of Worcester, Mass., are thus doubly protected—first, by the legislation noted, and second, by the consistently, honorable and liberal policy, which has characterized the management of that famous old organization since its incorporation in 1844. The annexed illustration tells its own story:

Thirty-Year Endowment policy—Age 30. Amount, $10,000. Annual Premium, $312.50

		Cash Value. (Guaranteed.)	Paid-up Endowment.
After Two Years,		$257 40	$631 80
"	Three "	442 30	1,056 50
"	Four "	654 80	1,475 50
"	Five "	885 50	1,887 90
"	Ten "	1,968 90	3,852 00
"	Twenty "	5,075 50	257 20
"	Thirty "	10,000 00	Full Amount Payable in Cash

The above amounts will be increased by the Company's *Annual Dividends*, or the premium will be diminished.

This company is one of the oldest, strongest and best in the United States, and as shown by the official report for 1888, has $1,187.08 assets for each $1,000 of liability. The wisdom shown in its investments is evidenced by the fact that the interest derived therefrom, has exceeded all its death claims since its organization—more than forty-five years ago. The Newark office is in charge of Mr. Samuel Wright, General Agent for New Jersey and Southern New York, (with the exception of New York and Kings Counties.) It is located at No. 802 Broad street, where full and explicit information concerning the company's resources and methods will cheerfully be given on application. Mr. Wright is a native of Brooklyn, N. Y., and is thoroughly familiar with life insurance in every detail. He has the rare faculty of making its sometimes puzzling features perfectly plain, even to those who "have no head for figures," and an interview with him will prove both pleasant and instructive, and his claim that nothing better in the form of life insurance, than the policies of that company, can be obtained anywhere at any price, is fully justified by the facts.

L. STILWELL & CO., MACHINISTS,

Manufacturers of Jewelers', Silversmiths' and Watch, Pen and Pencil Case Makers Machinery and Tools, Special and General Machinery, 30 and 32 Franklin Street, near Broad Street, Newark, N. J. This firm has long been known throughout Newark and its neighborhood, as being a house of no little importance to the business interests of the city. It is in fact among the foremost establishments of its kind in this vicinity, on account of the immense variety of tools and different kinds of machinery, etc., made here, as well as the general excellence of the stock. Any kind of delicate or heavy machinery can be had at this house, or will be made to order. Tools of all sorts, especially those in use among jewelers and silversmiths, lathes of every variety, rolls, presses, drops, draw benches, and tools and machinery of every nature can be obtained at this establishment. We cannot pretend to give any but the most meagre account of the business of this house. The list of tools, etc., made here, is a long and comprehensive one, far too much so far as to attempt any detailed description. Suffice it to say, that the list embraces nearly every kind of tool used in the industries above mentioned, as well as others. The firm was founded in 1875, under the name of Stilwell & Pierce. Twelve years later it was changed to L. Stilwell & Co. The business is very large, aggregating from $30,000 to $40,000 yearly. The factory is located at 30 & 32 Franklin street, near Broad street, and comprises two stories and a basement, each 25x60 feet dimensions. Employment is given to twenty skilled workmen.

J. T. WOODRUFF, WALL PAPERS,

White Lead, Colors, Mixed Paints, Varnishes, Brushes and Window Glass, Machinery and Illuminating Oils, 350 Mulberry Street, Newark, N. J. House painting and papering has risen to the dignity of an art, of late years, and those who are content to go on in the old ruts, producing the same kind of work over and over again, and making no effort to keep up with the times, must not expect to receive the patronage of a public that have learned to demand better things. Fitness and originality are the characteristics most popular in modern painting and papering, and it is to the great success attained in producing work of this kind that Mr. J. T. Woodruff owes his present prosperous position. Mr Woodruff is a native of Newark, and has carried on business in this city since 1878. The business premises occupied by him are located at No. 350 Mulberry street, being 20x60 feet in dimensions, and containing a large stock of wall papers, white lead, colors, mixed paints, varnishes, brushes and window glass, also machinery and illuminating oils. Employment is given to ten thoroughly competent assistants, and the facilities at hand enable orders to be filled at short notice, while the prices are invariably moderate and fair. One does not need to go far to see many specimens of this gentleman's handiwork, for many business houses and private residences display Mr. Woodruff's excellent taste and the variety is as noticeable as their number. The excellence of the stock used secures durability, as well as beauty, and, as only skilled workmen are employed, the results attained are uniformly satisfactory.

JAS. J. McGUIRE, CUSTOM TAILOR, 825

Broad Street, Newark, N. J. The advantages gained by having one's clothing made to order have been too frequently stated not to be entirely familiar to our readers, and we will not waste space by repeating them here, but simply say that those who wish to enjoy the full benefit of them, should not forget to use discrimination as to the establishment they patronize. Between what is commonly known as "cheap tailoring" and first class ready-made work, all persons of taste would prefer the latter, but there is certainly no occasion for the residents of Newark to make such a choice, for we have merchant tailors here who rank with the most skillful in the United States. Prominent among them is Mr. Jas. J. McGuire, and the productions of his establishment will compare favorably with the work turned out by the best custom tailors in New York, or any large city. The premises occupied are located at No. 825 Broad street, and comprise a store 25x70 feet in dimensions. Mr. McGuire employs four assistants in his store, and fifteen in his workroom. He is prepared to fill orders at short notice, and at the lowest prices consistent with strictly first-class work. His assortment of foreign and domestic suitings is too large to describe here, but suffice it to say, that it includes the latest and most seasonable novelties, and for fit, shapeliness, durability, and general excellence, the clothing furnished by Mr. McGuire deserves unstinted and cordial commendation.

FRANK ILIFF, WHOLESALE AND RE-

tail Dealer in Cream, Milk, Butter, Eggs, &c., also Choice Family Groceries, No. 490 Broad Street, Newark, N. J. It may readily be imagined that a very large quantity of groceries is required to supply the demand in this city and vicinity, and, as a matter of fact, the grocery business is one of the most extensive of all branches of trade here conducted. Mr. Frank Iliff occupies a leading position among our local dealers in these goods, and has been identified with his present business since 1889, having at one time been a member of the firm of Iliff & Hedges, assuming full control of the business in 1890, and it has since attained great magnitude, both a wholesale and retail business being done. Mr. Iliff was born in Sussex county, N. J., and is too well known here to render extended personal mention necessary. The premises made use of by him are located at No. 490 Broad street, and are of the dimensions of 100x50 feet. A very heavy stock is carried, and employment is given to three assistants, all orders being carefully filled, and customers being assured immediate and painstaking attention. The assortment of goods offered comprises cream, milk, butter, eggs, etc., also choice family groceries of all kinds, and the prices quoted are at all times in accordance with the lowest market rates. Mr. Iliff has always made a practice of handling first-class goods only, and the fact that articles coming from his store are sure to prove as represented, has much to do with its popularity.

H. CATION, GROCER, 32 EAST KIN-

ney Street, Newark, N. J. Among enterprises of the most highest usefulness must be reckoned such an undertaking as that new carried on by Mr. H. Cation, for at the establishment to which we have reference, there is to be found an extremely varied and desirable assortment of such indispensable articles as groceries of all kinds. These goods are offered at remarkably low rates, and are strictly reliable in every respect, being, in fact, guaranteed to prove as represented. This business was started by Mr. Cation in 1869. The premises occupied are located at No. 32 East Kinney street, and comprise a store 20x70 feet in dimensions. Particular attention is paid to the filling of all orders, and we can confidently recommend this house to anybody seeking supplies of the kind mentioned, for long experience has made Mr. Cation very expert in knowing the peculiar demands of this class of trade, and he is consequently able to supply them without annoying delay, and at the lowest market rates. Mr. Cation is a native of Newark, and has been very successful in building up a large retail trade, for his stock always contains a large and complete assortment of standard commodities.

JOHN H. KEAST, DECORATOR, FINE

Wall Papers and Window Shades, No. 973 Broad Street, corner Marshall, Newark, N. J. No more convincing proof of the great advance in culture that has been made during the past score of years could be asked for, than that afforded by a comparison of the wall papers of 1893, with those of twenty years ago. The designs, the coloring, the general effect attained—all are essentially different, and the difference is similar to that between a painted photograph and a water color. New and artistic designs in paper hangings are constantly being produced, and when placing orders for such goods it is well to exercise discrimination in order to be assured the opportunity of choosing from the latest and most successful novelties. Mr. John H. Keast is conceded to carry as desirable a selection of fine wall papers as can be found in the city, and as goods are cheerfully shown, a visit to his handsome store, corner of Broad and Marshall streets, is sure to prove pleasant as well as profitable. He handles the productions of the leading American and foreign manufacturers, and quotes the lowest market rates on the various grades dealt in. Mr. Keast has carried on his present enterprise since 1881. He not only handles wall papers and window shades, but also does a general decorating and painting business, employing twenty assistants and being prepared to fill all orders at short notice, and in a uniformly superior manner. Designs and estimates for interior decoration will be furnished promptly, and as Mr. Keast gives personal attention to the execution of such commissions, he is in a position to guarantee satisfaction to his customers.

ISAAC ROSENSTRAUCH, IMPORTER

and Jobber in Hosiery, Fancy Goods, Notions, etc., No. 836 Broad Street, Next Door to C. R. R. Station, Newark, N. J. Mr. Isaac Rosenstrauch is one of the leading importers and jobbers of hosiery, fancy goods, notions, etc., in New Jersey, having built up a very large business during the score of years that operations have been carried on, and it is generally understood among the trade, that he is in a position to quote bottom prices, and fill the largest orders without delay, but probably the large majority of our readers will be more interested in the retail branch of his business, this being located at No. 81 Market street, while his wholesale warehouse is at No. 836 Broad street, next door to C. R. R. station. Mr. Rosenstrauch carries a large stock, but it is more remarkable for quality and variety, than for magnitude, it comprising the productions of some of the foremost foreign and domestic manufacturers, and including many goods it would be difficult to find elsewhere. Those who are particularly interested in the latest fashionable novelties, find a visit to this store especially enjoyable, for Mr. Rosenstrauchs' facilities and methods are such, that no dealer in New Jersey offers his patrons more late and desirable novelties to choose from. A competent and adequate force of assistants is employed, so that prompt and polite attention is assured to every caller.

A. J. SIMPSON, PLUMBING, STEAM and

Gas Fitting, Tin, Copper and Sheet-iron Worker, Galvanized Iron, Cornice made and put up at short notice, No. 223 Clinton avenue, Newark, N. J. Telephone No. 876, Mr. A. J. Simpson is conducting a trade of extensive proportions, as plumber, steam and gas fitter. The premises occupied for this business consists of a store 40x125 feet dimensions, situated at 223 Clinton avenue. It is neatly and appropriately fitted up, and contains a full line of steam fitting, gas and steam fitters supplies, besides all the many tools and appliances pertaining to this trade. Mr. Simpson is a native of Newark, and has been in business for himself for the past four years, having served twelve years at the plumbing trade with the late M. H. Smith. Mr. Simpson is already well-known as a skillful and reliable representative of his trade. He is prepared to compete with his contemporaries in every way, and may be implicitly relied upon to execute all orders and fulfill every contract with promptness, and in a faithful and workmanlike manner. Special attention is given to sanitary plumbing and steam fitting, making water and sewer connections, setting bath tubs, etc., etc. In addition to the regular plumber's trade, Mr. Simpson does any kind of work in tin, copper and sheet-iron, and is prepared to make galvanized iron cornices and put them up at the shortest possible notice. A force of fifteen skilled mechanics is employed in the different branches of the business, so that all patrons may be assured of being quickly and well served.

T. H. POLLOCK, BRUSH MANUFAC-

turer, Jewelers' and Watch Case Makers' Brushes a Specialty, 13 and 15 Franklin Street, Newark, N. J. The business of the brush manufacturer is of far greater magnitude and much more importance than is ordinarily recognized. Toilet brushes of different kinds, such as hair, nail, and tooth brushes, form but a small part of this industry. In manufactures of almost every kind, brushes are essential articles, and these are made specially for certain purposes. Mr. T. H. Pollock is one of the merchants of this city, who devotes himself to the manufacture of these indispensable articles. He makes a specialty of the fine grades of brushes, such as are used by jewelers and watch case makers. These require to be made most carefully, of the imported bristles and goat hair, and they are used in great quantities. Mr. Pollock has been carrying on this business since 1876, and he has acquired so great a degree of perfection in his products, that he supplies many of the largest jewelers' establishments of this city. The factory is situated at 13 and 15 Franklin street, where an entire floor is occupied, and fourteen workmen are employed. This business is both wholesale and retail, and Mr. Pollock has his hands full attending to orders. Mr. Pollock is a native of New York city. He is a well known citizen of Newark, and is Assemblyman of the Third District of Essex County, N. J.

W. CAMPFIELD, DEALER IN FINE

Teas, Coffees, Groceries, Provisions, Flour, Foreign and Domestic Fruits, Canned Goods, Wooden and Willow Ware, Corner Sherman Avenue and Wright Street, Newark, N. J. In the staple and important lines of general groceries, this is a well known representative house. It was started in 1874, by Mr. Joseph Holton, who was succeeded in 1878 by Mr. William Campfield, the present proprietor. For the past fifteen years, Mr. Campfield has had the reputation of keeping a thoroughly reliable grocery store, and he has many patrons who have dealt with him since he began business. The line of trade is one having a broad basis, comprising most of the indispensable commodities such as groceries of all kinds, teas, coffees, sugars, provisions, flour, foreign and domestic fruits, canned goods, and a long list of articles too numerous to mention. Mr. Campfield also keeps a full stock of wooden and willow ware. The store is situated at the corner of Sherman avenue and Wright street. It consists of two floors, 24x55 feet in dimensions. The business is exclusively retail, and employment is given to two assistants, customers are served promptly, and orders are carefully delivered. Mr. Campfield is a native of Columbia, Morris Co., N. J. He has long been a Newark man in every sense of the word. He, and his house, are well known here, and they are both equally well spoken of and respected.

A. K. FIELD, MANUFACTURER, Im-

porter and Wholesale Dealer in General Sporting Goods, No. 9 Central Avenue, Newark, N. J. It used to be said that Americans were so devoted to money making that they had no time for sports of any kind after they left school, but such an assertion would now be very far from the truth, for within the last twenty years there has been a decided change for the better, and the result is an immense and rapidly increasing demand for sporting goods of all kinds. Mr. A. K. Field carries on the only wholesale sporting goods house in Newark, and as he is a manufacturer and importer as well as a wholesaler, it is natural that he should be able to meet all honorable competition, and to quote bottom prices on all the almost endless variety of articles included under the head of general sporting goods. He is a native of New Jersey, has been in business in this city for the past six years, and founded his present business in 1886. Spacious premises, located at No. 9 Central avenue, are occupied, and a large and complete stock is constantly carried, the productions of the leading domestic and foreign manufacturers being well represented. Orders are assured immediate and careful attention, and the prices quoted are uniformly as low as the lowest, so it is natural that an extensive trade should already have been built up.

A. ALLING REEVES, Successor to Isaac

A. Alling & Co., Maker of Fine Jewelry, Factory in Newark, Office 21 Maiden Lane, New York. This prominent establishment has undergone numerous changes since its foundation, nearly half a century ago. In 1841 it was known as Messrs. J. & J. Alling. Thirteen years later the name was changed to Alling Brothers & Company. These gentlemen were associated in the management of the house until 1881, when another change took place, the firm becoming Isaac A. Alling & Company. The company has now been dissolved and Mr. A. Alling Reeves has succeeded to the proprietorship, after having been one of the partners for several years. Mr. Reeves is a native of this city, and is well known and respected throughout the vicinity. He is a large manufacturing jeweler, the factory being located in Newark. This building covers an area of 35x90 feet. It is fitted with all the modern machinery and appliances used in this branch of industry, and the work produced here is well known for its beauty of design and excellence of finish. A large force of men is constantly employed, who are selected for their skill and accuracy in the handling of the precious metals. The office is situated at 21 Maiden Lane, New York, and contains a large assortment of the most beautiful ornaments in gold, silver and precious stones. The terms will be found extremely moderate for the class of goods dealt in, which are certainly unsurpassed by any other firm in this neighborhood.

H. TOBELMANN, STAPLE AND FAN-

cy Groceries, Teas, Coffees, Sugars, Spices, etc., Fine Butter a Specialty, corner Orchard and Camp Streets, Newark, N. J. We know of no establishment in the city, of a similar character, more worthy of commendation than that of which Mr. H. Tobelmann is the proprietor, located at the corner of Orchard and Camp streets, and we are sure that it only needs a careful trial of the accommodations he supplies to convince any unprejudiced person that our favorable opinion has excellent foundation in fact. Mr. Tobelmann is a native of Germany, began business here in 1881, and has a large circle of friends in this city. The premises occupied by him cover an area of some 1,500 square feet, having been recently enlarged and improved. The stock on hand is made up of fine staple and fancy groceries, especially selected for family trade. Choice teas, coffees, sugars, spices, etc., as well as fine butter, are also handled at all times. Mr. Tobelmann owes much of the reputation he enjoys as an honorable business man, to his invariable practice of never misrepresenting any article in the slightest degree intentionally. Errors may sometimes occur, but such will be cheerfully rectified when attention is called to them, and no trouble is spared to satisfy every customer. There are three efficient and polite assistants employed, and orders can thus be filled without delay, and will be delivered, if desired, to any part of the city, and as the goods handled are all sold at the lowest market rates, it is but natural that a large retail business should be done.

A. BUSCH, Manufacturer of Mattresses,

Dealer in Spring Beds, Cots, etc., 66 Market Street, Second door from Plane Street, Newark, N. J. One of the most important points of house furnishing is the selection of good bedding. To have a house filled with handsome furniture, pictures and ornaments, is most pleasing to the eye, but what person is in a mood to admire or appreciate these things, however beautiful they may be, if he has tossed all night on a hard, uncomfortable bed, and tried in vain to get much needed rest. Therefore we maintain good bedding is the first question to be considered. A well woven wire mattress or other kind of spring bed, of which there is a great variety to choose from, is a good thing to begin with. Then follows a thick hair mattress, or two if you can afford them. They are most expensive items, not on account of the covering, which is cheap enough, or the amount of work put upon them. The expense is principally in the carded hair used as stuffing. This comes in various qualities, the finest of course doing the best service. Once bought it never needs replacing, for a mattress can be made over and over again, and each time be equal to new. Therefore a good maxim is, to buy the best if you can possibly do so. To procure the best, it is necessary to go to a dealer known to be honest in his transactions. There are plenty of these in Newark—men who sell their goods for what they really are. Many of these houses are supplied by A. Busch, manufacturer of mattresses, and dealer in spring beds, cots, etc. The factory, situated at 66 Market street occupies one floor of 25x143 feet in dimensions. Mr. Busch is a native of Germany. He began operations in this country in 1884 as A. Busch & Co., continuing to do a partnership business until two years ago, when he assumed sole control of the enterprise. Mr. Busch employs experienced workmen in this branch of trade, and he aims to produce the best at as reasonable rates as any other manufacturer in the country.

J. LEWIS WHYTE,

Art Store, Stamping Designs,

Materials for all Needle-work.

835 BROAD STREET,

Newark, N. J.

Mr. Whyte was born in New York, but is one of the best known business men in Newark in his line of trade, being perfectly familiar with every department of the business. He has spent considerable time abroad, and is familiar with the manufacture and sale of all foreign articles in his line. His establishment, at No. 835 Broad street, is an old stand, having been opened in 1854; is the oldest in Newark and as every popular among all classes of purchasers, for it always contains an extensive and complete stock of art goods, stamping patterns, embroidery materials, etc., which are offered at the very lowest market rates, while the assortment is so varied and comprehensive as to enable all tastes to be suited. The premises have an area of 1,500 square feet, and the stock is displayed to excellent advantage, while a sufficiently large force of competent assistants is employed to assure immediate and careful attention to every caller. Mr. Whyte is associated with Mr. Moore in the handling of gum labels, tans, advertising novelties, etc., for all kinds of business, and the firm carry on operations on an extensive scale, having warerooms at No. 139 Clark street, Chicago, and No. 15 Park Row, New York, besides those in this city. They have exceptional facilities for filling the heaviest orders at short notice, and quote positively bottom prices at all times. The great convenience of gum labels has caused them to come into universal use, and there is not a line of business in which they cannot be employed to advantage. Messrs. Moore & Whyte can furnish them in all sizes, grades and styles, and they are "warranted to stick" under all circumstances. Advertising novelties of the latest and most attractive design are also furnished in quantities to suit, a full line, varying from the simplest to the most elaborate, being constantly on hand to choose from.

NEWARK PURSE FRAME M'F'G. CO.,

Manufacturers of Purse and Pocket Book Frames, No. 329 Market Street, Newark, N. J. No doubt many of our readers have wondered at the remarkably low prices quoted on purses and pocket books nowadays, for the cost of these articles has been very considerably reduced of late years, and an excellent purse may now be bought at what seems an absurdly low price. This reduction in cost has been brought about, chiefly by the use of improved machinery, and the economy gained by dividing the work of manufacture up into specialties. This has been observed by a visit to the shop conducted by the Newark Purse Frame Manufacturing Company, who give exclusive attention to the production of purse and pocket book frames, and utilize a plant of the latest improved machinery. Employment is given to some twenty assistants, the company being prepared to furnish anything at their line at short notice, in quantities to suit, and at positively the lowest market rates. The business was founded about the year 1875, by Mr. Gustave Wuesthof, who was succeeded in 1888 by Mr. E. B. Vliet, he giving place to the present company, May 18, 1889. The proprietors are Messrs. W. P. Blasius and Emil Poeter, both of whom are residents of this city. Well-equipped premises located at No. 329 Market street, are made use of, and orders are assured immediate and careful attention.

A. T. LOOKER, MANUFACTURER of and

Wholesale and Retail Dealer in Furniture, Carpets, and Oil Cloth, 817 Broad Street, Newark, N. J. There are furniture houses not 100 miles from Newark that make much greater pretensions than are made by the gentleman whose card we print above, and those who are easily influenced by extravagant statements may be persuaded that they are the only concerns which may be trusted to supply customers with reliable goods at lowest prices, but still Mr. Looker's business methods are appreciated by many of the most careful buyers, and his trade will compare favorably with that enjoyed by any dealer in similar goods in Newark. Indeed, the magnitude of his stock goes far to prove this to be the case, for notwithstanding that five floors are occupied, each of the dimensions of 50x200 feet, the premises are none too spacious to properly accommodate the large business done. This comprises the manufacture of furniture as well as dealing in furniture, carpets and oil-cloth, at both wholesale and retail, and it is notable for this fact—it does not include articles which cannot be guaranteed to prove as represented. The business carried on by Mr. A. T. Looker was founded by Samuel Brown in 1790, who was succeeded in 1859 by the firm of McDermit & Looker, and they by Mr. Looker in 1884. The establishment is located at No. 817 Broad street, where nine competent assistants are employed, and we would most earnestly advise such of our readers as wish to furnish a house wholly or partially, to step in here, and see what inducements are offered. Remember that Mr. Looker carries a complete assortment of furniture, and that he offers it at the lowest market prices, quality being considered. Mr. Looker has also a branch establishment at Passaic, N. J.

MARTIN & CO., ENGRAVING, DIA-

mond Dealers and Setters, No. 135 Market Street, Room No. 1, Newark, N. J. Every one knows that there is a great difference in diamonds—leaving the matter of size out of the question—but every one does not know, apparently, that the setting of a diamond is second in importance only to the quality of the stone itself, and so true is this that an expert can point out many cases where a fine gem is surpassed in appearance by one of apparently inferior quality, owing to the more skillful setting of the latter. It is said that no two diamonds are precisely alike, and this being the case it is obvious that the conditions of setting must be changed to suit the stone in every instance, if the best results are to be attained. Such of our readers as wish to have diamonds reset, to purchase them, or to have diamond jewelry of any description made to order, would do well to call on Messrs. Martin & Co., at No. 135 Market street, for this firm make a specialty of diamond setting, and have the experience, the taste, the skill and the mechanical facilities to suit the most critical trade. Mr. M. I. Martin was born in this city, and is very generally and favorably known in the jewelry trade. A sufficient force of assistants is employed to enable orders to be filled at short notice, and engraving, etc., will be done at the lowest rates consistent with first-class work.

UNITED STATES INDUSTRIAL IN-

surance Company. Home Office, Nos. 843 and 845 Broad St., Newark. The phenomenal extension of the business of the United States Industrial Insurance Company during the comparatively short time that operations have been carried on, is significant of many things, but above all of the fact that the people—"the common people," as Abraham Lincoln used to delight to call them—are appreciative of true insurance principles, and will heartily support an enterprise which really carries them into practical effect. The tendency of late years has been to combine life insurance and investment, and the result is that the market is flooded with policies, so involved in meaning and technical in style that they are beyond the comprehension of any ordinary man; and even trained lawyers find room for honest differences of opinion as to their meaning. The Insurance Commissioner of Massachusetts has officially deprecated the practice of combining life insurance and financial investment, and has given it as his opinion that it is best to save money by means of the facilities afforded by savings banks, and to keep your life insurance entirely independent of other considerations. The popularity of the plan followed by the United States Industrial is due in a great measure to its low cost, and this low cost is the natural result of the skillful and economical carrying out of pure insurance principles. The men identified with the company are prominent merchants, manufacturers, etc., used to handling affairs of importance, and possessing the full confidence of the business and social communities, as will be seen from the following list : *Officers*—Edward N. Crane, President ; Chas. A. Lighthipe, 1st Vice-President and Treasurer ; F. B. Mandeville, M. D., 2d Vice-President and Medical Director ; T. Elmer Gay, Secretary ; Frederic W. Ward, Counsel. *Board of Directors*—Chas. A. Lighthipe, ex-President Orange National Bank ; Hon. George A. Halsey, 8 Halsey & Sons ; William Clark, Clark Thread Co. ; John H. Ballantine, P. Ballantine & Son ; Gottfried Krueger, Gottfried Krueger Brewing Co. ; Edwin M. Douglas, President German National Bank ; E. O. Doremus, Vice-President American Insurance Co. ; William T. Rae, William T. Rae & Co. ; J. C. Smith, J. C. Smith & Co. ; Edward N. Crane, Crane & Co.; E. Luther Joy, L. Joy & Co.; George B. Swain, Swain & Jones ; Matthew T. Gay, Blanchard Bro. & Lane ; Frederic W. Ward, Stevens & Ward ; F. B. Mandeville, M. D., Medical Director ; Lawrence T. Fell, State Labor Inspector ; George R. Jenkinson, T. B. Peddie & Co.; Geo. Spottiswoode, Geo. Spottiswoode & Co., Orange, N. J.; James H. Hart, Tolar & Hart, New York. We could fill pages with glowing testimonials from beneficiaries of the Company, setting forth their gratitude for the promptness and fidelity with which obligations have been discharged, but space forbids, and we will leave our readers to form their own conclusions of the ability and good faith of the Company from the especially rapid development of its business in precisely those sections where it has been called upon to pay most losses. The following figures will prove interesting and instructive :

UNITED STATES INDUSTRIAL.

New Policies in 1889,	65,849
Policies Lapsed in 1889,	39,050
Increase in 1889,	2,449

We can only make comparison with the business in the State of New Jersey of the *previous* year, of the two oldest companies, as officially reported, which is as follows :

METROPOLITAN.

New Policies in 1888,	85,062
Policies Lapsed in 1888,	52,102
Increase during 1888,	32,960

PRUDENTIAL.

New Policies in 1888,	80,069
Policies Lapsed in 1888,	57,280
Increase during 1888,	23,289

The comparison speaks for itself. The first annual statement of the Company, issued December 31, 1889, showed it to be in an excellent financial condition, and more than realized the expectations of its friends. The capital has been increased, with the view of extending operations to other States, and the indications are that the next annual statement will show even more remarkable progress. The home office is at Nos. 843 and 845 Broad street, and full information will be given on application by mail or in person. Many experienced agents are employed, and the advantages of insurance are placed within the reach of all.

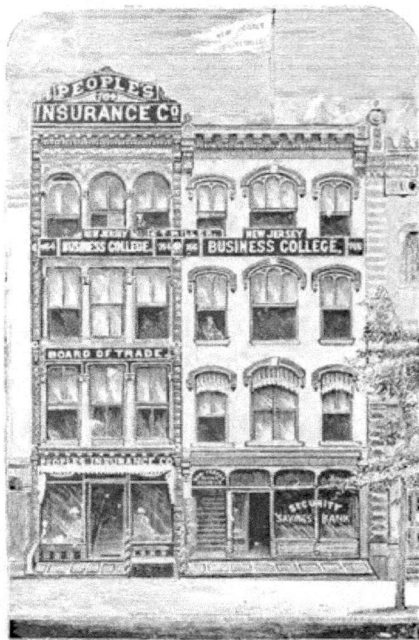

NEW JERSEY BUSINESS COLLEGE, 764

and 766 Broad street, Newark, New Jersey. Business Studies, Short-hand, Type-writing, German, Drawing, etc. Cards written, Resolutions engrossed. Divested of all unessential details, the question which confronts the young man who has received a common school education, and contemplates entering commercial life, is simply this: "Shall I get the practical training indispensable to success in business by attending a business college, or shall I get it during an indefinite term of ill-paid office drudgery?" There is but one sensible answer to this question, and that many young men answer it incorrectly, is due simply to the unfavorable impression they have formed of all business colleges, by what they know concerning some, unworthy of the name. The New Jersey Business College was established in 1871, and its graduates are now occupying responsible and profitable positions throughout the country. To say that graduation from this college insures immediate and pronounced business success would be absurd, but to say that graduates who have made proper use of the facilities provided are possessed of a thorough practical training, which could not have been got during a narrow round of office duties, excepting after years of painful effort, is a simple and demonstrable statement of fact. It is the purpose of Mr. C. T. Miller, Principal and Proprietor of this college, to give students a practical education in the full sense of the term, and to attain this end he has gathered about him a corps of eight experienced and successful teachers, and furnishes tuition in business studies, short hand, type-writing, German, drawing, etc. Our space is too limited to admit detailed description of the course of study, etc., but full information is contained in an illustrated catalogue which will be sent free to any address. Mr. Miller is a native of Manchester, Md., and has been identified with the New Jersey Business College since its original establishment. For eight years he shared its ownership with Mr. G. A. Stockwell, and from 1882 to 1886 he was associated with Mr. W. E. Drake, but since the latter date he has been sole proprietor. Commodious and well-equipped premises are occupied, at Nos. 764 and 766 Broad street, and all interested are cordially invited to call and personally inspect the many facilities provided.

RUSSELL & SAYRE, BUILDERS, SASH,

Blinds, Doors, Moldings, and Machine Work, Nos. 38 and 40 Crawford Street, Newark, N. J. Telephone, No. 445. The business carried on by Messrs. Russell & Sayre, was established in 1876, and this concern has long ranked among the leading builders and contractors in the State. Mr. C. M. Russell is a native of Morristown, and Mr. J. M. Sayre, of Madison, N. J., both these gentlemen being very generally known in business circles throughout this section. The firm are prepared to figure very closely on plans and specifications, being aided materially by the fact of their carrying on a well-equipped shop for the manufacture of Sash, Doors, Blinds, Moulding, etc., the premises utilized being located at Nos. 38 and 40 Crawford Street, and comprising two floors of the dimensions of 53x75 feet. They are fitted up with a very complete plant of improved machinery, power being furnished by a forty-horse engine. Orders for machine work will be filled in a superior manner at short notice, the charges being always in strict accordance with the lowest market rates. Employment is generally given to about fifty assistants, and the most extensive commissions can be executed with very little delay when haste is desirable. Messrs. Russell & Sayre have carried out many important building contracts, and have a most enviable reputation for faithfully and skillfully performing all duties undertaken.

W. L. TEUSH, Photographer, 695 Broad

Street, Newark, N. J. Mr. Teush is prominent among first-class photographers, and is worthy to stand as a representative for producing all that is best and most advanced in the several departments of the art of photography. He occupies a spacious and attractive studio, which is 20x80 feet in dimensions. It is very conveniently fitted up with every facility for executing this work in all its branches. Mr. Teush is a thoroughly experienced photographer and has consequently met with brilliant success. He requires the services of three skillful assistants to meet the demands of his numerous patrons. Great skill and judgment are shown in the arrangement of individuals and groups, so that a glance at his work reveals originality and excellence. Mr. Teush is familiar with every detail of this business and gives his personal attention to all work entrusted to him. His selected assortment of finely executed work proves that he is master of his profession, and that he has the facilities, and also the ability, for producing anything in his line which could possibly be required. Orders for portrait pictures, whether large or small, interior views of halls or small rooms, outdoor pictures of buildings or of landscapes, will be attended to with promptness, and satisfaction will be warranted as far as circumstances will admit.

WM. M. SMITH & CO., Agents for

American Watches, Diamonds, Jewelry, Silverware, Clocks, Lamps, Rugs, Etc., Watches and Clocks Repaired, Cash or Installments, 32 Clinton Street, Newark, N. J. A reliable watch is without doubt as valuable a companion as a man can have in these days, and the missing of a train, or the failure to keep an engagement with one whose minutes are worth dollars, and who cannot, therefore, afford to wait for a laggard, may seriously injure one's prospects. As watches can be bought for a very little money, nearly all who would profit by punctuality, are able to procure one. Mr. William M. Smith & Co., are agents for American watches of all descriptions, and those who are about to purchase one, would do well to visit this store and examine the stock which they can show. The premises are located at No. 32 Clinton street, and are 20x25 feet in dimensions. Besides the large assortment of watches to be seen here, you will find a full and fine display of diamonds, jewelry, silverware, clocks, lamps, rugs, etc. They offer some very desirable novelties in each of these lines. Watches and clocks are repaired in a skillful manner, no exorbitant charges being made. Mr. Smith & Co. employ two competent assistants, and all goods as well as all work is strictly guaranteed. Goods are sold or cash or on installments.

HEATH & DRAKE, Dry Goods, Cloaks, Millinery, Carpets, Upholstery, etc., 777-779 Broad Street, Newark, N. J. The business carried on under the firm name of Heath & Drake, was founded very nearly half a century ago, and has long held a leading position, not only in this State, but throughout this section of the country. Operations were begun in 1841, by Mr. S. R. W. Heath, and in 1847 the firm name became S. R. W. Heath & Co., the present style being adopted in 1867, when Mr. E. C. Drake was admitted to partnership. On the decease of Mr. Heath, in 1889, his interest in the business passed into the hands of his estate. Mr. Drake is a native of Mendham, N. J., and is universally known in business and social circles. Under the present skillful and liberal management, the high reputation of the enterprise is fully maintained, and it is safe to say that a more generally popular establishment cannot be found in New Jersey. The magnitude and scope of the business are so great that detailed consideration of even its more prominent features is impossible within the necessary limited space at our command, the firm selling both at wholesale and retail, and handling everything in the line of imported and domestic dry and fancy goods, cloaks, millinery, carpets, upholstery, etc., together with carriage trimmings and linings, enamelled cloth, patent and enamelled leather, etc. The premises utilized are located at Nos. 777 and 779 Broad street, in one of the handsomest and most commodious mercantile buildings in the city, furnished with large and elegant plate glass windows, and equipped with the most improved facilities for the accommodation of customers, including two large elevators and a comprehensive cash system driven by a steam motor. The building comprises six floors and a basement of the dimensions of 28x160 feet, and every available inch of this vast amount of space is fully utilized, for the stock is as complete as it is varied, and all classes of trade are catered to, and all tastes and purses can be suited. Employment is given to more than one hundred assistants, and large as this force is, it is by no means unwieldy, the duties of the various employees being so well apportioned and carefully systematized that the service is more prompt, efficient and courteous than at the large majority of much smaller establishments. Uniform politeness to all is the cardinal principle of the management, and this fact, taken in connection with the absolute reliability of goods, and the lowness of the prices quoted, explains the great and increasing popularity of this truly representative store. The very latest novelties are always to be found here, together with full lines of staple goods, and the policy of the management is such that the most inexperienced buyers may confidently rely upon receiving full value for every dollar expended.

DOTY'S CARPET EMPORIUM, 159 to 161 Market Street (Formerly Isaac N. Doty & Co.) Newark, N. J. The popularity of Doty's Carpet Emporium is not at all difficult to account for, for the purchasing public are quick to appreciate special and genuine inducements, and those offered at this establishment are many and pronounced. The enterprise was formerly carried on under the firm name of Isaac N. Doty & Co., and has been in existence long enough to be known and appreciated throughout this section of the State. The premises made use of are located at Nos. 159 to 161 Market street (up stairs), and have a total area of about 12,000 square feet, opportunity being thus afforded for the carrying on of a very extensive and complete stock of floor coverings, comprising Wilton, Axminster, moquette, velvet, body brussels, tapestry brussels and extra ingrain carpets, rugs, art squares, mattings, linoleums, oil cloths, etc. The firm makes a specialty also of making over and re-laying old carpets; all the work being superintended by E. Hanson, formerly of Jancovius & Hanson. The productions of the leading manufacturers are represented, and the latest and most artistic Novelties are offered at positively the lowest market rates. All classes of trade are catered to, and all tastes and all purses can be suited at this store, as a call will amply demonstrate. The Drapery Department deserves special mention, unsurpassed service being offered in the line of making and hanging shades, Curtains, Portieres, Venetian blinds, etc. Lace and Nottingham Curtains in all the latest designs may be found here, together with Turkoman, Chenille, and East Indian portieres, Shades and shade hollands. Employment is given to a number of experienced and well informed assistants, and prompt and courteous attention is assured to every caller. In addition to their other business, they make a specialty of Church Carpets, Cushions and Upholstering, and can refer to more than a hundred Churches which they have furnished in this immediate vicinity.

FRANK HARRISON, Stenographer, 721 Broad Street, Newark, N. J., and 239 Broadway, New York. There is a great and growing demand for the services of expert stenographers, and, indeed, so general is the use made of stenography nowadays, that it is difficult to understand how business could ever have been successfully conducted without it, excepting on a comparatively small scale. Those wishing accurate reports made of trials, examinations, arguments, sermons, conventions, debates, etc., or desiring to engage a stenographic amanuensis, can do no better than to communicate with Mr. Frank Harrison, of No. 721 Broad street, Newark, or 239 Broadway, New York. Mr. Harrison is one of the most experienced and skillful stenographers in the country. He is a native of Springfield, Ohio, and was stenographer for the United States Courts in New York city for years, opening an office in Newark in 1885. Mr. Harrison employs four assistants, and utilizes many offices, a very important branch of his business being the teaching of practical stenography, he having 250 pupils. His charges for tuition are moderate, and the advantages of such teaching are so obvious, that it is not at all surprising that they should be so largely availed of. Orders may be sent by Long Distance Telephone, No. 941, Newark, or 725 New York, and will be assured prompt and painstaking attention.

GEORGE DeVORE, Real Estate Broker, 693 Broad Street, Newark, N. J. From the inception of the above house, it has been recognized as among the principal real estate concerns in this section of the city, where could be found an extensive list of the most desirable city and suburban property, farms and land. Since 1869, the proprietor of the enterprise has been intimately connected with the business interests of this section of New Jersey, and he has in consequence made the venture a great success. His office is prominently located at No. 693 Broad street, where he is pleased to meet and accommodate in any way those interested in the purchase, sale, or renting of property. In addition to his real estate business, he is prepared to loan money at lowest rates on approved securities in any amount, and he will be found a safe medium for transacting business of this nature. Mr. Geo. D. DeVore, is a native of Mendham, N. J. He is as well and favorably known throughout Newark as an enterprising and honorable real estate broker.

LOOKING NORTH FROM
NEWARK & NEW YORK R. R.

COLEMAN NATIONAL BUSINESS

College, 858 Broad Street, Newark, N. J. The advantages and facilities for obtaining a superior business education cannot be equaled elsewhere in this country. Our boys, and, indeed, many of our girls, must learn to take care of themselves. In comparatively few countries education is compulsory, and this is what makes the average American citizen more intelligent than his foreign contemporaries. Many parents do not care for their sons to have a classical education. Many boys have no taste for it, and then much precious time is wasted; especially is this the case if a youth expects to lead a business life. In most of the colleges, a business course is provided for those who wish to take it, but now we have business colleges, where a complete course in the different branches of business is taught. Among these institutions, which exist in most of our large cities, is the Coleman National Business College, in Newark, New Jersey, established more than a quarter of a century ago, as one of the first links of the Bryant and Stratton chain of business colleges, and purchased by the present manager, Mr. H. Coleman, in 1881. Since the institution has come under Mr. Coleman's management, the course of study has been modernized, and put upon a more practical business basis. This change of management resulted in a largely increased patronage from year to year, so that in April, 1890, larger accommodations became necessary, and the school was moved to its present splendid and commodious apartments, 858 Broad street, in the N. J. Central R. R. buildings. Mr. Henry Coleman, the president, is a native of Whitehall, N. Y. He is a man of wide experience, having been principal of a similar college for nearly seventeen years, at Poughkeepsie, N. Y. The building at 858 Broad street is commodious, and well adapted for the purpose, having over 10,000 square feet of flooring. Mr. Coleman's aim is to provide a thorough business education for young men, that on graduating they may be prepared to fill positions of trust, requiring intellectual training. Since 1865, when Mr. Coleman's experience in fitting young men for business began, more than 30,000 pupils have been under his care, which speaks volumes for the methods he employs. We wish him every success in so worthy an enterprise.

N E W A R K

ABOVE cut shows building now occupied by "The Bee Hive" and on each side part view of buildings to be occupied Spring of 1891.

PART view of Mammoth Clock Department occupying one entire floor.

VIEW of grand Stair-Way leading to upper floors.

SECTION of Shoe Department, the Finest and Largest in New Jersey.

B E E = H I V E

L. S. PLAUT & CO., The Bee Hive, 711,

713, 715, 717 and 719 Broad Street, Newark, N. J., the Largest Fancy Goods House in the State. Owing to the proximity of Newark to New York, the merchants of the former city are practically obliged to compete with the leading houses of the greatest commercial centre of America, and the simple fact that under these conditions, the establishment known as the Bee Hive, has become the largest fancy goods house in New Jersey, speaks volumes for the ability and enterprise of the management, and at the same time, proves that the residents of Newark and vicinity are appreciative of liberal and honorable business methods. This enterprise was inaugurated in 1870, by Messrs. L. Fox and L. S. Plaut, in a two story frame building located at No. 721 Broad street, next to the canal, and it is a noteworthy coincidence that in May, 1891, the year that the business will attain what may be called its majority, this site will again be occupied, for the premises then utilized will extend from 707 to 721 Broad street, inclusive, and have a frontage of 150 feet, and an area of 50,000 square feet; it including all the buildings from canal bridge to Cedar street. Mr. Fox retired in 1882, and, at the death of Mr. L. S. Plaut, April 26, 1886, the business was willed to the present proprietors, Messrs. E. Plaut, L. Plaut, M. Plaut and O. Michael, who have greatly developed it, and are constantly striving to render the service even more comprehensive and efficient. The firm import most of the goods they handle, as such a practice enables them to offer just such articles as experience shows their trade demands, and also enables them to quote lower prices than would otherwise be possible. An immense stock is carried, including boy's clothing, suits and cloaks, dress goods, upholstery goods, oil cloths, baby carriages, boots and shoes, gentlemen's furnishings, gloves, hosiery, fancy articles, and, in short, a comprehensive assortment of such goods as are usually found in a first-class metropolitan dry and fancy goods house. Employment is given to 275 assistants, and as the premises are equipped with improved cash carriers and other facilities, all undue delay is avoided, the service being prompt, efficient and courteous at all times.

ESTATE OF P. HAYDEN, Importer, Manu-

facturer of and Dealer in Saddlery Hardware, Agent for Bown's Newmarket Clipper, Manufacturer and Patentee of the Celebrated Hayden's Tubular Iron Hames, Horse Clothing in all styles and qualities, 48, 50, 52, 54, 56 and 58 Mechanic Street, Newark, N. J. The enterprise carried on by the estate of P. Hayden was inaugurated in 1827, and has attained very extensive proportions, it being now one of the most important and most widely known undertakings of the kind in New Jersey, and this is no light praise, for the manufacture of saddlery hardware is a leading industry of this State, and is carried on with such enterprise and ability that both brains and energy are indispensable to the management of a business that is to retain a prominent position in this field of labor. Mr. P. Hayden was a famous importer, manufacturer of and dealer in saddlery hardware, and was especially well-known as the patentee and manufacturer of a large variety of hames, wood and iron. One of the latest improvements in this line is that known as "Hayden's Tubular Iron Hames," that was and is widely celebrated for strength, lightness, durability and convenience. Its manufacture is still a prominent feature of the business, for as yet it remains unrivalled in its special line. The main factory is located at Nos. 48, 50, 52, 54, 56 and 58 Mechanic street, the premises being four stories in height and 100 feet square, giving a total floor space of 40,000 square feet. They are equipped with an elaborate plant of the latest improved machinery, driven by an engine of sixty horse-power. Employment is given to 100 hands here, and to eighty more at the branch factory in Bloomfield. A simple catalogue of the productions of these two establishments would cover some 350 pages of our space, for all classes of trade are catered to and an almost endless variety of styles is turned out. Not only are goods shipped to every section of the Union but many are exported, customers being found in Canada, West Indies, Mexico, Australia and Europe. The extent of the export trade is due to the fact that the wants of foreign consumers have been carefully studied, and such customers have been and are supplied with goods suited to them, and not with articles with whose peculiarities they were unfamiliar. This house are agents for Bown's Newmarket Clipper, and deal heavily in horse clothing of all styles and qualities.

The business is so thoroughly systematized that every order is assured immediate and painstaking attention, and we need hardly add that the facilities available enable the lowest market rates to be quoted on all the articles manufactured and dealt in.

W. H. & R. BURNETT, Manufacturers of

Fine Furs, Seal-Skin Garments a Specialty, 17 & 19 Academy Street, Newark, N. J. The many advantages of fur garments, especially for ladies' use, create so extensive a demand as to make the fur business one of national importance, but it is safe to say there is not a concern in the country having a higher reputation in connection with the furnishing of fine furs at low prices than that of W. H. & R. Burnett, of No. 17 and 19 Academy street. This business was founded in 1866, by Misses C. F. & R. Burnett, and the existing firm name dates from 1870, when Miss C. F. Burnett was succeeded by Mr. W. H. Burnett, her brother. The enterprise has steadily developed until it has reached large proportions, customers being found throughout the country, although retail orders only are filled, much of the business being transacted through the mails. The firm manufacture fine furs in general, making a specialty of seal-skin garments, and one very important factor in their success is the fact that they make all their own goods, and sell direct to the consumer, thus saving him the paying of at least one profit, and enabling the firm to quote positively bottom prices on strictly first-class work. The premises made use of comprise four floors of the dimensions of 24x110 feet, and, besides having all necessary facilities for manufacturing, contain very extensive storage accommodations, the firm doing a large business in the storage of furs during the warm season. A large force of experienced assistants is employed, and orders can generally be filled at comparatively short notice, and in a manner which cannot fail to satisfy the most fastidious.

FRED I. WATKINS, Druggist, 191 Clin-

ton Avenue, Newark, N. J. Mr. Frederick I. Watkins has had many years practical experience among drugs, and in dispensing medicines and compounding prescriptions. He is therefore familiar with all the details connected with this business, is competent to prepare the most difficult prescriptions, and is a good man to go to for medicines and advice in case of illness. He has a neatly arranged and well fitted store at 191 Clinton avenue, Newark, which occupies one floor of 14x25 feet in dimensions. The establishment was founded in 1875 by Mr. J. E. Schussler, who carried it on successfully for some years, and at his death, Mr. Watkins succeeded to the proprietorship. The business is retail, and employment is given to two assistants. Everything that pertains to the druggists' trade is to be found at this store, including, besides pure drugs and fresh medicines, toilet requisites, the various articles needed by physicians in their practice, and the proprietary remedies of standard value and merit. Mr. Watkins is well known in Newark, and occupies a prominent position in his business.

WEBER'S, Wholesale and Retail Confec-

tionery and Ice Cream Parlors, 45 Market Street, Newark, N. J. The great advantages gained by going to the manufacturers of confectionery and ice cream are obvious. They are more likely to be pure and fresh if made on the premises, than if bought from a dealer who obtains them from somebody else. Newark people are not slow to recognize where the best articles may be found in any branch of trade, and the consequence is that Mr. Weber's confectionery and ice cream parlors are one of the favorite gathering places of many of the citizens. This establishment is located at 45 Market street, conveniently situated for people to drop into when they are tired of shopping and need refreshment. The business was started by Mr. Weber in 1884. He is a native of Newark, and has been well-known here for many years. The store is commodious, being 20x50 feet dimensions, and nicely fitted up for the purpose, with neat little tables, where one may sit and eat the most delicious ices and creams. These may be ordered in any quantity, either at wholesale or retail prices, large amounts being furnished at remarkably low rates. The confectionery is most attractive, the variety great, and the charges invariably moderate.

"FIRE INSURANCE."

Reliable Companies Represented.

Prompt and equitable adjustments of loss guaranteed. Lowest obtainable rate, and satisfactory form of Policy secured.

HIGHEST NEW YORK AND NEWARK REFERENCES GIVEN.

Over Twenty-Five Years in the Business.

Member of the Metropolitan Board of Fire Insurance Brokers.

New York Office, No. 69 WILLIAM STREET.

Regularly licensed by the Secretary of State. Business solicited for the following named Companies, all regularly authorized to transact business in the State of New Jersey.

Alliance Insurance Association of New York.
Greenwich Fire Insurance Company of New York
Nassau Fire Insurance Company of New York.
Firemen's Fire Insurance Company of Baltimore.
Exchange Fire Insurance Company of New York.
North River Fire Insurance Company of New York.
National Fire Insurance Company of New York.

JAMES G. ALDEN, AGENT,

765 Broad Street,   **Newark, N. J.**

HENRY KELLER, Dealer in Choice Family Groceries, Provisions, Teas, Coffees, Sugars, Spices, etc., Hamburg Place, corner Merchant Street, Newark, N. J. If one were to have as many dollars as there are groceries in Newark, he could safely start up another with the capital so acquired. It is, however, natural that a city of this size should have many of these useful establishments, especially in view of the fact that it is somewhat spread out, and that it has several immediate suburbs. In this particular section, the grocer's sign greets the eye from many quarters, and we wonder how in the world they can all make a living. The reliable ones do, in fact, but the others find it up-hill work. One of the most prosperous is that conducted by Mr. Henry Keller, at No. 5 Hamburg Place, corner of Merchant street. This gentleman began business operations in the grocery line at the above stand, in the year 1880. This is ten years ago. Ever since its inception the store has found favor with the public, and it has thrived. This has been the direct outcome of hard work on Mr. Keller's part to satisfy his customers that at all times he would furnish none but strictly reliable goods at fair prices. Dealing squarely with the people is what has told the story of Mr. Keller's success, and we are pleased to congratulate the residents of the neighborhood in having in their midst an establishment so high in reputation. Mr. Keller is a native of Newark. He employs three hands, and his store is 27x42 feet in dimensions.

H. CHARMBURY, Manufacturer of Special Machinery, Models, Experimental Work and General Repairs, Sweat Leather, Tip and Over-stitch Machines, No. 271 Market Street, Newark, N. J. One of the most successful inventors of the present time is reported to have said that he found it almost as hard to get satisfactory models of his inventions made as to devise the machinery in the first place, and probably there is no inventor but what has experienced more or less trouble in this respect, for skilful and painstaking model makers, who will faithfully carry out instructions, and rigidly adhere to the plans submitted to them, are by no means common. We, therefore, take pleasure in calling attention to the facilities offered by Mr. H. Charmbury, doing business at No. 271 Market street, for he makes a specialty of manufacturing models, experimental work and special machinery, and has an enviable reputation for skill and reliability. His shop is fitted up with all necessary machinery to carry on operations to the best advantage, and as three competent assistants are employed,

orders can be filled at short notice. Mr. Charmbury is a native of England, and has carried on his present enterprise since 1888. He is moderate in his charges, and has built up quite an extensive business, of which the manufacture of sweat leather, tip and over-stitch machines is an important feature. General repairing is also done, no pains being spared to secure neatness and durability in every detail of the work.

DR. FRANK GILBERT GREGORY, Dentist, 740 Broad Street, Newark, N. J. If it is true that our American people have more trouble with their teeth, induced by climatic influences, or possibly by want of care, than any other nation, it is equally true, and universally recognized, that no dentists in the world can compete with the superior excellence attained by our countrymen. There are many of them settled in all the prominent European cities, who have more work than they can attend to. Even the late Czar of Russia, Alexander II., travelled from St. Petersburg to Paris, expressly to have his teeth put in order by our most famous American dentist, then stationed there, on receiving a despatch from this gentleman in answer to a command from His Imperial Majesty, that he had no time to travel, even to meet the wishes of this august personage. When we think of the tortures endured by our fathers and grandfathers, of the horrible turn-screws, and other barbarous instruments then in vogue, we cannot be too thankful to science and the genius of the professional men who have done so much for the public good, and the advancement of their profession. The modern dentist is no torturer, but a skilful surgeon and doctor, who watches ever, and treats the teeth as a physician does the body, and is ready to do the most elaborate and delicate work whenever occasion requires. It takes people a long time to realize that they are not saving trouble or expense by neglecting their teeth. If they would consult a good dentist for themselves and their children more frequently, they would find themselves better off in the end, both in health and pocket. In this connection we take pleasure in calling attention to the facilities at the command of Dr. Frank G. Gregory, of 611 Broad street. This gentleman has recently moved to Newark, having been practicing his profession prior to 1889, in Brooklyn, N. Y. His office and laboratory are fitted with the appliances and instruments used in modern dentistry, and by the conscientious performance of every operation, the doctor has gained a reputation that he may well be jealous of.

P. BALLANTINE & SONS, Fine XX &

XXX Ales and Porter, Stock, India Pale and Burton, foot Fulton Street, Newark, N. J. New York Office, 134 Washington Street. Ballantine & Co., Export Lager Beer, Freeman Street, Newark, N. J. If the testimony of the great majority of competent physicians, and the results of practical experience, are to be regarded as conclusive, then it may be stated as an established fact, that the reasonable use of pure malt liquors is as healthful as it is agreeable. The demand for such liquors has increased with phenomenal rapidity of late years, and some idea of its present magnitude may be gained from a few figures concerning a representative establishment engaged in their production—that of Messrs. P. Ballantine & Sons. The business conducted by this firm was founded some forty years ago, and their productions have long held their present leading position in the market, being conceded by chemists, by expert brewers, and by consumers in general, to have few equals, and no superiors, either in this country or elsewhere. There is certainly every reason why they should be equal to the best in every respect, for the firm have exceptional facilities, use the choicest selected material, and make it a rule to have every detail of the various processes incidental to production carried on by experienced workmen under close and skillful supervision. The premises utilized cover an area of about ten acres, and a number of substantial buildings, from four to eight stories in height, are made use of, the ale and porter brewery being located at the foot of Fulton street, while the plant employed in brewing Ballantine & Co's famous "export lager beer," is located on Freeman street. Fine XX and XXX ales and porter, stock, India pale and Burton are produced at the Fulton street brewery, an average of 1,200 barrels of ale being sent out daily, while 7,000 barrels of lager beer are sent to New York every day, besides a large number distributed among other cities. Employment is given to about 1,200 men, and though 200 horses are owned by the firm, and used to convey the product to the railway, a large proportion of that work has to be done by hired teams. In spite of its great magnitude, the business has by no means reached the limit of its growth, for orders are rapidly and steadily increasing, and will probably continue to do so as long as the firm maintain their present policy of keeping the product at the highest standard of excellence. **(SEE NEXT PAGE.)**

UNION STEAM LAUNDRY, 888 Broad

Sreet, Between Fair and Green Streets, Newark, N. J. Thomas F. Crowley, Proprietor, Telephone 344. One need not be very old to remember the storm of opposition which hailed the advent of the first public laundries, or rather the first machine laundries, for the introduction of the washing machinery now in general use, is of comparatively recent date, and few industries have developed so rapidly as has the laundry business during the past fifteen or twenty years. The public were warned, that the machinery would rip clothes to pieces, that fine linen would be burned beyond repair, the strongest materials would be rotted by chemicals, and havoc and ruin generally would result from patronizing these establishments, but still they were supported so liberally that their number has increased with phenomenal rapidity, and this increase is still going on—so the natural presumption is that the service they afford is efficient and satisfactory. The truth is, that some laundries destroy clothes, the same as some washerwomen working at home do, but in one case as in the other, the fault lies in the *abuse*, and not in the *use* of the system employed. The Union Steam Laundry, located at No. 888 Broad street, between Fair and Green streets, may be cited as a representative establishment of this kind, for it is one of the most liberally patronized laundries in the State, and offers a service unsurpassed for reliability, and general efficiency. The proprietor, Mr. Thos. F. Crowley, is a native of Newark, and has had long experience in his present line of business. The premises utilized, comprise four floors, measuring 40x40 feet, and are fitted up with a complete plant of the most improved machinery. Employment is given to forty assistants, and the various duties and responsibilities are so definitely placed that the greatest possible accuracy is attained, mistakes in delivery, etc., being of very infrequent occurrence. Laundry work will be called for and delivered in any part of the city, orders by mail or by telephone, No. 344, receiving prompt and careful attention. The price list is very equitably made up, and the charges will compare favorably with any quoted by other laundries turning out equally desirable work.

THOMAS WESTON, Boot and Shoe Fit-

tings, 78 Market Street, Newark, N. J. Notwithstanding that Massachusetts is the great shoe manufacturing centre of the country, there are other States where this industry is widely carried on, and in some cities it forms one of the principal branches of trade. Newark is far ahead of her neighbors in this branch of manufactures. It not only possesses a great number of wholesale and retail shoe stores, but large establishments which produce only certain parts of shoes. It is owing to this fact of large houses devoting themselves exclusively to the production of one class of articles and the economy of material, etc., thus attained, that the finished product can be purchased at such wonderfully low rates. If you were told the shoe you wear had been made partially at three or four different factories, you would undoubtedly at first be much surprised, yet not hundreds, but hundreds of thousands of shoes are made in this way, not differing in any particular from the shoes begun and finished under the same roof. Prominent among the houses engaged in the manufacture of boots and shoe fittings in Newark, is Mr. Thomas Weston. He is a native of Northampton, England, where he learned his trade. He came to this country some years ago and settled in Newark, where he began practicing his present trade in 1879. Since that time his business has gone on steadily increasing until he has all the orders he can attend to. The premises occupied are at 78 Market street, in the midst of the manufacturing interests of the city. Occupation is given to twelve employees, who are competent to turn out first-class goods. Any kind of boot and shoe fittings are made here, and all orders receive prompt and careful attention.

WILLIAM E. GRAY, Tailor and Draper,

792 Broad Street, Newark, N. J. The establishment conducted by Mr. William E. Gray, at No. 792 Broad street, is one of particular interest to those who desire to dress correctly, for Mr. Gray is one of the leading tailors and drapers of New Jersey, and the garments produced by him will compare favorably with any of which we have knowledge, for they are unexceptionable in cut, fit and making, and will give entire satisfaction to the most fastidious, while the prices quoted are as low as is consistent with the maintenance of the high standard of merit essential to the attainment of such results as these. Mr. Gray is a native of England, and has carried on his present enterprise since 1880, during which time he has built up an extensive and select patronage, and largely increased his facilities for production. The premises utilized are 24x75 feet in dimensions, and contain a heavy and very carefully selected stock of foreign and domestic fabrics for gentlemen's wear, including the latest fashionable novelties as well as a full line of staple goods. The productions of some of the leading manufacturers are represented, and many exclusive patterns are provided—a policy appreciated and availed of by those who prefer individuality of dress. Employment is afforded to thirty experienced assistants, so that despite the magnitude of the business, orders can be filled at short notice, no pains being spared to deliver them promptly when promised.

S. A. DARRACH, Inventor and Manufac-

turer of Orthopedic Apparatus, 626 Broad Street, Newark, N. J. Medicine can do much when skillfully used, but it is limited in its powers, and the most successful physicians will be the first to admit that some diseases and many weaknesses are best cured and most surely relieved by mechanical means. Unfortunately some of the trusses and other specimens of orthopedic apparatus in the market are so poorly designed or badly constructed as to be more harmful than beneficial, and it cannot be too strongly insisted upon that whatever mechanical appliances are used, should be of the most approved design and most honest and skillful manufacture. We take pleasure in calling attention to the productions of Mr. S. A. Darrach, as they are designed and constructed on sound scientific principles. Mr. Darrach has carried on the business which he is now engaged in since 1872, and has invented many new and important appliances, which he manufactures. Among his leading specialties are "Darrach's Wheeled crutch" and "Darrach's apparatus for the treatment of spinal curvature and other deformities." Both of these have received the endorsement of the most eminent and practical physicians and surgeons, and have proved their value by the superior results attained.

P. BALLANTINE & SONS ALE BREWERY AND MALT HOUSE.

BALLANTINE & CO.'S LAGER BEER BREWERY.

PRICE'S ✳ NEW ✳ PHOTOGRAPH ✳ STUDIO,

923 Broad Street, Newark,

Next Door to Old Stand.

Everything New and Elegant, Best Light in the City, Fine Toilet Room with Every Convenience,

A-1 WORK AT POPULAR PRICES.

Most people have no difficulty in determining whether they like a photograph or not, but when they are asked to tell their reasons for admiring one and condemning the other, they often find it hard to put them into words. And, indeed, there are so many things going to make up a really artistic and satisfactory photograph that it is no wonder that something is lacking in a great deal of work of this kind. Mr. Price has been very successful in suiting the most critical among his patrons since he began operations in Newark, and in our opinion, the results attained at his studio will compare favorably with the work of the leading photographers. He has the most improved facilities at his command, and produces portraits which are clearly worthy of the name, as they are not only all that could be desired as regards perfection of me-

chanical finish, etc., but reflect the individuality of the sitter in a remarkably faithful manner, light, posing, the arrangement of accessories, etc. All these details are carefully attended to by Mr. Price, and the re-touching of the negative, the prominence given one feature, and the softened effect given another, all are carried out in a manner that indicates careful study, wide experience, and an earnest desire to come as near perfection as possible. Crayon portraits are made a specialty. Mr. Price gives employment to four thoroughly competent assistants, and is prepared to fill all orders at the shortest possible notice, and at moderate prices. His new gallery will be found the best lighted, finest appointed and most convenient in this section.

A. C. BECKWITH, Practical Metal Pattern Maker, for Malleable, Grey Iron and Composition Castings, Special Attention Given to Experimenting and Perfecting Inventors' Ideas, 271 Market Street, Newark, N. J. One need not be a mechanic to be able to appreciate the fact that the value of a casting depends greatly upon the accuracy of the pattern from which it is made, but there are many, even among those who are classed as mechanics, who have no adequate idea of the difficulties to be overcome in some kinds of pattern making. In some branches of this trade the very nicest accuracy is absolutely essential, and in order to attain the desired results, the nature of the material from which the casting is to be made must be thoroughly understood and allowances made to suit the circumstances of the case. It is hardly necessary to add that thoroughly first-class pattern-makers are not common, and that, therefore, it is well to use discrimination in the placing of orders calling for special skill and intelligence. In this connection it is fitting that we call attention to the service offered by Mr. A. C. Beckwith, who has a shop at 271 Market street, and is a practical metal pattern maker of long experience. He is a native of New York State, and is very generally known in mechanical circles, among his customers being some of the leading iron and brass founders in this section. Mr. Beckwith makes patterns for malleable, grey iron and composition castings, and gives special attention to experimenting and perfecting inventors' ideas. He employs three assistants, and is in a position to fill orders at short notice, and at reasonable rates. Among his references are the following well known concerns: Barlow, Condit & Morris, iron founders; S. J. Meeker, iron founder; Dehart & Clark, iron founders; E. Jost, machinist and brass founder; Pratt & Letchworth, Buffalo, N. Y.; George M. Ballard, iron founder; Miles Sweeney, brass founder; Edward Zust, brass founder; Oscar Barnett, iron founder; Oriskany Malleable iron company, N. Y.

WM. ZIMMERMANN & BRO., Stationers and Newsdealers, Books, Games, Toys, Fine Confectionery, Cigars, etc. Daily and Weekly Papers, Magazines, etc., Delivered Prompt and Early. No. 98 Clinton Avenue, corner Thomas Street, Newark, N. J. The man who does not read the newspaper, most certainly deprives himself of one of the best and most easily attained means of acquiring a liberal education, and it is beyond doubt, that this neglect, will, sooner or later, prove a drawback to his ultimate success in business. The United States is more of a newspaper

country than any other, for our people wish to be well informed, and to know what is going on in the world. All this wealth of information may be obtained for the nominal price of a few cents per day, and he is foolish who begrudges this small outlay. All the leading daily and weekly papers and magazines are to be found at No. 98 Clinton avenue, corner of Thomas street, where the Messrs. Zimmermann Bros. have a most attractive and well stocked establishment. Their business is retail, and their premises comprise an entire floor. They also have a great variety of fine stationery—confectionery of all kinds, cigars and a large stock of books, games and toys. Employment is given to ten carriers, who attend to all customers promptly and courteously. The firm consists of Messrs. William and Alfred Zimmermann, the former being a native of New York city, the latter of New Jersey. They have carried on this business since 1882, and have become one of the most popular houses in this part of the city.

PATRICK McCABE, Merchant Tailor, 870 Broad Street, Newark, N. J. It is not necessary to have a great deal of experience in buying, in order to appreciate the fact that the first cost of an article by no means always indicates whether it is "cheap" or not, for it soon becomes evident that durability, as well as lowness of cost, must be considered in order to invest money to the best advantage. Take it, for instance, in the matter of clothing, and there is no one but what will concede that some garments are dear at any price. There are many who have always worn ready-made clothing, and who think that garments made to order must necessarily be expensive and beyond their means, but were they to have a suit made by an experienced and skillful tailor, they would soon change their minds, for a custom made suit will wear longer, look better, and in short, give more lasting satisfaction than one ready-made possibly can. Our readers can easily make a trial anyway, for Mr. Patrick McCabe is prepared to fill orders for custom clothing at short notice, and at moderate prices, and guarantee satisfaction to his customers. He began operations in 1882, and carries on a well equipped custom tailoring establishment. We are happy to be able to say that his enterprise has been appreciated, and a thriving trade built up. Callers may depend upon receiving immediate and polite attention. Mr. McCabe is thoroughly familiar with his business in every detail, and his garments are not only cut in the latest style, but are warranted to fit to the satisfaction of the most critical.

BENJAMIN F. HURD, Architect, Room
3, No. 1 Cedar Street, Newark, N. J. The advisability of employing an architect in building operations depends considerably, of course, upon the circumstances of the case, but, in the vast majority of instances, it is perfectly safe to assert, that money spent for an architect's services is very profitably invested, inasmuch as the result is the saving of time and trouble, the assurance of having things carried out as you want them, and very often the saving of considerable money in the items of material and labor. Of course, it is assumed that the architect is competent and reliable, and, happily, this is generally a safe assumption to make, for the profession is on a par with that of medicine or of law, and attracts many able and honorable men. Mr. Benjamin F. Hurd has carried on operations as an architect in this city since February 1, 1880, and his work has excited much favorable comment among those who have had occasion to become conversant with it, for Mr. Hurd is very thorough and painstaking in his methods, and as he is excellently grounded in the principles of his profession, he attains results which give the best of satisfaction. Plans and specifications for new buildings, alterations, etc., will be drawn up at short notice, the interests of clients being carefully guarded in every legitimate way. The work of construction will be personally supervised if desired, at a small additional charge, and material and workmanship will be kept fully up to the agreed standard. Mr. Hurd has an office at No. 1 Cedar street, room 3, and all communications are assured immediate and careful attention.

EHRLICH, HEINZ & SINNOCK, Manu-
facturers of Fine Jewelry and Diamond Mounting, 331 Mulberry street, Newark, N. J. Jewelers say that a large proportion of the diamond jewelry sold, loses much of its possible effect by reason of the unskilful setting of the stones, and it is generally known that a really fine diamond may be made to compare unfavorably with a decidedly inferior stone, by being set to poor advantage. Of course, fashion has much to do with the setting of all precious stones, but those who may truthfully be called artists in this line of business can always succeed in setting a stone prominently and securely as well. Messrs. Ehrlich, Heinz & Sinnock are prominent manufacturers of fine jewelry and diamond mounting, and the fact that among their customers are numbered some of the leading dealers, is of itself enough to indicate the character of their work. The business was founded in 1884 by Messrs. Ehrlich & Heinz, the present firm having begun operations in January, 1888. Messrs. Ehrlich and Sinnock are natives of New Jersey, and Mr. Heinz of Germany. The shop is located at No. 331 Mulberry street, and is equipped with improved machinery, etc., employment being given to twenty assistants, and orders being filled at short notice, and at uniformly moderate rates.

BIMBLER, VAN WAGENEN & CO.,
Hog Slaughterers and Packers, 50 and 52 Plane Street, Newark, N. J. There is a decided contrast in the methods employed in the handling of meats nowadays to those in vogue comparatively a few years ago, and we need hardly add that the result of the contrast is all in favor of existing modes of procedure. One of the best equipped pork packing houses in this State is that carried on by Messrs. Bimbler, Van Wagenen & Co., at Nos. 50 and 52 Plane street, and some idea of the magnitude and perfection of the equipment may be gained from the fact that the firm handle about 150 hogs per day without the least straining of their resources. The concern is made up of Messrs. F. G. Bimbler, V. Van Wagenen and the firm of Swift Brothers, known throughout this country and also across the sea. The business was founded in 1885, and as the concern are prepared to meet all honorable competition in their special line, it is natural that their trade should have reached large proportions, it now necessitating the employment of thirty-eight assistants. The works are equipped with a fifty-horse engine and two fifty horse boilers, and have every facility for shipping, including a spur track running to the door of the packing house. Pork products of standard quality are wholesaled at the lowest prevailing rates, orders by mail or by telephone No. 334 being assured instant and careful attention, and the goods furnished being suited to the most critical trade.

R. W. BOND & CO., Wholesale Liquors, 11
Fair Street, Newark, N. J. The business conducted by Messrs. R. W. Bond & Co., is of very long standing, and it is safe to assert, that no local house in the wholesale liquor trade, bears a more enviable reputation for supplying goods of standard merit, at the lowest market rates. Many prominent retailers obtain the bulk of their supplies at this representative establishment, and dealers who are dissatisfied with their present service, and wish to secure goods that will enable them to cater successfully to the most fastidious trade, may profitably place an order here, for Messrs. R. W. Bond & Co., are prepared to furnish the choicest whiskies and the leading brands of imported and domestic wines, liquors, etc., at prices as low as can be quoted on goods of equal merit. The premises occupied are located at No. 11 Fair street, and constantly contain a very carefully chosen stock, the firm being in a position to fill the most extensive orders without delay. Employment is given to three assistants, and all communications are assured immediate and painstaking attention.

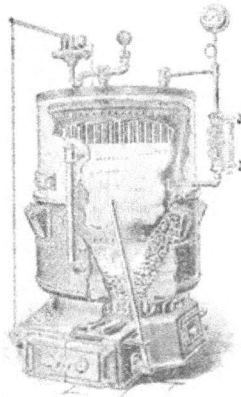

SUTCLIFFE & NOON, Steam Heating
Engineers, Jobbing promptly attended to, Steam Fitting a specialty, 872 Broad St., Newark, N. J. Practically all dwelling houses of the better class, as well as all factories, stores and public buildings in general, constructed nowadays, are equipped with steam heating apparatus, as this affords by far the most economical and manageable method of supplying artificial heat, but it sometimes happens that the efficiency of the plant is seriously interfered with by its being improperly set up, and, therefore, it is well to entrust such work only to those who make a specialty of it, and are known to be skilful and reliable. Messrs. Sutcliffe & Noon have an unsurpassed reputation in this respect, and have all necessary facilities to enable them to fill orders promptly and satisfactorily at moderate rates. The firm are practical plumbers, gas and steam fitters, and have carried on operations since 1878, the partners being James Sutcliffe and James Noon, the former a native of Pennsylvania, and the latter of this State. Jobbing of all kinds is promptly attended to, employment being given to eight assistants, and a specialty being made of steam fitting. The firm will furnish any style of steam-heating apparatus desired, but recommend the Gorton side-feed boiler for house heating, as it is especially designed for that purpose, is very economical in the use of fuel, and being automatically self-feeding it requires but very little care. The feed arrangement is such that choking is impossible, and the coal is evenly distributed over the entire grate, while the coal pockets are so placed that the reservoir can be as easily filled as an ordinary range. These boilers are thoroughly well made from selected material, and are durable and absolutely safe from explosion. They are adapted for both steam and hot water heating and are guaranteed to do all that is claimed for them.

DRAKE & CO., Attorneys in Patent Cases

before the United States Courts, 166 Market Street, Newark, N. J. It is, of course, not absolutely necessary for a person seeking to get out a patent on some recent invention, to solicit the aid of an attorney, but it is certainly for his interest to do so. There is always a certain amount of "red tape" about any such business, and a novice in such matters who tries to manage everything for himself, is more than likely to find himself "plucked" by some sharper, such as are always lurking about looking for prey. Then, again, a man who gives his special attention to these matters is more likely to succeed than an inexperienced one, no matter how clever and wise he may be in other matters. There is no need for Newark people to go out of their way to find such a man, for there are firms in their midst who devote themselves to this class of business, foremost among which we would mention Messrs. Drake & Co. This house commenced operations in Newark in 1867; later the partnership was dissolved, Mr. Oliver Drake becoming the sole representative, and in 1879 it again became Drake & Co. The members of the present firm are Oliver Drake, a native of New Jersey, and Charles H. Pell, of New York. They are attorneys in patent cases before the United States courts, and solicitors of American and foreign patents. Added to this, they are mechanical and electrical engineers and experts, having a thorough knowledge of this business, which is so often of extreme importance in regard to patent cases. Messrs. Drake & Co. occupy an office at 166 Market street. Here they are pleased to welcome anyone in need of their services. A consultation can do no harm, especially as it is free, and it may prove of great benefit.

A. H. BURKHARDT, Dealer in Fine

Groceries, Teas, Coffees, Sugars, Spices, etc., Fruits and Vegetables in Season, Flour, Feed and Grain, 246 Ferry Street, corner Ferguson, Newark, N. J. A representative enterprise in this neighborhood is that conducted by Mr. A. H. Burkhardt, dealer in fine groceries, teas, sugars, spices, etc., fruits and vegetables in season, flour, feed and grain. It was inaugurated in the year 1877, by Mr. Burkhardt in person, and under his skillful management it has thrived since its very inception. Mr. Burkhardt is a native of Germany, but as he has resided here and been in business in our midst so long (twenty-three years, he has made a large circle of both business and social friends. He was for four years one of the Board of School Commissioners, a fact which shows that he is a highly esteemed member of the community. He gives employment to four courteous and competent assistants in his business, and his store is 25x45 feet in dimension. He also utilizes a store-house 16x52 feet in dimension, for duplicates, etc., his hay and feed being stored in a spacious shed. Mr. Burkhardt has acquired an enviable run of custom during his business career. His invariably and strictly honest business methods and policy is what told the story of his success, and which tells it in any business. Our readers need but place a trial order with this establishment to be convinced that our favorable mention of it is not out of place. Remember the place, No. 246 Ferry street, A. H. Burkhardt, grocer.

ALEX. M. LINNETT'S Lincoln Park Phar-

macy. Prescriptions a Specialty, Clinton Avenue, corner Washington Street, Newark, N. J. An establishment in which the residents of Newark put great confidence, is that of which Mr. Alexander M. Linnett is the proprietor, for during the twenty years that this house has been in existence, it has been invariably managed in a straightforward and painstaking manner, that is worthy of unreserved commendation. Mr. Linnett was born and brought up in Newark, and settled himself in business here in 1880. Two years ago he moved into his present quarters, which are handsomely and conveniently fitted up for the purpose. The store is conveniently situated at the corner of Clinton avenue and Washington street, and covers an area of 20x70 feet. Mr. Linnett lets no element of chance enter into the operation of the prescription department, for he makes a specialty of this, having the most improved facilities for it, and employing only experienced and trustworthy assistants. These average about four. They know their business, and, thus, annoying delays rarely occur. The charges made are always as reasonable as could be expected, where only the best drugs and materials are used.

THE SEARLS-RANDALL Co., Successors

to Searls Manufacturing Co., of Newark, N. J. and P. D. Randall & Co., of Troy, N. Y. Manufacturers of Whip Sockets, Carriage and Sleigh Mountings. Newark, N. J. The Searls-Randall Company is of comparatively recent origin, having been organized in 1889, but the enterprise with which it is identified is of much longer standing, it having been inaugurated in 1874, by Mr. Anson Searls. Ten years later the Searls Manufacturing Company was formed, this concern being succeeded by the existing company, of which Mr. Anson Searls is President; Mr. P. D. Randall, Vice President, and Mr. Frederick Woodruff, Secretary and Treasurer. Messrs. Searls and Randall are natives of New York State, and Mr. Woodruff of this city. All these gentlemen are too well known in business circles hereabouts to render extended personal mention necessary. The Searls-Randall Company is really the result of a consolidation of the Searls Manufacturing Company, and P. D. Randall & Company, of Troy, N. Y., and is very extensively engaged in the manufacture of whip sockets, carriage and sleigh mountings; producing a full line of these goods of standard merit. The premises utilized comprise three floors of the dimensions of 55x350 feet, and are fitted up with the very latest improved machinery, employment being given to fifty assistants. Many attractive and some exclusive designs are shown, and both as regards workmanship and material, the product will compare favorably with any in the market, no pains being spared to attain uniformly satisfactory and dependable results.

E. T. ANDRUSS, Watchmaker and Jeweler,

350 Broad Street, Newark, N. J. Particular attention given to repairing. It is a mistake to suppose that it is always possible to make a saving in the purchasing of goods by buying them in large city establishments, for in not a few instances it will be found that quite the contrary is the case, and that actually better bargains are obtainable of our local dealers, than are to be had in more pretentious city establishments. But without entering into any argument on this subject, we may at least point out an establishment where the prices are uniformly low, the goods uniformly reliable, and the treatment accorded to callers, uniformly courteous, and this store may be found at No. 350 Broad street, under the control of Mr. E. T. Andruss. The enterprise was inaugurated in 1874, by the present proprietor, who has no small reason to congratulate himself on the manner in which his business has increased since its inception. His store covers an area of 540 square feet, and the stock carried is an extremely varied and desirable one, including watches, clocks, jewelry, etc., which we have before stated, are offered at very low rates. Mr. Andruss is a native of Newark, and is very well known throughout the city. Three competent assistants are employed, and particular attention is given to repairing. We can heartily commend this establishment, as every effort is made to combine satisfactory and durable results with low prices.

CHRIST. A. FISCHER. Masquerade and

Theatre Costumes, Wigs, Beards, etc., etc, 158 Mulberry Street, Near Market Street, Newark, N. J. **The Largest Assortment in the State.** There is probably not a resident of Newark, at all interested in private theatricals or masquerades, that does not know Mr. Christian A. Fischer, by reputation at least, for this gentleman, although a native of Germany, has been a Newark costumer for thirty years, and is, unquestionably, more widely and favorably known than any other costumer in New Jersey. Perhaps this may seem an extreme statement to those not acquainted with Mr. Fischer's standing and methods, but it is fully justified by the facts, and investigation will simply prove it. The premises made use of are located at No. 158 Mulberry street, near Market street, and comprise two floors of the dimensions of 20x60 feet. They are fitted up with all necessary facilities, and as employment is given to eight assistants, Mr. Fischer is prepared to make costumes of anything in his line to order, at surprisingly short notice, in cases where haste is essential. He carries a very heavy stock of masquerade and theatre costumes, wigs, beards, etc., the assortment being the largest and most complete in the State. We need hardly add, that he is in a position to quote bottom prices, and to faithfully carry out every agreement made, order work being delivered promptly at the time promised.

EMIL HERRMANN, 225 Plane Street.

Newark, N. J. If the public were as easily frightened as some writers seem to think it is, it would before this have almost abandoned the use of groceries, for certain newspapers have of late years devoted columns of space to a consideration of the alleged adulteration practiced in such articles. But the American people have, fortunately, too much common sense to be easily panic-stricken, and, indeed, the report of the commission of experts employed by the government to investigate the subject of food adulteration is, of itself, enough to squelch the alarmists, who would persuade us that we are all getting poisoned every day, for it sums up the result of the careful tests made in this sentence: "We find that the rumors of food adulteration are, in few instances, based on facts, and that the percentage of harmful adulterations is so small as to be practically unworthy of consideration." These are not the exact words, but they indicate correctly the conclusion arrived at. If a reputable house be patronized, there is no danger of being supplied with other than wholesome groceries, and as reliable an establishment as is conducted in this city is that of which Mr. Emil Herrmann is the proprietor, and which is located at No. 225 Plane street. The enterprise under consideration was started in 1887, by Messrs. Herrmann & Stern, and so continued until April, 1890, when Mr. Emil Herrmann assumed entire control of the business. A thriving retail trade has been built up, requiring the services of three competent assistants. This has been done by the handling of goods of excellent quality and by supplying the same at rates that will bear the severest comparison with those of other dealers. A fine assortment of family groceries is at all times on hand, and all orders are filled with an accuracy and despatch well worthy of notice.

ANDREW'S ART GALLERY, 701 Broad

Street, corner Cedar, Newark N. J. Finest Portraits in Water Colors, Crayon, Pastel and Oil. Crayon portraiture, as an art, at the present day, has been sadly abused. The many would-be artists, whose work has been almost wholly done for them by the photographer, have put before the public such inferior specimens, that faith in any good work of this kind has been greatly shaken. Real artists in crayon are few. To make a perfect likeness requires not only a natural taste for the art, and a thorough knowledge of the manner of execution, but also a study of all the minutest details which go to make up that wonderful effect—expression. In entrusting an artist to make a likeness in water colors, crayon, pastel, or oil, only those of the greatest ability can be relied on for satisfactory results. The work in either of the above named lines is displayed at Andrew's art gallery, is of the best. The gallery has been established for more than twelve years. Portrait work of every description is here executed with perfect correctness, taste and finish, as is testified by the portraits being found in the homes of the most influential and prominent business men, lawyers and clergymen of Newark. Andrew's art gallery is located on the second floor of the building, 701 Broad street, corner Cedar. It is of ample dimensions, and there is every facility for executing the finest portraits in pastel, water colors, crayon, oil and India ink, from locket to life size, from original pictures or from life. Special attention is invited to the life size pastel portraits at $25, and to a line of crayons from five dollars upwards. Specimens will always be cheerfully shown. A large and fine collection of portraits may be seen of notable men, Gen. Grant, Horace Greeley, Bishop Starkey, and others. No portrait is allowed to leave the gallery until perfect in every detail. The gallery is open until nine on Saturday evening, and visitors are always welcome.

WM. G. KUGLER, Ph. G., Druggist, 1123

Broad Street, corner Parkhurst, Newark, N. J. The drug store conducted by Mr. Wm. G. Kugler, is already well and favorably known to a large portion of the public, and under his able management we believe that it is bound to steadily gain in popularity and patronage. Mr. Kugler has gained his experience in New York city, graduating from the N. Y. College of Pharmacy. He is a native of New Jersey, and has a large circle of friends and patrons here in Newark. The undertaking in question was founded by him in 1889, and is located at No. 1123 Broad street, corner of Parkhurst street, comprising one floor, 20x70 feet in dimensions. Two thoroughly competent clerks are constantly employed, and the stock of drugs, medicines, chemicals, etc., is unusually complete, being made up of selected articles from the most reputable sources. Mr. Kugler makes a specialty of the compounding of physicians' prescriptions, and, therefore, sparing no trouble or expense in preparing himself to satisfactorily meet all demands that may be made upon him. He is a pharmacist of skill and experience, and may safely be entrusted with the most difficult and unusual prescriptions. No precaution is neglected, and error is thus made practically impossible. The charges made are very reasonable, and the stock of toilet goods, fancy articles, etc., is also quoted at very low prices.

C. SULLIVAN, Mechanical Engineer, 187½

Market Street, Residence, 75 Arlington Street, Newark, N. J. There is a right way, and there is a wrong way to generate and to utilize steam power, and as the circumstances vary so in every case, that few set rules can be laid down, the only satisfactory method to pursue, is to employ the services of an experienced and able engineer, whose training will enable him to take advantage of all favorable conditions, and reduce to a minimum, the effects of unfavorable conditions. He can thus save money for his customers by avoiding waste of power and of fuel, to say nothing of the saving made in wear and tear when a mechanical plant is arranged and adjusted as it should be. Mr. C. Sullivan, mechanical engineer, is an acknowledged expert on all questions pertaining to the use of steam, and being thoroughly practical in his methods, offers a service, whose value to manufacturers and steam-users in general can hardly be overestimated. He is a native of Vermont, and has had long experience in his profession, but has been identified with the machine-shop, etc., he carries on at No. 187 1-2 Market street, only since February 1, 1890. The premises made use of comprise two floors, measuring 25x80 feet each, fitted up with improved machinery, and containing all necessary facilities to enable orders to be filled in a thoroughly workmanlike manner at short notice, and at reasonable rates. Mr. Sullivan is prepared to furnish all kinds of machinery, boilers, etc., at the lowest market rates, and gives special attention to all kinds of pipe fitting and steam heating. Pipe will be cut and threaded from one-fourth inch to eight inch, inclusive, and repairing in all its branches, and general jobbing promptly and skilfully done. Old plants will be reconstructed on modern and economical principles, satisfaction being confidently guaranteed. Mr. Sullivan resides at No. 75 Arlington street, and communications addressed there or to 187 1-2 Market street, are assured prompt and careful attention.

BROAD STREET GRANITE WORKS.

G. A. Williams, Granite Works, No. 412 Broad Street, near M. & E. R. R., Newark, N. J., Residence, No. 118 Orange Street, American and Scotch Granite, also Galvanized Iron Railings, Cemetery Furniture, etc. Granite is one of the most durable of all building stones, and is used to a greater extent than any other, at least such is the case here in New Jersey. Its chief cost, of course, always has been that of working it, for it is one of the hardest of stones, but by improved tools and appliances, it can now be prepared much more readily than was formerly the case, and is coming more and more into use, not only as a building, but also as an ornamental stone, being used in tablets, monuments, etc. The Broad Street Granite Works, of which Mr. G. A. Williams is the proprietor (located at No. 412, near M. & E. R. R.), is one of the best known in this city. The enterprise under question, was inaugurated nearly twenty years ago, being founded by Messrs. Church & Williams, in 1871. In 1874, Mr. G. A. Williams, the present proprietor, assumed entire control of the business. American and Scotch granite are extensively dealt in, both at wholesale and retail, also galvanized iron railings, cemetery furniture, etc. Monumental, building and cemetery work of every description is also done in the most satisfactory manner. The premises occupied are 50x160 feet in dimensions, and are fitted up with all requisite facilities for the proper conduct of the business, these being operated by an eight horse-power engine. Eight skilled assistants are employed, and judging from the past record of this house, all customers may depend upon receiving prompt and careful attention. Many tasteful and original designs in the way of monumental work, etc., are to be seen at these spacious granite works.

LINNETT MFG. CO., Manufacturers of Fine Shirts, 45 and 47 Mechanic Street, Newark, N. J. A shirt seems a very simple garment to those who have never examined closely the various parts constituting it, but as a matter of fact it is probable that no other one article of wear has attracted so much attention, and been the subject of so many efforts to improve it. Many thousands of dollars are invested in shirt manufacturing, and a representative concern in this line of business is the Linnett Manufacturing Company, located at Nos. 45 and 47 Mechanic street, where two floors are utilized, each measuring 50x75 feet. This company manufacture fine shirts in general, and make a specialty of custom work, their facilities enabling them to fill the most extensive orders at short notice, and to attain results which cannot fail to prove entirely satisfactory, even to the most fastidious. Employment is given to seventy-five operatives, and every process incidental to production is so carefully supervised as to insure the maintenance of the high standard so long associated with the productions of this well known establishment. Operations were begun by Messrs. Jolley & Linnett in 1878, and this firm were succeeded by the present company, who, with enlarged facilities, are better prepared than ever before to promptly fill the heaviest orders to the entire satisfaction of all parties concerned.

ROBERTSON & LEBER, Gold, Silver and Platinum Refining, Jewelers' Sweepings a Specialty, 13 and 15 Franklin Street, Newark, N. J. In a city where the precious metals are so extensively worked as is the case in Newark, it is not surprising that there should be a number of establishments somewhat similar to that conducted by Messrs. Robertson & Leber, for the premises made use of by this concern are equipped with all necessary machinery and appliances for the refining of gold, silver and platinum. They comprise two floors, each measuring 40x160 feet, and are located at Nos. 13 and 15 Franklin street. The firm is constituted of Messrs. William L. Robertson and Leopold L. Leber, both of whom are natives of Newark, and are extremely well known here, particularly in trade circles. Although doing gold, silver and platinum refining in general the firm make a specialty of the handling of jewelers' sweepings, and can treat such at short notice and in the most approved manner, their charges being as low as the lowest. The business is rapidly increasing, and under present methods of management is evidently destined to continue to do so for an indefinite period.

HOWARD A. SMITH, Bicycle Supplies, Oraton Hall, Newark, N. J. The wonderful development of cycling during the comparatively few years that bicycles have been introduced into this country, is one of the most noteworthy and encouraging signs of the times, for it indicates that as a nation we are alive to the importance of outdoor recreations, and are ready and willing to welcome anything that will tend to popularize physical exercise in the open air. Of the delights of cycling, this is not the place to speak, suffice it to say, no one who has once mastered the steel horse will willingly give up riding, and every rider is sure to entreat his non-riding friends, to "go and do likewise." Although but little more than a decade has elapsed since the American advent of bicycles, their name is now legion, and the would-be purchaser is apt to be bewildered by the almost boundless opportunity for choice presented to him, but, although one's personal tastes will best determine whether a "high wheel," "safety," "crank" or "lever" machine is best suited to him, one rule applies to all, and that is, get a strictly high-graded machine at all events, for "cheap" bicycles are not only dangerous, but are far the most expensive in the long run. One of the leading dealers in bicycle supplies in this section of the country, is Mr. Howard A. Smith, doing business in Oraton Hall, where very commodious and finely equipped premises are utilized. This gentleman began operations in 1883, as a member of the firm of Bacharias & Smith, and assumed sole control three years later. He occupies a prominent position in wheeling circles, being a successful inventor of cycling accessories etc., and a member of the New Jersey Wheelmen, Atalanta and Business Men's clubs. Mr. Smith is prepared to fill all orders without delay, and every article furnished by him is sure to prove just as represented, and to be supplied at the lowest market rates.

F. R. SMITH'S Carpenter Shop, also, The New Bridge Feed Co., Hay, Straw, Grain, Oats, Bran, Feed, etc., 92 and 94 Clay Street, corner Mount Pleasant Avenue. Mr. F. R. Smith is a well-known carpenter and builder, and his shop at No. 94 Clay street, is one of the most largely patronized establishments of the kind in the city, for the proprietor has a well earned reputation for filling jobbing orders in a skillful and satisfactory manner, and for the prompt and faithful carrying out of building contracts, but it is not our purpose to speak especially of the carpentering service he is prepared to offer, but rather to call attention to the inducements held out by the New Bridge Feed Company, of which he is proprietor. This enterprise was inaugurated in 1890, and is already an assured success, for the public have learned that the company are prepared to furnish hay, straw, grain, oats, bran, feed, etc., in any desired quantities without delay, and at the very lowest market rates, the quality of the goods being strictly dependable in every instance. The premises occupied are located at 92 and 94 Clay street, corner of Mt. Pleasant avenue, and constantly contain a heavy and varied stock, while the employment of two assistants insure immediate and careful attention to every caller.

JAMES. W. DECKERT, Leather Splitting. Wet Stock and Finished Leather, Seal, Morocco, Sheep and Grain Leather Split as Required. Dealer in Russet Buffings, Grain, Pocket-book and Book-binders Leather, etc. Agent for Porter Belt Knives, Waltham Emery Wheels, New and Re-covered Rubber Rolls, No. 355 Ogden Street, Newark, N. J. The establishment conducted by Mr. James W. Decker, at No. 355 Ogden street, is not only one of the most useful in the city, but is positively unique, it being the only one in the entire country devoted exclusively to leather splitting. Mr. Deckert is a native of Tennessee, and founded his present business in 1887. That it has steadily and rapidly developed may be readily imagined from the fact that employment is now given to thirty-five assistants, aided by the most efficient leather splitting machinery in the market. The premises made use of comprise seven floors of the dimensions of 60x150 feet, and are fitted up with all necessary facilities for the splitting of wet stock and finished leather. Mr. Deckert is prepared to split seal, Morocco, sheep and grain leather as desired, and pays expressage one way on all lots of ten dozen or more. He respectfully solicits the patronage of manufacturers of leather goods, being confident that in the majority of instances he can save them money, and in every case can guarantee prompt, accurate and reliable service. He deals in russet buffings, grain, pocket-book and bookbinders' leather, etc., furnishing them in quantities to suit at bottom prices. Mr. Deckert is agent for Porter Belt Knives and Waltham Emery Wheels, and can furnish these and new and re-covered rubber rolls at manufacturers' prices, and at very short notice.

G. W. WARD, Manufacturer of Confectionery and Ice Cream, 61 Pennsylvania Avenue, Newark, N. J. An unfailing sign of the metropolitan character of a city is the existence of a first-class confectionery and ice cream establishment in its midst. The expenses of such an establishment are necessarily large, and unless it receives extended and continuous support, it cannot long be maintained in proper condition. It is gratifying, therefore, in preparing this review of Newark's business houses, to be able to point out such an establishment as that carried on by Mr. G. W. Ward, for the more one is acquainted with what constitutes a well equipped confectionery and ice cream establishment, the more thoroughly convinced he will be of the excellence of that mentioned. Mr. Ward is manufacturer of confectionery and ice cream, and has carried on his establishment since 1871, and has constantly added to his facilities until they have reached their present magnitude. His premises are located at No. 61 Pennsylvania avenue, where confections and ice cream of all kinds are made and sold, in connection with stationery, etc. The store occupied is 20x70 feet in dimensions, and an extensive retail trade is transacted in these goods, which require the services of six assistants. Those wishing pure and freshly made confectionery and ice cream should by all means give Mr. Ward a call, especially as his prices are uniformly reasonable.

THOMAS & COURTER, Manufacturers of Machinery, Superior Cylinder and Signal Oils, non-Corrosive boiler Compound, Wholesale and Retail Dealers in Paints, Oils, Varnishes, Window Glass, Chemicals, Anilines, Dye-woods, etc. Agents for Dundee Chemical Works, Hatters' Supplies of every description, 209 Market Street, Newark, N. J. Telephone 612. In every manufacturing and mercantile centre, there are certain old established houses generally known, and conceded to be leaders in their special lines of business, and Newark is no exception to the rule, for in every standard department of trade she can show concerns truly representative in every sense of the word. Prominent among these, is the firm of Thomas & Courter, which was established in 1862, and has held a leading position in the oil, paint and chemical trade. The partners are Messrs. George A. Thomas and Albert C. Courter, both of whom are so generally known in business and social circles throughout this vicinity, as to render mention quite unnecessary. The firm manufacture a line of cylinder, machine, and signal oils, belt grease, boiler fluid, shellac, varnishes, hatters' size marks and tanners' tools, and are wholesale and retail dealers in paints, oils, varnishes, window glass, anilines, chemicals, etc., and to transact their business, employ eleven men, and use three horses and wagons. Their spacious store, No. 209 Market street, corner Beaver, covers 4,500 square feet, and their warehouse, No 157 South Canal street, covers 6,700 square feet, is completely stocked with goods, comprising sperm, lard, whale, neatsfoot, olive, cod and other oils used in manufacturing, also, belting, glue, emery, cotton waste, window glass, sponges, drugs and a large line of supplies for hat and leather manufacturers use. All orders placed with this well known firm, have their personal attention, and is carefully and promptly attended to.

O. E. VAN WERT, Boarding and Exchange Stables, 19 Division Place, Newark, N. J. Mr. Van Wert carries on one of the most widely popular stables of which we have knowledge, and no one can do business with him for any length of time without conceding that the popularity referred to is by no means the result of luck and chance, but, on the contrary, is the legitimate result of straightforward methods, and an evident desire to treat every customer fairly and liberally. Mr. Van Wert has conducted this business since 1884, and it has steadily developed from the beginning. His business consists exclusively of the boarding of horses, their owners knowing they are assured comfortable quarters and the best of care. A very important department of his business is the buying, selling and exchanging of horses, wagons, livery goods and similar articles. He sells many horses and vehicles on commission, and as his stable is very favorably known to the purchasing public, he is able to dispose of animals entrusted to him for sale, without delay, and to make prompt returns to owners.

L. MENDEL & SONS. Wholesale and Retail Dealers in Choice Fancy Groceries. City Dressed Beef and Choice Cigars at Wholesale, No. 82 New Street, corner Warren Place, Newark, N. J. No one can blame a man for wanting what belongs to him, and, therefore, no one can blame anybody for trying to find an establishment where all agreements made are strictly adhered to, and where honor and fair dealings prevail. We can render our readers efficient help in finding such an establishment, for these are precisely the kind of business methods that have given the store conducted by L. Mendel & Sons, its present popularity, and we feel confident that they will be steadily continued. Mr. L. Mendel began operations in his present field of usefulness in 1855. The premises now occupied by L. Mendel & Sons comprise a store 1,540 square feet in dimensions, located at No. 82 New street, corner of Warren place, and a branch store at the corner of Bloomfield avenue and High street. These gentlemen carry as choice and varied a stock of fancy groceries, city dressed beef and choice cigars as any one could wish to see, for it is selected under the personal supervision of the proprietors, and will be found strictly first-class in every respect, and those who want choice goods at moderate prices should by all means give this firm an early call. They are prepared to give prompt and accurate delivery, and we feel sure that none who may favor them with patronage will have the least reason to regret it. Polite and experienced assistants are employed, and the minutest details of the business, which is both wholesale and retail in character, are most ably and honorably handled.

FILLMORE CONDIT, Manufacturer of the "Condit" Patent Refrigerator Door Fasteners, 320 Market Street, Newark, N. J. The "Condit" patent refrigerator door fastener is one of those inventions which it seems as though everybody ought to have thought of—they are so simple, practical and efficient. Other things being equal, the value of an invention is in direct proportion to its simplicity, and it would be impossible to devise a fastener more simple than the "Condit," while the most costly and elaborate arrangement could not possibly more efficiently perform all the duties required. It is so easy to operate that no one can be too lazy to use it, and the fact that it can be opened or shut with a pair of ice tongs, or a stick as well as with the hand, is by no means the least of its good points, for this ensures the using of the fastening in many cases where otherwise the door it is intended to secure would have been left open. In short, these fasteners save cold air, save ice and save money, and are conceded to be the only fasteners suitable for heavy ice room doors. They are used by all the more prominent refrigerator manufacturers, and more than 255,000 of them are now in use. The trade is supplied by Mr. Fillmore Condit, who has carried on his present business since 1880. He is located at No. 320 Market street, and has all necessary facilities to enable him to fill orders without delay. The fasteners are made in five sizes, and in four styles of finish, japanned, galvanized, brass and nickel. Orders for the larger sizes, with inside or double levers, will be promptly filled, and with such orders the thickness of the refrigerator walls must be stated. Goods will be delivered by freight, free, to any part of the United States, and dealers run no risk in ordering a full line, for Mr. Fillmore stands ready to take back from hardware dealers at any time, all his fastenings they may have, at cost price.

SHOEMAKER, PICKERING & CO., Manufacturers of Fine Jewelry, 23 Marshall Street, Newark, N. J. The manufacture of jewelry is so extensively carried on in this city, that any one house engaged in this line of industry, stands but little chance of gaining special prominence, and yet such prominence is undoubtedly held by the firm of Shoemaker, Pickering & Co., and is the legitimate result of sixteen years' skilful and conscientious work in the manufacture of fine jewelry. Operations were begun in 1874, the partners being Messrs J. H. Shoemaker, Silas W. Pickering and David E. Bidell, the two former being natives of New York, while Mr. Bidell was born in Newark; all are widely known here, both in business and social circles. The concern utilize spacious premises at No. 23 Marshall street, the shop containing an elaborate plant of machinery, including appliances of the most improved type. A full line of fine jewelry is manufactured, the productions of this establishment always comprising many attractive novelties, and finding favor among the most fastidious trade. Employment is given to fifty experienced assistants, and the heaviest orders can generally be filled at short notice, but whatever the necessity for haste may be, the workmanship is always up to the high standard, so long associated with this representative house.

MRS. R. HARRIS, Fine Millinery, 579 Broad Street, corner Central Avenue, Newark, N. J. Among the many enterprising and successful establishments engaged in this line of trade in Newark, the store which is conducted by Mrs. R. Harris, at 579 Broad street, stands as fine a sample of what a lady of energy and taste can do. Mrs. Harris started this business in 1870, and that she has been successful in it not necessary for us to say, as her numerous and desirable patrons testify to that. She carries a large and choice assortment of fine millinery, which embraces everything that is ever used in the construction of a bonnet or in the trimming of a hat. Her goods are new and fashionable, as she is constantly replenishing her stock, and selecting such novelties as the taste of her customers require. The premises are 25x20 feet in dimensions, and are conveniently arranged. Employment is given to ten assistants, that every visitor may be politely attended to and assisted in selecting such goods as she may desire. Orders for custom work are carefully filled, and every effort made to give entire satisfaction. Mrs. Harris is a native of this city, and is most highly esteemed among her many friends.

THE VREELAND BOTTLING CO.,

Manufacturers of I. C. Vreeland's Celebrated Soda and Mineral Waters, Office, 37 Court Street, Factory, 4 Nevada Street, Newark, N. J. The business of bottling soda and mineral waters has reached enormous proportions of late years, and is still rapidly increasing, but, like many other popular industries, it has suffered to some extent by the questionable practice of a few of the many engaged in it, and the public are beginning to appreciate the fact that some discrimination in the placing of orders is necessary if one wishes to be sure of getting just what he pays for. Hence the older and better known concerns are steadily increasing their trade, and this is especially true of the Vreeland Bottling Company, which carries on a business established by Mr Isaac C. Vreeland, away back in 1849. I. C. Vreeland's celebrated soda and mineral waters need no introduction to the residents of Newark and vicinity, these goods having been the standard of purity and excellence for many years. The present company was organized April 1, 1890, operates a well equipped factory at No. 4 Nevada street, and is prepared to fill both wholesale and retail orders without delay, and at the lowest market rates, the bulk of the business being wholesale, however. The proprietors are Messrs. R. L. Fisher and H. R. Vreeland, the former a native of Brooklyn and the latter of Newark. They will spare no pains to maintain the reputation of the product, and as they have the requisite capital, facilities, experience and ability, there is every reason to believe that the popularity of their goods will continue to increase in the future as it has in the past.

GUS WIDMAN, Sporting Goods, Fishing

Tackle, etc., Rifles, Revolvers and Ammunition, Fine Cutlery and Stationery, 286 Orange Street, corner Norfolk Street, Newark, N. J. Telephone 710. The establishment conducted by Mr. Gus, Widman at No. 286 Orange street, is very popular among those who use the rod and gun, for one may always find here a complete and attractive stock of sporting goods, fishing tackle, etc., including rifles, revolvers and ammunition of the most approved make; while bottom prices are quoted on all the articles dealt in. Fine cutlery and stationery are also well represented in the stock, many late novelties being shown. Another department of Mr. Widman's business is the doing of mercantile, book and job printing, he being prepared to turn out work equal to the best, at the lowest market rates. Every facility is at hand to insure uniformly artistic and satisfactory results, particularly in the line of ball and society work, of which a specialty is made. Estimates will be promptly and cheerfully furnished on application, and as Mr. Widman is prepared to figure very closely, and to guarantee satisfaction to the most critical, those having a printing order to place cannot afford to neglect giving him an opportunity to bid. Work will be delivered at short notice, and orders by mail or telephone, (No. 710), will receive prompt and careful attention. Mr. Widman is also agent for the Germania Fire and German American Insurance Companies.

E. ALSDORF & CO., Dealers in Bicycles,

Pianos, Parlor Organs, Sewing Machines, etc., 10 and 12 Academy Street, Newark, N. J. An interesting example of how a progressively managed business enterprise will develop, is afforded by the growth of the undertaking carried on by Messrs. E. Alsdorf & Co., at Nos. 10 and 12 Academy street, for, when this was founded, in 1876, the business was confined to the handling of sewing machines, whereas now it comprises the sale of various other important commodities, as, for instance, bicycles, children's tricycles, pianos, parlor organs, etc., while sewing machines are still extensively dealt in. Operations were begun by Mr. E. Alsdorf, and in 1888 the present firm was formed by the admission of Mr. J. A. DuBois. Spacious premises are occupied, and a large and varied stock is constantly carried, for an extensive business is done, and all classes of trade are successfully catered to. Safety bicycles for ladies or gentlemen, girls or boys, of the most improved type may be bought here at the lowest market rates, a specialty being made of machines adapted to ladies' use, although all classes of riders will here find goods suited to their needs. The leading makes of pianos and cabinet organs are also well represented, together with sewing machines combining all the latest improvements. Callers are assured prompt and courteous attention, any desired information being cheerfully given.

R. J. O'CROWLEY, Practical Plumber and

Roofer, Hot Air Furnaces; Stoves and Ranges. Orders and Jobbing Promptly Attended to, 552 Broad Street, Near Lombardy Street, Newark, N. J. Mr. R. J. O'Crowley has been identified with his present business for the past twenty-two years, and, having said this, it is unnecessary to enlarge upon the fact of his being thoroughly familiar with it in every detail. He is a practical plumber, roofer and gas fitter, and also handles the leading makes of hot air furnaces, stoves, ranges, etc., and, being conversant with the strong points, and also with the weak points of the several varieties, is prepared to supply customers with the kind best suited to their needs, a point worthy of note, from the fact that a stove which will give the best of satisfaction under some circumstances, may be quite unsuited to use in other positions, where the conditions are different. Mr. O'Crowley deals in a sufficient variety to enable him to suit all tastes and purses, and he quotes bottom prices on every stove or furnace handled. The business under consideration was established in 1857, by Mr. D. G. Rutherford, the firm of Rutherford and O'Crowley being formed in 1873, and was continued until the death of Mr. Rutherford (which occurred in 1888), at the old stand, No. 574 Broad street, now the site of the First Baptist Church. The premises now occupied by Mr. O'Crowley, at No. 552 Broad street, comprise two floors, each 25x75 feet in dimensions. An extensive plumbing and roofing business is done, requiring the employment of twenty thoroughly experienced workmen. Mr. O'Crowley gives close personal supervision to the details of his business, and all orders and jobbing are promptly attended to, while his establishment is a representative one in every sense of the word.

WILLIAM S. SWAIN, Custom Tailor. 827

Broad Street, opposite First Presbyterian Church, Newark, N. J. There are a large number of people in Newark and vicinity, who are not satisfied with ready-made garments, and yet do not feel willing to pay the prices demanded by some custom tailors. It is to this class that we especially appeal in this article, for we are confident that the work turned out by Mr. William S. Swain, will give complete satisfaction, and we know that his charges are considerably below those made in the majority of tailoring establishments where garments of equal merit are produced. Mr. Swain founded his present business in 1887, and has confined himself to the second floor owing to large rents in this location. Since that date he has largely increased his trade, and will doubtless continue to do so as long as his present liberal methods are adhered to. The assortment of foreign and domestic woolens on hand bear evidence of careful selection, and will well repay an examination from those appreciative of stylish and desirable fabrics for gentlemen's wear. The clothing produced under Mr. Swain's direction is very thoroughly as well as fashionably made, and perfection of fit is guaranteed, while orders can be filled at short notice, as ten competent assistants are constantly employed. This popular establishment is located at No. 827 Broad street, and is patronized by the best class of customers in Newark as well as suburban towns.

TRAVIS & SHARPE, Wholesale and Re-

tail Manufacturing Confectioners, No. 58 Academy Street, Newark, N. J. It is apparently very difficult for some persons to discriminate between the use and abuse of a thing, or to draw the line between honest and meritorious articles, and those which are the reverse, hence candy eating has been denounced as unhealthful, and candy has been condemned as impure, and even poisonous. But the great majority of people have common sense enough to see that the eating of candy in reasonable moderation is rather healthful than otherwise, and that reputable manufacturers may be depended upon to produce wholesome confectionery, and so the consumption of candy steadily increases with the growth of population, and reliable manufacturers are encouraged to continue to produce pure and attractive goods. Messrs. Travis & Sharpe, of No. 58 Academy street, are wholesale and retail manufacturing confectioners of established reputation, their productions having gained wide popularity since operations were begun in 1888. The firm are prepared to furnish choice confections in quantities to suit, at the lowest market rates (quality considered), and both wholesale and retail orders are assured prompt and careful attention.

WM. H. EVANS. Sale and Exchange Stables, 105 Frelinghuysen Avenue, Newark, N. J. We hear a great deal about the fraud and deception practised by those who sell horses, but hear very little about the deception practiced by those who buy them. A man who purchases of the irresponsible dealer so common in this country, practices deception insomuch as he deceives himself, for he convinces himself, against his better judgment, that such a dealer can and will give him more for his money than one who is known in the community, and has a business and a reputation to maintain. An honest and a reputable dealer will give full value for money received, whether he handles horses or houses. To say that a horse dealer is necessarily dishonest or at the least fond of "sharp practice," is to confess your own ignorance or prejudice. Mr. Wm. H. Evans is extensively engaged in the sale of horses, and those at all acquainted with him, even by reputation alone, need not be told that his methods are as honorable as they are enterprising. He has a large stock of carriage teams, road, speed and general business horses constantly on hand, and can always furnish a good, reliable team at a reasonable price. The premises occupied are 25x100 feet in dimensions. He has on hand thirty horses, and employs two men, callers being assured immediate and courteous attention. All horses sold by Mr. Evans are guaranteed to be what they are represented to be.

THE DELTA ENGINEERING & MANU- facturing Co., 78 & 80 Mechanic Street, Newark, N. J. Manufacturers of Exhaust Fans, Blowers, Rotating Fans, Steam Radiators, Steam Coils for Indirect Radiating Systems, Electro-Plating Machines, Electric Motors, Dynamos for Isolated Lighting Plants, Water Motors, etc. The Delta Engineering & Manufacturing Company began operations in 1889, and the success of the enterprise was assured from the start, for the service offered is in some respects unique in its character, particularly as regards its completeness, and is so obviously valuable that it could not but be appreciated by investors, manufacturers and the public in general. The men identified with the company are widely and favorably known in mechanical and business circles, and their experience, skill and responsibility are the best possible vouchers for the ability and integrity of the concern. The President is Mr. John L. Seward, the Treasurer Mr. Francis S. Scharff, and the Secretary and General Manager, Mr. Joseph H. Scharff. Spacious and thoroughly equipped premises, located at Nos. 78 and 80 Mechanic street, are utilized, the most improved facilities being at hand for the manufacture of exhaust fans, blowers, rotating fans, steam radiators, steam coils for indirect radiating systems, electro-plating machines, electric motors, dynamos for isolated lighting plants, water motors, etc. The company are consulting engineers and contractors for all work in connection with heating, drying, ventilating and the supplying of power of all kinds, and gives special attention to the designing and construction of labor-saving appliances, and conveniences. Combining as they do, the duties of engineers, manufacturers and contractors, it is obvious that they are fully responsible for the results attained, and our readers need not be told that undivided responsibility is one of the surest guarantees of efficiency. The company are prompted by every consideration to spare no pains to ensure absolute accuracy in each of the many details incidental to their work, and are in a position to figure very closely on contracts, as they can eliminate all elements of chance, from the comprehensive view they take of the attending circumstances. Another very important advantage gained is the possibility of practically ensuring the execution of commissions within a certain period, for having shops of their own, and skilled workmen under their immediate direction, there is no danger of construction being indefinitely delayed by the pressure of other orders or the indifference of those in charge of affairs. All communications, by mail or otherwise, are assured immediate and careful attention, and manufacturers who wish to improve the efficiency of their plant, to put in electric lighting machinery, to transmit power to any distance, or to secure or extend heating or ventilating facilities, will best serve their own interests by communicating with this well-equipped and responsible concern.

The tool and specialty department, now in charge of Mr. S. D. Barnett, manufactures the "Essex Brand" of contractors' paving, and slaters' tools, and furnish iron forgings of any shape or size.

KELLOGG & VAN HOUTEN, Manufacturers of Lead Pipe, and Dealers in Fine Plumbing Materials and Sanitary Specialties, Supplies for Plumbers, Gas Fitters, Machinists, Factories and Mills, 45 and 47 Mechanic Street, Newark, N. J. The firm of Kellogg & Van Houten are widely and favorably known in Newark and vicinity, particularly among the plumbing trade, for this concern is extensively engaged in the manufacture of lead pipe, and do a heavy wholesale business in fine plumbing materials, sanitary specialties, and supplies for plumbers, gas fitters, machinists, factories and mills. The premises made use of are located at Nos. 45 and 47 Mechanic street, and are fitted up with all necessary machinery, including a steam engine of seventy-five horse power. The firm carry a complete stock at all times, and are thus in a position to fill orders without the least delay. They are agents for the Sanitas Manufacturing Company's plumbing appliances, and furnish the same at manufacturers' rates. These goods have received the endorsement of physicians, and of practical sanitary engineers, and are generally conceded to have no equals in their special line. Messrs. Kellogg & Van Houten are also agents for the Tanite Emery Wheels and Grinding Machines, too well known among machinists and others to need eulogy in these columns. The firm employ twenty assistants, and are in a position to execute all commissions at very short notice, and to quote the lowest prices that can be named on goods of standard quality.

THOMAS B. ALLEN, Confectioner and Caterer, Ladies' Restaurant, No. 691 Broad Street, Newark, N. J. Mr. Thomas B. Allen is one of the best known confectioners and caterers in the State, for he has carried on operations ever since 1869, and has long held a leading position in his line of business. The premises utilized by him are located at No 691 Broad street, and are spacious and very conveniently arranged, while every facility is provided to aid in securing prompt and accurate service at all times, and employment is given to thirty assistants, the result being that callers are assured immediate and careful attention, and the most extensive commissions can be executed at short notice. Mr. Allen does a general confectionery and catering business, and is very frequently called upon to furnish public banquets, suppers, lunches, etc., for the supplies obtained of him are always strictly first-class in every respect, and the cooking and service are beyond criticism. During the warmer months his establishment is a favorite resort of those in search of creams, ices, soda water, etc., and at all times of the year it is very largely patronized by the fair sex, for Mr. Allen maintains a first-class ladies' restaurant, which is highly and deservedly popular, for the bill of fare is varied and well chosen, the cooking is excellent, the service is prompt and courteous, and the prices are uniformly moderate.

JOHN B. JOYCE, Practical Tailor. Clothing to Order, Cleaning, Dyeing, Repairing and Pressing, 354 Broad Street, Opposite Washington Place, Newark, N. J. The establishment conducted by Mr. John B. Joyce is widely and favorably known hereabouts, and is well deserving of the liberal patronage it receives, for only strictly first-class work is turned out and uniformly reasonable prices quoted in every department of the business. This enterprise was started by its present proprietor in 1885, and is well worthy of being given prominent mention in these columns, for it has been the means of saving much money for the residents of this section, and was never so well prepared as now to continue the good work so long ago begun. Mr. Joyce is a practical tailor, making clothing to order, and also cleaning, dyeing, repairing and pressing the same, in the best manner possible, at very reasonable prices. The premises occupied are located at No. 354 Broad street, opposite Washington place, and measures about 800 square feet. Two competent and reliable assistants are employed, and all work intrusted to this establishment, whether the making of clothing or the cleaning or repairing of the same, will be done in a thoroughly satisfactory manner, and at a very moderate charge. Mr. Joyce is a native of Newark, and is very well known throughout the city, and makes a specialty of filling orders promptly, at the time promised, to customers.

J. T. HARTSHORNE & CO.,

COAL,

Office and Yard,

Nos. 49 AND 51 MURRAY STREET, NEWARK, N. J.

The firm whose card forms the heading of this sketch has been before the public a sufficient length of time to establish its deserved reputation as a house doing business on a strictly honorable basis. We therefore esteem it a pleasure to chronicle the success it has attained, and earnestly advise our readers to think of this article when about to buy coal—it will pay you. We do not intend to convey the idea that you can buy cheaper of this house than any other, for, as is well known, coal dealers in this city amicably and reasonably agree on regular market rates, so that as for *price*, that is the same anywhere. We *do* mean to say, however, that different dealers carry different *grades* of coal bearing the same name. This is the point we wish to bring out. The firm of J. T. Hartshorne & Co. has always dealt in first quality coal, trusting the public would recognize and appreciate its efforts to deal fairly by its patrons. Such has, in fact, been the case, for the liberal patronage which has been accorded this house since Messrs. J. F. Hartshorne and A. Turnbull (the company), assumed control, forcibly illustrates the reaction, looking at the matter in the light of a *cause* and an *effect*. Poor coal is dear at any price, therefore, it is economy to patronize a house known to be reliable, in the coal it carries. Such a house is that of Hartshorne & Co. The coal they carry is warranted to be free burning and free from slate. A specialty is made of Blacksmiths' and Manufacturers' coal, and in this connection a trial order is solicited. The service of the house is accurate and prompt, there being a large force of men and horses in readiness and attendance at all times. The yard is conveniently located at Nos. 49 and 51 Murray street. Its dimensions are spacious and well adapted for the purposes for which they are intended. A neatly fitted up office is a feature of the establishment, and the scales therein *invariably register 2,000 pounds per ton,* as the load leaves the yard for its destination. Honesty and square dealing have had much to do with the success Messrs. Hartshorne & Co. have thus far attained. With such a record, the business of this firm should continue to increase. We hope the residents of this neighborhood will appreciate the faithful endeavors of Messrs. Hartshorne & Co.

H. ADDISON HICKOK, Mechanical Engineer.

Plans, Specifications and Estimates for Bridges, Roofs and Structural Iron Work, Office, 762 Broad Street, Newark, N. J. To those not keeping themselves fully informed as to the methods of modern architectural construction, the constantly increasing number of structural uses to which iron is being put, cannot fail to be a continual source of surprise and admiration. This increased use of iron is doubtless perhaps due to the comparative ignorance of former builders as to its excellence as a building material, than to the wonderful improvements in the manufacture of, and in the methods of working iron and steel. The profession of mechanical engineering is a distinctive outcome and an accompanying growth of this age of iron. There are departments to mechanical engineering, as there are to all other professions, and that to which Mr. Addison Hickok gives particular attention is the designing of bridges, roofs, and structural iron work. Mr. Hickok is a native of Washington county, N. Y., and has practiced his profession in Newark since 1888. He has had a thorough technical training at the Stevens Institute of Technology, and also wide and varied practical experience in extensive bridge works, so that he is well qualified for the discharge of any responsible duty he may undertake. Plans, specifications and estimates will be furnished at a short notice for any engineering project, every detail of the work being carefully and skillfully carried out. Mr. Hickok's office is located at No. 762 Broad street, and all communications to that address are assured immediate and painstaking attention.

ORLANDO GREACEN & CO., Manufacturers

of Coach, Carriage and Hearse Hardware and Trimmings, Nos. 229 and 231 Mulberry Street, Newark, N. J. The business carried on by Messrs. Orlando Greacen & Co., is not only one of the most extensive of the kind in the State, but is also one of the oldest established, it having been founded by Mr. Orlando Greacen in 1861. This gentleman is associated with Mr. Walter J. Harper, who became a member of the firm in 1888. The manufacture of coach, carriage and hearse hardware and trimmings is very extensively carried on, many of the leading carriage manufacturers obtaining the bulk of their supplies of this kind from this representative concern, who turn out a very complete line, comprising not only a full assortment of staple styles, but also many attractive novelties. The premises utilized are located at Nos. 229 and 231 Mulberry street, and have a total floor space of about 5,000 square feet, they being fitted up with all necessary facilities to enable operations to be carried on to the best advantage, so that every order is assured immediate and careful attention, and will be accurately filled at the lowest market rates. Employment is given to twenty-five experienced assistants, and careful supervision is exercised in connection with every process incidental to manufacture, no pains being spared to fully maintain the high reputation so long associated with the product.

JOHN SEILER, Dealer in Dry and Fancy Goods,

291 Lafayette Street, Newark, N. J. The dry and fancy goods store conducted by Mr. John B. Seiler, at 291 Lafayette street, opposite J. Hensler Brewing Co., in this city, is worthy of extended mention in "Newark and its Leading Business Men." Although not as large as similar establishments in town, it contains practically everything which is usually carried in first-class dry goods houses, in fact, it is the best stocked store of its class in the "Iron Bound District." The premises utilized are 25x90 feet in dimensions, and are admirably adapted for the purpose for which they are built. A heavy stock, well arranged and displayed, enhances the general appearance of the establishment, which requires five clerks to attend to the wants of its patrons, as an extensive business is done. Mr. Seiler is a resident of this city since 1851. The date of the inauguration of his business, 1874. He is an esteemed citizen, and deserves the liberal patronage of his neighbors. The writer likes to see a community patronize an old resident, for they are the people who have made Newark what it is. In chronicling the leading business men of Newark, we place Mr. Seiler in the foremost ranks of those of her citizens most worthy of praise. He has spent many years working faithfully to serve the public honestly, and this is the least we can say for him. Trusting the public will place entire confidence in Mr. Seiler, and his business methods, we earnestly invite them to trade with him when in need of anything in the dry goods line.

WILLIAM SELBY, Wholesale and Retail Provision Dealer,

367 Broad Street and 8 Centre Market, Packing House, 90 Seventh Avenue, 5 Centre Market Place, Newark, N. J. The colossal provision business, both wholesale and retail, which Mr. William Selby carries on in this city, was inaugurated by him in 1862. His establishment at Nos. 367 Broad street and 8 Center Market, and 5 Centre Market Place, and packing house at No. 90 Seventh avenue, are well known to represent an enormous meat business. No better proof of this fact can be advanced than the enumeration of what Mr. Selby has constantly on hand in his numerous places of business, viz.; dressed hogs, smoked hams, shoulders and bacon, fresh loins, fresh pork sausage, lard (tierce or tub), leaf lard, bolognas, head cheese, corned pork, tongues, pigs' feet, pigs' heads and pressed beef. This list surely embraces all that is usually to be found in wholesale provision establishments, and the retail meat men of our city should take advantage of Mr. Selby's fine stock. Having a practical experience of over forty years in the handling of meat, both wholesale and retail, Mr. Selby, with the assistance of a large corps of employees, furnishes meat to the citizens of Newark as cheap as his buying in large quantities will permit. No other house in the same line of business in this city can quote the uniformly low rates which Mr. Selby is prepared to quote. His retail market is 30x50 feet in dimensions, and equipped with the best and most modern meat market improvements. Mr. Selby is a native of England, and widely known in New Jersey. He was for two years a local school commissioner, and is at present the president of the Consumers Hygenic Ice Manufacturing Co. At the packing house on 7th avenue, Mr. Selby manufactures his own ice. An ice machine is something worth seeing to those who have had an opportunity. Mr. Selby's ice is made from well water, three hundred feet deep. Cold storage room is also a feature of the establishment, and meat is cured for other parties.

J. THOME'S Music Store, 261½ Market Street,

Newark, N. J. The value of everything which tends to add harmony and artistic beauty to our busy life, and exercise such refining influence as the art of music, cannot be too highly estimated. The people of New Jersey, and in Newark in particular, have shown great appreciation of all that is best and highest in musical art, as the popularity and success of the establishment conducted by Mr. J. Thome, at No. 261 1-2 Market street, gives decisive evidence. He opened his store in 1887, and has met with abundant and deserved success, and we would advise all desiring to purchase anything in the line of musical merchandise to go to Mr. Thome's before concluding purchases elsewhere. He carries a valuable stock of sheet music and musical goods of all kinds, which are quoted at the lowest prices, and goods not found in stock will be cheerfully ordered and delivered for customers. Mr. Thome was born in Europe, and has met the wants of this community to such a degree that his trade has rapidly increased, and now requires the services of three intelligent and reliable assistants. Prompt and painstaking attention is given to every caller, and the high reputation of the past will be fully maintained in the future.

JOS. AUTENRIETH, Dealer in Fresh and Smoked Meats,

and Manufacturer of Autenrieth's Celebrated Bolognas and Sausages, No. 72 Orange Street, Newark, N. J. It needs no argument to prove that an establishment at which fresh and smoked meats, etc., of superior quality can be bought at the lowest market rates, is a decided public convenience, and as just such an establishment is carried on by Mr. Jos. Autenrieth, we take pleasure in making prominent and favorable mention of it in our columns. Mr. J. Autenrieth is a native of Germany, and has been identified with his present undertaking since 1885, when he succeeded Mr. F. Autenrieth, who had carried it on since 1854. The premises made use of include a store 18x22 feet in dimensions, located at No. 72 Orange street, also, a manufactory 24x70 feet in size, where the celebrated Autenrieth's bolognas and sausages and smoked meats are made. Four competent assistants are employed, and an extensive business, both wholesale and retail in character, is done, and such of our readers as have had dealings with Mr. Autenrieth, need not be told that prompt and polite attention is shown to every caller, and that while the commodities furnished are of uniformly excellent quality, the lowest cash prices are quoted at all times.

LOUIS RICKERT, Dealer in Confectionery, Stationery, etc., Newspapers, Periodicals, etc., No. 221 Clinton Avenue, Newark, N. J. One of the many retail business houses recently established in this city, and to which we take pleasure in calling attention, is conducted by Mr. Louis Rickert. He is a native of New York city, but like many others, prefers to work his way and gain his reputation as a merchant in this city, rather than in the vast metropolis, where almost every branch of industry is overstocked. Mr. Rickert occupies a store of 18x50 feet in dimensions, at 221 Clinton avenue. Here will be found choice confectionery of every kind, ranging from the fancy French bon-bons, to the more simple and wholesome, and to some tastes equally delicious, pure sugar and molasses candies. In confectionery, more than in a great many articles of consumption, everything depends upon the making, and that this process involves much experience and skill is generally acknowledged, especially by those who have tried experiments at home, attended by ignominous failure. The confectionery at Mr. Rickert's establishment is so attractive in appearance and taste, and the prices are so moderate, that persons who call there once, are sure to return, and are never again attempted to try "economical" home experiments. A full line of fine stationery is also kept in stock, besides the leading newspapers, periodicals and various other commodities. Mr. Rickert employs two assistants, whose business it is to see that all orders are promptly attended to, and who serve every customer with uniform courtesy.

KROEPLIN BROS., Saddlers and Harness Makers, Repairing Neatly and Promptly Done, No. 210 Clinton Avenue, corner Wright Street, Newark, N. J. Kroeplin Brothers are one of the recently established firms in this city. They are both natives of Newark, but have only carried on their present business since 1889. They have already gained the reputation for being skillful saddlers and harness makers, and for being able to compete, in the excellence of their work, with firms of much longer standing. The line of trade comprises the manufacture of fine saddles, harness and nearly all the varied articles needed for the care of horses. These comprise bridles and collars, of the most improved styles, whips, blankets, fly nets and sheets. They also keep an assortment of curry combs, brushes, sponges and feed bags, and everything that goes to make up a comprehensive and complete stock of this nature. The business is entirely retail. The store is situated at 210 Clinton avenue, corner of Wright street, and is of 15x50 feet in dimensions. A specialty is made of custom work and repairing, which is neatly and promptly done. The Messrs. Kroeplin use none but good stock, they employ well trained assistants, and they neglect no means to assure satisfaction to their customers, both as regards the quality of the work done, and the promptness with which orders are filled. The charges are uniformly moderate, and we feel sure that all dealings with this firm will be entirely satisfactory.

NEWARK STEAM DYEING & SCOURing Establishment. Theo. W. Neiman & Son, 153 Mulberry Street, near Hamilton, Newark, N. J. The business carried on at the Newark Steam Dyeing and Scouring Establishment was founded in 1872, and for some years was conducted by Mr. Theodore W. Neiman, who subsequently took Mr. Frederick W. Neiman into partnership, under the firm name of Theo. W. Neiman & Son. Mr. Frederick W. Neiman became sole proprietor in 1885, and has fully maintained the high reputation of the establishment for excellent work, prompt billing of orders, and moderate charges. From the very first it has been the policy of the management to quote as low prices as are consistent with the attainment of thoroughly satisfactory results, and the extent and character of the patronage prove that this practice is endorsed by the discriminating public, who know that money spent on inferior dyeing and cleaning work is practically thrown away. The premises made use of are located at No. 153 Mulberry street, near Hamilton, and are equipped with all necessary facilities for the dyeing and cleaning of ladies', gents' and children's garments, etc. and entire satisfaction is confidently guaranteed. Goods may be sent by mail or express, and all orders, however received, are assured prompt and careful attention, and will be delivered at the time promised.

A. N. HARNED, Book Binder and Blank Book Manufacturer, 872 Broad Street (Kremlin Place), opposite City Hall, Newark, N. J. The practical value of a book is dependent even more upon the manner in which it is bound than upon its typographical appearance, and if some of our publishers would pay more attention to the binding of their books, the public would be better satisfied even if wide margins and handsome type were sacrificed to compensate for the additional expense. Improvements in machinery and in methods have materially reduced the cost of binding of late years, and when a large order is given, the work can now be done at remarkably low rates. No book binder in the State has a higher reputation for turning out uniformly excellent work at a moderate price, than Mr. A. N. Harned, and as he makes a specialty of binding for the trade, he has provided every facility for filling extensive orders at short notice. Mr. Harned is a native of New York, and began business in Newark in 1882. He was formerly at No. 201 Market street, but for some time past has occupied his present well-equipped quarters at No. 872 Broad street (Kremlin Place), opposite City Hall. Book binding and blank book manufacturing in all their branches are extensively carried on, an adequate force of experienced assistants being employed, and all orders being assured prompt and painstaking attention. Mr. Harned gives the business careful personal supervision, and knowingly allows no defective work to leave the establishment.

J. ILIFF & CO., General Commission Dealers in Live and Dressed Stock, Sheep, Lambs, Calves, Cows, Pork, Poultry and Game. Also Fruits, Vegetables, Hay, Grain, Butter, Eggs, etc. Office, 70 Orange Street, Newark, N. J. The firm of J. Iliff & Co., is of comparatively recent origin, it having been formed in 1886, but the enterprise with which it is identified is of much longer standing, it having been inaugurated in 1850, at which time Messrs. Rhodes and Iliff opened the first live stock market in the city, it being located at the corner of Plane street and Railroad avenue. The present concern is constituted of Messrs. J. and M. Iliff, both of whom are natives of Sussex county, N. J. The firm are general commission dealers in live and dressed stock, sheep, lambs, calves, cows, pork, poultry and game, and also in fruits, vegetables, hay, grain, butter, eggs and country produce in general, giving special attention to the handling of beef, in which they deal both at wholesale and retail. Extensive stock yards are maintained at Harrison, and the Newark office and store are located at No. 70 Orange street, where one floor measuring 18x60 feet is utilized, together with a large basement. Employment is given to five competent assistants, and despite the magnitude of the business, orders are filled with a promptness and accuracy, that might profitably be imitated at many smaller establishments.

R. HEINISCH'S SONS, Manufacturers of their latest Patent Tailor Shears, Scissors, etc., 109 to 121 Bruce Street, corner 13th Avenue, Newark, N. J. The enterprise conducted by R. Heinisch's Sons is entitled to prominent mention in any review of Newark's leading industrial undertakings, for this enterprise was inaugurated away back in 1825, and has steadily developed until it has reached very large proportions, and, what is more, has done much to build up Newark's reputation as a manufacturing center, for the business owes its growth to strictly legitimate methods, the productions of R. Heinisch's Sons being sold strictly on their merits, and being conceded to be unsurpassed in the market. The sole proprietor is Mr. R. Heinisch, who was born in Newark. Mr. Heinisch was an officer in the army during the Rebellion, and has served two terms in the New Jersey Legislature. The firm manufacture a full line of tailor shears, scissors, etc., most of their productions being protected by patents, and all of them being made from carefully selected material, in a skillful and painstaking manner. The factory is located at Nos. 109 to 121 Bruce street, corner 13th avenue, and comprises three and one half floors of the dimensions of 230x100 feet. It is equipped with a sixty horse engine, two sixty horse boilers, and all other necessary machinery, and employment is given to 100 assistants, so it will readily be believed that the annual product is large in amount and great in value. These shears and scissors are the standard throughout the country.

JOHN F. HOUGH, Plumbing Contractor, 402 Washington Street, Newark, N. J. Close Estimates Furnished, and Thorough Work Guaranteed. Jobbing Promptly Attended to. Telephone 929. The inception of the enterprise of which Mr. John F. Hough is the proprietor, took place in 1875. This gentleman pays especial attention to plumbing, and we need not say that the work which he does is executed in a workmanlike and irreproachable manner. With full knowledge of theoretical, practical and sanitary plumbing, and the necessary appliances to facilitate the work, Mr. Hough turns out some of the best plumbing jobs in the city. Tin roofing is the next thing which takes up the time and attention of Mr. Hough and his large force of men, and in this as well as other work which is performed by it, the firm has a high reputation. Galvanized cornices are set up whenever orders are received, and a good job of cornice work, every mechanic will say, is something worthy of admiration. In close affiliation to plumbing comes gas fitting, which is dispatched with a care and precision worthy again of the "same" this establishment has. Still continuing, steam heating presents itself to our inspection; we will simply say in this respect that the firm has long since been out of its apprenticeship, and are prepared to "go ahead" with orders in confidence of being able to do themselves credit. A particular study is made of sanitary appliances, and a variety of these articles are kept constantly in stock. Ventilation is not slighted either, for better posted knowledge than possesses Mr. Hough on this subject, is scarce. Pumps of all kinds are repaired if "out of gear," and a stock of new ones can be found at the shop. Furnaces and ranges come next, and none but the latest and best are kept. Sheet metal work of all kinds is executed upon order. Jewelers' utensils are repaired, and the house enjoys quite a trade in this line. To conclude with, both electric and coppersmith work is done, and well done too. Hot air heating is also paid attention to. We see, then, that Mr. Hough is engaged in a diversity of undertakings. We are willing to trust in his fifteen years of business experience, however, and not mention what knowledge he might have possessed previously. Employment is furnished eight men regularly. The premises occupied are 20x30 feet in area. Mr. Hough was born in Newark, and is esteemed by its citizens. Those having work to be executed, which comes under his line of business, would do well to profit by his large experience, and leave their orders with him.

SETH B. RYDER & CO'S., Carpet Cleaning Works, No. 22 Mechanic Street, Near Broad Street, Newark, N. J. Carpets while in our possession insured against loss by fire. The advantages gained by patronizing Ryder & Co's. carpet cleaning works, may be very briefly summarized as follows : 1. Carpets of every description are thoroughly cleaned, all dust, vermin and moths, being absolutely removed. 2. The work is done in a manner that cannot injure the most delicate fabric, no steam or fluid of any kind being used, and the machine utilized being so constructed and operated that tearing or stretching the carpet is impossible. The "Ferry Patent Carpet Cleaning Machines" used by this firm are the safest, simplest and most efficient machines of the kind ever invented, and Messrs. Ryder & Co. (who have the sole right to use these machines in this county), cordially invite the public to call at their works, No. 22 Mechanic Street, and see them in operation. 3. As the work is done under cover there is "no postponement on account of the weather," and hence carpets are returned when promised, and when haste is essential will be taken away, cleaned and returned the same day. 4. Carpets are fully insured against loss by fire while in the custody of the firm, and when stored on their premises are insured against moths also. 5. Carpets will be called for, and delivered free to any part of the city, and expressage will be paid one way on carpets sent from a distance, the charges for cleaning, etc., being twenty per cent. below New York prices. Other advantages might be cited, but we have named enough already to account for the popularity of the service rendered by this representative enterprise, which was started a quarter of a century ago. The proprietor, Mr. Seth B. Ryder, is a native of Albany, N. Y., and held a commission as Major during the rebellion. He has served as Sheriff of Union County, and is widely known throughout this section. Mr. Ryder gives his business close personal supervision, and maintains the service constantly at the very highest standard of efficiency.

MRS. O. C. SMITH, Toys, Candies and Fancy Goods, Union Steam Laundry Agency, 454 Washington Street, Newark, N. J. As it takes all kinds of people to make a world, so it takes all kinds of business to compose the industries of a city. Some people are more or less pretentious, while others spend their lives on earth in a quiet and more humble way, and endeavor to live in such a way that they may contribute their humble mite towards the grand spirit of enterprise, which is so characteristic of this country, and of the American people in general. Even the women, animated with a spirit of enthusiasm, which they no doubt copy from their countrymen, launch themselves into business, and oftentimes meet with a success which fairly tinges with blushes the efforts of the opposite sex. It is a fact, that the American woman has more business inclination than any upon the face of the universe; and is it not a characteristic of which our nation may be proud ? We believe so, for it is a good trait to see in a woman other inclinations than desires of "parlor and society" life. These are very well in their place, and to a certain degree, but too many of these inclinations in women do not contribute to a nation's good; on the contrary, we believe the tendency is in the opposite direction. The establishment conducted by Mrs. O. C. Smith, and which she inaugurated in 1886, is a typical illustration of the idea we mean to convey, for this lady manages her affairs with such skill, that the success which has attended her efforts is worthy of our admiration. Her establishment is the agency for the Union Steam Laundry of this city, and a fine assortment of toys, candies and fancy goods are offered for inspection. Mrs. Smith is a native of Newark, and is assisted by a courteous attendant in her business. The premises she occupies are 20x50 feet in dimensions. We earnestly call the attention of the public to this establishment, and hope it will encourage the efforts of this lady in her line of business.

BROAD STREET TEA WAREHOUSE, L. Lehman, Wholesale and Retail Cash Grocer, Flour and Butter Depot, Wines and Liquors, No. 461 Broad Street and 52 Orange Street, Newark, N. J. This business was founded in 1880, by Messrs. Scheuer & Lehman, and carried on by them till 1888, when the present proprietor, Mr. L. Lehman took its management, as the "cash" grocer, at No. 461 Broad street, and 52 Orange street. The assortment of choice family groceries, flour, butter, wines and liquors, are as complete as could be desired, for Mr. Lehman's long experience has made him perfectly familiar with the requirements of city trade, and prepared him to cater to it, with the best possible advantage. Fine tea, coffee, sugar, flour, meal, pork, lard, hams, butter, cheese, eggs, wines, liquors and fruits of all kinds are to be found here, and the goods are sold as low as the lowest, as the terms are "for cash." Mr. Lehman offers liberal inducements to purchasers, and he has every facility at hand to enable orders to be filled promptly. Goods are delivered in any part of the city free of charge. Mr. Lehman is a native of Newark, and does a wholesale, as well as a retail trade, employing some fifteen competent, courteous and obliging assistants, and the premises occupied measure 80x50 feet in size.

JOSEPH F. IMFELD, Manufacturer of Fine Gold Chains, Nos. 355 and 357 Mulberry Street, Newark, N. J. The business carried on by Mr. Joseph F. Imfeld has been under his sole control, only since the early part of the current year, but it was founded in 1875, and the enterprise has long held a leading position among similar undertakings in this section. Operations were begun by Mr. Oren A. Hendrick, and in 1880 Mr. Imfeld was admitted to partnership under the firm name of O. A. Hendrick & Co., and became sole proprietor on the death of Mr. Hendrick, in 1890. Mr. Imfeld is thoroughly familiar with every detail of the business, and has both the ability and the disposition to fully maintain the high standard so long associated with the enterprise. He is extensively engaged in the manufacture of fine gold chains, producing a full line, comprising not only staple styles, but also many tasteful and attractive novelties. The factory is located at Nos. 355 and 357 Mulberry street, and as it is very thoroughly fitted up, and employment is given to twenty-seven efficient assistants, the most expensive orders can be filled at short notice, and at prices that will compare favorably with those named by other manufacturers of equally desirable goods.

GEO. KUNDEL & SON, Harness Manu-
facturers and Dealers in Whips, Blankets, Brushes, etc., etc.,
263 Springfield Avenue, Newark, N. J. All Goods Warranted as Represented, at the Lowest Market Price. Repairing
Neatly Done at Short Notice. Everyone who owns a horse,
or who has the care of one, is interested, or should be, in the
harness his animal wears. Harness for horses, like clothing for men, are made both ready and custom, and it is just
as reasonable to put some harnesses on these poor animals, as
it is to put some suits on men. We see some that inspire
admiration, almost, and some that inspire pity, so awkward
are they. Now, there is no reason for buying cheaply made
harness, any more than for buying cheaply gotten-up clothing, for both are, at the present day, sold at reasonable
prices, and well made, too, but care should be exercised in
patronizing houses of reputable standing, if we do not wish
to be "takenin," as the expression goes. Patronize such an
establishment as that which Geo. Kundel & Son carry
on, and you will buy what is right, at prices which will surprise you when quoted. These gentlemen are workmen of
recognized superior ability, and the work which they do is
the only advertising they need. Besides the manufacturing
of harness, repairing is done, and work of this kind is dispatched with all the celerity which the assistance of three
competent workmen can offer. The store, which is 15x55 feet
in dimensions, contains a select assortment of whips, blankets, brushes, etc. Anything which a horse wears or needs
can be found at this establishment. Call and see for yourself.

CONRAD KRIPPENDORF, Machinists'
and Jewelers' Tool Maker, No. 19 Green Street, Newark, N.
J. Rolls, Dies, Cutters and Drawplates of Every Description Made and Repaired. This gentleman's career is one of
deserved credit, and his record is that of a self-made man.
His trade is that of machinists' and jewelers' tool maker, in
which branch of industry he is an acknowledged expert.
By energy and perseverance, together with native skill, he
has made a reputation for being one of the most satisfactory
men to have dealings with, as his tools are invariably made
of the best material, and finished with care and accuracy.
These make a superior rolls, dies, cutters and drawplates of
every kind and size, besides the innumerable tools needed
for the machinists' and jewelers' arts. Mr. Krippendorf established himself in Newark in 1871, in his present business.
He occupies premises of 20x30 feet in dimensions, at No. 19
Green street. These are fitted with a steam engine of eight
horse power, which runs all the machinery used in this
trade. Employment is given to three skilled workmen, but
all the operations of the establishment are under the direct
supervision of the proprietor. The goods will be found
of extremely moderate cost. All orders are filled
promptly, and we can safely say, that all articles made at
this establishment are more than worth their cost, and will
prove satisfactory in every respect.

L. L. CARLISLE, Dealer in Masons' Materi-
als and Coal, Newark, N. J. Manufacturers' Agent for Standard Ohio, Vitrified, Salt Glazed Sewer Pipe, Terra Cotta
Goods, Fire Brick and Tile, Office and Wharf, foot of Clay
Street. Telephone Call 158. The enterprise conducted by
Mr. L. L. Carlisle, in this city, was founded in 1865, by Mr.
Edward Sayre. Mr. Carlisle assumed control in 1879, and
through his able management, push and enterprise, the business has increased ten-fold. He is one of Newark's marked
business men, and was born in Monmouth County, New Jersey. For four years he was a member of the Board of Education, and for three years sat an honored member of the
city's aldermanic chamber. The premises he occupies are
located on the Passaic River, at the foot of Clay street, and
measure 225 feet on the street and 300 on the river. A finely
appointed office is to be found here, as well as a good wharf,
where vessels are easily anchored. Mr. Carlisle affords employment to fifteen hands the year round, and all orders
receive prompt attention. The business as that of masons'
materials and coal, chiefly. These articles are A-1 in quality,
and are sold at the lowest market rates. Mr. Carlisle is also
the manufacturers' agent in town, for the Standard Ohio,
vitrified and salt glazed sewer pipe, terra cotta goods, fire
brick and tile. The attention of the readers of the "History
of Newark and Its Leading Business Men," is respectfully
called to this establishment.

L. M. MOLL, Carpenter and Builder, Walnut
Counters, Book Cases, Desks, Wire Screens for doors and
Windows Made to Order at Shortest Notice. Jobbing a
Specialty. Orders by Mail will Receive Prompt Attention,
87, 89, 91, and 93 Parkhurst Street, Newark, N. J. Among
the numerous carpenters and building contractors doing
business in our prosperous city, mention should be made of
the enterprise conducted by Mr. Lewis M. Moll. This gentleman gave inception to his business some ten years ago,
and the many buildings he has erected since then are proof
sufficient that he has shown himself thoroughly master of
the most complicated plans, and exacting specifications.
Many, when deciding on building, like to have a house that
will not look precisely the same as a dozen others in the
same locality, in other words, individuality is sought after.
When the supply of money is unlimited, such a house is very
easily obtained, but as the majority have to calculate closely
in building, the contractor one selects to execute the work
has much to do in the case, which has, in result, a financial
bearing on the man's pocket book. In introducing the subject of this sketch to the reading public, we desire to say
that we know Mr. L. M. Moll to be a man practical and
thorough in every detail of his business. Schooled by master
mechanics, while learning the trade in his youth, he has ever
had in mind the old proverb, which says that, "Whatever is
worth doing at all, is worth being done well." There is a
great deal in this, and none know how much, until they have
personally gone through the period of building. Mr. Moll
makes a specialty of building private residences, and buildings destined to business and manufacturing industries, and
his experience in such matters is as reliable as the pilot at
the wheel of a vessel. He also pays attention to fine cabinet
work, and is prepared to execute all kinds of jobbing in his
line. Mr. Moll is a draughtsman of no mean ability, and is
as close an appraiser on plans as the Newark Business' Exchange can boast of. He cheerfully furnishes estimates, and
when quoted these are invariably found to be as low as the
usage of good materials and superior workmanship will
allow. The shop occupied by him at the address given in
the card which heads this article, is 2,100 square feet in area.
A sufficient force of assistants is employed to enable all orders to be filled at short notice, the number, of course, varying with the time of year. Walnut counters, book cases,
wire screens for doors and windows, mantels, etc., are all
built with great taste, at low figures. In chronicling the representative business men and their enterprises in the "History of Newark and its Leading Business Men," we place high
confidence in the gentleman to whom we have alluded. Any
work which our readers may entrust to him is sure to be
promptly and accurately executed in a commendably satisfactory manner. Mr. Moll is at present erecting a beautiful residence for Mr. Carl F. Seitze, the well known hat
manufacturer. It is to cost $20,000, and is located upon the
elegible site of 13th avenue and High street. It will be three
stories high, and of brick, with brown stone and terra-cotta
trimmings. An octagonal corner is a feature of the style of
architecture. This extends the entire height of the three
stories, and towers off at an apex. The building will be finished in the most elaborate manner, and will be a model of
modern improvements. The plans are of Mr. Moll's own
design, and do justice to any residence on High street.

MYRON B. MARSH, Butcher and Grocer,
Fruit and Vegetables, No. 53 Bleecker Street, Newark, N.
J. The establishment now conducted by Mr. Myron B.
Marsh, was inaugurated thirteen years ago by Mr. G. E.
Lawrence, who died in June of 1890. Mr. Marsh, who had
been with Mr. Lawrence for six years previous to his decease, came into possession of the establishment, and will
endeavor to continue giving the patrons of the stand the
satisfaction they have been accustomed to receive. Mr.
Marsh employs three courteous and social assistants, who
attend to the meat and grocery route of the house. Two
teams are circulating constantly, calling for and delivering
orders in all parts of the city. The store is well stocked
with a fresh supply of groceries, and a large ice box contains fine city dressed and Chicago beef. Mr. Marsh is a
native of Newark, and has hosts of both business and social
friends, who join us in hoping that his present prosperity will
continue as well as it has begun. Mr. Marsh is also an
artist of recognized high merit, and his customers receive
at his hands works in oil painting, which if purchased would
cost more than many could afford. A trial order is respectfully solicited.

HANSON, VAN WINKLE & CO., Es-tab-

lished 1830. Acids, Chemicals, Dye Stuffs, etc. Manufacturers of Nickel and Electro-platers' Materials, Manufacturers of the "Little Wonder" and "Wonder" Dynamo-Electric Machines, for Electro-plating and Electrotyping, Nos. 92 and 94 Liberty Street, New York. Nos. 219 and 221 Market street, Newark, N. J. The general public are comparatively familiar with dynamo-electric machines in connection with the electric light, but it is not commonly known that electro-plating and electrotyping are now carried on by the aid of such machines instead of batteries, which not very long ago were exclusively used. Electro-plating dynamos are made expressly for the service for which they are used, and the old-established firm of Hanson, Van Winkle & Co., have met with great success in introducing the "Little Wonder" and "Wonder" Dynamo Electric Machines, of which they are manufacturers, for these machines have demonstrated their practical value beyond the possibility of a doubt, and are now used in some of the largest shops in the country. They are thoroughly well made of carefully selected material, and as their design is simple and strong, the liability to get out of order is reduced to a minimum. The firm are extensive manufacturers of nickel and electro platers' materials, and deal largely in acids, chemicals, dye stuffs, etc., maintaining an establishment at Liberty street, New York, besides the one in this city at 219 and 221 Market street. The business was established in 1830, and its present magnitude is the legitimate result of extensive facilities judiciously utilized. Messrs. Hanson, Van Winkle & Co. are prepared to quote the lowest market rates on the various commodities they handle, and to fill all orders without delay. The partners are Messrs. Joseph Hanson, Abraham Van Winkle and Frederick S. Ward, all of whom are widely known in mercantile circles.

T. MASCHY, Carriage and Wagon Maker,

Jobbing and Horse Shoeing, Steel and Iron Forging, 219 Clinton Avenue, opposite Elizabeth Avenue, Newark, N. J. All experienced horsemen appreciate the advantages of having their carriages and other vehicles made to order, as in this way they can have their own ideas of beauty, style and durability fully carried out. This is no doubt more costly than ready-made work, but it generally gives greater satisfaction to all parties concerned. Many of our readers may have had dealings with Mr. T. Maschy, but for those who have not had any experience with this excellent carriage and wagon maker, we wish to venture the advice of a speedy call upon him. He occupies premises at 219 Clinton avenue, opposite Elizabeth avenue, 50x50 feet dimensions, with an annex measuring 15x30 feet. He employs competent workmen, who assist him in making any kind of carriage or wagon that may be desired. Besides this, he is fully prepared to do all kinds of steel and iron forging at short notice. These comprise factory, mill and builders' forgings, extension and slide coal shutes, steel or iron awning, and other frames, etc., etc. Estimates will be promptly furnished for this as well as other work. Jobbing done quickly and neatly, and the prices will be found as moderate, if not more so, than any like establishment in the city.

EDWARD DUNN, Plumber and Sanitary

Engineer. Special Attention Given to the Draining, Ventilation and Sanitary Condition of Private and Public Buildings, No. 101 Market Street, Newark, N. J. The rapid increase in population in our cities and towns, has made the subject of sanitary plumbing and ventilation of the utmost importance for the welfare of the race. System after system has been invented and tried, only to prove faulty sooner or later, thereby causing illness and endless trouble. Intelligent and practical men have set themselves to work to solve this difficult problem, each one vying with the other to produce the best. In consequence, we have many experienced sanitary engineers who are well fitted to discover where the fault lies in localities that have proved unhealthy, and to put our houses into such condition that we may no longer be afraid to live in them. Mr. Edward Dunn has been identified with the interests of this business since 1865. Four years later he associated himself with his brother, the firm being known as E. Dunn & Brother. In 1881, this partnership was dissolved and Mr. Edward Dunn has since carried on the business alone. Mr. Dunn came originally from Ireland. He has long been settled in Newark. As plumber and sanitary engineer, Mr. Dunn is prepared to give special attention to the draining, ventilation and the general sanitary condition of any building, public or private. He is also manufacturer of an improved low pressure steam heating apparatus for buildings, such as churches, schools, stores and private houses. In addition to this Mr. Dunn does a retail business in stoves and ranges, of which he keeps a full assortment. He occupies premises at 101 Market street, comprising four floors and a cellar, 22x100 feet dimensions, he employs forty hands, and has a steam engine of eight horse-power. Mr. Edward Dunn was awarded several silver medals from 1879 to 1883, by the State Board of Health and the Agricultural Society, at Waverly, N. J., for exhibits of the best methods of sanitary work and ventilation.

CARROL PH. BASSETT, C. E., PH. D.,

Firemen's Building, corner Broad and Market Streets, Newark, N. J. The principle of division of labor has latterly made itself prominent in professional fields. Professional engineering has felt it. Increased complexity of social problems fostered by the rapid growth of urban populations has developed a branch of the engineering profession distinctively termed Municipal Engineering. The field embraces such engineering constructions as are specially required by the denser populations. The design and construction of water works, sewerage and drainage are now almost invariably in intelligent communities committed to the hands of engineering specialists. Hap hazard and rule of thumb must give place to intelligent calculation and design. Carrol Ph. Bassett, C. E., Ph. D., whose offices and laboratory are located corner Broad and Market streets, has turned his professional attention particularly to that branch of municipal engineering embraced under hydraulic and sanitary work. He has accomplished much towards building up a national reputation for himself in his specialties. He has designed or constructed (or both) water works or sewerage systems in the following towns. Long Branch, N. J.; East Orange, N. J.; Phillipsburgh. N.J.; Orange, N. J.; Englewood, N. J.; South Orange, N. J.; Summit, N. J.; Plainfield, N. J.; Somerville, N. J.; Middletown, N. Y.; Corning, N. Y.; Monticello, N. Y.; Watkins, N. Y.; Reading, Pa.; Williamsport, Pa.; Wilmington, Del.; Parkersburg, W. Va., beside consultations on public works at Altoona, Pa.; Mt. Holly, N. J.; Elmira, N. Y., and other places. In his practice he has introduced special features involving sewage purifications at Long Branch and East Orange, which were new in municipal works in this country. Mr. Bassett is a member of the American Society of Civil Engineers, N. J. San. Association, acts as Consulting Engineer for the city Board of Health, and is Chief Engineer for the Commonwealth Water Company. He is an extremely busy man.

PETTY'S PHARMACY.

Pure Drugs and Chemicals, "Petty's Famous Soda," Prescriptions a Specialty. All hours, Day or Night, 925 Broad Street, Newark, N. J. From the very earliest ages, the art of preparing the compounds that allevate and remove pain and heal the sick has been regarded among the highest of human functions, and this is the reason that so much interest and importance attaches to the calling of the apothecary in our own times. It would be a serious oversight not to mention Mr. Petty among Newark's prominent men, for his pharmacy, situated at 925 Broad street, near Hill street, is one of the best known and most popular in the city. Mr. Petty does a very large retail trade in drugs, medicines, and the various branches of the apothecary's business, but he makes a specialty of keeping only the purest drugs and chemicals, from which he compounds his prescriptions. He enjoys an excellent reputation for accuracy and vigilance in this work, as well as in the general exercise of his profession, receiving as a consequence, the favor of many of the foremost medical practitioners, as well as the prominent citizens of Newark. Mr. Petty's soda water has become famous, and is very generally appreciated throughout the city. The fountain is very handsome, and the list of refreshing drinks is an unusually long and complete one. We append it, as it shows what a great variety of things are to be had in this excellent establishment.

Petty's "List" of Cream Soda Syrups. Ambrosia, Apricot, Blackberry, Blood Orange, Banana, Chocolate, Coffee, Ginger, Grape, Lemon, Maple, Nectar, Orange, Peach, Pine Apple, Raspberry, Sarsaparilla, Sherbert, Strawberry, Vanilla, Wild Cherry. Lime Juice and Soda, Malto, Root Beer, Fluid Oats, five cents.

Very Tart and Popular. Phosphate, with Petty's Raspberry, Orange or Lemon, five cents. Egg Phosphate, Seltzer Lemonade with Shaved Ice. Calisaya and Soda, ten cents. Egg Lemonade, Ginger Ale, fifteen cents.

Natural Mineral Waters on Draught: Saratoga Vichy, Geyser, High Rock, Seltzer, Waukesha, Bethesda. five cents, Large Glass, ten cents. Hunyadi Water, ten cents.

Hot Drinks: Chocolate, Coffee, Ginger, Lemon, five cents. Bouillon, Clam Broth, ten cents.

Customers may have more or less syrup by instructing the attendant when ordering.

The prices, as will be seen, are moderate. For the benefit of smokers, we may add Mr. Petty keeps a line of very fine cigars.

J. W. WOLF & CO.,

Jobbers in Cloths, Cassimeres and Tailors' Trimmings, 26 Academy Street, Newark, N. J. In Newark, as in every other large purchasing center, the clothing business has attained enormous proportions, the manufacture of custom and ready-made clothing representing the investment of hundreds of thousands of capital, and the employment of many hundred hands. Of course the demand for cloths, cassimeres and tailors' trimmings is proportionately large, and among the various houses engaged in supplying it, that of J. W. Wolf & Co. deserves honorable and prominent mention, for this concern are both jobbers and retailers, and are prepared to furnish articles of standard merit, in quantities to suit, at positively the lowest market rates, filling orders promptly and sparing no pains to fully satisfy every customer. Mr. John W. Wolf is a native of Newark, and has been identified with his present enterprise since 1887, he being well and favorably known in trade circles throughout this vicinity. The firm utilize premises located at No. 26 Academy street, between the post office and Halsey street, and always carry a very attractive and complete stock, which will be found well worthy the inspection of those interested in fashionable and dependable fabrics for gentlemen's wear.

HUGH SMITH & CO., MANUFACTUR-

ers of Oak Tanned Patent, Enameled and Fancy Colored Leather, Hoyt Street and Central Avenue, Newark, N. J. There is an immense and growing demand for the finer grades of leather, and among those concerns engaged in this important line of manufacture, not one bears a higher reputation than that of Hugh Smith & Co. It would be more strictly accurate, however, to refer to this concern as a corporation, with Mr. Hugh Smith as president, it having been regularly incorporated January 1, 1889. The business was founded in 1862, by Messrs. Hugh and Charles Smith, the former gentleman assuming sole control in 1867, and retaining it until the organization of the existing company, which owns the buildings utilized, and has a capital of $100,000 paid in, with a surplus. The premises are located on Hoyt street and Central avenue, and the buildings comprise two floors of the dimensions of 40x125 feet, and four floors measuring 68x125 feet, two buildings 50x100 feet each. The plant of machinery is very complete, and is of the improved type, all necessary facilities being provided for the manufacture of oak tanned, patent, enameled and fancy colored leather of all descriptions. Employment is given to 150 assistants, and under corporate management the business is so thoroughly systematized, and carefully supervised, that orders can be filled more promptly, and with more uniform accuracy than ever before.

M. PRICE, Manufacturer of all Varieties of

Hatchets, Adzes, Brick Trowels, etc., etc., 338 Mulberry Street, Newark, N. J. As the actual quality of such articles as hatchets, adzes, and other edge tools cannot be accurately determined, even by an expert, without practical test, it is obvious that the retail purchaser must depend upon the honor of the dealer, and the dealers upon that of the manufacturer, for the assurance that the tools will prove serviceable and satisfactory. No reputable dealer can afford to handle inferior edge-tools at any price, but as competition in the sale of hatchets, adzes, etc., is very close, it is important for him to know where he can get tools of uniformly dependable quality, at the lowest market rates, and this knowledge may be satisfactorily obtained by placing a trial order with Mr. M. Price, for he is prepared to furnish tools of standard merit, at prices as low as the lowest, quality, of course, considered. He occupies premises measuring 75x300 feet, equipped with all necessary machinery, power being furnished by a sixty horse engine. Employment is given to fifty experienced assistants, and the most extensive orders can be promptly and accurately filled. The product comprises all varieties of hatchets, adzes, brick trowels, etc., the goods being very widely and favorably known among the trade, as they have been on the market many years, and are uniformly first-class in material, temper and workmanship, great pains being taken to maintain the enviable reputation they have long since won. Mr. Price's office is at No. 338 Mulberry street, and all communications to that address are assured immediate and careful attention.

VAN STEENBERG & CLARK, Dealers in Blue Stone for all Purposes, Ogden, corner of Gouverneur Street, Telephone No. 597, Newark, N. J. Blue Stone is utilized for so great a variety of purposes that the demand for it is something enormous, and as new applications of the stone are constantly being made, the demand is continuously and rapidly increasing, so it is not surprising that a great deal of capital should be invested in the quarrying, marketing and working of this popular stone. A leading house among those engaged in handling it is that of Van Steenberg & Clark, doing business at the corner of Gouverneur and Ogden streets, where premises measuring 425x100 feet are utilized. This firm was formed in 1881, and is constituted of Messrs. William Van Steenberg and Jacob Clark, both of whom were born in New York State. Mr. Van Steenberg served two years as Alderman in this city, and both he and Mr. Clark are extremely well-known, not only in business, but also in social circles. Mr. Van Steenberg resides at No. 292 Mt. Pleasant avenue, and Mr. Clark at No. 172 Summer avenue, orders sent to, or left at either of these addresses being assured as prompt attention as those delivered at the works. The firm deal in blue stone for all purposes, both at wholesale and retail, and are prepared to furnish mantels, hearths, sills, steps, chimney caps, coping, tombs and dressed stone in general. Flag stone will be laid and curb stone set in first class style and at bottom rates, and estimates will be cheerfully furnished on application, and orders by mail or telephone promptly attended to, employment being given to thirty competent assistants.

GEO. D. RANDELL & CO., Wholesale Dealers and Jobbers in whiskies and Fine Imported and Domestic Wines, Liquors, etc., 18, 20 and 22 Fair Street, Newark, N. J. There is a very extensive demand for wines, liquors and cordials for medicinal use quite apart from that of those who use liquors as a beverage, and it is obviously of the first importance that stimulants used for medical purposes should be pure and wholesome, so that those wishing anything in this line would do well to take advantage of the facilities offered by Messrs. George D. Randell & Co., for this concern are very large wholesalers, jobbers and retailers of whiskies and fine imported and domestic wines, liquors and cordials, and are prepared to supply goods of guaranteed quality, in quantities to suit, at the lowest market rates. This business was founded in 1857. The high reputation of the enterprise has been fully maintained under the present management, and the concern consequently do a very large business, both at wholesale and retail. They utilize very commodious premises, at Nos. 18, 20 and 22 Fair street, and carry a heavy and exceptionally complete stock at all times. Employment is given to nine efficient assistants, and all orders, large or small, are assured prompt and careful attention.

W. G. GLOVER, Bread, Cake and Pie Baker, 128 Orange Street, Newark, N. J. Economy is a virtue beyond a doubt, but like charity, it "covers a multitude of sins," or, at least, a multitude of mistakes, for some people never seem to be able to practice true economy, although they deny and stint themselves in a hundred ways. That it is not economical to do yourself what can be more cheaply and better done by somebody else, would seem to be plain enough for the merest child to understand, and yet there are many housekeepers who bake their own bread, cake and pastry, when they are so circumstanced that it would be much cheaper to buy these articles at a public bakery. The objection may be raised that home cookery is superior to that practiced at such an establishment, but that does not apply to the bakery conducted by Mr. W. G. Glover, at No. 128 Orange street, for the cookery here will compare favorably with the best of that done in private families, and should any one of our readers doubt this fact, let them remember that "the proof of the pudding is the eating," and make a practical trial of Mr. Glover's productions. The premises made use of comprise a sales-room 25x18 feet, and a bakery of the same dimensions. A full assortment of bread, cake and pastry is always on hand to choose from, and is constantly fresh and appetizing. Three competent assistants are employed, and all goods handled are sold at the lowest rates consistent with the use of the best materials.

AUG. GOERTZ & CO., Manufacturers of Bag, Purse and Pocket Book Frames, all kinds of Fancy Metal Goods, 280, 282 and 284 Morris Avenue, near South Orange Avenue, Telephone 426, Newark, N. J. The manufacture of bags, purses, pocketbooks, etc., is by no means so simple as would at first appear, for even the simplest articles of this kind are not made by any one concern, but are the product of several separate establishments. Some idea of the magnitude of the demand for these goods may be gained by visiting the factory of Messrs. Aug. Goertz & Co., at 280, 282 and 284 Morris avenue, near South Orange avenue, for, although this concern makes merely the frames for bags, purses, pocketbooks, etc., they maintain a very large and finely equipped establishment, employ 150 assistants, and are capable of turning out an immense amount of goods in the course of a year. Their factory is three stories in height, and is fitted up with a steam engine of eighty horse power. Besides making pocket book frames, etc., the firm manufacture all kinds of fancy metal goods, including many late and attractive novelties, and are prepared to supply anything in their line at short notice and at bottom rates, their superior facilities easily enabling them to meet all competition. The partners are Messrs. Aug. Goertz, Ed. Kuecht and Ed. Wester, all of whom are natives of Germany.

C. G. WOLFF, Commission Dealer. Staple and Fancy Groceries. Corner Orange and Gray Streets, Newark, N. J. Groceries! We are all of us more or less interested in the subject, for we are also more or less inclined to be particular about what we eat, and quite right it is to entertain certain scruples in this direction, for a great many groceries who furnish the public with these articles of our diet, are not as scrupulous in what they sell, as they might be. We mean to convey the impression that many men who are engaged in this line of business, frequently take advantage of the unsuspecting public, and deal out to it inferior goods at high prices. There is one, and only one way to avoid being taken in, in this respect, and if our readers will lend us their attention, we would say to them, buy your groceries of a store known to do business in an upright, straightforward manner; a house that is known to keep none but those goods calculated to be a fair equivalent for the money you are obliged to pay for them, a house which, seeing that a certain line of goods is not as it should be, will not palm it off on its customers, just the same as though they were all right. In other words, patronize a grocery store where none but strictly honorable business methods are employed. Such a house you will find in that of C. G. Wolff, commission dealer and grocer, at the corner of Orange and Gray streets, in this city. It was inaugurated in 1886, by Mr. Wolff, who employs three competent assistants. The store is 40x25 feet in dimensions, and a first class line of everything choice in groceries is kept in stock at all times. Mr. Wolff makes a specialty of fine creamery and dairy butter.

UNIGLICHT & BRO., Hat Sizing Factory, Nos. 46 to 50 Fourth street, Corner Dickerson Street, Near Central Avenue, Newark, N. J. Telephone No. 262. As Newark is undoubtedly one of the largest hat manufacturing centres in the country, it is hardly surprising that the processes for making these indispensable articles should be divided and subdivided. This naturally facilitates the manufacture, and increases the amount of goods. There is a special art in the sizing of hats, as well as in every other process, through which a hat must pass before it is ready for the market. In this art, the Messrs. Uniglicht are specially skillful, and the number of hats which pass through their hands in the course of a year is almost incredible. The firm in question, Messrs. Benjamin and Morris Uuglicht, have been established in this business in Newark since 1887. In a remarkably short time they won a name for producing excellent work, and their trade increased rapidly. The factory is situated at Nos. 46 to 50 Fourth street, corner Dickerson street, near Central avenue, and is 40x80 feet in dimensions. The firm is always busy filling the large orders that are constantly coming in. Orders sent by telephone, No. 262, receive as prompt attention as those given in person, and we but echo the public sentiment when we testify to the high esteem in which this firm is held by Newark business men.

PETER SCHUCKHAUS,

(Successor to J. Rittscher,) Dealer in Furniture, Bedding, Carpets, Oil Cloth, Best Feathers, Window Shades, Upholstering Goods, Stoves, etc., 196 Ferry Street, Newark, N. J. The stock carried by Mr. Peter Schuckhaus, doing a furniture business at No. 196 Ferry street (Turn Hall), is as large as it is attractive, and shows evidence of care and skill in its selection; but what makes this establishment an especial favorite with the purchasing public, is the fair minded and accommodating spirit displayed in its management. Mr. Schuckhaus sells furniture and household goods of all kinds, for cash or on easy terms, and since beginning operations in 1890, this house has made a record of enterprise and honorable dealing, which commends it to all who appreciate straightforward business methods. Every article sold at this store, is guaranteed to prove just as represented, there is no evasion, no attempt to shift responsibility. If certain goods be warranted to have certain qualities, the guarantee is strictly adhered to, and should it prove not to be justified by the facts, the matter will be made right, promptly and cheerfully, for Mr. Schuckhaus acts on the policy, that *he cannot afford to lose an honestly dissatisfied customer,* and he does not propose to if he can help it. The store is 50x75 feet in dimensions, and comprises in its stock, parlor suits, chamber sets and such kindred goods, all A 1 for the money. Of course, different people have different tastes, and *purses,* consequently a large stock must be carried. Reliable clerks are engaged, and furnish all information cheerfully. Furniture, carpets, bedding, feathers, window shades, upholstered goods, stoves, etc., can all be obtained at this establishment, much cheaper than elsewhere as "Broad" and "Market" street rents do not prevail on Ferry street. Mr. Schuckhaus succeeded Mr. Rittscher in this business during the current year. The public should patronize an establishment when the management tries so hard to please patrons.

EDWIN G. BACHMAN,

The Gents' Furnisher, 119 Market Street, Newark, N. J. Neckwear, Underwear, (light and medium weight,) Flannel Shirts, White and Colored Shirts and all the Latest Styles of Linen Brand Collars and Cuffs, Overalls, Jumpers and Working Shirts. Strangers in Newark (or indeed, in any other place, are frequently at loss to know just where to purchase certain articles of which they stand in need, for while they, of course, desire to deal with a trustworthy house, still they do not feel like paying an extra profit for a name. Gents' furnishings are among the commodities in most common request, and those stopping in Newark and wanting anything in this line, can possibly do no better than to visit the establishment carried on by Mr. Edwin G. Bachman, at No. 119 Market street. This gentleman began operations here in his present line of business in 1889. The premises utilized are 15x75 feet in dimensions, and contain a fine stock of gents furnishings, including neckwear, underwear, white and colored shirts, and all the latest and most desirable styles of collars and cuffs, and also, overalls, jumpers and working shirts. These goods will all be found to be excellent in quality and low in price, and as Mr. Bachman employs two efficient and experienced assistants, he is able to serve customers without delay. Mr. Bachman makes his own shirts.

B. R. BAILEY & SON,

Oysters, Clams and Produce, Commission Merchants, 46 Commerce Street, Newark, N. J. One of the largest and oldest established enterprises of the kind in this section of the State is that carried on by Messrs. B. R. Bailey & Son, at No. 46 Commerce street, for this representative firm are very large wholesale dealers in oysters, clams and produce, and conduct an undertaking founded very nearly thirty years ago, operations having been begun in 1862 by Messrs. M. Dehart & Co., who were succeeded by the present concern in 1889. Both members of the firm are natives of New Jersey, and are extremely well known in Newark and vicinity, not only in business, but also in social circles. A large force of men is employed, and every facility is at hand to enable the largest orders to be filled without delay, for the firm supply many prominent dealers, and must be prepared to meet the heaviest demands upon their resources promptly and satisfactorily. They utilize an extensive storage warehouse at City Dock, and constantly carry an immense stock of oysters, clams and produce, consignments being received from some of the leading producers throughout this section.

JOSEF WEIL,

Artist, Studio, 222 Market Street, Newark, N. J. The history of Newark should have recorded in its annals, the work of one of its most eminent artists. This beautiful accomplishment is possessed but by a very few men in our city, and foremost of them all is Mr. Josef Weil, who established his studio in our midst in the year 1889. Mr. Weil, from early childhood, was of an artistic turn of mind. As the years rolled around, his desire to perfect the talent which nature had bestowed upon him, grew so strong, that he resolved to devote his entire time to art. He finally concluded to go abroad and study the masterpieces of past great artists. Selecting Munich, that world renowned city of fame, as the best seat of learning, he became a member of the Royal Academy of Art in that place. For a number of years he studied at this institution, coming in contact with the teachings of the greatest artists of the present age. Having completed his course, Mr. Weil received congratulations from his faculty as having shown marked talent in art. He traveled extensively through Europe, visiting the most celebrated museums of art in the principal cities of the Continent. As we have said, he opened his studio in 1889, at No. 222 Market street, in this city. Mr. Weil, through the fine art work he has already executed in this city for his patrons, has made for himself, even in this early day, a reputation which assures him complete success. Mr. Weil is a native of Newark, and has hosts of friends who wish him success. His studio is a "bijou" of art, and is about 25x40 feet in dimensions. The work he does is chiefly oil painting and crayon. Orders for this kind of art work are executed with the greatest of artistic skill, and at short notice. Mr. Weil has a number of students, all of whom make rapid progress. The readers of the History of Newark who are inclined to art, are respectfully invited to interview Mr. Weil with reference to taking lessons. His class is already large, but a few more could be accommodated. The terms are reasonable, and satisfaction is generally experienced by the students. It is not out of place to mention that Mr. Weil is worthy of patronage. We should encourage home talent. Portrait and landscape work are executed in the most artistic manner. Mr. Weil has recently opened a "life" school at his studio. The school work will be from *life models,* on the same plan as Parisian and Munich schools. A large number have already joined the class.

BARBER & CO.,

Choice Meat and Poultry Market, 383 Plane Street, Newark, N. J. The ordinary run of people are inclined to have a preference for tender meats, and what can be more vexing than a piece of tough meat? Occasionally a dealer may be excused for having unknowingly sold a piece of such meat, but if he exercised the care which Messrs. Barber & Co. do at all times, the occurrence would be even rarer. There are a great many provision dealers in this city, but not all of them have the facilities to serve the public, as these gentlemen have, at their store. Equipped with all the latest and most convenient meat market fixtures, they keep about their establishment an atmosphere of neatness and purity, not always to be found in other meat markets, who pretend to sell good meats. We mean to convey the idea that good meats and vegetables are to be found at Barber & Co.'s market, then, and if any doubt the veracity of our statement, we invite them to give this market a trial, and they will be convinced. The firm does such a large business, that its stock of meats is continually in rotation, and does not have time to become unsalable. All the choicest meats kept in an A 1 shop will be found here, as well as the year-round vegetables, game and spring delicacies in their season. Three pleasant clerks are always at the store ready to fill your orders, and prompt service is a characteristic of the house. The prices on Messrs. Barber & Co.'s meats and other goods, are as low as can be quoted anywhere else in town, if not actually lower, and we feel sure that they are as reasonable as could be expected, considering the superior grades of meats furnished. The company has a finely equipped market and plenty of room, for its dimensions are 20x50 feet. Messrs. Barber & Co. inaugurated their present business in 1882. They employ two courteous and reliable clerks, who attend closely to the wants of the firm's patrons. We invite all those in this vicinity and elsewhere, who have not yet tried their establishment, to do so at their earliest convenience, as the advantages to be derived in trading with this house are plainly evident.

L. J. LYONS & CO., Manufacturers of Steam
Boilers, Brewers' Tanks, Chemical Pans, Oil Stills, etc., 191
to 195 Commerce Street, Newark, N. J. An enterprise which
has been carried on for more than forty years, and has held
a leading position almost from the very first, cannot but be
well and favorably known among the class to which it
caters, and as the undertaking conducted by Messrs. L. J.
Lyons & Co., manufacturers of steam boilers, etc., has just
such a record, it follows that Steam-users and manufacturers in general are well conversant with it, and give it
the hearty support to which its years of faithful service, and
the unsurpassed advantages it now offers so clearly entitle
it. Operations were begun by Mr. L. J. Lyons in 1847, and
in 1880 the present firm was formed by the admission of Mr.
Owen McCabe, both he and Mr. Lyons being too generally
known in business and social circles to render extended personal mention necessary. The firm occupy commodious
premises at Nos. 191 to 195 Commerce street, equipped with
the latest improved machinery, for the manufacture of steam
boilers, brewers' tanks, chemical pans, oil stills, etc., employment being given to fifty assistants, and the business being so
thoroughly systematized, that every order is assured prompt
and careful attention, and every detail of the work of construction or repairing is carried out under close and skillful
supervision. Boilers of all kinds will be made to order in a
superior manner, and repairing will be done at short notice,
and at moderate rates. A large stock of second-hand boilers is constantly on hand, and any ordinary size can be furnished without delay, and at a very low figure.

ALBERT F. KAZENMAYER, Successor to
John Pfister, Jr., Druggist and Apothecary, Deutsche
Apotheke, Corner Van Buren and Market Streets, Newark,
N. J. The drug business carried on by Mr. Albert F. Kazenmayer, at the corner of Van Buren and Market streets, was
founded in the year 1889. Mr. Kazenmayer is a native of
this city, and is well known in both business and social
circles. Despite the comparatively short time he has been
identified with the business at his present establishment, he
has the entire confidence of those who have thus far availed
themselves of the facilities he offers, for Mr. Kazenmayer
is very careful and thorough in his methods. As he has had
practical experience in the prescription line for a number of
years, he is excellently well qualified to meet all cases
brought before him. A large, complete and carefully selected
stock of drugs, chemicals and medicines is carried, and it is
obtained from the most dependable sources, and is noted for
its purity and freshness. Physicians' prescriptions are compounded at the shortest possible notice, consistant with the
exercise of the watchful care so essential in insuring against
even the most trival errors. All charges made are uniformly
moderate and satisfactory, and sufficient assistance is in attendance to insure polite and painstaking attention to every
caller. Mr. Kazenmayer has a nice looking pharmacy, the
fixtures being admirably adapted for the purposes, for which
they were intended. Mr. Kazenmayer also carries toilet
soaps, toilet articles, perfumeries and druggists' sundries.
Prescriptions are compounded day and night. We trust the
readers of our work will bear this establishment in mind,
whenever in need of anything to be procured of the pharmacist. We know of no better place to recommend to the
public residing in this immediate vicinity.

G. ELLERMAN & SON, First-class Bread,
Cake and Pie Bakery, No. 297 Market Street, Newark, N. J.
This popular establishment is well known in this vicinity as
a first-class bakery, for a specialty is made by the proprietors
of supplying families with goods that are of that even excellence which is so much appreciated. The premises occupied
will measure 25x99 feet. Employment is given to four competent assistants, as an extensive business has been built up.
A very large assortment of bread, cake and pie is at all
times carried, which cannot be surpassed in excellence and
variety. All orders for bread, cake, etc., will be executed
at short notice, and filled and delivered accurately, to bke
customers are served in a polite and attentive manner. Mr.
Ellerman, who is a native of Germany, started this business
in Brooklyn, in 1865, and it was in 1884 that the establishment
was founded in Newark, N. J., by G. Ellerman and Son. Mr.
G. Ellerman served in our army during the late rebellion,
as Corporal in the 8th New York Regiment.

THE OLIVER MANUFACTURING CO.,
H. M. Oliver, Manager, Manufacturers of the Oliver Patent
Wagon and Wagons of Every Description, Repairing in all
of its Branches, Factory, Foot of Clay Street, Newark, N. J.
Telephone 943. The Oliver Manufacturing Company was
incorporated in the year 1889, with Messrs. John Wegle as
president, Henry M. Oliver as treasurer, and William
Jacoby as secretary. Messrs. Wegle and Jacoby are natives
of Germany, but have resided here many years. Mr. Oliver
is a native of this State, Mr. Wegle at one time was honored
in the aldermanic chamber of the city government, but after
serving a short time, resigned the office, his business demanding his undivided attention. Though never having held public office, the other members are highly esteemed citizens
and business men in the community. In the prosecution of
their business, these gentlemen find that the employment of
fifteen skilled mechanics becomes necessary. The specialty
manufactured is the "Oliver Patent Wagon," well known on
the market. This wagon is noted for its elegance of construction, beauty in finish, and general appearance. Other
makes also receive attention, and repairing is done in all its
branches. To business men, the question of buying a new
wagon, or even that of repairing the "old one," should be a
"point" where a little discriminating thought is advisable.
None but reliable firms should be given the work, as it
means dollars and cents saved in both instances. Buy and
have your wagon repaired by the Oliver Manufacturing Co.,
at the foot of Clay street, in this city, and we guarantee you
will receive satisfactory work. The main building is 45x60
feet in dimensions; the blacksmith shop is 20x50 feet,
and the paint shop 18x50 feet in dimensions, and a 20 horse
power engine furnishes power.

MARTIN BROS., Wholesale and Retail
Grocers, and Dealers in Teas, Coffees and Spices, 29 Belleville Avenue, Newark, N. J. Those who have had extended
dealings with this house, do not need to be told of the advantage of placing orders here, but the many who are in
search of a well equipped and thoroughly reliable grocery
store, will thank us for calling their attention to that conducted by the Martin Bros., No. 29 Belleville avenue, for it
will be found to "fill the bill" in every particular, and both
as regards the completeness of the stock, and the efficiency
of the service, merits far more extended mention than our
space enables us to give it. This business was established in
1876. The store occupied measures 75x20 feet, and contains a well chosen stock of teas, coffees, spices, flour and
other articles too numerous to mention. These goods are
especially adapted to family use, and guaranteed to prove
as represented in every respect. The Messrs. Martin are
natives of Ireland, and have many friends here. They are
careful buyers, and are in a position to quote low market
rates on all goods handled, and to furnish goods satisfactory
to the most fastidious. Sufficient help is employed to assure
prompt service to all.

S. W. THOMPSON, Dealer in Flour, Feed,
Grain, Hay, Straw, Salt, etc. Manufacturer of the Manhattan
Feed, 383 Market Street, and 190 Commerce Street, Newark,
N. J. There is an immense amount of grain and feed handled
in Newark every day. Among the wholesale and retail dealers
in these commodities now bear a higher reputation than Mr.
S. W. Thompson. This gentleman handles flour, feed and
oats, and enjoys such relations with producers as to
enable him to fill all orders without undue delay at the very
lowest market rates. Mr. Thompson has been engaged in
his present line of business since 1884. He has gained a high
place in the confidence and esteem of his customers by the
integrity and ability shown in executing orders, and the
large wholesale and retail business now done is only the
legitimate outcome of the enterprising methods followed
from the beginning. The premises made use of by Mr.
Thompson are located at No. 383 Market street, and comprise two floors, each 22x77 feet in dimensions. He has
gained increased facilities from year to year, and was never
better prepared to guarantee satisfaction to customers than
at the present time. Four efficient and courteous assistants
are employed, and the most extensive orders can be filled at
short notice, and every care is taken to insure accuracy as
well as celerity.

JAS. McGUINNESS, First Class Boarding and Livery Stable, 209 and 211 Clinton Avenue, Telephone 853, Newark, N. J. One of the most reliable boarding and livery stables in this section of the city is kept by Mr James McGuinness, at 209 and 211 Clinton avenue. The stable is a commodious two-storied building, 50x150 in size, containing a large number of well-appointed and ventilated stalls, and in the generally complete equipment of the premises, all the modern adjuncts of convenience and utility are well represented. First class carriages and horses, for both business and pleasure driving, are furnished at short notice, and at the most reasonable prices, the "turn-outs" of this establishment being well known for their excellence in point of style and quality. Mr. McGuinness is the owner of ten excellent horses, and employs four assistants. He makes a specialty of boarding horses, and in this particular is able to give complete satisfaction, having an abundance of room, and large box stalls, if these are desired. Besides the stable on Clinton avenue, Mr McGuinness has a storehouse on Somerset street. This establishment was founded in 1887, by its present proprietor, who is a native of New York city, but is already well known and thoroughly respected in this city and vicinity. Orders can be sent by telephone to the stable, and will receive immediate attention.

WILLIAM MURRAY & CO., Dealers in Machine Oils, Anilines, Acids, Shellac, Alcohol, Dye Woods, Dye Stuffs, Wood Alcohol, Naval Stores, White Lead, Window Glass, Paints, etc., 180 Mulberry Street, corner Hamilton Street, Newark, N. J. Messrs. William Murray & Co. deal very extensively, both at wholesale and retail, in machine oils, manufacturers' supplies, painters' supplies, etc., carrying a heavy and varied stock, and quoting bottom prices on all the commodities handled. Mr. Murray is a native of New York State, and has been identified with his present enterprise since 1880. The store is located at No. 180 Mulberry street, corner of Hamilton, and is commodious and very conveniently fitted up. Standard extra quality short lap oak leather belting is a prominent specialty with this house, and is highly commended by all who have given it a trial, as it is made from butt pieces only, not over four feet in length, patent rivited, and thoroughly stretched by powerful machinery, and is consequently exceptionally strong, durable and reliable. The firm are prepared to supply belting made from pieces five and six feet long, same as made by other belt manufacturers, if desired. A full assortment of machine oils, anilines, acids, shellac, alcohol, dye woods, dye stuffs, wood alcohol, naval stores, white lead, window glass, paints, etc., is constantly carried, these goods being furnished in quantities to suit, without delay, and at positively the lowest market rates.

MISS LENA KELLER, 673 Broad Street, Newark, N. J. Every lady knows that the cutting and fitting of a dress or cloak, have much more to do with its appearance, than the material of which it is composed, for it is possible to make a very presentable garment from comparatively inferior goods, if the cutting and fitting be first-class; while on the other hand, the most rich, tasteful and costly material may easily be (and frequently is), spoiled in its effects by unskillful handling. Those of our lady readers who do their own dressmaking, in whole or in part, will find it greatly for their interest to call upon Miss Lena Keller, 673 Broad street, as she teaches cutting and fitting by the new French system, conceded by experts to be the most perfect and complete ever invented. It is the only system that drafts the back and front at the same time; is adjustable to every measure, fits every form, entirely obviates the necessity of alterations, and gives the same style as that attained by the best French dressmakers. Miss Keller is the Newark agent for this system, and will cheerfully give full information concerning it on application. Such of our readers as have not the time or the disposition to do their own dressmaking, would also do well to place their orders with Miss Keller, for she has an unsurpassed reputation, as an artistic and fashionable dress and cloak maker, and while giving personal attention to the filling of all orders, employs a sufficient force of competent assistants to enable commissions to be executed at short notice. Her charges are moderate, and we can confidently guarantee satisfaction to every customer. Miss Keller is a native of Morristown, N. J. and has built up an extensive and select patronage here in Newark.

NEWARK EMBROIDERY WORKS, H. Bornemann, Proprietor, Manufacturers of Embroideries of Every Description. Embroidered Flannel and Ladies' Flannel Skirts, Infants' and Children's Cloaks, Shawls, Wrappers, Skirts, Sacques, Dresses and Slips. Factory: 78-84 Shipman Street, Newark, N. J. New York Office and Salesroom: 86 Walker Street. Some of our readers may have wondered how the elaborate embroideries so common in the market can be sold at such low figures, and wonder is perfectly excusable in this connection, for these low prices would be impossible were it not for the exceptional ability and enterprise of the leading houses in this line of business. The Newark Embroidery Works produce an enormous amount of embroideries of every description in the course of a year, for the most improved facilities are utilized, and employment is frequently given to as many as 150 assistants at one time, the demand for the productions of this establishment having rapidly and steadily increased since operations were begun in 1881. The proprietor, Mr. H. Bornemann, is a native of Germany, and is very widely and favorably known in trade circles, both on account of the excellence of his goods and the reliability of his methods, as he sells goods on their merits, and faithfully carries out every agreement. The New York office and salesroom is at No. 86 Walker street, the factory being at Nos. 78-84 Shipman street, Newark. Embroideries of all kinds, and embroidered flannel and ladies' flannel skirts, infants and children's cloaks, shawls, wrappers, skirts, sacques, dresses and slips are very extensively manufactured in a great variety of attractive patterns, including many late and tasteful novelties. Workmanship and material are excellent, and Mr. Bornemann supplies many of the leading dealers throughout the country, being able to quote bottom prices on goods of standard merit. SEE OPP. PAGE.

MRS. T. DEVINE, Fancy Goods and Notions, 49 Sherman Avenue, Newark, N. J. There is but little need of our advising the well-informed ladies of this vicinity to visit the establishment of Mrs. T. Devine, at No. 49 Sherman avenue, Newark, for they are no doubt acquainted with some, at least, of the many advantages accruing to those who purchase supplies at this house, but as this book will come before the attention of many not so well informed, we are convinced that much good may result from naming a few of the inducements offered to patrons of the enterprise alluded to. Business was begun in 1890, and a growing patronage is being built up, as Mrs. Devine is unremitting in her efforts to convince the public that she is prepared to furnish everything in the line of fancy goods and notions, stamping and embroidery at the very lowest market rates for first-class articles. The advantage of dealing with a lady of Mrs. Devine's knowledge and experience is fully appreciated by those who have become her regular patrons. Two competent assistants are constantly employed. All orders are carefully attended to, and all efforts made to give full satisfaction.

A. T. STEFFENS & CO., Manufacturers of Saddlery Hardware, 260, 262, 264 and 266 Morris Avenue, Newark, N. J. Many thousands of dollars are invested in the manufacture of saddlery hardware in Newark alone, and one of the most important of the various local establishments devoted to this branch of production is that conducted by Messrs. A. T. Steffens & Co., at Nos. 260, 262, 264 and 266 Morris avenue. The business here located was founded in 1880, and came under the control of the present proprietors in 1886, the partners being Messrs. A. T. Steffens, J. O. Amberg, G. A. Thiessen and J. I. Amberg. The concern utilize four spacious buildings, comprising one containing three floors and a cellar of the dimensions of 50x40 feet, and three one story in height and measuring 25x40, 25x50 and 25x89 feet respectively. These premises are conveniently arranged and very completely fitted up with improved machinery, power being furnished by a fifty horse engine. Messrs. A. T. Steffens & Co. manufacture so many styles of saddlery hardware, that even to catalogue their productions would more than exhaust our available space, and we will simply say that their 1st comprises many valuable novelties as well as a full line of staple goods, and that their articles will bear the closest comparison with those of other dealers, both as regards excellence of material and workmanship, while the firm are prepared to wholesale them at the lowest market rates, and to fill even the most extensive orders without undue delay.

NEWARK EMBROIDERY WORKS, 78-84 SHIPMAN ST, NEWARK.

THE STAR SHOE WORKS. John Heath.

Proprietor, Boots and Shoes Made to Order from $3 up. Fine Repairing a Specialty. A Large Assortment of Gents' Fine Shoes Always on Hand, No. 140 Mulberry Street, Between Mechanic and Market Streets, Newark, N. J. It may safely be accepted as a general rule, that a boot or shoe showing fine workmanship, is composed of superior stock, for, although of course poor material may be made to present a good appearance by skillful handling, still ordinarily speaking, it does not pay to combine skilled labor and inferior stock. For illustrations of the truth of this statement, visit the Star Shoe Works, carried on by Mr. John Heath, at No. 140 Mulberry street, and you will see that the stock there shown comprise every variety of boot and shoe, designed for fine city trade, and also that the unusually careful workmanship displayed in the goods handled has its parallel in the care which has been used in the selection of the material composing them. As a consequence, a pair of shoes chosen from this assortment is bound to wear well, and look well, and it is owing to the general knowledge the people possess of this fact, that the large business has been built up. A specialty is made of fine custom shoes to measure, also of all kinds of fine repairing. Equal inducements are offered to ladies and to gentlemen, and for those who prefer ready-made goods, an immense assortment is carried. Two well-informed assistants are employed, and every caller is assured prompt and courteous attention.

LOUIS SCHLETH (Successor to Julius Gerth), Manufacturer of and Dealer in Looking Glasses, Portrait and Picture Frames, 233 Washington Street, Half Block from Market Street, Newark, N. J. Old Frames Regilt Equal to New. All Orders promptly attended to. No better opportunity for the display of taste in selection could be wished, than that afforded when choosing a looking glass or picture frame, for these articles should harmonize with their surroundings, and they play so important a part in interior decoration, that they may easily mar the whole appearance of an apartment if injudiciously selected. But the most cultivated taste cannot obtain the best results without ample material to work with, and therefore we take pleasure in calling the attention of our readers to the facilities afforded by Mr. Louis Schleth, at No. 233 Washington street. The machinery used in the works are the most modern, and Mr. Schleth having the "facilities," can do work at exceedingly low prices. The stock of mouldings is exceptionally large and varied, comprising in addition to staple goods, in gilt and carved wood, all the latest novelties in old oak, ivory and silver edging. Looking glasses and picture frames, of any size and description, can be made to order at the shortest possible notice, and beautiful work is also done in the line of easels, fancy tables, etc. Mr. Schleth is a native of New York city, and is thoroughly acquainted with his present business in every detail. His trade is steadily increasing, and no one in need of anything in this line, can afford to slight the opportunities he offers. Those uncertain as to what kind of frames to get, will find Mr. Schleth ready to advise them to the best of his ability, and as he has had much experience, his advice is well worth having. His stock, which is very large, enables customers to select any pattern which they may find to their taste. Mr. Schleth inaugurated his business in 1886. He employs competent assistants, and his premises are 1,500 square feet in area. Orders received will be given the most painstaking attention.

C. L. & T. H. FITHIAN Dealers in Beef, Veal, Mutton, Lamb, Pork, Vegetables, Fish, Oysters, Clams, Poultry and Game in Season, 45 and 47 West Kinney Street, Between Halsey and Washington, Newark, N. J. There is no disputing the standing of the establishment conducted by Messrs. C. L. & T. H. Fithian, at Nos. 45 and 47 West Kinney street, for this is universally conceded to be one of the most extensive enterprises of its kind in this vicinity. Business was begun here just about twenty years ago by the present firm. These gentlemen are both natives of New York city, and they have a thorough practical knowledge of the many details of the business in which they are engaged. The premises in use are of the dimensions of 40x50 feet, and contain a large and varied stock, comprising meats of all kinds, vegetables, fish, oysters, clams, and poultry and game in season. It is scarcely necessary to say that this firm deal in nothing but what they can conscientiously guarantee to prove as represented, as they have gained a high reputation for upright and honorable methods. Employment is given to eight competent assistants, and every order is assured prompt and careful attention, and goods are delivered free to all parts of the city. The Messrs. Fithian are in a position to quote the lowest market rates on all the commodities they handle.

PHILIP SLEE, Men's Furnishing Goods, No. 196 Market Street, Opposite Miner's Theatre, Newark, N. J. Assuming that the points of a first-class establishment of the kind conducted by Mr. Philip Slee, are the carrying of a varied stock of fashionable goods, the assurance of prompt and courteous attention to all callers, and the fixing of prices at fair and reasonable rates, it is difficult to see how the enterprise carried on by this gentleman could be greatly improved, for all the desirable features alluded to may be found therein, and that this fact is very generally appreciated by the residents of Newark and vicinity, is proved by the popularity of this representative store. Business was begun by Mr. Slee in 1887. He is a native of Newark, and is very widely known throughout this section of the State. Of the goods kept in stock may be mentioned, men's furnishing goods, and it may be stated that one of the most complete assortments is always to be found at this establishment, which is located at No. 196 Market street. The premises in use measure 15x30 feet, and employment is given to two well informed assistants. In closing we may say that no gentleman who desires to present a fashionable appearance, can afford to allow Mr. Slee's store to remain unvisited, for many novelties are offered there that it is hard to find elsewhere, and which are of importance to those wishing to dress correctly.

JOHN L. KINSEY, Park Pharmacy, 671 Broad Street, Four Doors Above West Park Street, Newark, N. J. The need of medicine has existed as long as man's human frailties, and will continue until he has reached a stage of absolute perfection and immunity. It necessarily occupies a most important and prominent place in the life of every community, and those who have charge of these vital commodities, need to be trained and reliable in the highest degree. These qualities are fully possessed by Dr. John L. Kinsey, one of Newark's leading druggists. Dr. Kinsey is proprietor of the Park Pharmacy, and is one of the most reliable and experienced druggists in this vicinity, having had an extended practice in this line of business. The stock of fine drugs of every description is very complete, and the most careful attention is paid to the filling of prescriptions, for which work Dr. Kinsey is peculiarly fitted by long practical experience, and for the thorough accuracy characteristic of this department, as well as purity of material, the store is widely noted. The premises are located at No. 671 Broad street, a few doors above West Park street, and are 20x80 feet in dimensions. A fine stock is carried, consisting of drugs, chemicals, patent medicines, fancy toilet articles and druggists' sundries. Five competent assistants are constantly employed and the large measure of patronage and success which the house now enjoys, is the highest tribute to the enterprise and reliability of its talented proprietor. Dr. Kinsey is a native of Morristown, N. J. He was in the Navy Medical Department for about eighteen months during our late war. He fully merits, as he has received, the confidence and esteem of his fellow citizens and professional confreres.

NOYES & BOULWARE, Mnfrs of

Ladders and Poles, cor. Norfolk and Orange Sts., Newark, N. J. It may surprise some of our readers to learn that the manufacture of ladders and poles is an industry by itself, but such is the fact, and, indeed, were such not the case, these highly useful and popular articles could never be sold at the low rates now quoted on them, for it is only by making a specialty of their production, that the expense of manufacture can be reduced to a minimum. Noyes & Boulware occupy a prominent position among the concerns engaged in this line of work, for they produce a large variety of ladders, poles, etc., and quote the lowest market rates on goods of standard quality. This business was founded by Mr. Noyes in 1888. The premises occupied are located cor. Norfolk and Orange streets, Newark, and comprise a shop 50x40 feet, a store-room 50x18 feet, and a shed 24x50 feet in dimensions. These are fitted up with the most improved facilities, and employment is given to eleven assistants. All orders by mail, or otherwise delivered, will receive prompt attention, and be filled at very short notice. They are prepared to meet all honorable competition, and those wanting anything in the line of step-ladders, trusses, painters' and masons' scaffolds, ropes, blocks and falls, flag, scaffold and awning poles, masons' horses, tubs and mortar boards, patent extension step-ladder and truss, will find it to their advantage to communicate with this firm. They make a specialty of the manufacture of fire department ladders, and are prepared to furnish estimates for scaffolding for churches, halls, etc. Mr. Noyes is a native of Bangor, Me., and is well known throughout Newark, and conducts one of the most complete ladder manufactories in this vicinity.

THE EAGLE WINKER MANUF. CO.

Sole Manufacturers of the Celebrated Eagle Winkers, also Drops, Face Pieces, tug ends, Bridle Fronts, pad Housings, Boots, etc. etc., Fancy Patent Leather Work in General. Office and Factory, 35 and 37 Mechanic Street, Newark, N. J. The Eagle Winker manufacturing company, report a large and steadily increasing demand for their productions, and it is not surprising that such should be the case, for the celebrated eagle winkers, of which the company make a specialty, are remarkably efficient, handsome and convenient in design, and are honestly and skilfully made from selected material, as are all the company's productions. The office and factory are located at Nos. 35 and 37 Mechanic street, the premises being of good size, and equipped throughout with the most improved machinery. Besides being sole manufacturers of the popular eagle winkers, the company makes drops, face pieces, tug ends, bridle fronts, pad housings, boots, etc., and fancy patent leather work in general. Winker plates will be made to order from paper patterns or measurement, and all commissions can be executed at short notice, employment being given to thirty assistants. The president of the company is Mr. John S. Lyles, the secretary and treasurer being Mr. James H. Robley. Both these gentlemen are well and favorably known in business circles throughout this vicinity, and to their enterprising and honorable methods the high standing of the company is chiefly due. No trouble is spared to maintain the high reputation now enjoyed, and uniformly reliable goods will be furnished at short notice, and at uniformly moderate prices.

A. C. NAVATIER, Wholesale and Retail

Dealer and Jobber in Confectionery, Fine Chocolates and Bon Bons a Specialty, 214 Mulberry Street, Near Green Street, Newark, N. J. It is true there are some people that "don't care anything for confectionery," but they miss a good deal of innocent enjoyment, and are certainly not to be envied in the least. The time when confectionery was believed to be hurtful is now gone by, and it is generally acknowledged that pure candies may be of positive benefit to the health. Some little care should be exercised to assure that they are pure, however, and as good a way as any is to buy from those handling only such goods, then you know that the candy is fresh as well as good in other respects, and the price is also as low as can be named anywhere. Mr. A. C. Navatier, of No. 214 Mulberry street, near Green street, Newark, has gained a high reputation as a wholesale and retail dealer and jobber in confectionery since he opened his present establishment in 1880, and we would most certainly advise every lover of well-flavored, fresh and pure candy, to give him a call. His assortment is a varied one, and the prices quoted are sure to prove satisfactory. Among other delicacies, Mr. Navatier makes a specialty of fine chocolates and bon bons, and has a large line of penny goods always on hand, which he guarantees pure and fresh. He gives close personal attention to the many details of his business, and has the satisfaction of seeing it steadily and rapidly increasing.

THE C. McINTIRE CO., C. H. McIntire,

Manager, Manufacturers of McIntire's Patent Connectors, Terminals and Specialties, Nos. 13 and 15 Franklin Street, Long Distance Telephone 882, Newark, N. J. The uses of electricity seem to be without limit. For many years we were content with it as used with telegraphy, now new machines and inventions are constantly appearing before the public for the practical use of this great power, and we have ceased to be astonished at anything. All our towns and cities are now furnished with electric companies, and the need in Newark is very great. Hence we find companies of very high standing located here, foremost among which must be mentioned The C. McIntire Co., formerly C. McIntire & Co., the name being changed recently to the one it now bears. Mr. Chas. H. McIntire is the manager, and proves himself the right man in the right place, as he is efficient and well fitted in every way to carry on the business of the company. The premises situated at Nos. 13 and 15 Franklin street, cover an area of 40x150 feet, and are fitted with abundant steam power, and every kind of machinery used in this business. Electric supplies of every description may be had here, comprising electric fixtures, insulated wire, electric wire, etc., the principle manufacture being the McIntire Patent Connector, and terminals of an improved kind. This company supplies all the largest telephone, telegraph and electric light companies in the United States and Europe, among which are the Long Distance Telephone Co., Western Union Telegraph Co., Bell Telephone Co., of Canada, International Bell Telephone Co., of Antwerp, Belgium, The Pennsylvania R. R. Co., and electric companies of all systems. Their stock comprises a full line of the McIntire patent specialties and supplies. Twenty skilful workmen are in the company's employ, who are ready at a moment's notice to attend to each and every detail of the business. The company is well known throughout the country. They have received the John Scott medal and premium, awarded by the Franklin Institute of Philadelphia, Pa., to the most deserving for patent specialties.

CYRUS F. LAWRENCE, Boarding and

Sales Stables, and Dealer in Fine Saddle, Carriage and Driving horses, 53 and 55 Austin Street, Newark, N. J. Telephone 488. There are few persons who do not enjoy driving. As an exercise it is certainly both pleasant and healthful, and those who are fond of horses, and who know how to treat them, are genuinely enthusiastic about this pastime. Riding is still more exhilarating, and is becoming more and more popular, as people recognize the advantages derived therefrom. It is not always possible to attain just the kind of horse one wishes from a livery stable, but there are many establishments of this kind in Newark, where most excellent horses are to be had at any time, both for riding and driving, and among these we can cite no better example than the one conducted by Cyrus F. Lawrence, at Nos. 53 and 55 Austin street. The stable occupies two floors, each 40x160 feet in dimensions. It is fully supplied with every facility for carrying on the livery, boarding and sales business, and can easily accommodate thirty-five or more horses. Mr. Lawrence owns ten horses, and takes twenty-five boarders. The carriages, of which a large number is here kept, are on the second floor. Mr. Lawrence deals in fine saddle, carriage and driving horses, giving his careful, personal attention to all transactions. Ten competent and reliable assistants are constantly employed, and all orders sent by telephone, No. 488, will be promptly attended to. We recommend this establishment to our readers as one where both horses and service are good, and the prices uniformly fair.

HUNTINGTON MACH-
ine Works, Smith & Landell,
Successors to E. W. Roff, Steam
Engines, Shafting, Pulleys and
Wood Working Machinery, for
Cabinet and Box Makers, Planing Mills, etc., all with the latest improvements. Office Nos.
135 and 137 Halsey Street, Newark, N. J. The Huntington Machine Works of the city of Newark, N. J., not only enjoy a local
reputation of high standing in
the superiority of the work
which is turned out, but a very
wide one throughout the State.
It is a credit to the citizens of
our city, to know that Newark
ranks sixth, as the most important city engaged in the manufacturing industries of this country. This reputation is based
upon the existence in our midst
of such establishments as the
one we have alluded to. True,
there are many turning out work
of a similar nature, but no where
in our city do we find an establishment doing business pertaining to machinery, who execute their work any better than
the Huntington Machine Works.
A firm who carry on a business
manufacturing steam engines,
shafting, pulleys and wood
working machinery, and carry
it on successfully, must have at
its helm, men who are more than
ordinary mechanics. It is, of
course, well known, that the
highest degree of skilled labor
is necessary to be employed in
the construction of such machinery, and that none but first-
class work is allowed to pass
in establishments of high standing. Without exaggeration, we
can say that the Huntington
Machine Works possess all these
qualities, and it is a fact, that if
the firm has succeeded as well as
it has, that it is due to the truth
of this statement. Like all
things, good work finds its level,
and that turned out by the firm
in question, has found itself upon
a level with other reputable
machinery works in Newark.
The firm is composed of Messrs. J.
W. Smith and C. Landell. Both
these gentlemen have made
their mark as machinists of a
superior order, and the market
knows them too well to allow us
to dwell unnecessarily in intro-
ductions. Employment is afforded to twenty-five skilled mechanics the year round. Parties in business, or contemplating going into business, would
do well to investigate the advantages which the Huntington
Machine Works offer in the
machinery they manufacture.
Steam engines, shafting, pulleys
and wood working machinery
for cabinet and box makers,
planing mills, etc., are all specialties with the firm, who offer
upon this kind of machinery,
prices which, if known to all,
would furnish sufficient inducements to cause many to place
their orders with the firm.

COREY & STEWART, HATTERS and

Furriers, 711-713 Broad Street, Newark, N. J. It is universally acknowledged that the hat is one of the most important features of a gentleman's dress. There are three points to be considered in the purchase of a hat: 1. Its constant use, being handled more than any other article of attire. 2. Its low cost, considering its length of wear compared to necktie, socks or other articles of attire. 3. As it is the most noticeable article a man wears, it is well to have a durable, finely made hat at the start. A man can wear a shabby coat and still preserve his self-respect, but a rusty hat is out of the question. Among the business houses of this city, one of the greatest prominence and longest standing is the firm of Messrs. Corey & Stewart, hatters and furriers, of 711 and 713 Broad street, Mr. J. W. Corey has a record as manufacturer for thirty-eight years, during which time he has never reduced the wages of his employees. He started his business alone in 1882, and eleven years later took as partner Mr. Stewart, the firm having since been known as Corey & Stewart. They provide furnishings at wholesale rates, and do an immense business in hats and furs. Mr. Corey, besides having the most thorough knowledge as a manufacturing hatter, consequent upon wide experience of so many years standing, has invented a number of articles pertaining to his branch of trade, which have proved successful in every way. Among these are the Hat wire brim, invented in 1856; the inflexible hat, in 1869. In 1871 the justly celebrated "Corey Brim Hat" appeared. Five years later a new leather hat lining, and in 1888 the improved adjustable mourning band. To the inhabitants of Newark the establishment of Messrs. Corey & Stewart is so well known and appreciated, it is superfluous to recommend it. To strangers we recommend it as a house reliable in every respect, and one where they cannot fail to find what they seek. The store is large and well adapted for its purpose, being 30x75 feet in dimensions, and twenty competent assistants are given constant employment.

DR. C. D. MANDEVILLE, Retail Drug-

gist, 412 Mulberry Street, Newark, N. J. Residence, 218 Mulberry Street. The retail drug store conducted by Dr. C. D. Mandeville, is doubtless pleasantly familiar to many of our readers, for it has for some years ranked very high among local establishments, and is to-day unquestionably as well managed an enterprise of the kind as can be found in this city. The patrons of a pharmacy have a right to expect the utmost caution on the part of the management when they are called upon to compound physicians' prescriptions, and we are happy to say that this expectation is fully realized in the case of the establishment in question, for the proprietor spares no pains to guard against the possibility of even the slightest errors, and has provided the most elaborate and improved facilities for the measuring and general handling of the drugs and chemicals dealt in. The preparation of physicians' prescriptions is recognized as the most important feature of the business, and the many orders daily filled show that the public are appreciative of the advan-

tages here offered. Dr. Mandeville is a practising physician, and established his drug store in 1888, which is located at No. 412 Mulberry street, his residence being at 218 Mulberry street, where he may be consulted from 8 to 10 a. m., and from 2 to 4 and 7 to 9 p. m. He gives close personal supervision to the many details of his pharmacy, and employs two competent and polite assistants, so that despite the magnitude of the business, every caller is sure of receiving immediate and careful attention. The stock not only includes drugs, medicines and chemicals of every description, but also fancy toilet articles, etc., moderate charges being made in connection with all departments of the establishment.

DAVID RIPLEY & SONS, Steam Saw

and Planing Mills, and Manufacturers of Packing Boxes Timber and Lumber, Commercial Dock, Newark, N. J. A commercial centre of the size and importance of Newark, embraces in her limits all the leading manufacturers. One branch of industry creates or helps another, and they all tend to the prosperity of the city, and the good of the country. The majority of manufactories use packing boxes for the shipment of their goods, and for this reason, the manufacture of these cases has assumed large proportions in Newark. Prominent among those engaged in this line of business, we find David Ripley & Sons. This house has been in existence for nearly half a century, having been founded by David Ripley in 1845. During fifteen years he carried on the business alone, at the end of which time he took his sons into partnership, and the firm name became David Ripley & Sons. This name is still retained, though Mr. Ripley, Sr., died in 1887. The firm is now composed of William A. Ripley, Charles O. Ripley and J. Wattles Ripley, all natives of New York State. The mills owned and run by these gentlemen are three large buildings, located in a most favorable position, with water at either side. Fifty hands are employed by this firm in its operations, and a 100 horse power engine is used to operate the machinery needed in the business. This is both wholesale and retail, timber and lumber being supplied in large or small quantities. The steam saw and planing mills are the scene of busy action, and the number of packing boxes turned out by this house is very great. The position occupied by Mr. Ripley was from the first a prominent one, and the house has lost none of its prestige since the decease of the senior member of the firm. The advantages offered to manufacturers and others by this house, are recognized as very great, and they are unsurpassed by any other in the city. The members of the firm have figured in different political offices, the Legislature, Board of Aldermen, and Police Commissioners, besides being most favorably known in the business world.

CARLSON BROS., Dealers in Choice Fam-

ily Groceries, Teas, Coffees, Spices, Fruits, Vegetables, etc., Butter, Cheese, and Eggs a specialty, 150 Mulberry Street, Newark, N. J. The old proverb says "the nest way to a man's heart is through his stomach," and if this be the case the Carlson Brothers must be on the direct road to the hearts of their patrons, for they certainly make every effort to satisfy their stomachs, and as a result have built up a large and steadily growing retail business. These gentlemen have only carried on operations since 1888, but as we have before stated, they understand their business, and the public have already shown their appreciation of the fact, by the liberal support they have given the enterprise. Messrs. Adolph and Clarence Carlson are both natives of Sweden, and are thoroughly acquainted with the handling of groceries of all kinds. The premises occupied are located at No. 150 Mulberry street, and are 20x60 feet in dimensions. Employment is given to three efficient and accommodating assistants. Choice family groceries, teas, coffees, spices, fruits, vegetables, etc., are constantly carried in stock at all times, while a specialty is made of butter, cheese and eggs. Orders will be given prompt and careful attention, and particular pains taken to offer the choicest goods obtainable, and to supply them in quantities to suit, so that the most fastidious can be satisfied. A visit to the establishment of Messrs. Carlson Brothers will prove all we have said regarding it to be strictly and entirely true.

As may be seen from the accompanying illustration, the building is one possessed of a handsome architectural effect which inspires thoughts of the substantial. The large plate glass fronts are worthy of note, as they are as large as any in the city. The building is four stories high and is of the dimensions of 75 x 100 feet, the basement is neatly finished off also, so that in the store itself are 37,500 square feet of available space in which to accommodate the immense stock carried. We are forced to generalize rather than enter into detail upon the stock which this house carries. Suffice it to say, that the person who once pays the establishment a visit of inspection, becomes convinced that no other similar establishment in the city equals it in point of beauty and quality of the goods carried. The enumeration of the goods which we have given in the heading of our article will give an adequate idea of the goods handled. The great feature of this house is its *characteristic* of selling articles of superior merit at the most reasonable terms. This is what interests the public, and what has been the key of success to Messrs. Muller & Schmidt. Both these gentlemen are natives of Germany, but have resided in this country for many years. Mr. Muller came over in 1857, and at odd times had been superintendent in saw mills or engaged in the cigar business. Mr. Schmidt had been a cabinet maker of a superior order, and began business as a dealer in second-hand furniture. This experience these gentlemen found to be of great help to them when starting in business. Their knowledge of the furniture business would swell the yearly amount of business transacted by parties who are in the same line, and yet frequently are so ignorant of their business as not to be able to distinguish a cherry stained set from the genuine article. The employment of twelve competent salesmen and assistants is necessitated to meet the requirements of the trade. Three wagons and five horses are also kept on the go at all times delivering goods. These beautiful vehicles are familiar sights on the streets of our city. An elevator is a feature of the store, and does away with the tedious climbing of stairs. Electric lights

MULLER & SCHMIDT, Dealers in Furniture, Carpets, Oil Cloth, Live Geese Feathers, Beds and Bedding of Every Description, Stoves, Ranges, Baby Carriages, Refrigerators, Hair, Husk, Excelsior and Straw Mattresses, Store Nos 113, 115 and 117, and Warerooms Nos. 86, 88, 90, 92, 94, 96, and 98 Springfield Avenue, Newark, N. J. The well known establishment whose cut we print upon this page is worthy of our attention in this book. Its inception took place a little lower down on Springfield avenue, on the first of October, in the year 1885. Messrs. Muller & Schmidt, the present proprietors, were the inaugurators of the enterprise. The establishment was received with so much favor by the public that the increase in business demanded newer and larger quarters. A removal was accordingly effected on the first of April, 1890, the present spacious and handsome edifice being selected by the firm for the new location.

are found in every corner of the store for the better inspection of goods at night. A stock of $35,000 is carried and offered to the public at the lowest market rates. Our young friends contemplating "going housekeeping" would do well to remember that they will save money in trading here.

ARTHUR R. SCHAAF, Wholesale and Retail Grocer and Flour Dealer, Selected Teas and Coffees, Fine Creamery Butter a Specialty, 378 and 380 Springfield Avenue, corner Camden Street, Newark, N. J. Telephone 966. The grocery store conducted by Mr. Arthur R. Schaaf is worthy of special mention in the "History of Newark, and Its Leading Business Men." No store on the Hill engaged in this important branch of mercantile activity is a more representative one of its kind, for all proclaim it the best stocked and the cheapest to deal with. The inception of this new enterprise did not take place until the current year, but the favor with which it has been met by the public and the liberal patronage it has received, makes it worthy of an establishment of much longer standing. This is certainly high praise, but the reputation which Mr. Schaaf's grocery store has already attained as a reputable house to deal with, is as deserved as it is popular. The store is admirably adapted for the purposes for which it is intended, and is very spacious, its dimensions being 3,250 square feet in area. It is well finished off and lighted, and an atmosphere of neatness pervades the whole surroundings. The stock having been purchased but recently, is as pure and as fresh as running water. Four competent and courteous assistants are given employment and render faithful and prompt service. There is no disputing the fact that Mr. Schaaf has a nice store and a nice stock of goods to select from. His prices defy competition. With such favorable conditions he is certain to establish a large trade before many d iys. Mr. Schaaf is a native of New York city, and has hosts of both social and business friends in Newark. We recommend his store to the favorable consideration of the readers of the History of Newark. Mr. Schaaf, previous to his engaging into business himself alone, had for seventeen years been associated in partnership with his brother at No. 138 Springfield avenue. He had been acting all these years in the capacity of conducting the business, so that we see his experience has been great.

A. V. HAMBURG, New York Notion

Store, Hosiery, Underwear, Gloves, Corsets, Fancy Goods and Notions, 265 Broad Street, Newark, N. J. This well known house stands to-day among the most successful uptown business houses. Was established in 1886, and has been the first dry and fancy goods business to succeed in the upper portion of Newark. Mr A. V. Hamburg's experience covers a period of eighteen years in this line, and by close personal attention he has established a good business reput ation in the midst of a growing portion of the city. Hamburg's New York Notion Store carries a full line of ladies' and gents' furnishing goods, including a great variety of corsets, gloves, hosiery, underwear, kid gloves, collars, cuffs, dress trimmings, neckwear, jewelry and fancy goods and notions of every description. The kid glove department of this house is of special importance. Importing their own lines of kid gloves, they are enabled to offer their customers first-class goods in latest novelties, at favorable prices. The corset department in this house is conducted upon an extensive scale, having constantly in stock the leading makes and styles, which include ladies', misses' and children's. A large assortment of fancy goods and notions is also carried. The gents' furnishing department contains a well selected line of gents' wants, and the custom shirts manufactured by this house have a well earned reputation. Competent and courteous help is always employed by this house, and patrons enjoy their shopping tours when spent at Hamburg's New York Notion Store.

WOODSIDE PHARMACY, J. E. Janes, M.

D., Cor. Washington and Elwood Avenues, Newark, N. J. The Woodside Pharmacy was founded nearly fifteen years ago, by Dr. J. E. Janes, who at that time became a practising physician. Dr. Janes is a well known man in these parts. He has grown up with Woodside, and is in truth a part of the place. Graduating from the Western Reserve College in 1865, Dr. Janes went to New York and entered the Medical College. He served his time at Bellevue Hospital, and took his degree in 1870, when he settled in his present position. As a physician Dr. Janes has, in an eminent degree, demonstrated his skill and ability, and has built up a large and fine practice, while as pharmacist and chemist, he occupies a leading position in the profession. Dr. Janes pays particular attention to the compounding of physicians' prescriptions and family recipes, and conducts all business personally, thereby guaranteeing absolute accuracy in every instance. The pharmacy is fitted up with every convenience, and its appearance is neat and very attractive. For the convenience of patrons, Dr. Janes also keeps a postage stamp station upon the premises, which are located at the corner of Washington and Elwood avenues. Patients wishing to consult Dr. Janes professionally, will do well to call between the hours of 8 and 9 A. M., 1 and 2 and 7 and 8 P. M. Besides his record as a medical man, Dr. Janes served with distinction in our late war.

W. H. BENNETT, Wholesale and Retail

Dealer in Milk and Cream, Office, 51 Bank Street, Newark, N. J. Creamery, Andover, Sussex Co , N. J. Sole Agent for Howell's Purified Condensed Milk, Cream and Pot Cheese. Telephone 383. The establishment conducted by Mr. Wm. H. Bennett on Bank street, is worthy of extended mention in this, a history of the representative business enterprises of Newark. It is an important question, that of pure milk. In a large city like ours, where the farmers are "few and far adjacent," milk is not always milk. Those of our readers who have been "taken in" by their milkmen, will hail with delight, then, an establishment partaking of the nature of Mr. Bennett's. This gentleman is in close relation with the producers of this important article of our diet, and whatever you buy at his establishment, you may be sure is as pure and unadulterated as anything can be. Milk and cream are handled in greater quantities than by any other concern in the city, and the prices quoted are as low as can be expected on goods of relative value. The firm in question was inaugurated in 1887, by Mr. W. H. Bennett, who has built himself up a reputation envied by other dealers, who have been less successful. His creamery is in Andover, Sussex county, New Jersey. Mr. Bennett is sole agent for Howell's purified condensed milk, cream and pot cheese. These goods are too well known by the public for us to dwell unnecessarily upon their merits. Mr. Bennett's establishment is 25x50 feet in dimensions, and in it are employed seven competent and courteous attendants. The wants of the public are well met in the line of goods carried, so we deem it both a pleasure and a duty to point out the advantages to be derived in purchasing at Mrs Bennett's place of business. A wholesale and retail business is done in all that pertains to milk, cream, butter, cheese, condensed milk, etc.

C. M. MILLARD, Ecclesiastical and Domes-

tic Stained Glass, Architectural Decorator in Plaster, Memorial Windows a Specialty. Designs and Estimates Furnished on Application. Office and works, 145 Washington Street, Newark, N. J. A representative business carried on among the many industries of Newark, is that of stained glass windows. It is not many years ago when even the ordinary plain transparent glass received its highest perfection, to say nothing of stained glass. Hitherto our dwellings contained nothing in the line of ornamental glass, and the most costly edifices had all that the market afforded, plain glass. But to-day our buildings are improved 100 per cent. in their decorative appearance by the introduction and use of stained glass. In residences, front doors, storm doors, transoms and the squares of lattice work are generally receiving stained glass. Offices are also beginning to use stained glass, as, while admitting light, it shields the interior from the gaze of curious and inquisitive observers of what is going on inside. It is in large public buildings, libraries, city halls, depots, and especially in churches, where the genuine art work, which can be put into stained glass, has a wider and broader field, that we can appreciate the beauties of this invention. We have seen tableaux illustrated upon stained glass in the windows of churches which would do credit to Raphael or Michael Angelo's brushes. This is not exaggeration either, for we repeat, wonderful works of art have already been executed upon stained glass, and are to-day presently kept as lasting monuments of the progress of art in the present age, in our most celebrated art galleries and museums. To contractors of buildings, architects, etc., we wish to call the attention to Mr. C. M. Millard's stained glass works. It will pay you to visit his establishment and see what you can select that is tasty for the buildings you undertake. Two floors, 30x70 feet in dimensions are occupied, affording 2,800 square feet of available floor room. Ten skilled workmen receive regular employment, and orders are promptly and tastily filled. Mr. C. M. Millard is a native of England. Stained glass is cheap, decoratively and usefully ornamental. Below we direct our readers attention to some of Mr. Millard's work. Residences: Mr. Lawrence's house, at Flushing, Long Island; Mr. Wagner's house, at Red Bank, N. J.; Mr. J. E. Rowe's house, at Newark, N. J.; Mr. DeVausay's house, at Newark, N. J.; Mr. Carhuff's house, at Newark, N. J. Churches: First German Pres. Church, Mercer street, Newark, N. J.; Church of Carmelite Fathers, 29th street, New York; Church of St. Thomas the Apostle, 118th street, New York; Fewsmith Memorial Church, Hudson street, Newark, N. J. Public Buildings; Market Street Depot, Newark, N. J.; Second National Bank, Hoboken, N. J.

COCKEFAIR & DENMAN, Dealers in Groceries and Salt Meats, 483 Washington Street, corner Crawford Street, Newark, N. J. There are grocery stores in Newark to do justice to a city twice its size, almost, and were it not for a few like Cockefair & Denman's to redeem the reputation of the grocery business, we fear the public would have reason to complain. To furnish the public as it should be furnished with its groceries, a grocery, if it expects the patronage of people who purchase none but first-class goods, should have such high grade of goods in stock; but if it is inclined to be indifferent as to the quality of the stock selected, it must sooner or later wake up some fine morning and find that the trade has gone to patronize elsewhere. A great many men fail to succeed in business because they know not that the public is intelligent enough to detect their "little game" in their methods of doing business. Others who are in business, as Messrs. Cockefair & Denman, are fully aware that, if for no other reason than that of honesty, it is better to treat the purchasing public "on the square" (as the expression goes), than to attempt deception. It pays in the long run, and these gentlemen have found it so, not that we mean to infer that these men would perhaps possibly try the unfair methods if they thought they could make more by it, but because they are known and recognized in Newark as business men of the strictest integrity and conscientiousness of what is right to do by the people who leave their hard earned dollars with them. The founder of this establishment was Mr. E. M. Hopping, in 1868, the present proprietors having assumed control in 1886. Mr. Cockefair was previous to this ten years in company with Mr. Hopping. Four competent clerks are engaged in rendering faithful service in the store, which measures 18x75 feet in dimensions. Mr. John W. Cockefair is a native of Bloomfield, and Mr. G. Harvey Denman of Madison, N. J. The firm, besides carrying all the choicest articles to be found in a first-class grocery store, also carry a heavy stock of salt meats and vegetables of all kinds. Neatness and purity are features of the meat furnished. Families not quite satisfied with the stores they patronize for groceries and provisions, should call on Messrs. Cockefair & Denman at their earliest opportunity.

ROSA BLAASE, Dealer in Fine Cigars, Tobacco, etc., Newspapers and Periodicals, Stationery, etc., 64 William Street, Newark, N. J. The enterprise which Mrs. Rosa Blaase conducts at No. 64 William street, was inaugurated by her husband, Mr. Chas. Blaase, in 1883. In 1890 Mrs. Blaase began to continue the business herself. She is an estimable lady who needs the encouragement she solicits. We have seen her establishment, and pronounce it well stocked with all that heads this notice, viz.: fine cigars, tobacco, newspapers and periodicals. A fine line of stationery is also carried, and all in all, it is one of the best stores of its kind in this vicinity. We should all have a desire to further our education by reading the newspapers, and at Mrs. Blaase's will be found all the local and foreign papers, magazines and periodicals of the day. Users of the "weed" will find a veritable heaven for their tastes here, as all brands of the choicest cigars and tobacco are carried. Pay Mrs. Blaase a call and be convinced of the truth of our statements.

J. L. WHITNEY'S Pharmacy, 365 South Orange Avenue, corner 10th Street, Newark, N. J. Public Telephone 766. Night Bell. Mr. J. L. Whitney's pharmacy, on South Orange avenue, was not inaugurated by him until recently, but the liberal encouragement it has received makes it worthy of an establishment of much longer standing. The stock of drugs, medicines and chemicals carried by him are pure and fresh, from the most dependable sources and are of a superior quality. Mr. Whitney is a native of Orange county, N. Y., and is proficient in his chosen profession. Having devoted years of his life in the study of prescription compounding, he is prepared to meet the wants of the public in this respect, as no other establishment in the immediate vicinity can. He also carries a finely selected stock of fancy and toilet articles, cigars, perfumes, sachet powders, etc., etc. These may be purchased at prices which are as low as articles of merit will allow. Mr. Whitney has a magnificent store, the fixtures being admirably adapted for the purpose for which they are intended. We take pleasure in recommending this establishment to the readers of the "History of Newark and its Leading Business Men." Those of our readers who live in this neighborhood can find no better place to patronize for drugs and medicines. Courteous assistants are employed, and every one receives prompt attention. The store is open day and night, and prescriptions are filled at all hours. Public telephone 766. 365 South Orange avenue, Newark, N. J.

PHILIP ZEHNER, Baker, 302 Mulberry Street, Newark, N. J. There is no need of our pointing out the trouble which may be saved by purchasing one's supplies of bread, pastry, etc., from a first-class baker, for the majority of our readers have had practical experience of the advantages of pursuing such a course, and so need no argument to convince them. But still there are unquestionably some people who have a prejudice against "baker's bread," and it must be confessed that there is baker's bread in the market that is neither palatable nor nutritious, but what does that prove? We have seen "home made" bread which was better adapted for building material than for eating purposes, but that don't proves that all home made bread is unfit to eat, any more than the incompetence or carelessness of a few bakers proves that all who are in the business are equally unworthy. We have no hesitation in saying that the productions of Mr. Philip Zehner, doing business at No. 302 Mulberry Street, are good enough for the most fastidious person to eat, and to thrive upon, and the magnitude and steady increase of that gentleman's business proves that our opinion is that of many others. Mr. Zehner is a native of New Jersey, and has been identified with his present enterprise since 1890. He is successor to Mr. L. Kellner, and had had been with him for fifteen years previous to his coming into possession. The premises occupied by him, at the above address, comprise two floors, each 20x60 feet in dimensions. Three competent assistants are employed, and an extensive retail business is done. Mr. Zehner's prices are low, his productions first-class, and his facilities for the prompt filling of orders are well known in this vicinity.

JACOB GOLDBACH, Practical Watchmaker and Jeweler. Watches, Clocks and Jewelry Neatly Repaired. Spectacles and Opera Glasses a Specialty. 183 Ferry Street, corner Van Buren Street, Newark, N. J. Too much care can never be exercised in the selection of jewelry, for no article of personal wear is looked upon as more accurately representing the taste and position of its owner. Richness is to be sought for, while "show" is to be avoided, and the best way to obtain jewelry calculated to please the eye and not offend good taste is to patronize a jewelry store of high repute, nothing more nor less. Patronize an establishment of repute in this respect, and you are safe from the deceit so frequently practiced by second rate jewelers. (?) We can help our readers in their search for a reliable jewelry establishment. That conducted by Mr. Jacob Goldbach, at No. 183 Ferry street, is as worthy of your patronage as any in the city, for this gentleman deals in none but high class goods, and the prices quoted are also as reasonable as anywhere else in this city, if, indeed, they are not more so. Broad and Market street jewelers pay "big rents"; Mr. Goldbach does not, and he is able to take the difference in rents and divide it equally with his patrons. His store is just as spacious and attractive, the only difference is that it is on another street than Broad or Market. That does not impair the goods in the least. Watches, clocks and jewelry are neatly and promptly repaired. Two courteous and skilled assistants are employed. Remember the place. No. 183 Ferry street, Jacob Goldbach.

E. S. SHAWGER, Roseville Grocery, Fine

Grocer and Provision Dealer, Wines, etc., Meat and Vegetable Market, Corner Roseville Avenue and Orange Street. The vastness and importance of the grocery and meat trade of Newark can scarcely be over-estimated, and the total quantity of these goods retailed in the course of a year must be something enormous. Each section of the city has certain houses which are conceded to be the leaders in their several lines, and so far as Orange street is concerned, this position must be given to the establishment conducted by Mr. E. S. Shawger, at the corner of Roseville avenue and Orange street. This enterprise was founded in 1875, by its present proprietor. The undertaking has been steadily extended since its inception, for the methods praticed have been at once enterprising and conservative, and such as could not fail to inspire confidence and attract patronage. An extensive retail business is done, nine assistants being required to serve the many patrons, fill the many orders, etc. The premises occupied comprise a store 28x80 feet in dimensions, in addition to a store room 12x90 feet in size, and are stocked with a large and varied assortment of goods, including fine groceries and choice meats of every description, also wines, etc., and vegetables of all kinds in their season. The prices quoted at the Roseville Grocery are very reasonable, and economy is best served in the long run by trading at a reputable establishment like this. Mr. Shawger is a native of Rockaway, N. J., and is very widely known and highly respected in Newark. Orders will be promptly attended to, and delivered accurately as promised.

CHAS. UPTON, Cigar Dealer, 110 Orange St.,

Newark, N. J. There is but one sure way of distinguishing a good cigar, and that is to smoke it, for in spite of the claims of self-styled "experts," we question if there is a man living who can infallibly judge by any other means. Examination will tell whether a cigar is well or ill made, and whether it is well seasoned or not, but beyond this it avails but little, and, therefore, the smoker has only one surety that he will not be imposed upon, and that is the reputation of the dealer from whom he buys. Mr. Charles Upton has long had the name of selling thoroughly satisfactory cigars at moderate prices, and this name is so well deserved that we feel that we can do our readers no greater service than to call their attention to this gentleman's establishment at No. 110 Orange street, for here may be found a remarkably complete assortment of cigars, pipes, tobacco and smokers' articles of all kinds, and the prices are as satisfactory as the goods themselves. Mr. Upton makes a specialty of an excellent line of cigars which he calls the "Upton's Tactics Brand." These are made for the trade of this house, and were registered August 18, 1886, by Charles Upton. They are made from the finest selections of imported tobacco, and are warranted to contain full Havana filler, no artificial flavors of any description being used. The Upton's Tactics Cigars are a veritable bargain. They cost but five cents apiece and are worth more than many that are sold for double the price. They are largely sold to smokers throughout the city, and we have no hesitation in recommending them favorably to the public. The store occupied by Mr. Upton measures 600 square feet, and contains in addition to the tobacco, a fine assortment of confectionery. Mr. Upton has carried on this business since 1864, succeeding Wm. Duerniger, who started it in 1852. The present owner is a native of Newark, and is an energetic and reliable business man. Employment is given to three reliable assistants, and callers are assured prompt as well as polite attention.

LOUIS V. PFEIFER, Dealer in Choice

Beef, Veal, Mutton, Lamb, etc., Poultry and Game in Season, 561 Orange Street, Opposite 11th Street, Roseville. Every house keeper of any experience knows that much of the worry and trouble too often connected with marketing, is due to the questionable business methods of some houses engaged in furnishing family supplies, and, therefore, it is of interest to all to learn of an establishment, the management of which is characterized by the entire absence of "sharp practice" of any kind. We have no intention of asserting that the establishment conducted by Mr. Louis V. Pfeifer is the only enterprise of this kind in the city, of which this may be said, for such an assertion would be wide of the truth,

but we do say that its proprietor deserves great credit and liberal patronage, for the manner in which he has conducted affairs since 1883. Mr. Pfeifer's customers have learned that they may place absolute dependence upon the representations made to them, and also that the prices at which dependable goods are furnished at this market, will bear the severest comparison with those quoted at any establishment in the vicinity, on articles of equal merit. The premises occupied are 20x50 feet in dimensions, and an extensive retail business is done in beef, veal, mutton, lamb, etc., also poultry and game in their season. Business is carried on at No. 561 Orange street, opposite 11th street, and employment is given to three assistants, so that the large patronage enjoyed is quickly and easily attended to. The proprietor, Mr. Louis V. Pfeifer, has fairly won his exceptional success by hard work, combined with the habit of close personal supervision, of every department of his business.

LAWSHE & CO., Transporters of Heavy

Freight, Between Newark and New York, Offices 280 Market Street, Newark, N. J., 230 Pearl Street, New York. A careful examination of the many and extremely varied industries of Newark, shows us some important houses that cannot be classed among the manufacturers or the ordinary tradesmen. No work of this kind would be complete without the mention of these, as well as other prominent business houses, and in this connection we take pleasure in calling the favorable attention of our readers to Messrs. Lawshe & Co., transporters of heavy and light freight, between Newark and New York. This well known express company was established in 1864. From the first, it occupied a most prominent position among the other transportation companies of the country, and during more than a quarter of a century that it has been in existence, it has maintained this important position, and stood at the head of the express business between Newark and New York. Besides transporting heavy and light goods between the above named cities, Messrs. Lawshe & Co., have facilities for forwarding goods of any kind to all parts of the globe. The company maintains three offices, which are located as follows: 280 Market street, Newark, N. J., 51 to 55 Prospect street, Newark, N. J., 230 Pearl street, New York. Orders or goods sent to these addresses will receive prompt and careful attention. The individual members of the firm are L. B. and D. T. Lawshe. These gentlemen have been long known in business circles here and elsewhere, and are known to be both reliable and trustworthy in the work they execute. In closing we would say that shippers wishing to send goods to Newark from distant points, will save both time and money by entrusting them to Messrs. Lawshe & Co.

G. W. LAWRENCE, 611 and 613 Broad

Street, Opposite Trinity Church, Newark, N. J. Importer and dealer in Glass, China, Pottery, Lamps, etc. Goods direct from the best Factories in Europe and this country. The enterprise carried on by Mr. G. W. Lawrence, was established by him in 1870, and has therefore been under his able management for the past twenty years. The premises occupied are 23x51 feet in dimensions, containing a heavy and extremely varied stock of glass, china, pottery, lamps, etc., selected with care and taste, from the most reputable factories in Europe and this country also. Decorative glass and china ware is now produced at prices within the means of all, and the ornamental character of such ware has made it a favorite with all cultivated people. The chief objection to the use of decorative ware—the difficulty of replacing one or more pieces accidentally broken, is now to a great extent obviated, for there are certain stock patterns carried by first-class dealers constantly, and pieces can be matched for years to come, as easily as white ware. Mr. Lawrence is prepared to furnish outfits for hotels, restaurants, bars, etc., in fine glass ware, etc, of such patterns, in point of artistic beauty of shape, decoration and lowness of price, that they are impossible to surpass. He also makes a specialty of bonus in silver, glass, etc. Mr. Lawrence is an importer and dealer in the above named lines of goods, and the extensive retail glass and crockery business transacted, requires the services of ten competent assistants. The premises occupied are located at Nos. 611 and 613 Broad street, and contain a stock embracing many attractive novelties, which will be cheerfully shown, and prompt and courteous attention given to every caller.

H. W. SMITH, Manufacturer of The Domestic Shirt, Overalls, Jumpers and Engineers' Suits, also Hats, Caps, etc., Athletic Goods, Gents' Furnishings, No. 201 Market Street, Newark, N. J. The establishment formerly known as "The Smiths," has long been favorably known in connection with the manufacture and sale of the "Domestic Shirt," and the carrying on of a general furnishing business. This enterprise was inaugurated in 1860. Ten years later Mr. Harry W. Smith, now the sole proprietor, came into possession. The business has steadily developed, especially during the last decade, until it has become one of the most extensive and important undertakings of the kind in the State. Mr. Smith now offers more inducements than ever before, and his store is undoubtedly the headquarters for fine shirts, gentlemen's furnishings of all kinds, athletic goods, overalls, jumpers, engineers' suits, etc. He also offers great inducements in hats and caps, having continually in stock the latest styles in silk, derby and felt. These are made by the leading hatters in the country, such as Dunlap, Youman and Miller. Mr. Smith claims to sell the best line of $2 hats in the city. There is no excuse for not being suited at this house, for aside from the stock being varied, particular attention is paid to conforming hats to fit the head. This is the only way to attain comfort. To accommodate the extensive stock, the occupancy of two floors is necessary, these being each 35x105 feet in dimensions. Employment is given to eight assistants, and despite the magnitude of the business, callers are attended to with a promptness and care which might be profitably imitated at many a much smaller establishment. The store is located at No. 201 Market street, and those looking for the very latest fashionable novelties in gentlemen's furnishings, hats, caps, etc., may save time and trouble by going there, and the chances are that they will save money also, for Mr. Smith enjoys very favorable relations with manufacturers, importers and jobbers, and is content with a small margin of profit on all the many goods he handles.

W. W. LYON, Dealer in Fancy Groceries, Fine Cigars, Foreign and Domestic Fruits, Vegetables in their Season, 308 Mulberry Street, corner Mulberry Place, Newark, N. J. In compiling the various industries of Newark the retail grocery trade assumes a decided importance. Among those who supply fresh and first-class groceries is Mr. W. W. Lyon. His store is located at No. 308 Mulberry street, corner of Mulberry place, and is well stocked with fancy groceries, etc., also admirably arranged for the extensive business transacted. Five reliable clerks are employed, who wait upon customers in a polite and attentive manner, and all goods are delivered promptly as desired. This is one of the most reliable establishments in its line in Newark, and the stock carried comprises everything usually to be found in a first-class grocery establishment. In addition to groceries, Mr. Lyon deals extensively in fine cigars, foreign and domestic fruits and vegetables in their season, which will be found superior to some quoted at much higher prices at other establishments. Mr. Lyon is a native of Newark, and is well and favorably known throughout the community. The premises occupied are 30x100 feet in dimensions, thus affording ample space for the handling of the large and varied stock. Goods are sold in quantities to suit purchasers, and the prices will be found as reasonable as any in Newark for the same quality of goods.

NEWARK BLUE PRINT CO., Herbert F. Soverel, Manager, Corner Broad and Cedar Streets, Newark, N. J. The science of chemistry is the one which deserves most the attention of the learned, for, as one eminent writer has said, "It is really the only science." The rapid progress which it has made within the past few decades has demonstrated theories which had hitherto existed simply in embryo, and brought to light facts which have surprised the world. If we pause to reflect for a moment, we will note the important rôle chemistry plays in the world of business. Everywhere we find chemical agents employed to perfect the work which, without the knowledge of chemistry, would remain imperfect, if not impossible. In our rolling mills, dye works, laboratories, paint and oil works, etc., etc., knowledge of chemical properties forms the chief feature of the work, and makes millions for the capitalist. In complicated problems and in the simplest axioms, chemistry and the knowledge of it makes itself evident to scientists and manufacturers. In a thousand and one ways, then, can a knowledge of chemical properties be put to use, and good use too. Take the "Blue Print" business, for instance. Here is a gentleman, Mr. Herbert F. Soverel, who uses his chemical knowledge in the process of reproducing drawings, maps, pictures, writings, etc., by sun printing. This is one of the triumphs of a practical knowledge of chemistry. Nothing but a superficial knowledge of these things ever becomes known to those who are not students, and actual lovers of the study of chemical changes, so that we credit Mr. Soverel with a good deal of practical and useful knowledge. To architects, engineers, draughtsmen, patent lawyers and others who are likely to have occasion to have works of this kind executed, we heartily recommend Mr. Soverel, who stands at the head of his profession in the process of blue and sun printing, as manager of the Newark Blue Print Co., corner of Broad and Cedar streets, Newark, N. J.

GEO. W. THOMAS, Boarding and Livery Stable, 79 and 81 Bloomfield Avenue, Newark, N. J. Everything First-class, Prices Reasonable. The first important problem, and indeed the most important one, that confronts him who would maintain a private equipage is, "Where shall my horse and carriage be kept?" For in the majority of instances it is quite out of the question to think of keeping them on one's own premises. Every one at all acquainted with horses knows that not only the comfort of the animal, but also the enjoyment of his master depends in a great measure on the way in which the horse is fed and otherwise cared for; and, therefore, as we say, the question of how to secure to him proper treatment and food become of paramount importance. There are doubtless many reliable establishments in Newark where horses and carriages will be properly used, but we are sure that there are none in which more pains are taken to satisfy patrons than in that conducted by Mr. Geo. W. Thomas, at Nos. 79 and 81 Bloomfield Avenue. This enterprise was inaugurated in 1887, and since 1890 has been located at the above address. It has met with a high degree of appreciation, for the honorable and liberal methods of the proprietor quickly became manifest, and the result is a large and steadily growing business. Mr. Thomas is a native of Drakestown, N. J., and is well known as a good judge of a horse, and as a man who will not stand by and see one abused if he is able to prevent it. Mr. Thomas conducts a boarding and livery stable; particular attention and care is given to private teams, everything being first-class and the prices very reasonable.

P. LOWENTRAUT, Manufacturer of General Hardware, Mechanics' Tools, House Furnishing Goods, etc., and Sole Manufacturer of Eureka Club and Columbia Club Ice Skates, Office and Factory, Corner Kent and Bremer Streets, Newark, N. J. The city of Newark ranks third among the cities of the Union in the importance of her manufactories and manufacturing enterprises. This is an honor for our city which has been gained through the enterprising spirit of such men as Mr. P. Lowentraut. Possessed of a mechanical turn of mind, which has assured his success in business, Mr. Lowentraut inaugurated the establishment, at whose head we still find him, this was in 1869, or twenty-one years ago. He began on a small scale, as many men have done whom after years succeeded in doing an immense business. The success which Mr. Lowentraut has attained has not been a rapid outcome from any "streak of luck," either, but a hard earned success, for the management of an establishment of this nature demands the closest of personal application, and we doubt not but what Mr. Lowentraut passed many a restless and sleepless night to get to where he now is in the ranks of prominent and successful business men. He is a mechanic who has made his mark, and well deserves the success which has attended his efforts. General hardware, mechanics' tools, house furnishing goods, etc., are manufactured, and Mr. Lowentraut is the sole manufacturer of the Eureka Club and Columbia Club ice skates. Employment is afforded to 125 skilled workmen, and the factory is a large, three-story concern, taking up nine consecutive lots of land. An eighty horse-power engine is a feature of the establishment.

Established 1855.

MOCKRIDGE & SON,

DEALERS IN

FINE BUILDERS' HARDWARE,

Wood Mantels,

TILING AND BRASS GOODS,

Nos. 97 and 99 Market St.,   Newark, N. J.

O. B. MOCKRIDGE.   D. R. SPARKS.

FREEMAN & CO., General Commission Merchants in Fruits and Produce of all Kinds, Eggs, Butter, Poultry, Game, etc., 51 South Orange avenue, corner Howard Street, Newark, N. J. The commission house of Freeman & Co. was not inaugurated until the year 1890, but the success it has met with and the liberal patronage which it has received, makes it worthy of an establishment of much longer standing. Mr. Freeman is a native of this city, and is an energetic and enterprising business man. The manner in which he has so ably began his present enterprise proves our statement. There is so much competition now-a-days in the fruit and produce commission business, that he who succeeds in it must be pretty well informed, and know how to buy judiciously and sell reasonably. Mr. Freeman and his partner are equal to any and all emergencies which might arise, however, so they have launched themselves in the surging sea of competitors, and intend to run their chance in the great race for wealth. We prognosticate from present appearances that fortune will smile upon their efforts, for their business methods are honorable and their integrity is unimpeachable. They handle fruits and produce of all kinds, and eggs, butter, poultry, game, etc., are also paid attention to, meats being carried in Winter. The premises are 22x75 feet in dimensions, so that there is room enough to carry a large stock. We recommend this house to the readers of the History of Newark. The prices quoted are the lowest in the market, the goods are A 1 in quality, and come straight from the producers. Four courteous assistants take and fill orders.

A. MASON, Ice Cream, Candy, Cigars and Tobacco, 292 Orange Street, Newark, N. J. The luxuries of this life may be found, some of them, in the satisfaction which we give our tastes for sweet things, and what is pleasanter to the taste than a good plate of ice cream, a nice pound of confectionery, or a good cigar? These will fill the bill tolerably well to the average mortal. Now the question arises, where can we find good cream, confectionery and cigars? Well, may we ask it, too, for there are so many dealers who sell inferior goods in this line. But we know of a place where none but the purest unadulterated of these nice things are sold, and that place is at A. Mason's, at No. 292 Orange street, in this city. A large reception room 18x22 feet is there with all its coziness, and it makes a nice place to step into for refreshments. The business was inaugurated by Mrs. H. Mason in 1886, but two years later A. Mason took charge of the establishment. Call and be convinced, that the best ice cream, candy and cigars in the city may be had here. Fresh candies are kept in abundance at this establishment. All the confectionery is manufactured on the premises, and is guaranteed to be as pure as it is possible for candy to be pure.

HARTH & AHR, Dealers in Fancy and Staple Groceries, Choice Teas and Coffees, Wines, Liquors and Cigars, Flour, Feed, Hay and Oats, 248 South Orange Avenue. The grocery house of Harth & Ahr was inaugurated by these gentlemen in December of the year 1889. Mr. Joseph Harth and Mr. Frederick Ahr, are both natives of Newark, and are well known throughout the city as business men of ability and integrity. They employ four assistants and occupy two floors, each of the dimensions of 20x50 feet. This affords 2,000 square feet of available space, in which an extensive grocery and feed business is carried on. Though this enterprise is not of very long standing, the liberal patronage which it has received makes it worthy of an establishment of much longer standing. The stock of groceries carried by Messrs. Harth & Ahr is quite heavy, and is well selected for family purposes. Choice teas and coffees are carried, and canned goods, sugar, spices, molasses, kerosene and goods of like nature are sold at prices which the dealer cannot quote. Flour, feed, hay and grain, are also extensively handled and a superior line of these goods are also quoted at the low water mark. The reader of "Newark and its Leading Business Men," who reside in the immediate neighborhood, would do well to avail themselves of the advantages to be derived in trading at this reputable establishment. We know of no better place to recommend to them and take pleasure in so doing. Courteous and prompt service are features of the house at all times.

R. S. YOUNG.

⇒⊶ GROCER, ⊷⇐

And Dealer in Woodenware and Household Hardware.

No. 512 Orange St., Newark, N. J.

It is a very pleasant task to chronicle the continued success of an enterprise, always carried on in accordance with progressive and honorable methods, and steadily increasing in patronage and influence. Such an undertaking is that conducted by Mr. R. S. Young, at No. 512 Orange street, and so thoroughly does it deserve its present prosperity that its high standing is as much of a credit to the community as to the proprietor of the business in question. He is a native of New Jersey, and has been identified with his present business since 1888, having started it at East Orange, removing to Newark in 1889. The premises occupied are of the dimensions of 25x56 feet, thus affording ample opportunity for the carrying of a heavy stock, comprising choice staple and fancy groceries, also woodenware and household hardware, specialties being English Blend Tea, Excelsior Java Coffee, fresh butter and eggs, superior beef, ham and bacon. Employment is given to three experienced and courteous assistants, and despite the magnitude of the business, orders are filled with a promptness and accuracy, such as are seldom attained even at much smaller establishments. It is hardly necessary to say that a dealer of Mr. Young's standing and experience is able to quote the very lowest market rates on his goods, while at the same time fully guaranteeing them to prove as represented. Mr. Young has a very large number of regular customers, and spares no pains to maintain the enviable reputation his establishment has held so long.

Mrs. O. S. JENKINS, Bread, Cake and Pie Bakery, 591 Orange Street, Roseville, N. J. If Mrs. O. S. Jenkins does not know how to carry on a bakery by this time, it is certainly not from lack of experience, for she has been identified with that line of business since 1878, and should be familiar with it in every detail. As a matter of fact we believe that she is thoroughly conversant with the requirements of the public, and is liberal and painstaking in catering to them, for since she assumed control of her present establishment, she has made it one of the most popular of its kind, in this vicinity. Mrs. Jenkins is a native of New Jersey. She succeeded Mr. Williams in business, and is widely known personally in Newark and vicinity, where her energetic and straightforward business methods have made her many friends. An extensive retail trade is carried on, bread, cake and pie being supplied in quantities to suit, at the lowest market rates. Employment is given to competent assistants, and callers are assured prompt and polite attention. Mrs. Jenkins occupies premises located at No. 591 Orange street, comprising a store and bakery, each measuring 400 square feet, and fitted up with every requisite facility for the proper conduct of the business in all its many details. She gives her business careful personal supervision, and is continually trying to improve the service rendered.

R. V. CUEMAN, House, Sign and Ornamental Painter, Dealer in Paints, Oils, Glass, Decorative Paper Hanging, 507 Orange Street, Roseville, N. J. Much of the protective value of paints and varnishes depends upon the character of the ingredients used in their composition and as these articles are used quite as much for their preservation as for their decorative qualities, it follows that care should be taken to purchase them from a concern which may be depended upon to furnish honest and reliable goods. No paint and varnish house in this part of Newark has a better record in this respect than that now conducted by Mr. R. V. Cueman, and his customers enjoy an additional advantage in the fact that the stock carried is so large and varied that it is easy to find goods therein which are particularly suited to the present business in hand. The establishment in question was founded in 1865, by Messrs-

---

JACOB DeVAUSNEY, Plumber, 468 Orange St., Newark. The subject of this sketch, was born in Paterson, N. J., in the year 1853, he apprenticed himself to the firm of Horatio Moses & Son, who were the largest firm of plumbers, sheet iron, tin and copper workers in Paterson. He remained with them until 1857, when, owing to the hard times of that year, they failed, and were succeeded by the firm of McCullough & Wilcoxson, with whom Mr. DeVausney remained until the spring of 1859, when he left Paterson and came to Newark, N. J. He entered the employ of Messrs. S. B. Miller & Co. in April of 1859, and remained with them until June of 1861, when owing to the outbreak of the rebellion, work being dull, he left their employ and subcontracted to do the tinning on a church at Providence, R. I., the residence of Mr. Thos. L. Davis, then President of the Poughkeepsie bank, Poughkeepsie, N. Y., and a residence for Dr. Pinckney, (surgeon of United States), at Easton Point, Maryland. After having completed these he returned to Newark and opened a shop at (old) No. 81 Commerce street. In 1862 he took in partnership, Mr. Jacob Zepf, and moved to (old) No. 108 Ferry street, and there opened a large store under the firm name of DeVausney & Zepf. The firm was dissolved by mutual consent in 1863, and Mr. DeVausney moved to (old) No. 108 Mulberry street, where he remained one year, and then took possession of the large stores, No. 2 and 4 Commerce street, where he continued until 1877, having experienced the hard times '67 and '73, without failing to pay one hundred cents on a dollar to all his creditors, although he did not receive from his debtors, in some cases, one cent on a dollar. In 1877 his lease having expired, he removed to No. 20 Bank street. In 1880 his business having increased in Roseville, and by the earnest solicitations of many customers, he opened a branch in the rink building, corner Sixth and Orange streets. In May, 1890, the lease of his store, No. 20 Bank street, having expired, and the buildings torn down to make room for the Prudential building, he then consolidated both stores in one, at 468 Orange street, where he is now located. Mr. DeVausney having had an experience as above, is fully capable of being entrusted with any kind of plumbing, sheet iron or tin work. He has the reputation of doing only the best work, as he can not do a poor job at any price, neither will he undertake it. His motto is, "what is worth doing is worth doing well."

Perine & Cueman, and so continued until 1870, when Mr. R. V. Cueman assumed full control of the business. He is a native of New Jersey, and is very well known throughout Newark and vicinity. He served as brevet 2nd Lieutenant in New Jersey Volunteers. The premises occupied are located at No 507 Orange street, Roseville, and are 30x100 feet in dimensions. Employment is given to ten assistants, both a wholesale and retail business being done. Paints, oils, glass, etc., of every description will be supplied in quantities to suit, at the very lowest market rates, and special attention is given to handling decorative paper hangings. Mr. Cueman is a practical house, sign and ornamental painter, all orders for such work being accurately filled without delay, and executed in the most satisfactory manner possible.

J. BETZLER, Roseville Pharmacy, 503 Roseville Avenue, Corner Orange Street, Newark, N. J.

The Roseville pharmacy has been known and patronized for ten years or more, but to no such extent as is the case at present. Founded in 1880 by Mr. Whitewack, the establishment was purchased three years ago by the present proprietor. Mr. Jacob Betzler, who completely remodelled the business and the premises. The results are of the most favorable nature, for under the new regime, the Roseville pharmacy has grown in popularity, and the business has increased three fold. Mr. Betzler is undoubtedly the right man in the right place, for he has had thirty years experience in this branch of business, and is thus in a position to take a stand among the most prominent pharmacists in the country. Mr. Betzler was formerly associated with the well known Dr. Lott Southard, of whose property and store he took entire charge. He was also partner in the drug business for five years before his accession to the Roseville pharmacy. The premises in use are situated at No. 503 Orange street, corner Roseville avenue, and are of 25x50 feet in dimensions. They are conveniently fitted up and are neat and attractive in every way. Several skilled assistants are in constant attendance, and all patrons are assured of being both well and promptly served.

W. H. SHAWGER, Dealer in Meats, Vegetables, Fruits and Oysters, 501 Orange Street, Newark, N. J.

Orders Solicited and Goods Delivered Promptly. "Different people have different tastes" to be sure, and it would be foolish to expect everybody to prefer the same articles of food, but practically everybody likes meat of one kind or another, and is sure to give the preference to those dealers who furnish just the grade called for. Here is the main secret of the large business built up by Mr. W. H. Shawger, since 1885, for he has pursued but one policy from the first, and that is to give customers just what they ask for. Mr. Shawger was born at Rockaway, N. J., and is universally known throughout Newark. The premises occupied by him are located at No. 501 Orange street, and have an area of 1,000 square feet, and always contains a large and very desirable stock of meats of all kinds, together with a full assortment of vegetables, fruits and oysters in their seasons. Low prices rule in every department of the business, and as employment is given to three reliable and efficient assistants, callers are waited upon promptly and politely, no trouble being spared to suit all, while the goods sold will be found fresh and first-class in every respect. Orders are solicited and goods delivered promptly to any address in the city.

HENRY ARBOGAST, Dealer in Fine Groceries, Teas, Coffees, Sugars, Spices, etc., Fruits and Vegetables in Season, No. 46 Montgomery Street.

We knew of no more worthy example of the representative houses of Newark than the popular establishment conducted by Mr. Henry Arbogast. This house was established by its present proprietor in 1865, and was then located corner of West and Kinney streets. Since 1872 business has been carried on at No. 46 Montgomery street. Mr. Arbogast possesses a valuable and extended experience in the grocery interests, and by his liberal and honorable methods has gained the public favor. The premises are of the dimensions of 20x22 feet, and are well stocked and conveniently arranged, and the trade is strictly retail. The stock is made up of staple and fancy groceries, and fruits and vegetables in season. No inferior articles are sold and every effort is made to avoid adulterated goods. A competent assistant is constantly in attendance, thus insuring the patrons of the house prompt attention. The low prices and fine assortment carried have given this establishment the prosperous trade it enjoys. Mr. Arbogast is a native of France, is well known to Newark and commands the respect and esteem of this community.

JOHN RUCKELSHAUS, Manufacturer of and Dealer in All Kinds of Furniture, Carpets, Oil Cloths Mattresses, Feathers, Stoves and Ranges, Nos. 129 and 131 Market Street, near Halsey Street, Newark, N. J.

Prominent among the houses of enterprise and thrift engaged in the manufacture and sale of furniture in this city, is the reliable and popular establishment located on Market street. Nos. 129 and 131, near Halsey street. It was founded in 1860 by Mr. John Ruckelshaus, the present proprietor, who has shown himself, during these thirty years, fully conversant with every detail of the business, and the requirements of his many customers. The premises occupied comprise four entire floors, each 40x110 feet in dimensions. They are fitted up as salesrooms, with every appliance and facility for the display and accommodation of the large and valuable stock, which has few equals for quality of materials, finish, workmanship and style in Newark. All the newest designs in parlor, dining room and bedroom furniture are shown, besides any quantity of odd pieces. He also deals extensively in carpets, oil cloths, mattresses, feathers, stoves and ranges. These goods will be found to prove as they are represented. The business is retail, and seven assistants are employed, who are competent to fill orders in an acceptable manner. Mr. Ruckelshaus is well known throughout the vicinity for the superior excellence of his stock, and his uniformly fair dealings. At No. 124 Market street Mr. Ruckelshaus has a large factory, 25x80 feet in dimensions, where he manufactures all his own upholstered goods. In the loft of this building his mattresses are also made. Mr Ruckelshaus makes all his own parlor suits, sofas, lounges and easy chairs. He can warrant all his goods. This is an advantage which can not be had in dealing with many other houses.

FACTORY, NEW JERSEY R. R. AVE., BETWEEN GREEN AND ELM STS.

SEALY & CO.

Salesroom, 167 Market St.,

Second Floor, near Broad St.

NEWARK, N. J.

Sign of the large gold hat

HATS.

Everybody knows that some hats will retain their shape and color for an indefinite period, while others will become mis-shapen and shabby in a very short time, and as it is impossible for one not brought up in the business to distinguish the good from the bad by examination, the only sensible way to do is to buy of a manufacturer, who sells only his own goods, and hence knows just what he is offering. It is obvious that such a man could not afford to supply his customers with inferior headgear, even if he were willing to do so, and it is also obvious that a manufacturer is in a position to quote positively bottom prices. For practical proof of the advantages gained by dealing with "first hands," we would refer our readers to the establishments carried on by Messrs. Sealy & Co., at No. 167 Market street, near Broad street (sign of the large gold hat), and on New Jersey R. R. avenue, between Green and Elm streets. The latter is the factory of the firm, and is a large four-story structure, fitted up throughout with the most improved facilities. The same prices are quoted at both places, and these prices are in every instance as low as the lowest, quality considered. In fact, some styles, as for instance the $1.75 and $2.00 derby, are unequalled for elegance, durability and cheapness, and the stock is so varied that all tastes and purses can be suited. Hats will be made to order in three hours, and without extra charge, and repairing will be done in a superior manner, at short notice. Mr. Sealy has been engaged in the hat industry ever since 1885, when he learned the trade here in Newark. He makes all the goods he sells, and spares no pains to maintain the enviable reputation so long associated with them.

J. H. MERSFELDER, Sanitary Plumbing

and Heating, Stoves, Ranges, Steam Heaters and Hardware, Corner Barclay and Spruce Streets, Newark, N. J. The gentleman who carries on the plumbing business at the above address, has been in Denver, Colorado, and in Kansas City, to make a special study of this branch in these cities. Though yet a young man, he possesses an experience gained by travel and observation, which many men engaged in the business for years have never had the opportunity of receiving. Mr. Mersfelder is recognized by architects and building contractors, as a mechanic of superior ability, and he is busy at all times with a force of ten men who are also as skillful. His store is well stocked with plumbers' materials, builders' hardware and handsome stoves. There are some handsome stoves made nowadays, but were some of the most elaborate of them to be judged by the rule, "handsome is that handsome does," they would make a very poor showing, for beautiful as they are to look at, their interior arrangement is so poor that they are wasteful of fuel, and indeed, give out but very little heat anyway. Not that we mean to say all handsome stoves are inefficient, for such is not the case, there being some which are as useful as they are handsome, and the way to get such stoves is to place your order with a thoroughly informed and strictly reliable dealer, as for instance, Mr. J. H. Mersfelder, who is located at No. 148 Spruce street, corner Barclay. This gentleman began operations here only a short time ago, but he has had such practical experience in his business as to enable him to give his customers advantages which it would be hard to equal in this city. The premises utilized are 20x50 feet in dimensions and contain a fine stock of heating and cooking stoves, lawn mowers and general hardware. Mr. Mersfelder is also prepared to do all kinds of plumbing and gasfitting in a thoroughly reliable manner at short notice, and his charges for same will be found very moderate. Mr. Mersfelder is a native of Newark, and very well and favorably known throughout the city as a young business man of energetic push.

R. LOEPSINGER, Gilder, 326 Plane

Street, near Market Street, Newark, N. J. Ornamented looking glasses and Picture Frames of all kinds. Picture Frames made to order. Old Frames Regilded equal to new. The poorest homes have looking glasses and picture frames adorning their walls, and, in fact, it would be a cheerless and uninviting home that did not boast of something in the line of wall adornment. The reproductions of our past and present great artists can be had at such reasonable cost now that it lies within the reach of everyone to secure these objects of pleasure and of our admiration. In a parlor or drawing room, for example, what can be more appropriate and at the same time more useful, than a nicely framed looking glass, lined here and there with artistic stripes of gilding? And what can make a home more attractive than picture frames, and the subjects represented in them? The portrait may wait to our recollection sweet remembrances of one departed, or inspire with patriotism our souls in seeing a likeness of one of the nation's heroes; perchance the subject is that of a cataract or seething water-fall, a landscape, or the old homestead. These all tend to our happiness and refinement, and it is pleasant to note that, however, ignorant or uncivilized a person may be, every one in this world likes to linger long and even fondly over these pretty things. This proves that there are sweet things to live for, and makes this sometimes monotonous life brighter. We must not only think of the pictures, however, but cast a glance at its frame and see if it harmonizes with the surroundings of things. We have seen some very costly works of art robbed of all their beauty by a poorly selected frame, no taste seemingly having been displayed in the choosing of the mouldings or the workman (?) who made the frame. Let us exercise a little judgment in these things, and if we are not sure that ours is a proper one for the pictures we wished to have framed, ask men of experience, such as Mr. R. Loepsinger, of No. 326 Plane street, what their opinion is of our choice. Of course the matter is entirely optional with the buyer, but some people purchase the most ridiculous frames for beautiful pictures that it seems too bad that more care had not been exercised in the selection, and this is why we venture a suggestion of confidence in such reliable and experienced men in this line as Mr. R. Loepsinger, who has been in the business for years. This gentleman you will find at No. 326 Plane street, as we have said, and if you wish to be sure of receiving a thoroughly well made and well selected frame, patronize him. He may have equals, but no superiors in this line in the city. He also makes a specialty of regilding. Many articles in your homes would look as good as new if you had them regilded. Mr. Loepsinger is the right man to go to in this matter, as in the other we have been speaking about. He employs three competent men to help him, so that orders are dispatched at short notice. The prices quoted are as low as the lowest, and we feel that the public will receive general satisfaction in placing orders at Mr. Loepsinger's establishment.

J. B. STANABACK, Dealer in Staple and Fancy Groceries, 179 Verona Avenue, Newark, N. J. Everybody is familiar with the fact that some people can live comfortably on an income that others would starve on, and, of course, everyone knows that this is chiefly owing to superior methods of management. There is an art of buying as well as an art of selling, and many intelligent individuals never seem to learn that in order to buy to the best advantage, it is necessary to select a reputable and reliable house and deal with it entirely so long as the results are satisfactory. Mr. J. B. Stanaback has had full control of the store No. 179 Verona avenue, since May, 1889, and for the time which has passed, he has built up an excellent trade, and many of his patrons are to be ranked among the most careful and discriminating class of buyers. Family supplies, consisting of fancy and staple groceries, have been made a specialty from the first. The premises occupied comprise the first floor, measuring 25x50 feet, and the cellar of the building. Orders are called for and promptly delivered. The public are invited to kindly call and examine goods and prices before buying elsewhere. Mr. Stanaback is a native of Sparta, Sussex Co., New Jersey.

W. H. WARREN, Verona Avenue Pharmacy, 181 Verona Avenue, Near Summer Avenue, Newark, N. J. Prescriptions a Specialty. It is obvious that the entire community is interested in the question of obtaining pure and reliable drugs and medicines. Sickness is apt to appear in every family, and in spite of the charms made by those who argue in favor of "faith cure," most of us prefer to depend upon the means which the accumulated wisdom of years has placed at our disposal. Therefore, such an establishment as that conducted by Mr. W. H. Warren at No. 181 Verona avenue, is worthy of hearty endorsement and support. Mr. Warren started the "Verona Avenue Pharmacy" in 1890, and has proved to the satisfaction of all unprejudiced persons that he spares no pains to supply the most reliable drugs, medicines and chemicals to be obtained in the market. A large stock is carried, comprising, in addition to the articles mentioned, a fine selection of druggist's sundries, toilet articles, confectionery, etc. Prescriptions will be compounded in the most careful manner, as every facility is at hand to ensure perfect accuracy in the minutest details. The store is 20x50 feet in dimensions, and is finely arranged for this business. Employment is given to two careful assistants, that prompt attendance may be given every caller. Mr. Warren is a native of Newark, N. J., and has many friends in this vicinity.

JOHN E. ALBERT, dealer in Boots, Shoes, Rubbers, &c., repairing at reduced prices, corner Broad, State and Plane Streets, (Formerly at 563 Broad Street), Newark, N. J. Next to having enough money to buy everything you please and whenever you please, is the faculty of buying to the best advantage, and, indeed, we are not sure but what this should be placed first on the list, for he who knows where to buy, can get the kind of goods he wants, while he who has not the knowledge is very apt to be disappointed. As good a place as we know of to purchase anything in the line of boots and shoes, is that conducted by Mr. John E. Albert at the intersection of Broad, State and Plane streets. This enterprise was inaugurated in 1883 by Messrs. Albert & Bailey, but the firm subsequently dissolved and Mr. Albert now continues the business alone. Mr. Albert does a good business, and the rapidity with which the trade of his house has increased shows that many others share our opinion of the advantages offered by the proprietor. The premises occupied are exceedingly spacious in dimensions and five competent assistants are given employment. Repairing is done neatly and with dispatch, and work of this kind receives special attention. Mr. Albert served three years in the United States Navy during the rebellion. He has a wide circle of both social and business acquaintances, who recognize his straightforward business ways. Nothing but hard work and square dealing has brought him the success he has thus far attained, and as the public know that at Mr. Albert's boot and shoe store they can receive their money's worth, there is no doubt but what his future is assured in business. Mr. Albert was nineteen years in a New York wholesale house.

H. GERBIG, 41 Ferry Street, Newark, N. J., Books, Stationery, etc. It is nearly eleven years since the enterprise conducted by Mr. H. Gerbig was established. He is a native of Germany and is well and favorably known in this community. He occupies premises of the dimensions of 25x85 feet, which are located at No. 41 Ferry street, and an extensive stock of stationery, etc. is carried, and a large retail trade is done, orders being filled without delay. The stock comprises full lines of business and fashionable stationery, blank books and everything in this line of goods, all the leading daily, weekly and monthly papers and periodicals. Employment is given to four competent and well informed clerks, so that callers may depend upon receiving prompt attention. All goods handled are warranted to be first class in every respect and guaranteed to prove as represented. Mr. Gerbig gives personal attention to the many details of his business and endeavors to please all who trade at his store.

FRED L. GERBIG, Dealer in Musical Merchandise, 41 Ferry Street, Newark, N. J. Instruments repaired. Strings of all kinds. The history of Newark should chronicle the inauguration of an enterprise founded by Mr. Fred L. Gerbig in 1890, on Ferry street, No. 41. Mr. Gerbig is a young man of energetic ability and push, and, no doubt, will succeed with his new enterprise. It partakes of a musical nature, and as we are fond of music, we wish him success all the more. Musical merchandise of any description may be obtained at Mr. Gerbig's store, and instruments are repaired. Strings for violins, banjos, guitars, mandolins, etc., are carried in stock, and sold at reasonable rates. Mr. Gerbig is a native of Boston, Massachussetts. He occupies one-half of the store at No. 41 Ferry street. The musical world is invited to call and examine the stock. The inception of the business took place but recently and for this reason Mr. Gerbig will welcome all visitors. We earnestly hope our readers will patronize the establishment in question. We believe in helping the worthy.

ISAIAH C. WOLFE, Manufacturer of all kinds of Light and Heavy Wagons, No. 17 Belleville Avenue, Newark, N. J. There are some establishments which, while making no extravagant pretensions, still offer unsurpassed inducements to patrons, and we know that such of our readers as are competent to judge in the matter will agree with us in saying that that conducted by Mr. Isaiah C. Wolfe should rightfully be classed among those of this character. The business in question was founded in 1869 by Mr. I. C. Wolfe. The premises made use of are located at No. 17 Belleville avenue, and comprise two floors, each of the dimensions of 25x115 feet, part of which is taken up by a blacksmith shop. Particular attention is paid to repairing, orders being filled at the shortest possible notice and in a thoroughly workmanlike manner.

WILLIAM LANE, Dealer in Fancy and Staple Groceries, Corner Washington and Elwood Avenues, Woodside, Newark, N. J. Mr. Lane is a native of Hunterdon county, N. J., and is very favorably known in this vicinity. He commenced business here in 1889, and has gained the reputation of being an enterprising business man who employs strictly legitimate methods, and makes it an invariable rule to keep faith with his customers at all times. He occupies premises that are located at the corner of Washington and Elwood avenues, having an area of 1,000 square feet, thus affording ample room to carry a full stock of fancy and staple groceries. These consist of every thing in this line that is required for first class family trade. These goods are fresh and carefully selected, and will be sold at very reasonable prices. Two assistants are employed, and customers may be assured of prompt attention, and that goods will be found as represented.

VIEW OF SARGEANT MANUF'G CO.'S FACTORY, FROM COR. NEW AND SUMMIT STS.

SARGEANT MANUFACTURING COM-

pany, Manufacturers of Saddlery Hardware, etc., Newark, N. J. The manufacture of saddlery hardware is one of New Jersey's leading industries, and one of the most widely and favorably known concerns in it is the Sargeant Manufacturing Company, who utilize one of the most extensive and best equipped factories of the kind in the country. The buildings are substantial brick structures, three stories in height and covering an area of about four acres. They are well lighted, very conveniently arranged, and fitted up throughout with the latest improved labor-saving machinery, tools and appliances, thus putting the company in a position to easily meet all competition, both as regards the quality and the cost of their various products. Employment is given to about 300 persons, and large orders can be promptly filled, while all are assured immediate and painstaking attention. The productions of the company are handled by the principal dealers throughout the country, and are so universally known as to render detailed mention entirely superfluous. Suffice is to say that they are unsurpassed as regards material, design and workmanship, and include various specialties which are highly prized by practical men and are exclusively controlled by this enterprising and representative house.

CHARLES M. THEBERATH, Manufac-

turer of Fine Saddlery Hardware, 10 to 12 Ward street, Newark, N. J. The manufacturing of fine saddlery hardware is a specialty quite worthy of extended mention in a work of this nature, for an establishment engaged in an enterprise of this kind, and utilizing three floors of 50x65, or 9,750 square feet of available space, is certainly of importance in the list of the representative industries of this city. The inception of the business we refer to, took place in 1864, with Mr. Chas. M. Theberath as inaugurator. In 1866, Mr. Jacob H. Theberath, who had been in the former's employ, entered in co-partnership under the firm name of Chas. M. Theberath & Bro., which continued until 1877, when Mr. Jacob H. sold out his interest to Chas. M., who has continued the business under his own name to the present day. Chas. M. Theberath was born in Coblenz, Rhine province, Prussia, Germany, in 1837. Emigrated to America in 1850, and has lived in Newark ever since. The twenty-six years of actual and practical business experience which Mr. Theberath has had in saddlery hardware enables him to cope with the very finest of work in this line of goods. He employs between thirty-five and fifty men the year round, all of them are skilled in this particular work. The goods chiefly manufactured, are gold, silver and nickel plated, solid brass, German silver and aluminum bronze and leather covered centennial double-seam saddlery hardware. The reputation for the superiority of the goods in quality, style and workmanship.

is unquestionably second to none, and as this is well known to the trade, we will simply state that the Theberath establishment is well equipped with the necessary facilities to turn out harness mountings of the various different styles at very short notice. The leather-covered centennial double seam trimmings are considered by the trade here and abroad, as the most perfect covered harness trimmings in the market, and are secured by letters patent, on which marked improvements have been made since their first introduction. Mr. Theberath is highly esteemed by the citizens of our city. In politics he is a true Republican, and his party has honored him with the Delegation to the Chicago Convention, and also placed him on the Electoral ticket representing Essex County in 1880. In 1875 he was elected as a Freeholder, and in 1876, 1878, 1880 and 1882, successively elected Alderman, representing in Council the Fifteenth ward. By the Republican members of the Council he was elected as their representative in the Board of Trustees for the City Home at Verona, all these positions be filled with great credit to himself and to the entire satisfaction of his constituents. In 1886 he removed from the Fifteenth to the Eighth ward. Said removal relieved him of all political responibility and he has held no public office since. He is now a Director in the Security Savings Bank of this city. His father, a Presbyterian Minister, was the founder of the Second German Presbyterian Church in this city in 1854, where Mr. C. M. T. is still an active member.

D. DOUGLAS'S, Hat Forming Mill, 46, 48

and 50 Fourth Street, Corner Dickerson, Newark, N. J. One of the principal divisions of the hat manufacturing business is the process of forming. This branch of the trade is carried on most successfully by Mr. D. Douglas, who is the proprietor of a mill used for this purpose at Nos. 46, 48 and 50 Fourth street, corner of Dickerson street, Newark. This is in the centre of the hat manufacturing district, and the bats which pass through these factories in a month's time, may be numbered by thousands. At the establishment above mentioned, can be seen forms of every conceivable shape, and these are continually changing with the varying of the fashion. Mr. Douglas has been engaged in this business since 1887. The main building which he utilizes is 31x85 feet in dimensions. It is well equipped with all the machinery necessary for the manufacture of hat bodies, which is run by an eighty horse power engine. The boilers are of 150 horse power. The character of the work done at the establishment is first-class, and the bodies turned out are equal to those of any other house in the city. We take pleasure in recommending this house to the trade, as one whose work will prove eminently satisfactory in every detail.

AUGUST STEDENFELD, Manufacturer

of Carriages and Wagons, Practical Horse Shoer, Factory, 257 and 259 South Orange avenue, Newark, N. J. Sales Rooms, 79 Market street, Near Court House. Among the old established undertakings carried on in this section, is that conducted by Mr. August Stedenfeld. This enterprise was inaugurated about twenty years ago, having been carried on by its present proprietor since 1870. He is a native of Germany, and it is hardly necessary to add, is known throughout Newark, especially among horse owners, for Mr. Stedenfeld is a manufacturer of carriages and wagons, and is also a practical horse shoer. The man owning a carriage or wagon made by Mr. Stedenfeld, can feel assured that he has a vehicle which will stand any reasonable strain put upon it, will run easy and require but few repairs, and will be sound as a nut after the ordinary "cheap carriage" has gone the way of all poor work. Carriages and wagons of every description are carried in stock, and made to order. Repairing is promptly done, and all work warranted. Every detail of the business is carefully and skilfully attended to, selected materials are used, and when everything is taken into consideration the prices quoted must be called very low. The premises occupied consist of a salesroom located at No. 79 Market street, and a factory at Nos. 257 and 259 South Orange avenue, which are well fitted up for the manufacture and repairing of carriages, and, in fact, for horse shoeing and repairing in general, which is done in the most neat and durable manner, at short notice. Employment is given to twelve competent workmen, and the high standing so long ago established, will be fully maintained in the future.

F. SCHLUND & SON, Dealers in

Groceries, Teas, Coffees, Spices, Fruits, Flour, etc., 63 Tichenor street, corner R. R. avenue, Newark, N. J. Among the retail dealers in groceries, there are few who occupy a more prominent position than do Mr. F. Schlund & Son. The extent of their business is indicated by their numerous customers and their extensive stock. The store is located at the corner of Railroad avenue and Tichenor street. It is 20x50 feet in dimensions, and was opened by the present proprietor in 1887. The advantages to be obtained by trading here are obvious enough to require no explanation, and the steadily growing popularity of the house in question shows that the public appreciate the inducements there offered. These gentlemen are in a position to quote low prices as well as to supply desirable goods. In the sale of certain indispensible commodities, such as flour, sugar, teas, coffees and spices, they take especial care to satisfy the most critical customers, both as regards the quality of the articles and the prices named for them. Sufficient help is employed to attend to all customers promptly, and to fill orders accurately. Mr. Schlund & Son are well and favorably known in this vicinity, they are both natives of New Jersey.

B. F. WORRELL, Dealer in Fish, Oysters,

and Clams, Choice Cigars and Tobacco, Confectionery, Cider and Wood, 1238 South Broad Street, Newark, N. J. There are two great reasons why Mr. B. F. Worrell should do a large and prosperous business. First, because he deals in so universally popular an article as fish, and second, because he neglects no means to satisfy every customer. He began operations in 1884, and has already gained a high position among the leading houses in this city engaged in this line of business. Mr. Worrell is a native of North Carolina, and is very well known throughout Newark. The premises made use of by him are located at No. 1238 South Broad street, and measure 20x40 feet, a very varied stock being carried, consisting of fresh, salt and pickled fish, oysters, clams, etc. A specialty is made of the prompt and accurate delivery of goods without extra charge, and all orders are given immediate and painstaking attention. Employment is given to competent and polite assistants. Choice cigars and tobacco, confectionery, cider and wood are also largely dealt in, and the facilities at hand enable Mr. Worrell to handle his varied stock without confusion or undue delay. The lowest market rates are always quoted in all departments of the business, and purchasers are assured that every article sold will prove just as represented in every particular.

PETER CHARLES, ARCHITECT, 748

Broad Street, Newark, N. J. A well-known and successful Newark architect is Mr. Peter Charles, who began the practice of his profession here in 1883, and has already attained a leading position, and gained a high reputation for close devotion to the interests of those making use of his services. Mr. Charles was born in Scotland, but came to the United States at an early age, having resided in this country twenty-three years. He is a thoroughly practical and expert draughtsman, and general architect, having had wide and varied experience, and being a master of the art in all its branches. Plans for business buildings, city or country residences, tenement houses, and, in fact, buildings of all descriptions and classes will be executed in the most skilful and satisfactory manner, and designs and estimates in relation to any proposed work will be furnished at short notice. Mr. Charles has an office at No. 748 Broad street, and employs three competent assistants, all preparations of plans, specifications, etc., being done under his personal supervision. He will give personal attention to the construction of buildings if desired, taking pains to see that the specifications are strictly observed, and guarding the interests of whoever he may represent as carefully as though they were his own.

J. B. MARQUET & SONS, Manufacturers

of Paper and Packing Boxes, Nos. 36 to 46 Warren Street, Newark, N. J. Telephone 574. The J. B. Marquet & Sons paper and packing box manufactory was established in 1860, by the gentleman whose name first appears in the firm. For many years Mr. Marquet worked hard to establish a reputation and success attended his efforts. Having arrived at an age when the responsibilities of such a large business were more fit for younger men, Mr. Marquet quietly retired from the active management of his business and admitted his son, Mr. E. J. Marquet and his son-in-law Mr. Geo. E. Huebuer into partnership with him. Under the skilful management of both these enterprising young business men the business since transacted has increased two-fold. Employment is given to a force of 150 men and women, and paper and wood boxes are manufactured for the larger hat houses of the State, chiefly for those in Newark, New York and the Oranges. The firm uses 2,500,000 feet of lumber annually. This is stored at their large dock at East Newark. From six to seven hundred tons of strawboard are also annually used. The magnitude of the enterprise may be imagined from the above statements. No house in New Jersey turn out so many paper hat boxes and wood cases. The firm enjoys close business relations with the trade and supply its demands at rates which defy competition. Their factory which is three stories in height, covers a vast area of ground in the rear of 36 and 40 Warren street, in this city. The enterprise is the representative one of its kind in the State. We chronicle its history with pride, as its management and business methods have always won the applause of the business community of this section of the State.

C. W. HEILMAN, Successor to F. C. Hex-

amer. Established 1873, Furnishing Undertaker and Embalmer, 29 West street, corner Mercer, Newark, N. J. As long as the present method of disposing of the dead is continued and there seems to be no immediate prospect of its being superseded, the undertaker will hold a prominent and responsible position in the community, and it is gratifying to be able to state that as a general thing, those who assume the delicate and onerous duties of this profession are honorable and competent men. In calling attention to the facilities possessed by Mr. C. W. Heilman we feel that we are serving our readers, for it is always well to know the address of a thoroughly competent and reliable undertaker, and no firm in this city is better entitled to be so classed than the one in question. The business was established in 1873 by Mr. F. C. Hexamer, and so continued until 1886, when Mr. C. W. Heilman assumed ownership. This gentleman is a thoroughly competent and reliable undertaker and embalmer, his business premises being located at No. 29 West street, corner Mercer, comprising an area of 25x100 feet in dimensions, and being very thoroughly fitted up, enabling every order to be promptly filled, while the stock of coffins, caskets, and undertakers' supplies is varied and complete, so that all tastes can be suited. Four competent assistants are employed, and the proprietor gives close personal attention to every detail of his business. Mr. Heilman is very reasonable in his charges, and orders left at his place of business, will receive immediate and careful attention.

KING & CO., Manufacturing Jewelers, 355 Mulberry Street, Newark, N. J. The house of King & Co., manufacturing jewelers, was established in 1888 by the present firm. Since its inception the enterprise has succeeded in building up a trade worthy of an establishment of a much longer standing. This is due to the fact that Messrs. King & Co. have proven to the trade that they are capable of turning out just as superior work, if not more so, than concerns that have been known on the market for years. The jewelry business is not what it used to be. The trade now wants *something new* every time its representatives look over the samples of a factory. The younger men in the business have recognized the fact, and strive to meet the requirement in constantly getting up new designs. Prominent among the firms that have kept pace with the times, we can undoubtedly chronicle that of King & Co., for it is this very circumstance which has brought for it the recognition and high standing the house enjoys with the trade. Able management and superiority in excellence of workmanship is what has told the story for this house, we repeat, and we are happy to be able to congratulate Messrs. King & Co., through the columns of the "History of Newark and its Leading Business Men," upon the success they have thus far attained. The firm employ a large force of assistants who are skilled in their art. The power is furnished by a large engine, and the dimensions of the premises utilized are 25x60 feet. Every appointment calculated to facilitate the nature of the work is at hand in the factory, and the machinery and general apparatus are of the most modern and convenient pattern.

R. E. HARLOW, dealer in Staple and Fancy Groceries, also a full line of delicacies, 751 Market Street, Newark, N. J. Orders promptly attended to. All goods cheap for cash. Many a housekeeper is looking for just such an establishment as that carried on by Mr. R. E. Harlow at No. 751 Market street, and we take pleasure in commending this enterprise to such inquirers, for we know that Mr. Harlow's methods are sure to please, and we know those who have business dealings with this concern are outspoken in their approval of the accommodations offered. Operations were begun in 1888, and the trade since then has been steadily increasing. Mr. Harlow is a native of Newark, N. J., and has a large circle of friends in this vicinity. The premises used are 15x40 feet in dimensions and the stock on hand is not only large, but unusually varied as well, as it includes both fancy and staple groceries and a full line of delicacies. It will be seen that the greater part of the household food supply may be obtained of Mr. Harlow, and as his prices are all that can be reasonably desired as regards fairness, etc., it is well worth while giving the store a call. The groceries and provisions comprise the best the markets afford, as all goods are obtained direct from the producers.

ALBERT SCHURR, Oriental Pharmacy, 256 Belleville Avenue, Corner Oriental Street, Newark, N. J. Telephone No. 750, Newark. The Oriental Pharmacy has become a necessity to the neighborhood. Though recently founded, it at once took a high position among other establishments of a like nature and it fills a place hitherto vacant. It was established by August Drescher in 1889, who carried it on only a short time, when he was succeeded by George P. Lehmitier. Albert Schurr, the present proprietor, has recently purchased the entire establishment, and is already carrying on a flourishing trade. Mr. Schurr is a native of New York, and a graduate of the N. Y. College of Pharmacy. Ten years subsequent experience in New York render Mr. Schurr a competent judge of the requirements of the public, and an invaluable requisition to this neighborhood. He is a skillful pharmacist and chemist, and also makes a specialty of dealing in trusses, abdominal belts, supporters, braces, etc. of all kinds, which can be fitted on the premises. The store, situated at 256 Belleville avenue, corner Oriental street, presents a neat and most attractive appearance. It measures 25x55 feet, which gives ample room for the accommodation of a large and well selected stock of pure, fresh drugs, chemicals, patent medicines of acknowledged worth, and the latest novelties in perfumery, toilet articles and druggists' sundries. Mr. Schurr employs several competent assistants, whose duty it is to fill all orders carefully and promptly. He has already a long list of patrons, and this is daily growing longer.

C. VOLZ & SON, Furnishing Undertakers, 40-44 William Street, Newark, N. J., First-class Work, Embalming a Specialty, Coaches To Let for Weddings, etc., Open Day and Night. Telephone No. 602. The undertaking establishment whose card we print at the heading of this article is not unknown to the oldest citizens of our city, for they can remember its inauguration and its inception thirty-five years ago. Mr. C. Volz, now deceased, was the founder of the undertaking, and the establishment from the beginning has always been characterized by its refinement and courteous service, rendered in moments of supreme delicacy and sadness. In such moments, when bereavement calls for even more than sympathy and condolence, the services of an undertaker in whom utmost trust and confidence may be placed, become indispensable, and this is what has obtained success for the firm of C. Volz & Son, for as Mr. Volz, Sr., had been noted for his kind and sympathetic disposition in his business methods, so has the reputation of the house been sustained in as high a degree by Mr. Volz, Jr., who succeeds his deceased and honored father in the business to which both have consecrated their lives. The undertaker's duties are of the most onerous nature, and without wishing to introduce melancholy thoughts in the minds of our readers, we feel that it is not out of place in a volume of this kind to recall to the public that it is well to know the name and address of a first-class and highly reputable undertaker; and in this connection we would respectfully call our readers' attention to the gentleman who conducts the undertaking establishment which has so long been located at Nos. 40-44 William street in our city. Mr. Volz spares no pains to render the services connected with his business as highly refined as can be expected. He carries on all the departments affiliated with the business he is engaged in, and pays strict and especial attention to embalming; in this art Mr. Volz has no superior, if, indeed, any equal, and the public would do well to bear this feature of the establishment in mind. The entire supervision and direction of funerals is assumed, and carriages connected with the establishment are furnished on immediate notice. Coaches and carriages suitable to all occasions are also supplied for weddings, baptisms, etc. We wish to state in closing that we know of no firm engaged in this line of business in our city who so thoroughly has won the confidence and esteem of our citizens.

E. S. LYON, Boarding, Sale and Livery Stables, 370, 372 and 374 Halsey Street, Newark, N. J., Telephone 545, Dealer in Road, Coach and Draft Horses. Those who do not own horses of their own, and occasionally hire, and such as contemplate buying a horse, will be interested in being told that the best establishment to deal with in this line is that which is kept and managed by Mr. E. S. Lyon, at Nos. 370, 372 and 374 Halsey street, Newark, N. J. Horse dealers have had it said about them that they were "sharpers," and this may be so of some of them, but in this business, as in any other, we find honest and dishonest business methods employed. Mr. Lyon and his establishment, ever since its inception in 1882, have enjoyed the full confidence of the Newark public, as is shown by the liberal patronage which the house has received. Those who have had dealings with Mr. Lyon will testify to what we say as being so, and the large business which this house does in horse sales, considering the short time it has been in existence, is ample proof that honest and just representations are the rules of the establishment. Mr. Lyon deals in road, coach and draft horses, and his prices are as fair and reasonable as can be quoted on good horses. He also takes in boarders and does a general livery business, having the best of turnouts in the city for this purpose. Five assistants are employed, and prompt and polite service is extended to all. Mr. Lyon's salesman, Mr. Jacob Guerin, is an affable and social gentleman, who will advise impartially those who are not quite sure of the horse they wish to buy. As the success of the establishment has been due to its honest and fast dealing by all, the public may put explicit confidence in this house and buy to suit. All horses sold are warranted as represented. The public would do well to pay Mr. Lyon's stable a visit before buying or hiring. All of his horses are good roaders, and it does not take two to drive them—one to hold the reins and another to hold the whip—as they used to do in olden times with old fashioned flint-lock guns; one would aim and another would light a bon fire under the trigger to make it go.

JAS. McGUINNESS, Choice Meats and

Vegetables, 549 Market Street, Newark, N. J. Among the many meat and provision markets in Newark, it is perfectly safe to say there is not many known to enjoy as high a reputation for fair dealing, as the establishment conducted by Mr. Jas. McGuinness, at No. 549 Market street. This market has been in successful operation since 1885, for it was in that year that Mr. McGuinness established it. Since that time the business has steadily increased until now a large patronage of regular customers is enjoyed, the firm also filling orders for a considerable transient trade. The meats furnished by this house may be depended upon every time, for in making his purchases, Mr. McGuinness strives to obtain and receives no other than strictly wholesome meat, the purity and quality of which brings the people to trade with him at his place. Good goods tell the story of a man's success, generally, and so it has done in this instance. Mr. McGuinness employs three willing, able assistants, who furnish prompt and courteous assistance. The store is a nicely arranged one and contains a large, new ice box in which the meat is preserved. The dimensions of the place are 20x25 feet, so that a large stock may be and is admitted. We advise those who have not yet tried Mr. McGuinness' meat market to do so at their earliest convenience, as they will find it will be to their advantage.

GEORGE MAAG, Manufacturer of Fine

Saddlery Hardware, Silver Mountings a Specialty, 365 Market Street, Opposite Pennsylvania R. R. Depot, Newark, N. J. The saddlery hardware trade, as is well known, has long been an interesting and important specialty, and it is surpassed by no other branch of hardware manufactures, either in extent or value. The city of Newark has long been an important seat of this industry, and one of the oldest and largest houses engaged in the trade is that of Mr. George Maag, of No. 365 Market street. This firm is widely known as extensive manufacturers of fine saddlery hardware, also, of silver mountings; specialties being paid especial attention to. The house makes a leading specialty of fine silver trimmings and of new designs to order, and has been established here since 1885. The firm occupies a fine building 20x85 feet in dimensions, the machinery and mechanical appliances of which are of the most perfect and efficient character, operated by a 30 horse power engine. Employment is furnished to a large force of hands, the facilities of the firm for the prompt and perfect fulfillment of orders being unsurpassed, and the products turned out being noted for neatness of finish and excellence of general workmanship. The trade of the house extends throughout the United States and foreign countries, the goods being standard the world over; an immense stock is constantly carried, and the trade is promptly supplied to the full extent of its wants and at the very lowest prices. Mr. George Maag, the founder and proprietor of the enterprise, is a native of Switzerland, and has resided as a citizen of the country for many years. He is a practical man, having served his apprenticeship with thoroughly skilled workmen in the art of close silver plating; Mr. Maag is regarded with a respect and consideration only accorded to the more useful and reliable firms in the city. From its very inception this responsible house has been a favorite source of supply in this line of trade, and those forming business relations with it, will obtain advantages in goods and prices very difficult to be secured elsewhere. We therefore esteem it a pleasure to chronicle the success and high standing of this house in our work, statistics of the business interests of the

city. The enterprise in question has rapidly increased since its inauguration and its development is accelerated by the able and well managed business methods of Mr. George Maag, the proprietor. All correspondence receives prompt acknowledgment, and orders are filled at short notice with the most painstaking attention.

L. MERSFELDER, 405 Washington Street,

Retail Bakery, Newark, N. J. Pies, Cakes, Cookies, Crackers, Bread, and Confectionery. The public now generally understand that sickness is as often the result of eating improper food as of any other cause, and, as a natural consequence, more discrimination is exercised in the choice of food products than was formerly the case. That good articles are appreciated is proved by the success which Mr. L. Mersfelder has met with since beginning operations in Newark in 1888, for this gentleman spares no pains to supply his customers with bread, cake, pastry, etc., that is both healthful and palatable. He uses carefully selected materials, and follows the most approved methods in the manufacture of his goods, the result being that they are uniformly excellent in quality and cannot fail to prove satisfactory to the most fastidious. Mr. Mersfelder also deals in choice confectionery, etc., utilizing premises located at No. 405 Washington street, which comprise a store 25x30, and a basement 30x35 feet in dimensions, and a very complete stock is carried at all times. Employment is given three assistants, and callers are assured immediate and courteous attention, while the prices quoted are as low as can be named on goods of standard quality. Mr. Mersfelder is a native of Germany, and very well known and highly esteemed in Newark.

WOODSIDE COAL AND WOOD YARD.

J. F. Post, Proprietor, 122 Washington Avenue, Newark, N. J. Among the most important trades and business houses in this city there is none of more importance, than that of dealing in wood and coal, grain, hay, straw and feed. These commodities are used in almost all occupations and in most every home. If we were able to announce the quantity consumed even in our own State of New Jersey, it would surprise even those most familiar with such matters. It would be greatly to the advantage of consumers were they able to select for their use such as would be most economical. As it would be impossible for many to spend much time in this way, we are all inclined to trust to the coal dealer, and when we find the coal and wood to be what we require, and the price to agree with the market rates, we can but feel that we are trading with an honest man. Mr. J. F. Post is proprietor of the Woodside coal and wood yard. This business was established in 1875, and after two or three changes it passed into the hands of Mr. Post. The yard is 200x85 feet in dimensions, and has a six horse power Baxter engine. Employment is given to five assistants. The patronage he has received is proof that he is honest in his dealings, and the residents of this vicinity can testify to the promptness with which all orders are attended to.

DeHART & HALL, Grocers, 99 Belleville

Avenue, Newark, N. J. Of the grocery establishments on Belleville avenue, that kept by Messrs. DeHart & Hall, certainly deserves to be mentioned among the foremost. Started but a few years since, in 1886, this house at once took a prominent stand among those engaged in the business, and has gone on increasing in popularity to a marked degree. The trade is entirely retail, comprising all the usual articles which go to make up the stock of a first-class grocery. On examination, one finds that the stock is most carefully selected in every particular, and consists of every day necessities as well as the choicer table delicacies. Fine brands of tea and coffee, the best preserved and canned goods, fruits, and in fact, articles from every clime, here find a place, and a specialty is made of fruits and vegetables, which are always strictly fresh and first class. The firm is composed of Messrs. Lyman DeHart and Frank Hall, both natives of this State, the latter having been born and brought up in Newark, and both gentlemen have long been connected with the fruit and produce business. The store, situated at 99 Belleville avenue, is well adapted for carrying on this business, and is neatly and tastefully fitted up. It is of 25x60 feet dimensions, affording ample accommodations for a large stock. Messrs. DeHart & Hall give their close personal attention, so that the business may be carried in a thoroughly satisfactory manner to all parties.

McKIRGAN OIL CO.,

Manufacturers and Wholesale Dealers in all kinds of

Illuminating, Lubricating & Animal Oils, Deodorized Naphthas & Machine Gasolines, all Gravities,

94 TO 106 PASSAIC ST., NEWARK, N. J.

The illustration upon this page fitly introduces the works of the McKirgan Oil Co. to the attention of our readers. This house is one of the largest and most favorably known manufactories and wholesale dealers in illuminating, lubricating and animal oils in the country, and by reason of the heavy stock carried, the facilities provided and the large capital invested, it is exceptionally well prepared to fill the heaviest orders without delay. New and elegantly appointed offices have recently been fitted up and occupied, and are connected by Long Distance Telephone. This enables the many representatives of the company (who patrol the entire territory covered by the United States) to send in their orders as soon as taken, they in turn being filled as soon as received. Delays in shipping, therefore, seldom occur. The enterprise in question was founded a quarter of a century ago, operations having been begun in 1865. The present company was incorporated in the year 1885, and is essentially a Newark enterprise, as its officers are all citizens of this city. They are as follows: Mr. C. M. Coburn, President; Mr. C. E. Young Vice-President, and Mr. H. G. Tillou, Treasurer. The plant is located between Nos. 96 and 106 Passaic street, and measures 200x100 feet. There are included within this spacious areas two two story buildings, and four tanks holding approximately 7,000 barrels of oil. Employment is afforded to fifty work, men, and the factories and store rooms are fitted up with all the necessary and modern conveniences and facilities to enable operations to be carried on to the best possible advantage. A half dozen branch stores are maintained in different sections of the surrounding country, the trade of the company being as wide in scope as it is large in volume. Among the specialties handled are deodorized naphthas and machine gasolines of all gravities, "Brilliant" safety oil, and the Pratt Manufacturing Co.'s "Astral"—these, and, in fact all the oils carried being supplied to the trade and consumers in large or small quantities at short notice, and at the lowest market rates on goods of none but superior quality. Mr. C. E. Young, besides acting in the capacity of Vice-President, is also General Manager of the works. He is one of those men who have earned the position they occupy. The patronage of the business men who use oil in their establishments is respectfully solicited, and we are confident the long standing of this house will speak for itself.

JOHN KLENERT, Wholesale and Retail Dealer and Manufacturer of Fine Bolognas and Sausages, 59 and 61 South Orange Avenue, Newark, N. J. The best quality of Fresh Meats, Hams, Bacon, Shoulders, Lard, &c. Meats chopped to order. There are not many residents of this section of the city who have not partaken of the advantages to be derived in dealing with the establishment owned by Mr. John Klenert, at Nos. 59 and 61 South Orange avenue, for this meat, bologna and sausage market has been in existence twelve years, it having been founded in 1878. The proprietor, Mr. Klenert, is a native of Germany, but has resided here so long that he has become universally known in Newark, and has hosts of both social and business friends.

He keeps four men curing pork in Summer, and fourteen in Winter. A large six horse power engine is utilized in this work and greatly facilitates operations. Mr. Klenert's pork curing is quite a business in itself, but his bologna productions are no less worthy of mention, for he manufactures, wholesales and retails tons of this article yearly. He keeps in stock the best quality of fresh meats, hams, bacon, shoulders, lard, etc. As he keeps none but A 1 goods and quotes the lowest market prices, we recommend his market to the readers of the "History of Newark and its Leading Business Men." Patrons who deal here are sure of painstaking attention and courteous service. We know of no better place in this neighborhood to patronize, and respectfully invite our readers to bear Mr. Klenert in mind.

TWENTY-FIVE YEARS HANDLING REAL ESTATE.

JOHN M. BURNETT,

191 Market Street,

Newark's Real Estate Man.

Houses and Lots all over the City.

RICHARDSON BROS., Celebrated Saws. 15 to 27 River Street, Newark, N. J. It is questionable if any of the many productions of Newark are more widely distributed, and it is certain that none of them are more highly regarded wherever they have been introduced than the celebrated saws made by Messrs. Richardson Brothers, for the business carried on by this representative firm was founded thirty years ago, an the superior and uniform excellence of the product soon gave it a leading position in the market which has ever since been retained. Operations were begun in 1860, by Mr. Christopher Richardson, who, after some years was succeeded by the present firm. The enterprise was inaugurated in a comparatively small way, but has developed with surprising rapidity, and now ranks among the most extensive of the kind in the country, the works covering an area of about four acres, and employment being given to 200 assistants, aided by an elaborate plant of the most improved machinery obtainable. The trade-mark of the concern is a maltese cross, with an "R" in the centre, and on each of the four arms one of the letters going to make up the word "best." This trade-mark is not only neat but appropriate in design, for the saws bearing it are the best in fact as well as in name; that being the verdict of practical mechanics everywhere. Made from carefully selected material by skilled workmen, aided by the most improved facilities, it is not at all surprising that these saws should give the very best of satisfaction, both as regards cutting power and durability, and as they are handled by the leading dealers throughout the country and sold at reasonable figures, they have gone into universal use, and the demand for them is still steadily increasing.

M. E. WHITEHEAD,

Ladies' and Gents'

Oyster and Dining Rooms,

24 AND 25 CENTRE MARKET, NEWARK, N. J.

COMPANY'S BUILDING, BROAD AND MECHANIC STS., NEWARK, N. J.

WOOD & VAN SANT, General Agents

for New Jersey of the Liverpool and London and Globe Insurance Company, Broad and Mechanic Streets, Newark, N. J. D. Smith Wood, H. M. Van Sant. An insurance company which does a world-wide business, and which has paid out an average of more than a million of dollars a year in the United States alone for fire losses during forty-two years, not only without embarrassment but with such ease that its stock is now selling at a premium of nearly 2,000 per cent., is obviously in a position to offer the very highest class of protection to property holders, and as there is but one such company in the world, no one in the slightest degree acquainted with insurance matters needs to be told that we refer to the Liverpool and London and Globe, which was established as the Liverpool Insurance Company in 1836, and adopted its present name in 1864. An agency in the United States was established in 1848, and the progress of the Company in this country since that date is shown by the following table :

1848.	Net Fire Premiums,	$	4,519.00
1858.	" " "		471,988.00
1868.	" " "		1,739,630.00
1878.	" " "		2,422,126.00
1888.	" " "		3,938,030.00
1889.	" " "		4,273,371.00
1890.	" " "		4,496,999.00

A striking example of the advantages gained by insuring in a company doing a world-wide business and having a large accumulation of funds, was afforded by the Chicago and Boston fires of 1871-72. By the first conflagration the Liverpool and London and Globe lost $3,239,094 ; by the second it lost $1,472,290, and how these and other losses affected the standing of the Company in this country may be seen by the following statement :

U. S. Assets.

Year.	1st January.	Income.	Expenditure.	Excess of Expenditure.
1871.	$3,054,704	$3,103,901	$5,122,633	$1,958,732
1872.	5,040,450	3,723,101	4,484,999	751,898
1873.	4,105,550			

Thus showing Excess of Expenditure in the
U. S. in the two years, . . . $2,710,650.00
And Increase of Assets in the same time. . 1,110,939.00

That an immediate and very large increase of business should have been the result of the Company's action at the time referred to we need hardly add, for were the contrary the case the American people would but poorly deserve their reputation for keenly appreciating pluck and honor in business transactions. The Company's record in connection with the late disaster at Seattle, Spokane Falls, Lynn and Boston, has emphasized the lesson taught in '71 and '72, and plainly demonstrated that "the best is the cheapest"—in insurance as in other things. The State office for New Jersey is located in the Company's building, at the corner of Broad and Mechanic streets. This is a handsome and commodious structure, supplied with all modern improvements and facilities, including two elevators, which are running constantly during business hours. It contains a large number of finely-appointed offices, those not required by the Company being rented to lawyers, agents, etc., and being in active demand, as the location is central, and the conveniences unsurpassed. Messrs. Wood & Van Sant act as general agents for New Jersey, and receive applications for insurance, as do also local agents and brokers throughout the State. A large force of clerks is employed, and all business is assured immediate and careful attention, losses being promptly and equitably adjusted and paid. The present condition of the company's affairs in this country is clearly shown by the annexed statement :

Statement of United States Branch, Jan. 1, 1891.

ASSETS.

Real Estate, . .	$1,524,500.00
Loans on Bond and Mortgage, .	2,241,350.00
U. S. Government 4 per cent. Bonds,	1,804,400.00
State and City Bonds, .	729,375.00
Cash in Banks, .	686,367.88
Premiums in course of collection	705,169.44
Other Admitted Assets, .	104,952.82
	$7,459,995.14

LIABILITIES.

Unearned Premiums, .	$1,376,518.58
Unadjusted Losses, .	435,302.88
Perpetual Policy Liability, .	335,157.23
All other Liabilities, .	296,102.64
Surplus, .	$5,005,133.81
	$7,459,995.14

Directors in New York—Chairman, Charles H. Marshall; John A. Stewart, J. E. Pulsford, John Crosby Brown. Resident Manager, Henry W. Eaton; Deputy Manager, Geo. W. Hoyt.

WALTER J. KNIGHT.

Attorney and Counsellor at Law.

Supreme Court Commissioner, Special Master in Chancery, Notary Public. Practices in all the State Courts and U. S. Courts. Reference—Hon. Abraham V. Van Fleet, Vice-Chancellor of New Jersey.

800 BROAD ST., NEWARK, N. J.

No important manufacturing or mercantile enterprise can be successfully carried on nowadays without competent legal advice at times, for questions are continually arising which require extensive knowledge of the law and of precedents, in order to answer them satisfactorily, and the demands of modern business are so exacting that it is simply impossible for any man, however able, to properly attend to them, and at the same time to keep himself free from legal complications, without that assistance which only an experienced counsellor at law can render. The great majority of business men appreciate this fact, and the extensive legal practice enjoyed by Mr. Walter J. Knight is the natural consequence of this appreciation and of the general knowledge of his long and varied experience in his profession. He has had exceptional opportunities to become familiar with the practice of the courts. He is Special Master of Chancery and Supreme Court Commissioner, and is a director in some of the leading Newark corporations.

S. HEYMAN, Wholesale and Retail Dealer in Fancy Goods, Gents' Furnishings, Hosiery,

208, 210 & 212 SPRINGFIELD AVENUE, NEWARK, N. J.

Notions and Boys' Clothing.   Millinery Department, 195 Springfield Ave.   Clothing Department, Cor. Prince St. and Springfield Ave.

In compiling the "History of Newark and its Leading Business Men." our work would certainly be incomplete did we not make extended mention of the three large establishments conducted in this city by one of its most enterprising citizens, on Springfield avenue. **We have reference to Mr. S. Heyman.** As everyone who has resided in Newark any length of time knows, this gentleman began business in this section of the city some twelve years ago, and at first, on a comparatively small scale. We need but point out the three magnificent stores he conducts at the present day, as illustrative of the fact that nothing but his able management and business tact have won for him the success he has attained. We may truly state that Mr. Heyman is a self-made man, for his success in business is not due to any money he ever inherited from anyone, but is the direct outcome of his industry, perseverance and thrifty habits. These are the traits characteristic of self-made men, and they exist in the gentleman to whom we have reference. Were more of our citizens of this disposition the welfare of the community would be proportional. Mr. Heyman is a native of Hungaria, Austria, and has resided in this country for a number of years; his long residence in this city and his business relations have made for him hosts of both business and social friends. Mr. Heyman's dry and fancy goods store at Nos. 208, 210 and 212 Springfield avenue is an immense concern composed of three floors, each seventy-five feet square; this affords 16,875 square feet of available space and without entering into the endless details of the heavy stock carried, we can state that no store out of New York is better prepared to meet the wants of the public in the dry goods line. The ladies of Newark and especially of this section of the city have long since learned to visit this establishment when in search of the latest fashionable novelties. No satisfying explanation of the popularity of this dry goods establishment can be given in a few words, but the chief reason why Mr. Heyman's store has gained the confidence of the purchasing public, is simply because he has never spared pains to deserve it. From the very inception of the business; the business methods of Mr. Heyman have been uniformly reliable; no false representations have ever been made no fictitious values have ever been quoted; on the contrary, full faith has been kept with the public and every precaution has been taken to give each purchaser honest value for money paid. Closely affiliated with this important branch of industry is the millinery trade. In this connection Mr. Heyman has also launched out in a spacious and finely appearing store, located at No. 195 Springfield avenue. To form an adequate idea of the stock carried in this department of Mr. Heyman's enterprises, we would say that it must be seen to be appreciated. The store is under the superintendency of competent assistants, and the most fastidious tastes are given satisfaction. All the staple shapes and latest novelties in ladies' hats and bonnets are displayed, and the quality of the goods sold in this department, as in the others, may be depended upon. The stock is purchased from the most dependable sources and is sold at the most reasonable prices consistent with goods of honest grades. We take pleasure in inviting our readers' attention in a special manner to this department, for we have personally inspected the store and stock and we pronounce it irreproachable in every feature. We have thus far said nothing of Mr. Heyman's immense gents' clothing store, which may be found at the corner of Prince street and Springfield avenue. This is last, but not least, for no establishment in Newark engaged in this line is prepared to offer better inducements Some clothing stores may equal it in point of quantity of stock carried, but we doubt if there be one that can offer a more genuinely *honest* stock at the prices quoted. This store has developed from a small beginning to the leading position of which we speak, and the obvious conclusion must be that the public must have good reasons to be satisfied with their purchases. As goods vary in cost, the articles of clothing sold vary in price, but every garment is honestly and skilfully made. Competent and courteous assistants are employed, and every purchase is always guaranteed to prove as represented, the least misrepresentation not being countenanced. Mr. Heyman employs in all, about thirty-five salesmen and ladies. Courteous attention is paid to all visitors whether they purchase or not. Call and be convinced of the truth of our assertions.

E. HEYMAN, Dealer in FINE BOOTS AND SHOES,

218 & 220 Springfield Ave., Newark, N. J.

The gentleman whose card heads this article inaugurated his business in the year 1882. Mr. Heyman is a native of this city and is consequently well known to its citizens. The nature of his boot and shoe business partakes both of a wholesale and a retail nature, and requires the assistance of five skilled clerks to successfully carry it on. The premises utilized are embodied in two floors, each 30x60 feet in dimensions. This affords 3,600 square feet of available space, wherein an immense stock of boots, shoes, rubbers, slippers, gaiters, rubber boots, tennis shoes, patent leather goods, etc., etc., are kept in every variety conceivable. Mr. Heyman put $1,000 in this place when he started it. That was eight years ago, and the investment seems to have turned out to be a profitable one, as the house has stood the test bravely, and came out head and shoulders above competitors of much longer standing in the business. This is "business on the first floor," as the expression goes, but a great deal of hard work has been necessitated on Mr. Heyman's part to guide his store into the channels of success, in which it is now safely anchored. We congratulate the gentleman upon the success his establishment has attained, and we take occasion to inform the public of this city and surrounding towns that we know of no boot and shoe store in this section of the State where superior goods in this line may be obtained for so low prices. This is Mr. Heyman's lookout, however, and we think he is able to see his way through all right, and still sell cheaper than any where else. Call and give the establishment in question a trial and be convinced of the truth of our statement.

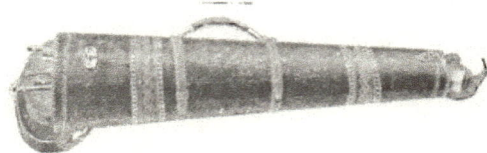

MAULBETSCH & WHITTEMORE, Manufacturers of Cases and Satchels for Musical Instruments, Brass, String and Reed, Web and Leather Drum Slings and Belts, Canvas Cases for Guitar, Banjo and Mandoline, Sample Cases and Leather Novelties, 108 to 114 N. J. Railroad Avenue, Corner Green Street, Newark, N. J. In presenting their new patent professional sole leather violin case to the trade, Messrs. Maulbetsch & Whittemore do so with the assurance that it will fill a long needed want, viz.: A case constructed entirely of leather, handsome in design, light in weight, strong and durable, and perfectly water and dust proof. As will be seen by the above cut, the case opens on the end and is accessible without placing either on the lap, table or chair. As it stands upright it is specially convenient in traveling, or when strings or rosin are needed. It can also be carried on the arm, or in the usual manner On the inside of the case, at the bridge, is placed a steel band, which makes it a perfect protection for the instrument. Two straps encircle the case, which are both ornamental and useful, as many things can be carried by their use. These cases will fit any model's point snugly, and are lined with a heavy flannel plush. They are made in colors of black, russet, orange and maroon, and are for sale to the trade by the manufacturers and jobbers. The leather industry in the city of Newark is one of its chief and representative enterprises, as everybody knows, and the many varied uses to which leather may be put is as well known. Take, for instance, the establishment conducted by Messrs. Maulbetsch & Whittemore; it is of the most interesting nature, for is there anything manufactured from leather any prettier than musical cases? We doubt it, for some of the finest pieces of leather work are in this line of goods, and the highest degree of skill and workmanlike execution are put into them. To the musical world these goods are of especial interest, and no good musician now-a-days can dispense with a proper case or satchel for his or her favorite instruments, for such cases are actually necessary for their preservation. Musical instruments, and especially string instruments, are very susceptible to the changes in weather, and should be kept, when not in use, in proper receptacles. Leather and canvas cases fill the bill, and are conceded to be superior to anything made in this line. The trade need no introduction to the house of Maulbetsch & Whittemore, for the standing of the establishment for the superiority of their goods is well known upon the market. It is not out of place, however, in a work of this kind, to call the attention of the public to the assortment of musical cases and satchels which this firm manufacture and carry, and all who need such goods would do well to pay the sample room of Messrs. Maulbetsch & Whittemore a visit of inspection before giving their orders. Catalogues are sent upon application, and the trade will find that the prices on these goods are very reasonably quoted. The establishment was inaugurated by the present proprietors in 1886, Mr. John Maulbetsch is a native of Germany, and Mr. Geo. D. Whittemore of Newark, N. J. Twelve assistants are given employment, and the premises are 2,500 square feet in area.

MRS. A. BOYLE, Confectionery, and also agent for Sun Laundry, 457 Washington Street, Newark, N. J. Mrs. A. M. Boyle began business in 1889, at the stand she now occupies, No. 457 Washington street. She keeps a fresh stock of pure confectionery at all times, and the best brands of cigars may also be found at her place of business. The premises she occupies consist of an area of 18x50 feet. She is agent for the Sun Laundry of this city, and her patrons in this line will all testify that she is painstaking in looking after their interests. This laundry is so well known as the best in the city, that we will not say anything further about it. We invite the people of this section of the city to leave their washing at Mrs. Boyle's store every Monday morning regularly, as this lady is estimable and worthy of the patronage she solicits from her neighbors. Gentlemen can secure the choicest cigars for themselves here, and the sweetest confectionery for their sweethearts or better halves as the case may be. We invite the public's attention to the laundry list below: Collars, 2c.; Cuffs, 2c.; Cape Collars, 2c.; Shirts, plain, 12c.; New Shirts, 15c.; Handkerchiefs, 1c.; Socks, per pair, 5c.; Undershirts, 5c.; Underdrawers, 5c.; Night shirts, 10c.; Vests, 30c.

HENRY SCHMITT, Groceries, Teas, Coffees, Spices, etc., 80 West Street, corner Morton, Newark, N. J. The grocery store conducted by Mr. Henry Schmitt at No. 80 West street, in this city, is well known to the people of this locality. The stand has been used for a grocery store ever since 1874, when Mrs. M. Fitzel and business here. Mr. F. J. Goebel came in 1882, and Mr. Schmitt in 1888. Mr. Schmitt is a native of Germany, but has lived in the United States ever since he was seven years of age. His long experience in the grocery business has thrown him in contact with many people who patronize his establishment as regular customers. Mr. Schmitt has a choice stock of groceries to select from at all times, and this is why his store is so popular. Honorable business methods are the rules of the house, and the service is prompt and accurate. Families can do no better than try Mr. Schmitt's grocery and be convinced of the truth of our statements.

FIEDLER'S HAT HOUSE, Junction Ferry

and Market Streets, Newark, N. J. It is no wonder that the firm of Edward Fiedler does a large business, for no discriminating buyer can visit this establishment without being impressed by two things, the magnitude and excellence of the stock on hand, and the low prices quoted on the same. A large and well selected stock will always draw custom, and the adoption of low prices is sure to stimulate trade. When both of these are combined it is not strange that the public are quick to perceive the fact, and be prompt in taking advantage of it. The firm to which we have reference is conducted by its proprietor on the principle of a fair equivalent for every dollar. This is what had most to do with the success which has attended Mr. Fiedler's efforts in business. He employs two courteous and efficient assistants who render honest and faithful service. The premises occupied are located at the Junction of Ferry and Market streets, and the fixtures are admirably adapted for the purposes for which they were intended. The assortment displayed comprises fine stiff, flexible, soft and silk hats. Childrens hats are also extensively handled. The latest novelties and styles, as well as the staple shapes, are all to be found here at low water prices. The firm was inaugurated in the year 1878, by Wm. H. Fiedler & Co., the present proprietor having assumed control in 1885. Mr. Fiedler is a native of Europe, but has resided in this country for a number of years. We respectfully invite our readers to bear this establishment in mind. It will pay you to trade here.

STROBELL & CRANE, Manufacturing

Jewelers, 211 Mulberry Street, Newark, N. J. The firm of Strobell & Crane was incorporated in the year 1884, by the same gentlemen who inaugurated the enterprise. From the very inception of their business the gentlemen have personally superintended every detail, and, as they are experts in their line, the result has been that all goods which have ever left the threshold of their establishment have been of a superior order of workmanship. Indeed, this feature has had much to do in securing for the house of Strobell & Crane the high reputation it enjoys. They make the finest quality of diamond jewelry, and there is nothing in the precious or semi-precious stone line which they do not employ with profit to the beauty of their productions. The trade learned to appreciate this firm's productions shortly after its inauguration, and the liberal patronage it has received proves that others have entertained before us a favorable opinion as to its being a reliable house to deal with. The jewelry trade is not what it used to be; so many have launched themselves into it that competition is sharp and to succeed in it, means to excel in it also, for this is a branch of the manufacturing activities in which the standing of a house is rated only upon the actual relative merits of the goods turned out. The trade is continually demanding something new, and unless a house makes it a point to introduce new designs frequently, as Messrs. Strobell & Crane do, it stands a poor chance of disposing of its goods. Mr. Strobell was born in Germany, and Mr. Crane in this country. Both are esteemed citizens in the community, and afford employment to twenty hands. Two floors, each 25x50 feet in dimensions, are utilized, and are equipped with all the facilities for dispatching the work to the best advantage. To those interested we advise the placing of a trial order with this firm. This firm are pioneers in a certain class of silver goods, which will tend much to popularize the wearing of silver jewelry in this country, as in Europe.

JOHN C. REISS, Saddle and Harness

Maker, Manufacturer of Calf Skin Horse Aprons, and Dealer in Robes, Blankets, Collars, Whips, etc. Orders promptly attended to at the Shortest Notice. Repairing Neatly Done, Corner Jones Street and South Orange Avenue, Newark, N. J. Among the various manufacturers of, and dealers in harness, etc., to be found in Newark, no one occupies a higher position than Mr. John C. Reiss, doing business at No. 1 Jones street, corner of South Orange avenue, for this establishment is second to none as regards the beauty, strength and durability of the work executed, and the prices quoted are as low as can be named on goods made from honest material, in a skillful and workmanlike manner. Mr. Reiss was born in Germany, and began operations in 1889, and has already built up a thorough trade, which is steadily and rapidly increasing. The premises in use are 15x25 feet in dimensions, and are well supplied with all necessary facilities for making and repairing harness of all kinds. Three competent assistants are constantly employed, and a well selected stock is always on hand to choose from, consisting of harness saddles, robes, collars, whips and horse goods in general, and, in fact, everything usually to be found in a first-class establishment of this kind, and the goods are warranted to prove as represented in every respect.

PETER J. McKIERNAN, Choice Beef.

Veal, Pork and Mutton, Fish, Oysters and Clams, Poultry, Fruits and Vegetables in Season, 859 Market Street, Newark, N. J. The meat market conducted by Mr. Peter McKiernan, at 859 Market street, is so convenient to reach that the establishment is liberally patronized. But there are other reasons besides convenience of location for the popularity of this market, and not the least of these is the fact that customers are sure to get just what they want. If you order first-class meat you may depend upon getting it every time, for Mr. McKiernan always carries a full assortment of choice cuts of beef, veal, pork and mutton, and has constantly on hand fish, oysters and clams, besides poultry, fruits and vegetables in season, which are supplied to customers at the lowest market rates. He established his business in 1890, and now has quite a large retail business, and caters especially to family trade, giving employment to two assistants, and filling large or small orders without delay. Mr. McKiernan is a native of this city, and occupies premises of the dimensions of 20x50 feet.

G. HELMER, Carriage and Wagon Maker.

470 South Market Street, corner Jefferson, Newark, N. J. For elegance in style, soundness in construction, and neatness in general appearance, the vehicles made by the gentleman whose card we print at the heading of this article, cannot be surpassed anywhere in this city, if, indeed, anywhere at all. This is a no mean tribute to pay to an establishment, but that carried on at No. 470 South Market street, by Mr. G. Helmer, is fully deserving of the highest praise, in a mechanical point of view. This gentleman undertakes the construction of the finest and lightest carriages, as well as the heavier work executed on wagons and trucks. The facilities which Mr. Helmer has for turning out work of a superior order, are well worth our attention. In the first place, we preface that he employs none but thoroughly competent, skillful and reliable workmen; in the second, that he has a large force the year round; and last, but not least, that he has one of the most finely appointed shops in town. With the employment of the best materials and the thorough knowledge which Mr. Helmer possesses in his chosen work, he is prepared, with the assistance of his men, to turn out as fine work as any one could wish for. He builds any sort of a vehicle, from a goat cart to a fire department truck. Testimonials from parties who have had work done by Mr. Helmer would fill a good sized book, and as our space is somewhat limited, we invite those of our readers who need work of this nature to be executed, to call at Mr. Helmer's establishment and he will furnish many of them. Mr. Helmer inaugurated his establishment in the year 1887, and has met with an ovation of success. He is a native of Sweden, but has resided in Newark several years. His shop is 30x40 feet in dimensions. Business men in need of vehicles of any description will find it to their advantage to have their work executed by Mr. Helmer. All orders receive immediate and painstaking attention. Remember the place and number, 470 South Market street, Newark, N. J.

OST & DRESCHER, Druggists and Pharmaceutical Chemists, Stores No. 108 Bowery Street, No. 288 Central Avenue and No. 27 Bowery Street. Among the many gentlemen engaged in the pharmaceutical profession in our prosperous and busy city, we wish to make prominent mention of the firm whose card we have given above. We will preface that the individual members are Messrs. Henry Ost, Ph. G. and August Drescher, A. B. Ph. G. Both gentlemen are of German parentage and scholars versed in their profession, as may be seen from the degrees of honor which there *alma mater* conferred upon them. Mr. August Drescher in addition, fills the highly responsible and honorable office of professional chemist for the State Board of Health. With such distinguished gentlemen at the head of the three pharmacies we have enumerated, the public may rest in assurance that all medicines sold and prescriptions compounded at these places of business will prove to be highly exact and efficacious. The physicians of our city have learned that Messrs. Ost & Drescher obtain their supplies from reliable sources, renew them often enough to prevent serious deterioration from age, and are scrupulously careful in the compounding of their prescriptions. As these things enable the effects of prescriptions put **up at** their establishments to be more accurately compounded **than** would otherwise be possible, and as the professional **reputation of the** physician is directly dependent upon **the pre-**scriptions having the desired effect, what should **be more** natural than that such thoroughly reliable men as Messrs. Ost & Drescher should have a large patronage? Nothing, and the success with which this firm has been favored is the direct outcome of their being men in whom the most explicit confidence may be placed. All three of the **stores** carry a heavy stock of drugs, medicines, chemicals, perfumery, cigars, fancy and toilet articles, druggists' sundries, etc., and the prices quoted are uniformly moderate. The readers of the "History of Newark and its Leading Business Men" would do well to bear Messrs. Ost & Drescher in mind whenever in need of pharmaceutical services or goods.

MRS. F. LIEBHAUSER, dealer in Fancy Cakes, bread and Pies, orders promptly attended to. Weddings and Parties given special attention. 28 Bloomfield Avenue, Corner Webster Street, Newark, N. J. It is always in order to give information as to where family supplies can be bought advantageously, and, therefore, we make no apology for calling the attention of our readers to the establishment now conducted by Mrs. F. Liebhauser. This enterprise was inaugurated by her in 1882, Mrs. Liebhauser having been identified with her present line of business in Newark for eight years. She is a native of Newark, and is well fitted to supervise such an undertaking as she is now connected with, being determined to handle only first class goods and serve the public to the best of her ability. Fancy cake, bread and pies are extensively dealt in, employment being given to six assistants. The premises occupied are located at No. 28 Bloomfield Avenue, corner of Webster street, and cover an area of 500 square feet. Customers will find the cakes, bread and pies baked and sold here to be of excellent quality and skillfully and thoroughly baked, and their superiority to the ordinary "baker's goods" is too marked to pass unnoticed. The bread is never heavy or sour, and, in fact, all the goods dealt in will be found particularly adapted to the use of families containing small children, being digestible and healthful in every respect. A specialty is made of supplying orders for weddings, parties, etc., at very short notice, and at reasonable rates, and the public are assured of receiving first class goods when ordering from this establishment.

THOMAS GRIMM, Dealer in Choice Beef. Veal, Lamb, Mutton and Pork. Poultry in season. All kinds of Bolognas and Sausages, No. 131 Springfield Avenue, Newark, N. J. One of the finest establishments in that important branch of commercial activity—the provision trade—is the market conducted by Mr. Thomas Grimm at No. 131 Springfield avenue. The establishment we speak of is admirably adapted for the purposes for which it was intended, and is fitted up with all the latest and most convenient tackle for the handling of meats. An elegant and spacious ice box or refrigerator is a feature of the establishment,

and the meats are preserved in it in as **fresh** state as is possible for them to be kept. A large **and well** selected stock of meats of all kinds, includes cuts of beef, veal, lamb, mutton, pork, etc., and poultry, game and vegetables in season are kept. Mr. Grimm endeavors to have in stock at all times, all the delicacies of his line for the table. He began business here in 1884, and the success he has attained is really worthy of our commendation. The public has seemed to appreciate Mr. Grimm's efforts to please the people, **and** we are glad to congratulate this gentleman for the high standing his market enjoys and the esteem in which he is held **by** the people. Mr. Grimm is a native of Germany, and has resided here for many years. The large regular trade which this market has, is proof that others besides us recognize the superiority of the goods quoted at so low figures. We advise all our readers to trade with Mr. Grimm if they are not satisfied with their present meat supplies.

F. P. GRUB, Wholesale and Retail Dealer **in** Flour, Feed, Grain, Hay and Straw, 530 Springfield Avenue, Newark, N. J. We need not state any special reason why we should make prominent mention of the above establishment, for it has become familiar to most of the residents in this section of the city, who are confident that it stands head and shoulders above all competitors in this line of business. It is not surprising to see that a large business is done and that two buildings are utilized. The store is 25x100 feet in dimensions and the store house on Tenth street is 37x38 feet in dimensions. Both these areas accommodate a large and extensive stock of hay, feed and grain. Four employees are constantly on hand, and no trouble is spared to deliver orders promptly, a fact greatly appreciated. The enterprise took its inception in the year 1870, with the present proprietor as inaugurator. Mr. F. P. Grub is a native of Newark, and is consequently widely known throughout the city. The best of everything usually kept in the hay, feed and grain line is the only quality kept at this establishment and this is what attracts the large trade enjoyed. Reasonable rates, honest dealing and good goods ought to prove an attraction, and has with Mr. Grub's business. We invite all who have **not** yet placed a trial order at this establishment to **do so** at the earliest convenience, as they will find **that it will** be to their advantage to do so.

FR. ANGELO-HAASE'S Prescription Pharmacy, 450 Springfield Avenue, near Jacob Street, three houses below old place, Newark, N. J. Too much caution cannot be used in the selection of the pharmacy that fills out our prescriptions, for the matter, as we are all aware of, is one of great moment. It is well to know the address of a skillful pharmacist in case we should suddenly be called upon to require his service, and this is why we wish to call the attention of our readers to the establishment conducted by Mr. Fr. Angelo-Haase. This gentleman's place of business is located at No. 450 Springfield avenue, and the public may depend upon the services rendered by the management. Two competent clerks are in attendance, and when in the filling of prescriptions are unknown. A choice stock of drugs, chemicals, etc., is carried, and all the patent medicines may also be found here. Mr. Haase is a native of Copenhagen, Denmark, but has resided here for some years. His store is admirably adapted for the purpose which it is intended, and the general appearance of the place denotes careful attendance to the minutest detail. Toilet articles of all kinds abound, as well as perfumeries, fancy goods, cigars, soda, etc. We know of no better place to recommend to our readers than Mr. Haase's pharmacy. It has stood the test since November 25, 1884, when its inauguration took place. This speaks well for it and shows that others besides us appreciate the advantages to be derived in trading here. Mr. Haase studied his profession during a term of five years in Copenhagen, Denmark, and in Germany, also. Subsequently to this, he practiced in these same countries for five years more. Arriving in America in 1872, he was employed in New York and Brooklyn pharmacies until 1876, when he went into business for himself in the latter named city. He remained in Brooklyn until 1884, when the establishment of the present enterprise took place in this city. Mr. Haase is to be congratulated upon the success which he has met in our midst.

EDWIN H. STONAKER, & CO., FUN-
eral Furnishers and Embalmers. Office and Warerooms, No. 906 Broad Street, and No. 103 Belleville
Avenue, Newark, N. J. Nothing is more distress-
ing than to have any mischance occur on the occasion of a funeral, and therefore it is useful to know of a
concern that possesses such facilities, and has had such wide
experience as to render any accident practically impossible
in the carrying out of arrangements under its direction.
Such a concern is that of Edwin H. Stonaker & Co., whose
office and warerooms are located at No. 906 Broad street,
corner of Green. Operations were begun in 1889 by Mr.
Edwin H. Stonaker, who is a native of Princeton, N. J., and
is now associated with Mr. J. W. Caldwell, a native of
Belleville, N. J. Employment is given to four competent
assistants, and all orders are assured immediate and painstaking attention, uniformly moderate charges being made,
and a full assortment of coffins and caskets being carried in
stock. Embalming will be done in accordance with the most
approved methods, and the firm is prepared to assume the
entire charge of funerals if desired, thus obviating the
necessity of giving that personal attention to the many details attending the preparations for such ceremonies that is
so unpleasant in time of grief. The utmost dignity and de-
corum will be maintained in cases where they have control of
affairs, and they may be depended upon to fully provide for
every contingency that is liable to arise. For the convenience of customers residing in that section a branch office
is maintained at 103 Belleville avenue

WILLIAM ROEMER. Manufacturer of
Trunks and Traveling Bags, Patentee and Sole Manufacturer of Roemer's Patented Frames, Locks and Trimmings. Salesroom: No. 82 Fifth Avenue, corner W. 14th
Street, New York; Factory, 269 to 277 Broome Street, Newark, N. J. Mr. William Roemer has been leading the market for the last twenty-five years in the manufacture of
traveling bags, and is the patentee and sole manufacturer
of over forty valuable improvements on such goods,
and is known to the trade as one of the most reliable
manufacturers in the business. His factory is located
in this city, at Nos. 269 to 277 Broome street, his
salesroom being at No. 82 Fifth avenue, corner of West
14th street, New York. The factory measuring 50x150 feet,
is equipped throughout with the most improved machinery, thus enabling the heaviest orders to be promptly
filled, and reducing the expenses of production to a minimum. Mr. Roemer uses carefully selected material and
spares no pains to fully maintain the enviable reputation of
his products for style, convenience and durability, Roemer's patented frames, locks and trimmings add materially
to the value of the articles to which they are applied.
One of his latest inventions is Roemer's cabin bag, which is
a new departure in bag making, and although it has been on
the market but a short time it is already an established
favorite, and adds one more to the long list of successes
which Mr. Roemer has attained in trunk and bag making

STANDARD CAB COMPANY. Stables

17 to 20 Essex Street. Office, 179 Market Street, Newark, N. J. Telephone 569. An efficient, reliable and economical cab service is one of the greatest public conveniences that can be afforded in a large city, and the residents of, and visitors in Newark, have reason to congratulate themselves on the facilities of this kind presented by the Standard Cab Company, for in the opinion of competent judges, these are not surpassed by those offered in any city in the Union. That they are appreciated, is proved by the rapid development of the business, for when it was founded, in 1887, three turnouts were enough to meet all demands, and the company now have eighteen turnouts, and propose to materially add to this number. The stable, 180x120 feet in dimensions, is to be equipped with the most improved appliances throughout, and will be the most commodious, as well as the most convenient structure of the kind in the city. Cabs will be furnished by the trip or hour, and elegant broughams, with drivers in livery, by the hour. A prompt and reliable baggage and transfer service is also maintained.

As this book will have a very extensive circulation among the class most interested in such a service as the company offers, we feel that we are doing our readers a genuine service by printing in detail, the rules and charges governing the practical workings of the enterprise as given below:

CAB SERVICE, MILE RATE. One mile or fraction thereof, each passenger, 25 cents. In service by the mile, no charge is made for a stop or wait of less than ten minutes; but for a stop or wait of more than ten minutes, an additional charge at the rate of $1 per hour will be made. All distances taken as shown by Holbrook's city map.

HOUR RATES. By hour within city limits, $1. Special rates for out-of-town work. In the hour service, if called from the stable, charge is made from time cab leaves the stable. Charges made by the mile, unless cab is engaged by the hour. No charge for ordinary hand baggage.

Subscribers to the Newark District Telephone Company, 182 Market street, can arrange for special signals to call a cab. Such calls at our expense.

Report any overcharge or discourteous conduct at once to the office.

PRIVATE EQUIPAGES. For weddings, calls, shopping, pleasure riding, etc. Elegant broughams with fine horses and drivers in livery. By the hour only, per hour $1.25. No service for less than the price of one hour. Fractions of an hour charged after the first hour. We desire to call special attention to these turnouts, and would simply say that they are the finest and most stylish to be had in the city of Newark, and are adapted to all the purposes for which the finest private carriages are used.

BAGGAGE AND TRANSFER SERVICE. Trunks, satchels and all kinds of baggage transferred, called for and delivered to all parts of the city. A responsible and trustworthy service at the following popular rates: To or from any depot or address, one mile or fraction thereof, each trunk, 40 cts. More than one, and within two miles, one trunk, 50 cts. More than one, and within two miles, two or more trunks, each, 35 cts. Traveling bags, satchels, etc., 10 and 15 cts. Orders should be left two hours before train time. All distances taken as shown by Holbrook's city map.

Patrons will best serve their own interests by making sure that their orders come to the STANDARD CAB COMPANY, whose office is now at No. 179 Market street, W. W. Ford, Manager; F. M. Lindell, Secretary. 569 is the telephone number, and orders sent in that way, or by mail, or telegraph, are assured as prompt and faithful attention as those given in person.

"KNOWN TO THE TRADE FOR HALF A CENTURY."

Under this heading comes the firm of Enos Richardson & Co., Jewelers, of this city, who have been well and favorably known to the jewelry trade of the United States for a period of fifty years. The firm, originally established in 1841, built their present factory, corner of Green and Columbia streets in this city, in 1848, and have occupied it since that time. They have a large and extensive plant for the manufacture of all kinds of jewelry. They were the first firm in the United States to use steam power in the manufacture of jewelry, and have always added every new and valuable improvement that has been made in tools or machinery that would improve the standard of their goods. Since 1849 they have occupied the same office in New York, No. 23 Maiden Lane—a thing almost unknown in the various changes of business life in that city. This year they are compelled to remove temporarily, as it has been decided to remove the present building and erect in its place an eight story fire-proof building, replete with every modern improvement. On May 1st, 1892, they will return to the old location, but to a new office and commence again a lease that we hope will continue as long as the last one did—forty-two years. See Opposite Page.

ENOS RICHARDSON & CO

23 Maiden Lane, N.Y.

W. MASKER.   C. WHITE

ENTERPRISE

Boarding and Livery Stables.

Horses kept by the Day, Week or Month

Special Attention Given to Gentlemen's Road Horses.

59 & 61 Mechanic Street,

Open Day and Night   Newark, N. J.

H. H. EHLERS, Hatter and Furrier. 63 Market Street, Newark, N. J. Childrens' Hats a Specialty. Just why a hat should be a favorite election bet has never been satisfactorily explained, although the ingenious theory has been offered that, as the winner has been proved to possess the better judgment, it is but right that his head should be adorned and protected. But, however this may be, it is at least sure that the hat is one of the most important features of the costume, and that those desiring to present a good appearance should be careful in the selection of so prominent an article. By general consent the establishment conducted by Mr. H. Ehlers, at No. 63 Market street, is considered the headquarters for hats, caps, furs, etc. and at no time during business hours can it be visited without finding a brisk trade going on. Mr. Ehlers has been residing in this city since 1849, and established his present enterprise here in 1869. A store 55x75 feet in dimensions is occupied, and employment is given to three competent assistants. The assortment on hand comprises full lines of the leading styles of men's headwear, and a specialty is made of children's hats. The latest shapes are placed on sale as soon as they make their appearance in the market, and the prices quoted are in accordance with the lowest possible rates on similar goods. Spring styles are offered at figures which commend themselves to every purchaser.

T. F. ROGERS, Carriage and Wagon Painter and Manufacturer, Rear 134 Mulberry Street, Newark, N. J. The money put into a thoroughly made carriage or wagon is always well spent, provided no fancy price has been charged for a "name," and as Mr. T. F. Rogers quotes the lowest rates consistent with the use of first class materials and the employment of skilled labor, those ordering a carriage or wagon painted or manufactured by him may be sure of getting the full worth of their money every time. He is prepared to make and paint light or heavy carriages and wagons to order at short notice, and they will be found stylish in design and easy running, and as durable as selected stock and superior workmanship can make them. Mr. Rogers is a native of Newark, and has carried on his present establishment since 1888, at that time succeeding Mr. Job Foster. The premises occupied are located at the rear of No. 134 Mulberry street, and have an area of 1,280 square feet. Employment is given to four efficient assistants, and particular attention is given to every order entrusted to this establishment, every facility being at hand and all commissions being carried out in first-class style at short notice and at uniformly moderate rates.

E. B. WOODRUFF, Undertaker, No. 846 Broad Street, Newark, N. J. Although good sense forbids there being too much stress put on the thought of death under ordinary circumstances, still it is but the part of common prudence to be prepared to act with promptness and decision in any emergency, and, therefore, we feel that the information that we propose to supply regarding the establishment conducted by Mr. E. B. Woodruff at No. 846 Broad street, will be neither out of place nor neglected. The establishment in question was founded in 1872, by Messrs. Irhind & Woodruff, and continued by these gentlemen until 1880, when Mr. Woodruff assumed the entire control of affairs. He is fully prepared to assume entire control of funerals and to supply everything required at equitable rates. All branches of the undertaking profession are carried on in a strictly first-class manner. The premises occupied at the above address are appropriately fitted up for the purposes for which they are used. Three reliable assistants are employed, and every facility is at hand that is necessary to the furnishing undertaking business.

FRED C. BOWLES, Grocer, No. 295 Belleville Avenue. In looking over a publication of this kind, it is most noticeable how important a part the grocery trade plays in business circles. Newark is fortunate in having not only a great number of groceries, but establishments that can compete in excellence and standing with those of any city of the United States. Truly they all bear somewhat of a family resemblance, but as in members of a household, it is wonderful how like, and yet unlike two individuals as well as two stores may be. The establishment conducted by Mr. Frederick C. Bowles, contains the same staples and fancy groceries as are to be found in many another store, but it is not always that they are to be found of as good quality and at such moderate prices as those kept by Mr. Bowles. The store has been well known and largely patronized by people in the vicinity for a number of years, it having been established in 1876 by Mr. James Bowles. This gentleman after a prosperous career of fourteen years, has been succeeded by his son, Mr. Fred C. Bowles. The methods of the concern are the same as formerly, honest dealing being the maxim, and we feel assured that Mr. Bowles will lose nothing by maintaining this policy. The store, situated at 295 Belleville avenue, is 15x15 feet in dimensions. Orders are promptly attended to, and customers are waited on by three polite assistants. Delicacies of many kinds, as well as all the staple goods are always in stock. Mr. Bowles is well known in Newark, having been born and bought up in the city.

DR. JOSEPH S. SUTPHEN, Orange Street Pharmacy, 290 Orange Street, Newark, N. J. There can be no question as to the representative character of the establishment now conducted by Dr. J. S. Sutphen, at No. 290 Orange street, for this pharmacy has held a high position among similar establishments for many years. The enterprise was inaugurated in 1888 by Messrs. Sutphen & Lyon, in 1870, and after one or two changes, came under the sole control of Dr. J. S. Sutphen in 1888. He was born in Somerset county, New Jersey, and is well and favorably known, having been a member of the Board of Chosen Freeholders of Essex county, N. J. for three years. Dr. Sutphen is a thoroughly competent and painstaking pharmacist, and this fact has, of course, much to do with the popularity of his establishment, for those conversant with his methods place the utmost confidence in his skill and carefulness. A very complete stock of drugs, medicines and chemicals is constantly carried, and prescriptions can be compounded at short notice, the ingredients obtained from the most reliable sources. Very reasonable prices are quoted in this department, and it is very largely patronized. A fine assortment of fancy and toilet articles, druggists' supplies, etc., is also at hand to select from. Moderate prices rule, and sufficient assistance is at hand to assure prompt and polite attention to every caller.

F. GARTZ & BRO., Dealers in Brewers'

Grains and Screenings, Flour, Feed, Grain, Hay and Straw. All Kinds of Farmers' Implements. Also Agents for the Celebrated Brands of Lister's Pure Bone Fertilizers, and the Walter A. Wood Mowing and Reaping Machine Co., 554 and 556 Springfield Avenue, Newark, N. J. Telephone No. 202. This book is descriptive of the leading business men of our city, and it is fitting to dwell somewhat longer upon the history of those of her citizens who are self-made men. Those who succeed in business by the inheritance of money accumulated by others who came before them, are certainly to be congratulated on their good fortune, but how much more worthy of admiration are the men who have reached the top round of the ladder by means of, and through their own efforts and perseverance! Both the gentlemen whose names head this article are men of this stamp, for what they have got to-day they have worked for; "early in the morning and late at night" was the programme for them for many a day, and success attended their efforts. We wish more of our business men had the schooling the Messrs. Gartz have, for the true value of money hard earned would be better appreciated. Mr. F. Gartz is a native of New York city; when quite a boy, even, the business in which he is yet engaged had great attractions for him, and when he left school he went into the employ of a man who was in the grain business in Elizabeth. He remained faithful in the employ of his employer until the latter died, and buying out the business he began the successful career of which we have spoken. The present establishment on Springfield avenue was inaugurated by him in the year 1874. Mr. F. Gartz admitted his brother, Mr. L. A. Gartz, of Elizabeth, into partnership with him in 1888. The latter gentleman had for sixteen years previously been acting in the capacity of shipping clerk for the Lehigh and Wilkesbarre Coal Company at Port Johnston, filling his position with honor to himself and credit to the company. Since the assuming of the brothers business has increased to a degree worthy of commendation in our columns. The premises utilized to-day by these gentlemen comprise two stores, each 25x100 feet in dimensions, and a storehouse of about 5,000 square feet. The Messrs. Gartz are dealers in brewers' grains and screenings upon an extensive scale. A proof of this is the fact that for the past eighteen or more years the firm has handled all of the grains and screenings from Krueger's large brewery on Belmont avenue. This is their principal business, but they also pay attention to the flour, feed, grain, hay and straw business. The lowest market rates are quoted on all goods sold by the house, which believes in handling none but goods of a high grade. Agricultural implements of all sorts are also dealt in, and everything from the common grass sickle to the most improved mowing machine may be found in the stock carried by this house. They are also agents for the Listers' standard fertilizers, known throughout the country as the best. In any dealings which the public may have with the house of F. Gartz & Brother, it may depend upon integrity. This is what has had most to do with the success of these gentlemen. We respectfully invite our readers to bear them in mind when in need of anything in their line.

GEORGE J. BUSCH, Watchmaker and

Jeweler, Dealer in Diamonds, Watches, Jewelry, Clocks, etc., No. 59 Springfield Avenue, Corner of High Street, Newark, N. J. Up to a comparatively recent period, nearly all the finer grades of watches and jewelry now in the United States were imported from Europe. Of late years, however, thanks to native skill and enterprise, American watches and jewelry have been so notably improved that they now stand unsurpassed, if, indeed, equaled for general excellence by the best foreign products of the kind; and in this connection attention is directed to the elegant and spacious establishment of Mr. George J. Busch, dealer in diamonds, watches, jewelry and silverware, where is always displayed a vast and varied assortment of gold and silver watches of the leading American manufacturers, the largest and finest stock carried by any house in this city, while patrons can at all times rely upon receiving excellent goods, honorable treatment and satisfaction. This house is one of the leading, largest and best equipped concerns devoted to this important branch of mercantile activity in Newark, its inception dates back to the year 1885, since which date Mr. Busch has continued the business with eminent success. The store is 25x30 feet in dimensions, handsomely fitted up and attractively arranged, a magnificent display being made, while a heavy and exceedingly fine stock is constantly carried, embracing elegant American gold and silver watches of every description, superb diamonds, beautiful jewelry of all kinds, clocks in unique and artistic designs, sterling silver and plated ware in great variety, gold and silver-headed canes, spectacles, eyeglasses, optical goods, art novelties, and a multifarious collection of scarf pins, sleeve buttons, rings, and small jewelry ornaments, American watches being the specialty. Several courteous and efficient assistants attend to the wants of customers, and expert workmen are also employed, fine watch and jewelry repairing being executed in the most superior and prompt manner, while no pains are spared to render the utmost satisfaction in every instance to patrons and purchasers, and, altogether, a very large and influential trade is done, the patronage growing steadily apace annually.

WILLIAM SCHAEFER, Dealer in Boots,

Shoes and Rubbers, two stores, Nos. 227 and 423 Springfield Avenue, Newark, N. J. Custom Work a Specialty and Repairing Neatly Done. There is no single article of dress which the average person exercises more care in choosing than that of footwear; and there is excellent reason for this, as not only our personal appearance, but our comfort is largely dependent upon the boots or the shoes that we wear. Those who have stopped to reflect upon this matter assert that no two individuals' feet are exactly alike, there being certain peculiarities of shape in every instance, the same as there are certain peculiarities of feature, which render every individual distinguishable from his fellows. As this is the case, it is evident that the only way to properly cater to all tastes and all requirements is to carry so large a stock that the most varying demands can be satisfied. In this connection we may properly call attention to the assortment offered by Mr. Wm Schaefer, at Nos. 227 and 423 Springfield avenue, for they are complete in every department, and are composed of the productions of the best equipped and most popular manufacturers. Mr. Schaefer is a native of Germany, but has resided here for many years, and inaugurated his present enterprise in 1888, having previously been associated with the firm of Ponto & Schaefer, since dissolved. Mr. Schaefer is well known by a large circle of both business and social friends, who recognize the superiority of his goods and trade with him as regular customers. We advice our readers to join in these ranks and enjoy the advantages to be derived from the purchasing of boots and shoes of Mr. Wm. Schaefer, at Nos. 227 and 423 Springfield avenue.

A. REINHEIMER, dealer in fine Kosher

Provisions and Delicacies. A fine stock of all kinds of Corned and Smoked Beefs and Tongues, Sausages, Hot Frankfurters and Sandwiches. Goods delivered free of charge to all parts of the city and suburbs. 142 Springfield Avenue, near Howard Street, Newark, N. J. Among those supplying the meat wants of the public, there are none more enterprising and more popular than Mr. Reinheimer, who keeps his market at No. 142 Springfield avenue. Care and attention is given to keeping this market neat and clean, and the purity and freshness of the meat sold is a characteristic feature of the establishment. It is daily supplied with the choicest cuts of beef, veal, mutton, lamb, etc., and also fresh vegetables when in season. The assortment of meats at this market also boasts of a large stock of salt and smoked meats. Mr. Reinheimer leaves nothing undone that pleases his customers, for it is his aim to furnish his patrons with every table delicacy in his line. Mr. Reinheimer started his present enterprise in 1890, and though it is yet comparatively in its infancy, the liberal encouragement which the public has given it makes it worthy of an establishment of much longer standing. The success which Mr. Reinheimer has thus far succeeded in attaining, is directly due to his ability as a manager in his chosen work. He is a native of Germany, and many of his fellow countrymen are his patrons. The premises occupied are located at No. 142 Springfield avenue, as we have said above, and are of the dimensions of 15x50 feet. This makes a nice sized meat market, and it is admirably fitted up for the purposes for which it was intended. A nice and large ice-box or refrigerator is a feature of the store, and the meats are kept fresh at all times. Mr. Reinheimer quotes the lowest market rates and respectfully solicits the patronage of the public

STEIN & BLAU, "The Fair," 196 and 198

Springfield Avenue, 57 Rankin Street, Newark, N. J. House Furnishing and Fancy Goods, Jewelry, etc., Wedding Presents, Birthday Gifts, and Holiday Goods a Specialty. "The Fair!" Who has not heard of it? Inaugurated only two years ago, and yet it is a household word in every family in Newark. This is progress, indeed, and shows that some where, at some time or other, somebody must have had great managerial powers to do this all in so short a space of time. The able management to which we refer emanated from Messrs. Stein & Blau, who launched themselves into this great enterprise in 1888. We need not dwell upon the success which has attended their efforts, for it is too well known, as we have stated. The assistance of twelve competent assistants is required to attend to the wants of customers, and house furnishing goods of all kinds are disposed of at prices which defy competition. Anything from a toothpick to a refrigerator can be obtained at "The Fair." We mean to convey the idea that household goods are kept, and that every conceivable thing in this line is carried in stock. If you need anything for the kitchen, for the library, the sitting or reading room, the hall or the parlor, the chambers or the walls of your house, you are sure to find it at "The Fair," and at "fair" prices, too. An idea of the magnitude of this establishment may fully be formed from the statement that the premises take up three doors, each 51x100 feet in dimensions. This we perceive affords an area of 2,300 square feet of available space in which the immense stock carried is accommodated. Tinware, ironware and woodenware for the kitchen abound in quantities which dazzle the inexperienced eye. The rapid growth of this establishment is proof of its popularity with the citizens of our city, and we take occasion to call our readers' attention to it. If the public wish to economize, let it trade with large houses like "The Fair," and they will obtain the rebate which large purchases allow the proprietors of this vast vast establishment to pass over to their patrons in selling them goods. To "The Fair," then, on Springfield avenue, for everything in the house furnishing line. If you want to give to any of your friends a birthday or a wedding present, there is no place where you can find a better assortment of such gifts and at lower prices than at "The Fair." Dolls and toys, games and other articles to make children happy are in abundance at "The Fair." It is the cry of every resident of Newark that "The Fair" deals fair with everybody.

JOHN WENGEL, Dealer in Choice Family

Groceries, 460 Springfield Avenue, Newark, N. J. Mr. John Wengel started in business in the year 1880. He is a native of New York city and has resided in this city for many years. The premises he occupies, at No. 460 Springfield avenue, cover an area of 2,000 square feet, so that we can see that quite a business is done. Mr. Wengel employs three competent and courteous attendants, who furnish prompt attention to all customers. A choice line of everything which goes toward making a grocery store a first-class establishment is kept on hand at all times, and teas, coffees,

spices, canned goods, table delicacies, soaps, pickles and provisions abound in great variety. Housewives need look no further than at Mr. John Wengel's store for first-class goods at bottom prices, for we believe he serves the public as well as any grocer in town. The citizens of his neighbourhood are to be congratulated on having an establishment of such high standing in their midst. We know of no better place in which to make our grocery and liquor purchases, and we advise all to give a trial order at Mr. John Wengel's store. Satisfaction is sure to follow, and once you have traded here a while you will be glad you have taken the step.

MORRIS & GRUNBERGER, Passage and

Exchange Agents. Fine Jewelry, Watches, Diamonds, Fire Insurance and Foreign Express. Steamship and Railroad Tickets, Tickets for All Ocean Steamers, Drafts and Money Orders, No. 205 Springfield Avenue, Newark, N. J. The citizens of the Hill need not be told of Mr. Grünberger's establishment, as its nature makes it conspicuous without advertising. We nevertheless wish to inform new comers that this gentleman deals in fine watches and jewelry, and that he repairs the same. He is assisted by a skillful workman, and the work turned out is of a superior order. He also sells tickets for foreign ports by the following lines, viz.: Bremen, North German Lloyd, Hamburg, American Packet Co., Red Star Line, Antwerp, Inman Line and the London and Liverpool Lines. Mr. Grünberger is a native of Austria, and came to this country in 1881. We advise all who intend going "across the pond" to call on Mr. Grünberger.

E. SCHOENFELDER, Crayon and Charcoal

artist and Photographer, No. 192 Springfield Avenue, Newark, N. J. The average man may not know a great deal about "art" in the broad sense of the word, but he knows pretty well what suits him, and knows that the work of the ordinary "artistic photographer" does not come under that head. We admire true art in photography as much as anyone can, but that "art," which results in producing a picture which is not a true likeness is not satisfactory, no matter how handsome the picture may be. There is no necessity for sacrificing faithfulness of portraiture in order to turn out handsome and truly artistic work, and if any proof of this statement is needed, it may be found in examining the productions of Mr. E. Schoenfelder, who has carried on operations in Newark since the year 1887. This gentleman has been in the photographing business for many years, and he has the most approved facilities at his disposal to attain results of the highest order. Mr. Schoenfelder is a native of Germany and studied his profession in that country. He is well and favorably known in Newark as a gentleman proficient in the knowledge and practice of the same, and we know of no artist photographer in the city to whom we would care to introduce our reader's attention than to the gentleman in question. Mr. Schoenfelder has a magnificent gallery and studio, and his prices are consistent with good work. Call and examine his work and be convinced that it would be to your advantage to place an order with him. Mr. Schoenfelder's wife, who has recently been to Europe, procured for her husband a $300 lense, by which Mr. Schoenfelder takes photographs 25x30 inches in dimensions.

A. D. HEYNE,

Architect,

COR. HIGH ST. AND SPRINGFIELD AVE., NEWARK, N. J

THE HYATT MEDICINE COMPANY, a Corporation. French, English, German, and all Domestic Medicines a Specialty, 30 New Street, Newark, N. J. We never think of medicines or, at least, we very seldom think of them until we are stricken down with illness. Then there is a general stampede for these remedies, and in the hurry and flurry of the moment we are really not prepared to know and to administer just what should be administered. It is prudent, therefore, and wise to think seriously of these things in moments when sober reflections are ours. It is not out of place in a work of this kind to point out to our readers all est disbursed where information of everything pertaining to medicines may be had. The Hyatt Medicine Company, a corporation, with Mr. Edwin F. Hyatt, of Newark, as president and treasurer, Mr. L. P. Hyatt, also of Newark, as secretary, and Dr. A. Barnett, of New York, as the company, own or control the following articles, viz.: Roe's DozzElm, for the teeth, mouth and breath, Dr. Z. Roe's Stomach Bitters and Liver Regulator, Le Roi Goat Cure, Oblipohn's Medjone Cough Cure, "The Gobbler" Corn Cure, Aunt Ann's Rheumatic Compound, and many valuable prescriptions, salves, liniments, etc., etc.,) in successful use over half a century. We also wish to call our readers' attention in a special manner to Hyatt's Life Balsams, the old reliable family medicines, established in 1848. As an alterative Hyatt's Life Balsam can be relied upon, as a curative for gout, rheumatism, scrofula, etc., it is certain, safe and speedy; sold by druggists. $1.00 per bottle, $5.00 half doz. Hyatt's A. B. Life Balsam $1.25 per bottle, $6.50 per half doz. Hyatt's Pulmonic Life Balsam, The Consumptive's Friend. In all complaints of the lungs, throat, chest and side, the Pulmonic Balsam will be found the most reliable of medicines $1.00 per bottle, $5.00 half dozen. Hyatt's Swiss Liniment. The Household Remedy, Never Fails. For ache, pain, bruise, wound, burn or scald a reliable relief and cure, 25 and 50 cents per bottle. Sweet Scoly Tea. As a tonic and sedative possessing rare excellence, and to the languid, nervous and debilitated affords refreshing sleep. An aid to digestion, and invaluable for Dyspepsia, Debility, Malaria and its Fevers, and to sufferers from Kidney troubles. Price, 25 cents. These medicines sent by express everywhere C. O. D. luzz has cured, does cure, will cure catarrh and its deafness. For cure $1. Box (often curing) 25 cents, by mail.

LOUISA FISHER, Retail Baker, 236 Bellemont Avenue, Newark, N. J. The proprietor of this establishment is a native of Germany, and started her present enterprise in 1878. Mrs. Fisher has long been identified with her chosen profession, and has always been successful in her undertakings. The premises utilized by her are situated at 236 Bellemont avenue, and are 20x24 feet in dimensions, allowing ample room for the facilities for the carrying on of an extensive business. Mrs. Fisher makes and handles all kinds of fine cakes and pies, and makes it a point to give every customer the full worth of their money. Employment is given to two efficient assistants, who attend to the filling of orders with promptness and dispatch. Prices are as low as any in the city.

LOUIS NUSBAUM, Vegetables, Fish, Oysters and clams a specialty. A large assortment of Canned Goods. All grades of fine Creamery Butters always on hand, and fresh Jersey Eggs, 235 Springfield Avenue, near Belmont Avenue, Newark, N. J. Mr. Louis Nusbaum had had considerable experience in his present line of business before he opened the store now conducted by him at No. 235 Springfield avenue. The premises utilized are 20x30 feet in dimensions, and contains a well selected stock of all kinds of fish, oysters and clams, which are constantly kept on hand, also all kinds of vegetables in their season. Most of us are rather particular about what we eat, and therefore it is no wonder Mr. Nusbaum's store is steadily gaining in popularity, for the articles there furnished are found to prove satisfactory to the most fastidious. The prices are uniformly low, for although Mr. Nusbaum does not claim to sell "below cost," he does claim to give patrons the worth of their money, and what more than that can we expect. He is a native of Newark, N. J., and began operations the current year and is already doing a thriving business, keeping in stock besides the articles named, a large assortment of canned goods, all grades of fine creamery butter and fresh Jersey eggs. He employs two competent assistants and every caller is assured of receiving prompt and courteous attention. Orders are delivered to all parts of the city.

THE JEAN TACK BLOCK, CORNER WAVERLY PLACE AND SOMERSET STREET.

EDWARD A. WURTH, Architect, Work Inspected and Superintended; Valuation and Arbitration a specialty; office, 748 Broad Street, Newark, N. J. The modern city architect is called upon to solve many complex problems, for the conditions he is obliged to consider vary more or less in every instance; and the question of how to furnish a maximum of accommodation with a minimum of building space available, and, at the same time to suitably provide for architectural beauty of design and excellence and perfection of every detail, both as regards strength and convenience, is one which requires thorough training and great natural ability to answer satisfactorily. Newark has its share of competent and progressive architects, and among them is Mr. Edward A. Wurth, who has an office at No. 748 Broad street. He is a native of this city and began the practice of his profession here in 1889. Mr. Wurth is a thoroughly well-equipped architect, and is prepared to execute commissions of all kinds coming within the scope of his profession, but he makes a specialty of valuation and arbitration, and his services are largely availed of in this connection, his ability and integrity being very generally known and appreciated. Another important department of his business is the inspection and superintendence of work, and those who wish to be sure that specifications and plans are accurately followed may gain that assurance by employing Mr. Wurth, for he is thoroughly versed in the practical details of building, and material and workmanship passing his supervision will prove satisfactory in every respect. Among the buildings which he has built are the large, extensive flats of Mr. F. J. Kastner, corner South Orange avenue and Camden street; large flats for Mr. Jean Tack, corner Waverly place and Somerset street; large brick, stone and iron building, corner Eaton place and Fourteenth street, East Orange, built on hotel plan for Mr. Wm. Hill, and his design for the new club house of the National Turn Verein has been accepted. He has also built houses for the following clients, who he can assure reference from: Mr. Wm. Fischer, Ridgewood avenue; Mr. Roemmele, corner Sherman avenue and Astor street; P. J. Moore, Astor street; Mr. P. Leonard, River street; Mr. Franchie, Comes' alley; F. J. Kastner, Springfield avenue and Fourteenth street, and Bank and Sixth streets; Mr. Koller, Ridgewood avenue; E. Popper, corner Thirteenth avenue and Wallace street; N. Levy, Sherman avenue; Mr. Fischel, Oliver street; S. Oury, Boston street; F. J. Timmes, Quitman street; G. Ambs, Bergen street; Ed. Funke, (two) corner Waverly place and Barclay street; J. V. Neehert corner Barclay street and Rose street; Mr. C. Korn, corner Springfield avenue and Jacob street; Miss A. B. C. Morris, corner Thirteenth avenue and Seventh street; Mrs. R. McEvoy, Eighth street; Paul Friedheim, Hunterdon street, and many more.

PHILLIP DILLY, Hats, Caps, Furs and

Umbrellas, 164 Springfield Avenue, near Broome Street, Newark, N. J. Established 1867. A leading and representative business enterprise in this city is that of Mr. Phillip Dilly, dealer in gents' furnishing goods, hosiery, gloves, jewelry, hats, caps and furs, umbrellas and canes. The inception of this business took place twenty-three years ago, in 1867. Mr. Dilly then did business on a small scale, but it has increased much since those days, for this establishment stands head and shoulders above firms who began business under more auspicious circumstances. The spacious premises, 18x94 feet in dimensions, are fitted up in a style representing all the modern elegancies and conveniences, and the immense stock, embracing all the best and most popular styles and grades in the goods above enumerated, is one of the finest and most complete to be met with outside of New York. Two clerks are employed and render prompt and efficient service. This house is the source of supply for the multitudes who follow the styles, and those who wear staple shapes in preference. The prices quoted by Mr. Dilly are as reasonable as can be expected on goods of relative value. We invite, in a special manner, the attention of our readers to this establishment, for we believe there is none better prepared to meet the wants of purchasers at so low rates. Call and be convinced.

M. RICHEIMER & SON, Wholesale and Re-

tail Dealers in Teas, Coffees, Sugars, Spices, Flour, Butter and Choice Groceries, No. 299 Springfield Avenue, Newark, N. J. The establishment conducted by Messrs. M. Richeimer & Son, in this city, is one of the representative ones of its kind, and we wish to call the attention of our readers to it in a special manner. It was inaugurated in 1880, and ever since its inception it has proved itself worthy of the patronage it has received so bountifully. The firm are German gentlemen of high standing in the esteem of the community, for they have hosts of friends among their countrymen and the American portion of our city as well. The house wholesales and retails groceries of the higher class of goods, teas, coffees, sugars, spices, flour and butter being paid special attention to. The "best" is kept in every department of the business, and this is what ranks the establishment so high in the estimation of those who trade with it. The premises utilized are of the dimensions of 25x75 feet, so that there is room to carry quite a heavy stock, and such is, in fact, the case. Three courteous attendants are employed, and the service rendered is of a pleasing character. The prompt filling and delivery of orders is a characteristic feature of the establishment, goods being delivered free of charge to all parts of the city. With one pound of baking powder are given three and one-half pounds of sugar; beautiful souvenir presents are also given with tea and coffee purchases. Those of the public who have not yet tried this establishment would actually favor themselves by so doing, for the advantages to be derived from a store which bears such a high standing are plainly obvious.

WILLIAM WENGEL, Dealer in Fine Boots

and Shoes, at 402 Springfield Avenue, Newark, N. J. Although there are many who consider themselves to be good judges of boots and shoes, not even a practical shoemaker can really estimate the true value after they are ready for the market. The appearance and feeling of the leather are some help, the general character of the workmanship is also a guide, but after all, nothing certain can be known before the article is put to the test of every day use. Therefore, the importance of buying your footwear of an experienced and reputable dealer, becomes manifest. Mr. Wm. Wengel has been engaged in business here since 1869. His store is located at No. 402 Springfield avenue, and is of irregular shape, being 35x25x20 feet in dimensions, and if you wish to see a carefully selected stock of reliable foot wear of all descriptions, just give this establishment a call and your wish will be granted. Mr. Wengel deals only with reputable wholesalers and manufacturers, and offers his patrons goods that will prove as represented in every respect, and as the prices quoted are as low as the market will allow, it is not surprising that his establishment should be one of the most popular in this city. Mr. Wengel is a native of New York State, but has many friends in both places. He employs two capable assistants, and assures all callers prompt and polite service.

D. MARX, Dealer in Dry and Fancy Goods,

Millinery, Gents' Furnishing Goods, Nos. 168-170 Springfield Avenue, Newark, N. J. The old residents of this section of the city would certainly consider our "History of Newark and its Leading Business Men" incomplete if we did not make extended mention of Mr. Daniel Marx's dry goods and gents' furnishing house in its columns. No better proof of the reliability of this establishment could be advanced than its age, for having been inaugurated in 1873, it is now in its eighteenth year of existence before the public. A house which has stood the test of the public's critical gaze for this length of time is certainly worthy of commendation. The establishment in question was inaugurated by Mr. Marx in person. He at first transacted business on a small scale, but as his goods and business methods soon found favor with the citizens of this locality his business so increased that he introduced several new departments. Prominent among these is the gents' furnishing department. The assortment carried in this line by Mr. Marx is conceded to stand head and shoulders above all others in the immediate neighborhood. It is a well known fact among buyers who are posted at all, that gents' furnishings goods can always be purchased cheaper of dry goods houses, than of regular furnishing stores. The latter have enormous rents to pay and cannot well do so on one department only, unless exhorbitant prices are quoted on goods which you can buy ever so much cheaper at the dry goods houses, who blend this department with their others to great advantage, both to them and their customers. We advise our readers to bear what we say in mind, then, and if they be in need of collars, cuffs, shirts, hosiery, underwear, handkerchiefs, neckwear, gloves, or any of the articles which men wear, to buy of Mr. Marx's dry goods store. You can buy cheaper here than anywhere else; one visit of inspection will convince you that what we say is not unfounded. We have come to this conclusion from experience and gladly pass the word to our readers. The great feature of Mr. Marx's establishment, however, is the dry goods part of it. We need not mention in detail the articles multitudinous which are carried by this house; suffice it to say, that in the immense stock carried may be found everything from the cheapest yard of calico to the costliest Lyons silk. Runs are made daily on special lots and genuine bargains are to be made from them every time one is advertised. Blankets, table linen, sheetings, cottons and calicos abound in large quantities and at low water prices. Our readers know as well as we can tell them what a well appointed dry goods house is, so we will simply state that the one conducted at Nos. 168 and 170 Springfield avenue, by Mr. Marx, is a model one, carrying the heaviest stock on the Hill. Mr. Marx is a native of Germany. He employs fifteen courteous and experienced assistants, who make it as pleasant for purchasers as possible. A visit of inspection is respectfully solicited. The millinery department of Mr. Marx's store is the largest and most complete on the Hill. Five assistants are employed in it and the stock carried is as varied as it is abundant.

F. McCORMICK, Wholesale and Retail Deal-

er in Butter, Eggs, Lard, Cheese, Poultry, Game, Fruits and Fine Groceries, corner Garside Street, 118 Bloomfield Avenue, Newark, N. J. Fine Butter a Specialty. The house of F. McCormick enjoys an enviable reputation in connection with the sale of groceries and fine goods in the line of produce, and on visiting the store carried on by this gentleman at No. 118 Bloomfield avenue, it soon becomes evident that his reputation is well deserved, for one meets with prompt and courteous attention, and the stock on hand to choose from is certainly large and varied enough to suit the most critical taste. It embraces a superior quality of butter, cheese, lard and eggs, also fine groceries of all kinds, and poultry, game and fruits in their seasons, and, in fact, everything usually included in a first class stock of this kind. The goods are all right, the prices are all right, and the service is all right, so the natural conclusion is that Mr. McCormick must be doing a very large business, a conclusion which we are happy to say is fully warranted by the facts. He began business operations in Newark in 1845, and since 1885 has been located at his present address. He is a native of New Jersey, and is widely known in social as well as mercantile circles. Giving close personal attention to business and employing efficient assistants, it is not to be wondered at that orders are promptly filled to the entire satisfaction of his customers.

LINCOLN A. VIRTUE

ARCHITECT,

No. 831 BROAD STREET

Second Floor.   Newark, N. J.

The above design has had a careful study, being drawn for a Classical City Hall and Court House building combined. I consider the classical architecture is more adapted to this class of building than any other ; even more so than the Romanesque, as commonly used. The Dome Tower, Columns, Pilasters, String Courses and Cornices, are the predominating features, and by a happy combination of all these, we arrive at one harmonious whole. The size of City Hall building being about 75x 100 and Court House being very little smaller, allows ample room in both buildings. The interior has been carefully studied so as to have the principal offices on the first floor, and Common Council, Committee Rooms and minor offices on second floor, allowing the entire third floor for the use of the Board of Education and City Civil Engineers' rooms. The Court House is likewise in size and description, having the entire second floor open for Court Room purposes. The elevators to both buildings are situated in the centre, being the most convenient place. The ventilation has been studied in every particular, so that a complete system of ventilation will be available in every square inch of buildings.

LYON & CO., Manufacturers of Awnings, Tents, Flags, Banners, Wagon, Truck and Horse Covers; Floor Crash and Awnings to let for Weddings and Receptions, Halls Handsomely Decorated for Balls, Fairs, Flag and Bunting Decorations, Calcium Lights, etc.; all orders by mail will receive prompt attention, 157 Market Street, Newark, N. J. A few years ago, the fitting up of a private residence with awnings would have been looked upon as a piece of extravagance unless the owner was known to be wealthy, but such action would now excite no comment whatever, for the simple reason that experience has proved that the saving in damage to carpets, furniture, curtains, etc., more than compensates for the cost of awnings, to say nothing of the comfort gained by their use. Well made awnings improve the appearance of even a handsome house; and one sure way of having them well made is to place the order with Messrs. Lyon & Co., doing business at No. 157 Market street, for this firm have the facilities and the disposition to do first class work, and may safely challenge comparison with any of their competitors. Mr. William J. Lyon is a native of Pleasantville, Westchester county, N. Y., and has had long experience in his present line of business. He has been identified with the firm of Lyon & Co. since 1887. The concern manufactures awnings of every description, and will put up, refit or do any repairs necessary on awnings already made at moderate charge. Tents, flags and banners are also largely manufactured, together with wagon, truck and horse covers, selected material being used and bottom prices quoted. Floor crash and awnings are to let for weddings and receptions, and all orders by mail are assured as prompt and careful attention as though given in person. Mr. Lyon gives personal attention to orders for decorating of every description, no pains being spared to fully satisfy every customer. The large number of halls, public buildings, etc., decorated by him give ample evidence of his ability and taste.

OSBORN PATENT PAPER BOX CO., Nos. 316, 318, 320 and 322 Market Street, Newark, N. J. Manufacturers of Paper Boxes of all kinds and Descriptions. It goes without saying, that the closer the competition is in any line of business, the more important it is to give careful consideration to even its most trivial details, and the ability and enterprise which certain manufacturers have displayed in giving this principle practical effect have borne fruit in a greatly increased demand for their products. For instance, many an article has gained its first hold upon the favor of the public, by being put up in specially attractive and convenient form, and we need hardly say, that paper boxes make at once, the handsomest and most useful package yet devised, so it is natural that the demand for them, vast as it now is, should still be rapidly increasing. The Osborn Patent Paper Box Company, utilize one of the most commodious and best appointed factories in New Jersey, and have need of all their facilities, for their business has attained great magnitude since its foundation, a score of years ago, and present indications are that it will continue to grow for some time to come. Operations were begun by Mr. B. Osborn, Sr., in 1870, and the present company was incorporated in 1886. Mr. Charles Scott, is President; Mr. E. D. Woodruff, Treasurer, and these gentlemen are associated with Mr. Fred erick Woodruff on the Board of Directors. The company utilize premises located at Nos. 516, 518, 520 and 522 Market street, fitted up with the latest improved machinery, driven by an engine of twenty-five horse-power. Employment is given to about one hundred assistants, and paper boxes of all kinds and descriptions are manufactured, orders being promptly filled, and bottom prices being quoted at all times.

W. H. MARCELL, Jobber of Fancy Grocer ies, No. 255 Market Street, Newark, N. J. It is an undoubted fact that the trade in groceries is one of the most important of the many branches of commerce pursued in any town, and it is obvious that a city as large as Newark must need many establishments which devote themselves to this business. Newark is essentially a business place, and progressive in every sense of the word. It has a vast number of manufactories, which make almost everything needful for the comfort and welfare of its citizens, and homes where these may be purchased at as reasonable a figure as can be expected or desired for good articles. Among the whole sale houses, Mr. W. H. Marcell occupies a prominent position as dealer in grocers' specialties. He has a large stock, comprising all the ordinary groceries for which there is such a constant and enormous demand; and, besides these, he is sole agent for a number of specialties, foremost among which may be mentioned the celebrated pickles and preserves put up by the H. J. Heinz & Co., the Keystone Pickling and Preserving Works, at Pittsburg, Pa. The demand for these goods is so great that it is hardly necessary to mention their claim to superior excellence. Having secured the gold medal at the Paris Exposition, they stand at the head of all condiments as the best. Mr. Marcell keeps an unusually large assortment of fine preserves, jams and jellies, both imported and domestic, made from the choicest fruits. He is also agent for one of the largest cracker bakeries in Philadelphia, handling fine goods at low prices. Added to these all the best German and domestic cheese are to be had in this establishment, fine smoked meats, lard, etc., etc. Mr. Marcell has recently removed into the large and commodious building northwest corner Broad and Plane streets, and employs a large corps of efficient assistants.

HALL IN NEWARK DECORATED BY D. BROCKIE & CO.

GARRY ZELIFF, Successor to James

Malone, Practical Horseshoer, No. 17 Belleville Avenue, Newark, N. J. The blacksmith shop conducted by Mr. Garry Zeliff, at No. 17 Belleville avenue, is not unknown to horse owners, for it has been a blacksmith's horseshoeing stand for a great many years. Mr. Zeliff, who now has the location, came into its possession about the first of March, 1890. He had previously done an extensive business on Summer avenue, where he went into business in 1886, but made the change to accommodate his large increase of business. Mr. Zeliff learned the horseshoeing trade when yet quite young, and has always followed it. Being in the prime of life, it is easy to see that the experience he has had, combined with his actual practical knowledge on the subject of horseshoeing which he possesses, entitles him to be ranked among the foremost of his craft in our city. Horses shod at Mr. Zeliff's shop are well shod in every sense of the word; the shoes are made to fit with as much pains and accuracy as shoes are made to-day for men and women; there is no difference. If a boot and shoe dealer should sell you a pair of ill-fitting shoes with nails sticking into your hide, you would suffer, wouldn't you? Well, the case is exactly similar in shoeing a horse; unless it is shod by a reputable blacksmith and horseshoer like Mr. Zeliff, unless it be shod by a person who knows his business, that poor dumb beast will suffer untold agonies, and ten to one a valuable animal is lost to you because you were not careful where and to whom you took it to be shod. See to this, hereafter, then, if you value your horse. Take it to Mr. Zeliff's shop, and you may be sure that there, if anywhere in the city, it will receive a shoeing irreproachable in every respect. Remember the number, 17 Belleville avenue.

L. E. TUTTLE, Sanitary Plumber, Tin and

Sheet Iron Worker, Furnace and Heater Work a Specialty. Sewer Connections Made, Estimates Cheerfully Given. 99 Bloomfield Avenue, Newark, N. J. Assuming a building to be furnished with steam, gas, and running water, it may be said to embody the greatest domestic conveniences of the Nineteenth century; but as convenient and self-nigh indispensable as these things are now-a-days, it should always be borne in mind that they entail duties, as well as afford comforts, and that among these duties must be mentioned that of seeing that the piping, etc., in use is kept in first-class condition. Fortunately this is an easy task, for there are experts who make a specialty of this line of industry, and who stand ready to render any assistance required at a moderate price. Prominent among such in this city is Mr. L. E. Tuttle, doing business at No. 99 Bloomfield avenue, and so well has he performed the duties of a sanitary plumber, that since he began operations in 1888 he has attained no small amount of popularity, and finds it necessary to employ thoroughly competent assistants to help him carry out the many orders received. The premises occupied by him are some 1,250 square feet in dimensions. Mr. Tuttle is a sanitary plumber, also tin and sheet iron worker, furnace and heater work being made a specialty. Sewer connections made and jobbing orders of all kinds attended to without delay, and carried out in a durable and neat manner. Estimates of all kinds of the above named lines of work will be cheerfully given. Mr. Tuttle is a native of Morristown, N. J., and well known among the enterprising business men of Newark, where his facilities equal the best, and his business is steadily increasing.

RIDLER & FISHER, Successors to A.

Ridler, Painters, Paperhangers and Decorators, Also Dealers in Paints, Oils, Glass, Putty, Wall Papers, etc., 18 Belleville Avenue, Newark, N. J. An interesting establishment to visit, is situated at 18 Belleville avenue. It is conducted by Messrs. Ridler & Fisher, who are both authorities in the particular line of business which they represent. The house was originally founded by Mr. A. Ridler, but since 1887, the joint proprietors have been Messrs. William H. Ridler and M. W. Fisher. Both members of the firm are natives of the State of New Jersey. The business of this house is to decorate houses in any desired style, with paint or the newest fashion in papers. Messrs. Ridler & Fisher have been most successful in carrying on this work, as they insist upon its being done in a first-class manner, and their charges are quite the reverse of exorbitant. They employ a force of eighteen skilled workmen, and give their personal supervision as well. We would like to call special attention to the large line of beautiful papers to be seen at this establishment. An examination of them will make one discontented forever with bare white walls. Besides a full line of these paper hangings, the firm deals in paints, oils, glass, putty, etc., which will be furnished in large or small quantities at short notice. The premises comprise two floors, each measuring 18x40 feet. These are conveniently fitted up so that the stock may be easily examined. Parties wishing to find first-class decorators will make no mistake in calling upon Messrs. Ridler & Fisher. Their estimates will be found moderate and the work equal to the best.

T. ATCHASON, Wholesale dealer in Pork,

Lard, Hams, Shoulders, Bacon, Sausages, Smoked Beef, etc., No. 447 Central Avenue, Newark, N. J. Among the truly business enterprises characteristic of this thriving and prosperous city, we wish to point out one in particular in this sketch. We have reference to the large establishment conducted by Mr. T. Atchason, who deals extensively in the goods enumerated in the heading of this article. One of the largest establishments of its kind in this city, it has a history which cannot but interest those of our readers who like to note the career of the self made men of their community. Mr. Atchason founded his enterprise in the year 1876, without capital. Drumming hard with a horse and wagon, he managed to get a start. The people who traded with him soon learned that his one aim was to deal honestly and squarely by all, and rest content in selling good goods at only fair marginal profits. This invariably brings success in any enterprise, and Mr. Atchason soon found his business developing and increasing in a degree which would have done credit to an establishment of much longer standing. Increase in volume of business necessitated increased room and facilities, and these were provided as fast as made manifest. Mr. Atchason, tired of "patching up" each year, however, and decided to build on a grand scale. His present large establishment at No. 447 Central avenue, is the result of his progressive ideas. The premises occupied measure 80x100 feet in dimensions, so that 8,000 square feet of available space is utilized to its fullest capacity. The main building is two stories in height, and presents a substantial, pleasing effect to the eye. The establishment is equipped with the most modern and improved machinery to facilitate operations, and this machinery is furnished motive power by steam generated from a forty-horse power Lyon boiler into the cylinders of a powerful horizontal twenty-five-horse-power engine. In addition to this is the ice manufacturing apparatus connected with the works. Mr. Atchason is one of the few Newark business men who have introduced the process of manufacturing into their establishments. The most of these ice machines use ammonia in the process of crystalization and congelation, but Mr. Atchason's uses sulphurous oxide, an agent less liable to taint meat than ammonia. The coils of piping in the "cooler" are perpetually covered with frost an inch thick. The capacity of the machine is ten tons per day, and, although, he does not make it a business, Mr. Atchason frequently accommodates business men with ice manufactured by his machine. The many thousands of dollars which have been expended in the building of such an immense plant, enables Mr. Atchason to successfully cope with his most powerful competitors. The curing of pork, purification of lard, smoking of hams, shoulders and bacon, and the manufacturing of sausages are all paid attention to, and dealers who have patronized the house for years will testify that the work is all executed in a thoroughly satisfactory manner. From eighty to a hundred hogs are cut up daily by this house, and the services of twenty-five men, twelve horses and six carts are required to furnish the promptness noticeable in the filling of all orders by this house. Mr. Atchason personally superintends his works and all his business, for he is an energetic business man in the prime of life. He never was afraid of hard work, and if there is any one thing to which we can attribute his success, it is, indeed, to this fact. He is an extensive real estate owner in this city, and owns the premises he occupies as his business establishment. We earnestly advise retail dealers who have not opened an account with this establishment to do so, as in so doing they will be consulting their own personal interests. Orders received by mail or telephone are promptly filled at short notice.

Harry Firth, Architect, opp. Brick Church Depot, E. Orange.

Every man is said to be the architect of his own fortunes, but if such be the fact, it must be confessed that there are many incompetent architects in the world, for the great majority of us find that the plan of our life needs frequent revision, and that things which seemed easy and desirable in theory are impossible to carry out in practice. Many a man who started to build a house after his own ideas, has met with a similar experience, and, as a general thing, the better informed a person is on the subject of building, the more strongly he is in favor of the employment of a competent architect, as opposed to the practice of placing the matter in the hands of a carpenter and builder, and allowing him to go ahead under general instructions only. We take pleasure in calling attention to the facilities offered by Mr Harry Firth, for we are convinced that those who make use of his services, will have abundant reason to thank us for the hint here given. Mr. Firth, who is located opp. Brick Church depot, began the practice of his profession here in 1889. He has had a very thorough technical training, having enjoyed a practical experience in steam heating, engineering and plumbing, to complete his architectural training, which he wished to have as thorough as possible, in every detail pertaining to the constructing, heating and ventilating of buildings, and has thus far been very successful in adapting means to ends, showing talent and ingenuity, as well as wide knowledge of available materials and devices. Plans and specifications will be prepared at very short notice, and personal supervision will be given to building operations, thus insuring that materials and workmanship are fully in accord with specifications A residence after the above style can be erected for $8,000 to $10,000, according to finish.

BELLEVILLE.

The township of Belleville is the most northerly of the suburbs of Newark. It is beautifully situated on the west bank of the Passaic river, and having for its southern boundary Second river, a stream which has an average width of forty feet. Second river is the dividing line that separates the township from Newark. The history of Belleville dates back to a time anterior to the Revolution. The place was once a part of Newark, but in 1812 Bloomfield was set off from Newark as a separate township and Belleville was included within its limits. Belleville was not created a separate township until several years later. Within the last two or three years new streets have been laid out, old streets paved and other improvements made. A number of houses are supplied with water by the Newark Aqueduct Board, whose pipes run through the town and whose pumping station is on the bank of the Passaic within its limits. There are also a number of hydrants erected for fire purposes. The town has a volunteer fire department, which consists of hose companies and hook and ladder companies. The affairs of the township are managed by a township committee elected annually by the people. There are a number of ancient houses within the limits of the township; the majority of them are situated on Main street, which is the principal thoroughfare of the township. Among the old families of Belleville whose descendants are still residing in old family mansions, or on property which was part of the old family homestead, may be mentioned the Spears, Van Ripers, Van Rensselears, Dows, Sandfords, and others. The Spears were among the earliest settlers of the place, and the name was originally spelled Speir. The Speir tract covered the heart of what is now Belleville. The Sandford family is also an old and influential one. Justice Theodore Sandford is now the oldest representative of that family, and is considerably over eighty years of age. The venerable

gentleman has been a Justice of the Peace for a great many years, and is the oldest magistrate in Essex County. He has always been prominent in public affairs, and is universally esteemed and respected. The Van Rensselaer family are descendants of the old patroon stock and are descended also from the Van Cortlandts of New York. The family is now represented by James Van Rensselaer, who resides not far from the old family mansion, which has now passed into other hands, and is now a hotel. One of the early ancestors of the Van Ripers was a blacksmith and wagon maker, who had his shop on the River road, a little south of where Christ Church now stands. When the British

visited the place during the Revolution, Van Riper melted all the work in his place into slugs to be fired at the Red Coats. When these slugs were exhausted he freely gave his tools to be used in place of ball. When the British officer commanding the troops saw the kind of missiles being used against him he cried out to his men, "For God's sake get out of here before they fire the anvil at us."

Belleville is connected with the opposite bank of the Passaic river by a substantial iron bridge. The first bridge across the stream there was built by a stock company in 1790. This company also constructed a turnpike road to Jersey City. In 1841 the bridge was carried away by a heavy freshet. Subsequently the bridge was purchased by Nicholas Joralemon. In 1851 he sold it to a stock company, who about 1873 sold it to the Boards of Chosen Freeholders of the counties of Essex, Hudson and Bergen. It is now free to the public, and is known as the Belleville Free Bridge. In 1879 the old wooden bridge was removed and the present substantial and handsome iron structure resting on piers of massive stone work was built at the joint expense of the three counties.

Belleville has five churches. The oldest of these is the Reformed (formerly Reformed Dutch). It is impossible to fix the exact date of the organization of this church, but records are extant dating back to 1720. The present church edifice

was built in 1852 and dedicated in 1853. From this church came the originators of the First Reformed Church of Newark, and the Reformed Church of Belleville is the mother church of the Classis of Newark. Christ Episcopal Church dates its history back to 1746 when a charter was granted by George II, King of England, for this church, as a part of Trinity Church Newark, the charter of Trinity Church requiring that one warden and five vestrymen be chosen from the section north of the Second river, which is now Belleville. For several years the congregation worshiped in an old store house. In 1811 the first step was taken towards a separation from Trinity Church, Newark, but the formal separation did not occur until 1835, when Christ Church, Belleville, was made a separate parish. The Catholic Church dates its history back to 1838. The other churches are of more recent date.

Belleville has several large manufacturing establishments within its limits. Among them may be mentioned the Hendrick's Rolling Mill, where copper is rolled in sheets and where wire, rivets and bolts are made. The mills were established about seventy-five years ago, and have been in active operation ever since. Another large establishment is that of the Fourdrinier Wire Works. This was established in 1877 by John H. Eastwood, William Buchanan and Charles Smith, under the name of Eastwood, Buchanan & Smith, the business being the manufacture of Fourdrinier wire cloth and all kinds of fine iron, copper and brass wire. In 1880 the concern was converted into a stock company, of which John Eastwood is president. The dye and acid factory of John Eastwood, which is near by, is also one of the important industries of Belleville. One of the largest establishments in the place is that of the DeWitt Wire Cloth Co., whose works are located on the Second river near the southern boundary of the township. The works of this company occupy a series of buildings and give employment to a large number of hands. The goods of this company are sold all over the Union as well as in foreign countries, and have a high reputation.

Leading Business Men of Belleville.

P. D. ACKERMAN, Planing and Molding Mill, Sash, Blinds, Doors, and Wood Turning, and Scroll Sawing. Also Contractor and Builder, Factory, Main Street, Near William, Belleville, N. J. It is a very useful piece of information, to know where lumber may be worked to order in first-class style, and at low rates, and hence we need make no apology for calling to the attention of our readers, the establishment of which Mr. P. D. Ackerman is the proprietor, located on Main street, near William street, Belleville, N. J. Mr. Ackerman has been engaged in this business for twenty-six years, and has conducted his present establishment since 1888. He has been patronized in so liberal a manner, as to conclusively prove that his management is popular, and the work turned out by him satisfactory. Two floors are utilized, each measuring 50x25 feet, and the necessary motive power is supplied by the Riverside Rubber Co., woodworking machinery of the most improved description being found on every side. Mr. Ackerman is a native of Paterson, N. J. He is very popular with those doing business with him, as he is always accommodating, and earnestly strives to give complete satisfaction to every customer. Mr. Ackerman is a contractor and builder, and also conducts an extensive planing and molding mill, sash, blinds, doors, wood turning and scroll sawing being made to order, at short notice and in a satisfactory manner. Employment is given to thirty-five workmen. The prices are reasonable in the extreme, being as low as can be found anywhere in the vicinity, and the character of the work done at this establishment is so uniformly superior as to challenge comparison with that of any similar enterprise.

J. F. WISSCHUSEN, Dealer in all Kinds of Fine Groceries, Provisions, Flour, Feed, Hay, Grain, Straw, etc., Main Street, Near the Bridge, Belleville, N. J. Probably very few, even the best of informed of our readers, have an adequate conception of the amount of groceries and provisions consumed in Belleville annually. There are many grocery and provision stores in town, and the majority of them do a good business, for "people must eat," and the goods comprised under the head of groceries and provisions from a large portion of the food supply of a civilized community. This fact is significantly indicated by an examination of the assortment offered at the establishment carried on by Mr. J. F. Wisschusen, on main street, near the bridge, for his stock is made up of fine groceries, provisions, flour, feed, hay, grain, straw, etc., fine creamery butter being made a specialty, there being hardly a food product of any kind that he is not prepared to supply. Mr. Wisschusen is a native of Germany, and has conducted his present enterprise since 1864. He is chairman of the Town Committee, and was connected with the Board of Education for five years, and is well and favorably known throughout Belleville. The premises occupied comprise two floors, each 50x50 feet in dimensions. There are two efficient assistants employed, and although an extensive business is done, callers can depend upon being served without delay. Mr. Wisschusen has from the first, catered particularly to family trade, and offers inducements unsurpassed by any available in this section. His goods are thoroughly reliable, they are offered in sufficient variety to suit all tastes, and are sold at the lowest market rates.

McCULLOUGH & CO., Golden Seal Tea Warehouse, Plain and Fancy Groceries, William Street, Belleville, N. J. There is no line of business but what profits by the personal attention of the proprietors, but we question if there is any other branch of trade in which the personal supervision is more marked than is the case in the retail grocery business. The vast amount of petty detail it involves is one reason for this necessity, for if such detail be not intelligently looked after, disastrous results will be sure to follow. A well managed and popular grocery store is to be found on Main street, opposite William street. It is conducted by Messrs. McCullough & Co., who started this business in 1890. They show by their personal attention to their customers that they desire to please them, and strive to give the best goods that can be bought, at very reasonable rates. They carry a full supply of plain and fancy groceries, which cannot fail to suit those who know what superior groceries are, and they have also a large stock of flour, feed and grain. This firm makes a specialty of tea of different grades. They have an extra good article of this kind, ranging in price from thirty-five cents to $1.25. They carry on this business as it is done in New York, giving to purchasers a handsome premium with each pound of the finest quality tea. The terms are strictly cash. Employment is given to two assistants, and orders are promptly and carefully filled. Mr. McCullough is a native of Belleville, and both members of the firm are well known throughout this locality.

C. F. STOLZ, Baker, and Dealer in Flour and Grain, John Street, Belleville, N. J. People used to think that baker's bread was only a commodity to be used in an emergency, but this, with a good many other old-fashioned notions, have been worn threadbare, and have been proved worthless in these modern days. The bread now to be obtained in our bakeries is as delicate and delicious an article as can be made in any private house, and, in fact, more so than in nine tenths of the houses in the land. The inhabitants of Belleville can easily prove this by specimens of this "staff of life" which so many of them enjoy, and which is made in their midst, by C. F. Stolz, the proprietor of the Original Belleville Bakery. The establishment in question is situated on John street, and comprises a shop 30x40 feet in dimensions which occupies the basement and a salesroom above. Mr. Stolz has been at the head of this enterprise since 1873. The business is both wholesale and retail. Employment is given to four assistants, and four wagons are in continual use for delivering goods. The cakes, pies, etc., made at this house, are justly celebrated for their delicacy, and no housekeeper in this vicinity need trouble herself to make these dainties at home. In addition to the bakery, Mr. Stolz keeps a large stock of flour and grain on hand, which may be had here, at as reasonable rates as anywhere in the neighborhood.

CHRIS. ORTHOLF, (Successor to H. J. Blaney, and formerly with Tonsor, Broadway, N. Y.), Shaving and Haircutting Rooms, Fine Cigars and Tobacco, William Street, Near Main, Belleville, N. J. Ladies' Shampooing a Specialty. What is more useful in a community than a barber shop? There may be some things that are equally as important, but none more so. A fellow gets through his work and wishes to go down town, and has not the time to shave (?) himself, or even if he has, he cuts himself so that when he meets the friends he calls on, they poke fun at him, and ask him if he has been taking mowing jumps through plate glass windows, and all that sort of thing. Now, such unpleasant occurrences can easily be avoided by patronizing a barber, a man who is on duty expressly to give you a nice clean shave in as short a time as it takes to say "Jack Robinson." It does not cost much and one's face is always so much the better off for it, that we have often wondered, why some men preferred cutting their faces all up in preference to patronizing a good barber. It's only a dime, and many a one we spend for less worthy use. In the future, boys, go to Mr. Chris. Ortholf to get shaved; he is a tonsorial artist of ability, and has a hand as gentle as a woman's. He has been on William St., near Main, for several months now and although he has a good run of customers already, he could add a few more to the list. Fine cigars and tobacco for sale, and its "your next." A skilled assistant is employed, and both gentlemen have a large circle of friends.

W. S. HAMLIN, Real Estate and Insurance, Main Street, Belleville, N. J. A constantly increasing proportion of business men place all their insurance through agents, for experience has proved this to be the most convenient and advisable method of procedure, aside from the fact that it is much easier to investigate the character and ability of a local agent than to judge accurately of the standing of several companies located in different cities. A responsible and reputable agent will avail himself of every facility to gain all the information possible concerning the different companies proffering insurance. Therefore, it is perfectly natural that Mr. W. S. Hamlin should be called upon to write a large proportion of the polices held in this vicinity, for since he established his office in 1889, he has gained a record for honorable dealing and careful attention to the interests of his customers. He is prepared to effect insurance to any desired amount, at the very lowest obtainable rates. He is agent for the Liverpool and London and Globe Insurance Company. This is the largest, and one of the best known fire insurance companies in the world! Its agencies are not only in nearly every country, but in all the large cities and towns, both on this side the ocean and in Europe. It owns many fine buildings, a prominent example of which is the one at the corner of Pine and William streets, New York. The amount of losses paid by this company is enormous, reaching forty million dollars in the United States alone. Mr. Hamlin is also agent for the Continental Fire Insurance Company, of New York, which stands very high among insurance corporations, and carries on an extended business throughout this country. Mr. Hamlin's office is conveniently located on Main street. All persons wishing to avail themselves of his services will find him, with his assistant, ever ready to give prompt and courteous attention. His facilities for rendering transactions in real estate are excellent, and those patrons who consult him as to these operations, will find them profitable to all parties interested.

SLATTERY & BRADY, Grocer and Liquor Dealers, Main Street, Belleville. Probably one of the best known establishments is that conducted by Slattery & Brady, on Main street. The proprietors have become thoroughly identified with the undertaking in question. The premises utilized comprise one floor and basement, and a large stock is constantly on hand to choose from, it being made up of choice staple groceries, fine teas and coffees, flour, lard, butter, eggs and spices, and many other commodities too numerous to mention, besides a fine line of liquors and cigars. They employ competent assistants, and are in a position to assure immediate and courteous attention to every caller. They cater to no special class of trade, but strive to offer a sufficient variety of goods to suit all tastes and purses, and quote positively the lowest market rates at all times. They have built up an extensive business, and have an unsurpassed reputation for selling goods strictly on their merits, no misrepresentation being practiced under any circumstances.

ISAAC B. BAKER, Dealer in all Kinds of Coal and Wood, Hay, Straw and Feed, Opposite Erie Depot, Belleville, New Jersey. As all residents of Belleville and the vicinity are well aware, one of the best places to procure coal and wood, is the establishment conducted by Isaac B. Baker. Mr. Baker has been carrying on his business in this place for about seven years, having succeeded in 1888 to a concern which had changed hands several times. His fair methods and good stock have rendered him a popular man, as well as a successful merchant, and his trade is ever on the increase. Mr. Baker owns large premises, comprising a yard, covering an area of 165x100 feet, and an office near by. This yard is stocked with all kinds of coal and wood, for which only moderate prices are asked. In addition to this stock, Mr. Baker deals in hay, straw and feed, for which he has a large demand. The premises are conveniently located opposite the Erie depot, and are fitted with every necessary, including an eight horse power engine, used for sawing. Mr. Baker is a native of Putnam county, N. Y., but is entirely identified with the State of New Jersey. He has filled acceptably several township offices, and is now fire commissioner on turpentine. He employs four assistants in his business, and it is needless to say, all orders sent to this house are attended to without delay.

A. B. PARSELLS, SR., Wagon Maker

and Wheelwright, Horseshoeing, Blacksmithing and General Jobbing, Main Street, Belleville, N. J. One of the most popular establishments of its kind in Belleville is that conducted by Mr. A. B. Parsells, Sr., located on Main street, and as many of our readers could doubtless have dealings with this house to the advantage of all parties concerned, we take pleasure in calling attention to some of the advantages to be gained by so doing. The enterprise to which we have reference, was inaugurated in 1846, and has thus been before the public long enough to prove that it is worthy of every confidence. The premises occupied comprise two floors, each covering an area of 660 square feet, and all necessary tools, machinery and other appliances are at hand to enable orders for anything in the wagon making and wheelwright line to be given that prompt and skillful attention to which the patrons of this establishment are accustomed. Carriages, wagons, etc., will be made to order and satisfaction guaranteed. Special attention is given to horseshoeing, blacksmithing and general jobbing, for which this house holds an exceptionally high reputation. The repairs that are made at this establishment are not only neat and handsome in appearance, but they are strong and durable when put to the test of actual wear, a point which those who have had much carriage repairing done will appreciate. The proprietor is very moderate in his charges, and well deserves the popularity he so long has enjoyed. Skilled and reliable assistants are constantly employed, and all orders in any branch of the business are promptly executed. Mr. Parsells is a native of Rockland county, N. J., and well known among the enterprising business men of Belleville.

GEO. F. THORNTON, JR., Plumbing,

Steam and Gas Fitting, Jobbing Promptly Attended to, Washington Avenue, Belleville, N. J. Mr. Thornton, who established this business here in April, 1890, is a practical plumber, steam and gas fitter, and those who have entrusted their work in this line to him since that time have no need to regret it. He is a native of Chicago, and has had some experience in this line previous to starting here. The premises occupied by him are 20x40 feet in dimensions. Employment is given to four competent assistants that orders may be attended to at short notice. He is prepared to undertake plumbing and all other kinds of house piping, either for small jobs or for large houses, stores or blocks of stores. As there is nothing upon which the health of the inmates of any building depends so much as the plumbing, it is necessary that only those who understand the business, and are thoroughly honest should be employed. There is no better way to learn about a workman than to judge of his work. If those having houses to build will inspect some of the plumbing which has been done by Mr. Thornton, they will find proof of his honesty and ability

F. W. TOLFREE, News Dealer, Books,

Stationery of All Kinds, etc., Main street, near William, Belleville, N. J. "Nothing succeeds like success," and in view of the success which has been won by Mr. F. W. Tolfree, since he established his present enterprise. We feel it to be quite unnecessary to present arguments to prove that he is both able and willing to supply first-class goods at bottom rates. Mr. Tolfree only established his present business in 1890, but he needs no introduction to a large portion of our readers, for there is hardly a business man in Belleville more generally known, and we may add more highly esteemed. The premises occupied by him are conveniently located on Main street, near William street, and comprise a store 15x55 feet in dimensions. He carries a large stock of books and stationery of all kinds; also, all daily, weekly and monthly publications, and, in fact, everything usually to be found in a first-class news dealer's establishment. Mr. Tolfree is a native of Bloomfield, N. J., and pursues but one policy regarding the goods he handles, his aim being to give the largest possible return for money received. This may seem incredible to those who believe in selling at as high a figure as possible, but Mr. Tolfree's experience has, no doubt, taught him that the public appreciate liberal methods, and at all events, no establishment in this section is more highly and deservedly popular. Employment is given two careful and attentive assistants, and all patrons are promptly attended to.

H. VREELAND & SON, Dealers in Meats,

Vegetables, etc., Washington Avenue and William Street, Belleville, N. J. The above and popular establishment is under the direct superintendency of Mr. Harry Vreeland It was established in the year 1885, and Mr. Vreeland, Jr., was identified with the enterprise for two years in succession. From 1885 to 1890, however, the business changed hands several times and the friends of Mr. Vreeland so importuned him to again take it up, that he finally did some few months ago. The old familiar "vim" has returned, and things look like "old times" now, for Mr. Vreelands old customers have all come back to him, and induced many of their friends to do likewise. A perceptible change for the better in the management is noticeable, and the business transacted is brisk. Mr. Vreeland deserves this popularity, for he is personally a genial fellow, and his sociability makes hosts of friends for him. The main reason why he succeeds, however, is because he keeps good meats and vegetables; this is the secret in a nutshell. He employs none but honest, fair and open business methods, and is as painstaking in filling small orders as larger ones. The market is neat and spacious, it being 25x50 feet in area. We know of no better market in Belleville which so well meets the meat wants of its citizens

JOHN CONLIN, Dealer in Fine Groceries,

Provisions, Flour, Feed, Hay, Straw, etc., Boots and Shoes, William Street, Belleville, N. J. This well managed and growing enterprise was established over thirty years ago, Mr. John Conlin, the present proprietor and founder having come to Belleville in 1876. He has had many years experience in trade, and has gained a thorough knowledge of the best way to conduct a first-class grocery and provision store, and how to cater to the many patrons who prefer this store to any other in this neighborhood. The premises occupied are 48x30 feet in dimensions, and are located on William street. The trade is entirely retail, and is carried on by Mr. Conlin with the help of three assistants. The stock consists of fine groceries of every description, provisions, flour, feed, hay, straw, etc. These goods are all fresh and desirable, and may be depended on in every instance for first-class family use. An equally important part of Mr. Conlin's business is his boot and shoe trade. He is the oldest dealer in this line of goods in Belleville, and has always done a large business, supplying many of the most prominent people in the place. The store is a double one, and one half is stocked with a full line of men's as well as ladies' and children's shoes, at very moderate prices. All customers are attended to promptly, and orders are delivered when desired. Mr. Conlin was a Township Committeeman for three terms, and has occupied the important position of Town Treasurer during two terms

HARRISON.

The town of Harrison is situated on the western border of Hudson County, on the east bank of the Passaic river, and though a separate municipality and in another county, is to all intents and purposes a suburb of Newark; indeed, for many years Harrison was known as East Newark and this name still clings to it. More people to-day know the place as East Newark, than Harrison. The place was, formerly, known as Petersborough, up to 1815, when it was known as Lodi. In 1840 the name was changed to East Newark and then to Harrison. In 1870 the town was incorporated with a common council instead of a town committee. The town now has a small but efficient police force, a good fire department and an excellent system of public schools. Harrison derives its chief importance from the fact that several large manufacturing establishments are located there, many of them being owned or largely controlled by Newarkers who have chosen this town as the site for their factories, for the reason that land is much cheaper and taxes lower than in Newark.

The situation of Harrison is an exceedingly favorable one for manufacturing industries, as it has an extensive water front along the Passaic, is reached by two of the leading railroads that pass through Newark, the Delaware, Lackawanna & Western and the Pennsylvania. The new branch of the latter road and the new line of the Lehigh Valley Railroad will also pass through this town. Both the Pennsylvania and Delaware, Lackawanna & Western Railroads have extensive freight yards in this town, and a very large proportion of Newark's freight business is done here. The town is growing rapidly and the indications are that at no distant day this will be a great manufacturing center. Entering the town by way of the Newark Free Bridge, which is the great thoroughfare of traffic between Newark and Harrison, the visitor strikes Harrison avenue, the principal street of the place, which is a broad and well paved avenue, through which runs a line of horse cars connecting with the City of Newark. This avenue is build up solidly with stores and residences for a distance of a mile and half, while even beyond this there are many beautiful villa sites. The lateral streets which cross Harrison avenue at right angles are also built up with neat and comfortable dwellings. The factories of the town are chiefly confined to the river front, though there are several large establishments well out upon the meadows. Near the Newark Free Bridge on the river front are several large stone cutting works, the chief of these being that of J. J. Spurr & Sons. In this yard some of the finest work of the country has been done, not only for large structures in New York, but for the homes of two millionaires on the Pacific coast. Another large manufacturing establishment is that of J. Lagowitz & Co., trunk and bag makers, which is situated on the river front near the Center street bridge of the Pennsylvania Railroad, and fronts on Harrison avenue. It is one of the largest factories in the place, and comprises an extensive system of brick buildings equipped with valuable and costly machinery. The plant is worth about $250,000. The factory gives employment to about five or six hundred people, and all the trimmings, frames, and, in fact, everything used in the manufacture of trunks and bags is made on the premises. Another large factory on the banks of the Passaic is that of Stannier & Laffey, manufacturers of brass and copper wire and wire cloth. The factory is one of the best known of its kind in the country and does a very large business. The Edison Lamp Co. occupy an extensive series of buildings on Third street. These buildings were formerly owned and occupied by the Peters' Manufacturing Co. as an oil cloth factory, but the Company met with several disastrous fires, which destroyed portions of their works, after which they abandoned their plant in Harrison and sold the property to the Edison Lamp Co., who have greatly improved the property and made many additions to the buildings. The manufacture of arc and incandescent lamps on Edison's patents is carried on here on a large scale.

Another important industrial establishment is that of Stewart Hartshorn, manufacturer of shade rollers. The factory has been in operation since 1870, gives employment to several hundred persons and turns out several hundred dozen shade rollers every day. Its products are known all over the United States.

The brewery of Peter Hauck & Co. is situated on Harrison avenue, between Fifth and Washington streets. It occupies a number of massive brick buildings, the main one fronting on Harrison avenue, being a very handsome structure architecturally. Its lofty turrets can be seen in all directions for miles.

and makes the brewery one of the landmarks of the town. Adjoining the brewery is the elegant residence of Mr. Hauck, which is the handsomest house in the place. Nearly opposite the brewery is the Davis Memorial Methodist Church, an imposing brick structure. Some distance farther west on Harrison avenue, is the superb edifice of the Catholic Church of the Holy Cross, one of the most massive and beautiful ecclesiastical edifices in New Jersey. Another church which is worthy of mention is St. Pius' Catholic Church on the corner of Jersey and Third streets, which for many years was the only Catholic church in the place. Christ Church on Fourth street, which is a pretty little Gothic frame structure, is the church home of the Episcopalians of the town, and is really a mission of Trinity Church, Newark. It is in charge of the Rev. Dr. Potter. The Presbyterian Church also has a flourishing congregation in this town. Harrison has also excellent public schools, as well as a fine parochial school attached to the Church of the Holy Cross. There is a flourishing German-English school on Hebden street.

Leading Business Men of Harrison.

CLARENCE T. VAN DEREN, office No. 307 Harrison Avenue, Harrison, N. J., dealer in Real Estate, Bonds and Mortgages. Commissioner of Deeds; Notary Public. Auction sales a specialty. Telephone 816. The business conducted by Mr. Clarence T. Van Deren in this town was inaugurated by that gentleman in the year 1885. Mr. Van Deren is one of Harrison's most active business men, and it would be looked upon as a strange

omission did we not make prominent mention of one who carries on as generally useful an enterprise as his. Its nature is that of real estate, bonds and mortgages and auction sales. The proficiency which characterizes Mr. Van Deren's ability in these branches of business is largely availed of by the residents of this section. The gentleman in question inaugurated his office in 1885 and since its inception his business has steadily found favor with the public. No one not

making a special study of the real estate of a place can keep pace with the numerous changes made in it from time to time, consequently it is well to go straight to a reliable agent when in need of information on the subject. Mr. Van Deren is "posted" on Harrison and Kearny property, and is just the man to see in regard to buying, selling or exchanging property. He is also a dealer in bonds and mortgages and those interested will find him reasonable as to terms, etc. Mr. Van Deren is a commissioner of deeds and notary public also. He has been for three years an assessor for the Third ward, and is at present the secretary of the Board of Health. He has a finely appointed office and employs two efficient assistants. The esteem in which Mr. Van Deren is held by the people is evidenced by the public offices he holds. The readers of this work would do well to call on him whenever they need services which he can render. "People who work in New York could hardly find a better place for a home than Harrison, N. J. Three railways, the Pennsylvania, the D., L. & W., and the Erie, run through the town. All have a magnificent suburban service, and every few minutes trains stop in the town on their way to or from New York. Fares are very cheap. An artisan, clerk or merchant can get a comfortable home here for less than half the price or rental he would have to pay for over-crowded quarters in New York. There are many very handsome houses in and about the town. Access to the most distant parts is made easy by a line of street cars. A man who has come to the front a good deal in Harrison lately is Mr. Clarence T. Van Deren. He was brought up in the town and when a lad of fifteen began to earn his own living in a real estate office. To this business he has kept ever since, and now at only thirty years old he is the principle real estate agent in the town. When he began business for himself he had only desk room in the old *Record* building, now he occupies a handsome suit of offices at No. 307 Harrison avenue, and his business keeps a big staff of clerks busy all the time. His business includes all manner of real estate transactions, buying, selling, exchanging and leasing, but he makes a specialty of auction sales. He also does a large insurance business and is a notary public and commissioner of deeds. Among the estates he represents are the Hebden, Van Sologen, Young, Zabriske, Williams, Dukes, Jackson, Banta, Juralemon, Ackerson, Jones, Heinsheimer and Phillips. These properties include building lots of every description, both factory and residence, at values ranging from $150 to $2,500. Being a notary he is able to draw up all contracts, leases, etc., called for by his business. He is sole agent in Harrison for the Liverpool and London and Globe and other insurance companies. An indication of his popularity and the estimation in which he is held is the fact that the volume of his business is $500,000 a year. He is not only enterprising but is also very popular, and is marked out for public office. At the present time he is secretary of the Board of Health. Greater honors are in store for him. His interests all lie in Harrison, in which he already has large holdings of property.—*New York World*.

JOHN T. McCLURE, House Sign and Decorative Painting, Paper Hanging, Hard Wood Finishing, Graining and Kalsomining, Shop, 405 Warren Street, Residence, 408 Warren Street, Harrison, N. J. It seems wonderful to those who have no special taste in that line to see the changing and attractive effects which may be attained by the judicious use of paints and paper hangings, and other home decorations, for by skillful management of such accessories small rooms may be made to look larger, dark ones lighted and unduly large apartments cosy and comfortable. Of course, in order to do this the means as well as skill must be provided, and in this connection it is natural to call attention to the establishment located at No. 405 Warren street, and conducted by Mr. John T. McClure. This gentleman possesses every facility for the doing of house and sign painting, and he is also prepared to do hard wood finishing, graining kalsomining and paper hanging in the most approved style, at short notice and at moderate rates. Six skillful workmen are constantly employed, and every order is guaranteed immediate and painstaking attention, the work being done in a satisfactory manner and with carefully selected and reliable materials. Mr. McClure is a native of Harrison and has been School Commissioner for one year. The business which he now manages was founded in 1887, under the firm name of Kleinknecht & McClure, but has been under Mr. McClure's sole control since the early part of the current year.

JORALEMON & HAZELTON, Dealers in Fancy Groceries, Tea, Coffee and Spices, Canned Goods, Fruits, and Vegetables in their Season, Corner South Fourth and Warren Streets, Harrison, N. J. The business now conducted by Messrs. Joralemon & Hazelton, was inaugurated in 1888 by Mr. A. V. Joralemon, who associated himself with Mr. Hazelton during the present year. Both gentlemen are natives of Harrison and are very well known and highly esteemed citizens. They have already built up an extensive trade, and it may be safely predicted that if they adhere to their present principal of governing affairs, the present steady and rapid growth of patronage will continue. People like to have a large stock of groceries, etc., to select from, and also like to feel sure that whatever they buy will prove as represented, and both these desires can be gratified by dealing with the firm in question, as many residents of Harrison have already learned. The premises made use of are located corner South Fourth and Warren streets, and are of the dimensions of 25x50 feet, and the stock on hand includes fancy groceries, teas, coffees and spices, canned goods of all kinds, and fruits and vegetables in season, all of which are quoted at the lowest market rates. Two competent assistants are employed, and orders are filled and delivered with a promptness and accuracy pleasant to see. Callers are attended to courteously and quickly, and care is taken to give no just cause for complaint.

JOHN CONNOLLY, Carpenter and Builder, Jobbing Promptly Attended to, Satisfaction Guaranteed, Woodland Avenue, off Kearny Avenue, Next to Township Hall, Kearny, N. J. Mr. John Connolly has carried on business in Kearny for a number of years, and is well known and highly esteemed. He became identified with his present business here in 1883, and has gained in the time elapsed since then an enviable reputation for upright and honorable methods in all his transactions, and is known to be one of the most reliable builders to be found in Kearny. His premises are located on Woodland avenue, off Kearny Avenue, and are of the dimensions of 28x18 feet, and all necessary facilities are at hand to give prompt and skillful attention to orders for buildings of all descriptions. Six assistants is the average number employed, and this force can easily be increased at short notice when occasion requires. Jobbing orders are given prompt attention, and work is executed in a thoroughly satisfactory manner. Mr. Connolly also deals in lumber of all kinds, and can furnish it in quantities to suit purchasers at the most reasonable prices. In fact his terms in every part of his business are very moderate, and his high reputation for fair dealing has been honestly earned. Mr. Connolly buys lots, builds on them and sells. He always has several desirable houses for sale or exchange, and parties wishing to procure a house of their own can do no better than consult Mr. Connolly.

EDWARD J. RICE, Dealer in Choice Family Groceries, Teas, Coffees, Flour, Feed, etc., 115 Harrison Avenue, near John Street, Harrison, N. J. The enumeration of the representative business enterprises of Harrison would certainly be considered incomplete by the residents of that town, did we not make extended mention of an enterprise carried on by one of its most prominent citizens. We have reference to the grocery store conducted by Mr. Edward J. Rice, at No. 115 Harrison avenue. Having been inaugurated in the year 1872 by Mr. Rice in person, from its very inception, the establishment found favor with the public, and increased in patronage and popularity. The success was well merited, for Mr. Rice spared no pains to deserve the reputation, and as the beginning was, so has been the continuation of the business. A word concerning the stock which Mr. Rice carries would not be amiss. It can be described in the statement that it comprises the choice staple and fancy groceries usually found in none but really first-class establishments engaged in this important branch of the mercantile activities. Special mention is particularly worthy of being made of the family flour which Mr. Rice offers his patrons. It is selected from the "cream brands," and tints with blushes all others on the market in its superiority over them. Imported teas and coffees, cream butter, nice fresh eggs, canned goods of every variety, etc., are of the purest quality and freshness. To successfully cater to the needs of his long list of regular patrons, Mr. Rice affords employment to two courteous assistants. The establishment is 25x50 feet in dimensions and is admirably adapted for the purposes for which it was intended. The fixtures are elegant and were made with a view of facilitating the manipulation of the goods to the best advantage. No house in Harrison is better prepared to successfully meet the grocery wants of the public. We esteem it a pleasure to recommend the establishment in question to the readers of the "History of Harrison and its Leading Business Men." Mr. Rice has occupied public offices, in this, his native town. He was for seven years in the aldermanic chamber, and for the past year has been sitting as Judge in the Police Court. We need not speak of the esteem in which he is held by his fellow townsmen, for the latter distinguished honor speaks for itself.

GUS SCHULTZ, Dealer in all Kinds of Meats, 131 Harrison Avenue, Harrison, N. J. A well regulated and reliable meat market is that of Mr. Gus Schultz, which was established in 1887 and has become the center of a very large trade. The store is finely fitted up and no pains or expense has been spared to place it in first-class order, with a large ice box for the preservation of all perishable articles. He has always in stock the choicest beef, veal, pork and mutton, and, though established not quite three years, he does quite a large trade and numbers among his patrons some of the best people in the vicinity. A competent force of skilled assistants are employed to attend to his numerous patrons. Mr. Schultz is a native of Germany and gives close personal attention to the many details of his business. The store is located at No. 131 Harrison avenue, and is 15x25 feet in dimensions, and gives accommodation to his large and well selected stock. Neatness, order and system are the leading features of this house, and courteous attention is accorded to all.

GEO. E. PETTIT, Staple and Fancy Groceries, 131 Harrison Avenue, Harrison, N. J. Mr. G. E. Pettit is a native of Newark, N. J., and began business here in 1889 in the retail grocery line, and by his able and popular management soon secured a fine trade. He brings long practical experience to bear in his business and is quick to discern the tastes and wants of his patrons, and has the ability to promptly and satisfactorily supply them. The premises are 15x25 feet in dimensions, and are finely fitted up, the stock is attractively displayed, and the store is thoroughly equipped with every appliance for the expeditious dispatch of its large business. Mr. Pettit carries a full and comprehensive stock of choice staple and fancy groceries, fine new crop teas, fragrant coffees, pure spices and Beatty's famous Ivory starch, which is one of the finest starches made; it is simple, harmless, economical, requires no cooking and does not stick.

ARCH'D McARTHUR, Plumber and Gas Fitter, Tin Roofing, Sheet Iron Work, No. 9 Kearny Avenue, Harrison, N. J. Hot Air Furnaces and Ranges. In the light of modern discovery, it seems odd that disease should be looked upon as inevitable, and an epidemic as a judgment upon the people, and in point of fact these views of such things have about passed away, and the people are coming to know that the plumber can do more to prevent disease than the physician can do to heal it. This, of course, is a general statement, and is not applicable to every call or to every plumber either, but, nevertheless, there is no denying that many a house is a hot-bed of disease, that, were it properly drained, etc., would be as healthful a tenement as could be wished for. Many people call themselves "plumbers." Many plumbers call themselves "sanitary engineers," but, after all, it is just as well to be on the safe side, and if you want to secure the services of a really reliable plumber, to employ one who has an extended experience as Mr. Arch'd McArthur has. This gentleman is a native of Scotland, and began operations here in Harrison in 1889. His premises are located at No. 9 Kearny avenue, and are of the dimensions of 36x18 feet. Here orders may be left for plumbing and gas fitting, tin-roofing and sheet iron work. Mr. McArthur gives close personal attention to all work entrusted to him, and can confidently guarantee satisfaction to every customer. Employment is given to four competent assistants. Mr. McArthur is also prepared to furnish and put up ranges and hot air furnaces. He uses the most improved devices, and is very reliable and moderate in his charges.

GEORGE H. SMITH, THE DAIRY, Butter, Eggs, Oysters, Clams and Milk, Wholesale and retail, Fresh Buttermilk Every Day, all Kinds of Canned Goods, No. 231 Harrison Avenue, Harrison, N. J. No resident of Harrison at all familiar with the town would consider our sketch of its history complete, did we not make extended mention of "the dairy" which can be found at No. 231 Harrison avenue, with Mr. George H. Smith as its genial proprietor. The business in question was inaugurated by this gentleman in the year 1890. Every housekeeper welcomed his new enterprise in this neighborhood, for it was an institution the need of which had long been felt by the neighborhood. Good butter, fresh eggs and pure milk are all articles in which the public are frequently "fooled," (if we may be pardoned in using the expression). We mean to say that some unscrupulous grocers and milkmen make it so unpleasant with their "good" (oleo) butter, "fresh" (decayed) eggs and pure (chalk) milk, that when a man comes and starts up an honest business in this line, he becomes popular with a hitherto outraged public. Such was and is the case in hand. Mr. Smith started out on the "square" with his customers, and before he knew it, he began to do a good business. He enjoys close relations with the farmers not many miles from here, and in this way supplies nothing but pure and fresh dairy produce. The prices he quotes defy competition, and tint with blushes those of other dealers. You should by all means avail yourselves of the advantages Mr. Smith offers to you. In the butter, egg and milk line they cannot be surpassed. Grocers have so many other details to attend to, that justice is rarely given to the dairy department. Mr. Smith makes it his sole business, and sees that the public is well, and, above all, honestly supplied in the goods we have reference to. Mr. Smith also carries oysters and clams.

MRS. D. KIRK, Millinery Goods, 214 Harrison Avenue, Harrison, N. J. Even the finest appointed and most generally known millinery establishments are frequently complained of for undue delay in the delivery of orders, and it would almost seem as though there must be something peculiar about the business that rendered it impossible to turn out goods at the time promised. Undoubtedly it is true to a certain extent that there is more detail to be looked after in this business than in almost any other, but that proper management will do much to assure promptness in this, is undeniable. Thus the experience of those who have had dealings with Mrs. D. Kirk, amply proves. This lady has carried on her present enterprise since 1888. She is a retail dealer in the latest styles in millinery work to order. No establishment in this vicinity turns out better work and at such reasonable prices. Mrs. Kirk is located at 214 Harrison avenue, where a beautiful stock is carried

and the very latest novelties are always represented. Mrs. Kirk employs a sufficient force of skilful assistants and makes it a rule to let no imperfect work leave her place. A very carefully arranged system of receiving and filling orders for custom work is in operation, and all confusion is avoided, the consequence being that orders are always sure to be delivered when promised.

P. J. BEHAN, Ready-Made and Custom Clothier, No. 212 Harrison Avenue, Harrison, N. J. A representative and reliable house actively engaged in the sale of fine clothing is that of P. J. Behan. This house was founded in the current year, and, although comparatively young, it has a large trade in both departments. Mr. Behan is a practical business man and gives the closest personal attention to his business, thus being enabled to fully guarantee the excellence of all goods leaving his establishment. The premises utilized are admirably equipped with every facility for the successful prosecution of the business. He pays the greatest attention to the selection of his goods and employs only the best talent in his line of business. Mr. Behan is a native of Ireland, having been born in the city of Dublin, and came to this country at an early age, and has had a long and varied experience in this business, and for years was in charge of different departments with Marshall & Ball, of Newark. Besides his extensive stock of ready-made clothing he has a large and growing custom trade, controlling the fine trade of Harrison. His garments are cut and made in the most artistic manner, at prices that range very low considering the quality of work done. His store is located at 212 Harrison avenue, and is large and commodious, being 25x60 feet in dimensions. There are competent workmen constantly employed to attend to the custom trade, as is also the case in the ready-made department.

WILLIAM LATIMER & CO., Ladies', Gents'
and Children's Fine Footwear of every description, No. 258
Harrison Avenue, near Third Street, Harrison, N. J. This
well known boot and shoe house was inaugurated in 1889.
The store these gentlemen occupy measures 50x40 feet in
dimensions and is elegantly fitted up with fixtures calculated to draw admiration and facilitate the handling of the large stock of boots and shoes carried.
These are obtained from the most reliable sources and are
purchased in large lots, which bring a large rebate to the
firm. This rebate, Messrs. Latimer & Co. share equally with
the patrons of the house. The prices of the goods are
strictly in proportion to the quality of the goods, and a fair
equivalent is given for every dollar. Some people expect a
dollar shoe to give as good service as a two dollar one.
Such are unreasonable and are not invited to this establishment. If good goods are expected to be better than inferior goods there is nothing more reasonably natural than that
they should cost the dealer more, and the buyer also. The
firm in question have had years of experience in their line,
they know their business, and it is conducted in a highly irreproachable manner; the strictly honest business methods
which have characterized this house since its inauguration,
is, in fact, what has made it popular with the public. Four

courteous assistants are employed and they are instructed
to represent the relative value of goods just as they really
are. All classes of trade are catered to. We know of no
better place to patronize in the purchasing of boots and
shoes in town, and recommend Latimer & Co.'s store to our
readers' favorable consideration.

IMPERIAL CUTLERY WORKS, Manu-
facturers of Table Cutlery, 707 North Fourth Street, Harrison, N. J. As it is practically impossible to judge accurately
the value of an article of cutlery from its appearance alone,
the purchaser has to depend upon the standing of the manufacturers for security that he is getting the value of his
money, and hence our readers would do well to
remember the name, "Imperial Cutlery Works,"
for this Company spare no pains to turn out goods of uniform and satisfactory quality, and a knife bearing that
name may be depended upon as regards excellence of material, fineness of tempering and thoroughness of workmanship. This business was founded by Messrs. Knight &
Heinold, in 1887, this firm being succeeded by Messrs.
Heinold & Co., in 1888, and the present Company being
formed in 1890. The factory is located at No. 707 North
Fourth street, Harrison, and has a total floor-space of some
six thousand square feet. It is fitted up throughout with
the latest improved machinery, driven by a forty-five-horse
engine, and as employment is given to forty-five assistants,
the Company are prepared to fill the heaviest orders at
short notice, the capacity of the works being very large,
moderate prices are quoted on all the styles produced,
and dealers will find the productions of the Imperial Cutlery
Works both pleasant and profitable to handle.

B. GREGORY & SON, Blacksmithing.
Wagon-Making and Repairing, 500 Passaic Avenue, Harrison,
Hudson County, N. J. A few years are considered ample
time in these days for the acquirement of any trade. Some
people learn to be skillful in a short time, others do not,
but when a man has carried on a certain line of business
for nearly half a century, his absolute proficiency in it is
almost a certainty. This is the case with Mr. B. Gregory, of
Harrison, N. J. He is a practical blacksmith, manufacturer
and repairer of wagons, and has been pursuing these industries since 1844. He carried on the business alone for
forty years, when he admitted his son, Everett M. Gregory,
into partnership, and the firm has since been known as B.
Gregory & Son. Natives of Morristown, in this State, both
father and son have lived in Harrison for many years, and
are well known throughout the place. The shop, situated
at No. 500 Passaic avenue, occupies two floors of 24x46 feet
dimensions, which are conveniently fitted up for the requirements of the trade. Employment is given to four workmen, who assist in the different departments. The work
done at this house is first-class in every particular, the
Messrs. Gregory giving their personal supervision even to
the details. Wagons are repaired promptly in a strong and
satisfactory manner, and orders for making vehicles can be
quickly filled. The charges will be found uniformly moderate, and will compare favorably with those of any house in
the vicinity.

S. SCHIFF, Dry and Fancy Goods, Carpets,
Oil Cloth, Linoleum, Ladies' and Gents' Furnishings, Boys'
Clothing, Hats, etc., 224 Harrison Avenue, between Second
and Third Streets, Harrison, New Jersey. The building in
which the above establishment does business is built upon
the site where once stood "Old Miser Rodwell's" rickety
shanty. This old fellow died some few years ago, here, and
was not supposed to have been worth a cent, when in reality,
he was worth a large fortune. He dealt in second hand
furniture, and was the quaintest, most eccentric individual
in town. Mr. Senior Schiff before entering his new store,
had previously been located at No. 119 Harrison avenue. He
inaugurated his present enterprise in 1888. His father, Mr.
Ludwig Schiff, was for eighteen years in the same line as his
son now is. Both gentlemen are business men of enterprise
and marked ability. Mr. Schiff's store is undoubtedly the
finest in Harrison in this line of goods. His store comprises two floors, each 25x70 feet in dimensions, and is
elegantly fitted up and admirably adapted for the purposes
for which it is utilized. The residents of Harrison can buy
as cheap of this establishment as they can either in Newark
or New York, and we advise them to give it a trial.

KEMP & RUTMAN,

HOUSE, SIGN AND ORNAMENTAL PAINTERS,

Dealers in Paints, Oils, Glass, Etc. Decorative Paper Hanging.

232 HARRISON AVENUE.

Much of the protective value of paints, oils, etc., depends upon the character of the ingredients used in their composition, and as these articles are used quite as much for their preservative as for their decorative qualities, it follows that care should be taken to purchase them from a concern which may be depended upon to furnish honest and strictly reliable goods. No house dealing in these articles in Harrison has a better record in this respect than that of Kemp & Rutman, and their customers enjoy an additional advantage in the fact that the stock carried is so large and varied that it is easy to select goods therein which are particularly suited to their tastes and to the business in question. Messrs. Kemp & Rutman also pay particular attention to painting, paper hanging, etc., and employ fifteen experienced and thoroughly reliable workmen in this work. The premises utilized comprise a floor 30x30 feet in dimensions and courteous assistants are in attendance to wait upon customers. Paints, oils, glass, wall paper, etc., are supplied in quantities to suit at the lowest market rates. All orders are accurately and promptly filled at short notice. Though this house is yet comparatively young in the race for wealth, the business it does is worthy of an establishment of much longer standing. A good job of painting or wall papering often borders on fine art work, and this is the only kind the firm of Kemp & Rutman execute. The readers of this volume are invited to avail themselves of the advantage to be derived in patronizing such a reliable house as that of Messrs. Kemp & Rutman. Their work is the best and their prices very low.

W. C. WOOST, Dealer in Groceries and Provisions, Fruit, Vegetables, Flour, Feed and Grain, No. 501 Harrison Avenue, Harrison, N. J. There is a familiar old saying to the effect that a stream cannot rise higher than its source, and it is equally true that the retail establishment devoted to any special line of business cannot offer first-class inducements if they are obliged to depend upon second-class wholesale houses to furnish them with their supplies. It is, therefore, clear that every resident of Harrison, N. J., and vicinity, is directly interested in the character of the local retail grocery houses, for groceries rank with the necessities of life, and it is of the first importance to be able to buy them to the best possible advantage. The house conducted by W. C. Woost was founded by him in 1879. Mr. Woost occupies very extensive premises at 501 Harrison Avenue, and a large stock is carried at all times, it being made up of staple and fancy groceries, provisions, fruit, vegetables, flour, feed and grain. The firm is in a position to meet all honorable competition, for it enjoys the most favorable relations with producers and has a well earned reputation for quoting bottom prices as well as for handling goods that will give the best satisfaction to the most select trade. Employment is given to six assistants, and orders are assured immediate and painstaking attention. Mr. Woost is well known in both business and social circles.

FRANK H. COYLE, Mason, Contractor and Builder, Residence, No. 316 Harrison Avenue, Harrison, New Jersey. One of Harrison's oldest families is that which bears Mr. Frank Coyle's name. This gentleman's father lived many years in this town and was considered as one of the "old settlers" of this place. He was for a long time the sole contractor in this immediate section, and it was from him that the subject of this sketch obtained his first knowledge of mason work. Mr. Coyle is a man who is thoroughly identified with the building interests of Harrison, and has built some of the finest residences and business buildings in it. A noticeable feature in his work is the workmanlike manner in which it is done; this, with the employment of conscientious men, and integrity in following out specifications, has built up for him an enviable reputation among contractors. Parties contemplating building would consult their own interests in consulting Mr. F. H. Coyle, for his experience in such matters is of long standing, and he possesses the faculty of being able to put it to practical use. Mr. Coyle is always ready to cheerfully furnish estimates, and all correspondence addressed to No. 316 Harrison avenue in his name, will be promptly acknowledged. This gentleman is one who has done much toward the present prosperity of Harrison, and we are pleased to say that there are none in his line who are more worthy of business encouragement.

MRS. A. BREITENBUCHER, Dealer in Beef, Veal, Mutton, Pork, Poultry and Vegetables, 205 Second Street, Harrison Central Meat Market, Harrison, N. J. There is probably no housekeeper but what has experienced more or less difficulty in obtaining entirely satisfactory meats, for the payment of the highest market rates by no means assures the purchaser of getting first-class goods, as many of our readers undoubtedly know from experience. This is not always the fault of the dealer, for mistakes are sure to happen in every line of business, and sometimes these mistakes are excusable, but, nevertheless, it is perfectly safe to say that, generally speaking, those who are willing to pay for first-class meats should be able to depend upon being supplied with such, and in this connection we may fittingly call attention to the facilities offered at the Harrison Central Meat Market, which is now conducted by Mrs. A. Breitenbucher, for here may always be found a first-class assortment of meats, Poultry, etc., and those who want choice articles in these lines should by all means give this establishment a call. The business was founded in 1871 by Mr. Adam Breitenbucher, who was succeeded by his wife, the present able proprietress. The premises are located at No. 205 Second street, and are 25x100 feet in size. A specialty is made of bologna sausage, which is manufactured on the premises, and for which purpose a 6 horse power Baxter engine is used. Vegetables are also largely dealt in, and every article sold may be depended upon to prove as represented. Three assistants are employed, and orders will be promptly and accurately delivered.

J. COOPER, Drygoods, Groceries, Meats, etc., 26 Johnson avenue, Harrison, N. J. Among the various and popular enterprises of Harrison which bear marks of increasing prosperity, is the establishment conducted by Mr. J. Cooper at No. 26 Johnson avenue. This establishment was founded by the present proprietor in 1887. The premises utilized are of the size of 25x50 feet, and a full and complete stock of drygoods, groceries, meats and provisions will be found constantly on hand. The facilities possessed by Mr. Cooper for obtaining a choice supply of goods are unsurpassed by any contemporary concern. The greatest care is taken by this gentleman in the selection of his choice and varied stock, which is highly esteemed by the residents of Harrison and vicinity for its excellence and low price. Employment is given to five clerks, who are polite and prompt in their attention to the many customers, and every facility is at hand for the conduct of the large and prosperous retail trade. Mr. Cooper is well known in this community as a very able business man, and through his prompt and honorable business methods, the present successful business has been built up.

HARTUNG & SANDFORD, Boat Builders.

Passaic Avenue, East Newark, N. J., Yachts, Working Boats, Canoes, etc., Built to Order, Spoon and Straight Oars Made. Boat building is one of the earliest industries of which we have any record. From the earliest ages the people who lived by the sea had boats, even if they had no houses to cover their heads. We hardly realize to what a state of perfection the art of boat building has been brought until we read of the rude and clumsy vessels used by our forefathers. The ordinary "land-lubber" does not know a good boat from a poor one, and, therefore, when wishing to purchase one, it is all important that he should apply to a firm whose word he can trust, and upon the products of whose house he may depend. As a prominent example of such, we take pleasure in recommending to our readers Messrs. Hartung & Sandford, of East Newark, N. J. Their business was established in 1880 by the late Mr. B. H. Price. After carrying it on for seven years Mr. Price retired, and was succeeded by the present proprietors, Messrs. George Hartung and Joseph Sandford. These gentlemen are both natives of Harrison, in this State, and are well known throughout the neighboring country. They are engaged in building boats of various kinds, yachts, working boats, canoes, etc., which they make to order. They also have a special line of fine hard wood row boats, which are fitted with spoon or straight oars, according to order. They occupy premises of 82x210 feet dimensions, and give employment to three assistants. Orders sent to Passaic avenue, East Newark, N. J., will receive prompt attention. Messrs. Hartung & Sandford have established a firm reputation for the quality of their products, and their business is rapidly increasing. A feature of the establishment is a large steam engine and boiler. Boats of all kinds are built, sold, exchanged and rented to private individuals, social parties and clubs.

HAMMOND BEEF CO., Commission Dealers

in Geo. H. Hammond's Western Dressed Beef, Mutton, Lamb, Etc., Harrison Avenue and Second Street, East Newark, N. J. Among the most prominent wholesale beef establishments in this city and its surroundings, is the one conducted by Mr. Henry F. Coffin, the commission dealer in George H. Hammond's western dressed beef, mutton, lamb, etc. Mr. Coffin is a native of Portland, Maine, where he is identified in the same business. He also figures prominently in the town of Dover, New Hampshire, where he carries on a large meat business. The inception of his Harrison enterprise took place in the year 1886, since which time the business has developed extensively, it being in a position to fill orders of any magnitude. It is only within a few years that western beef has been so universally used, but it is now considered the best, and Mr. Coffin deals in no other. His business demands the consumption of between 150 and 175 cattle per week, besides large numbers of sheep and a full stock of veal and pork meat. The premises utilized are situated on Second street, near the corner of Harrison avenue, Harrison, New Jersey, and are of the dimensions of 30x65 feet. A spacious and separate building is also utilized as a stable and wagon conservatory. Eight assistants are employed, and all orders receive immediate and careful attention. Mr. Coffin's establishment is equipped with every facility for the proper keeping and most advantageous handling of meats. The house is a popular one with all classes of dealers on the goods carried by it, for the proprietor is a thorough and square business man, and makes it a point to please his patrons by furnishing the best of everything in his line. Orders are received either by mail or telephone, (256). Mr. Coffin has a valuable assistant in the person of Mr. Melvin B. Dyer, a gentleman also a native of Portland, Maine. He has for many years been Mr. Coffin's bookkeeper.

G. H. WINANS, Manufacturer of Fine

and Medium Grade Crush Hats, Fancy Mixed Colors a specialty, Special Line of Soft Hats. 608 Passaic Avenue, East Newark, N. J. We have had occasion to note a large number of hat manufacturers in our review of Newark and its business men, and as we leave that busy city and turn our steps to East Newark, we find that the large enterprises, if not so numerous here, are quite as extensive and important. Noticeable among these is the manufactory of G. H. Winans, which is a large establishment engaged in the production of fine and medium grade crush hats, of which he

makes a specialty. The demand for this style of hat is increasing every year, and the companies engaged in the business are often hard pushed to supply the market. The house which is the subject of this article was founded in 1887, by G. H. Winans & Bro. The latter has since died and Mr. G. H. Winans is sole proprietor. Thoroughly familiar with this business, and not only supervising the workings, but taking an active part in all its practical details, Mr. Winans is prepared to compete with any other houses engaged in this industry, both in the quality of the goods and the prices charged for them. He does a large wholesale business, and is enabled to fill orders at short notice. The building used is two stories in height and is 75x200 feet in dimensions. The machinery, which is of the most improved modern kind, is operated by a 50 horse power engine. The business is divided in various departments, such as forming, coloring, blocking, trimming, etc., in which employment is given to sixty hands. Mr. Winans makes a special line of soft hats, in which the fancy mixed colors differ from the usual run of such goods. The factory is located at 608 Passaic avenue, East Newark, N. J.

E. BIERMAN, Dealer in Boots, Shoes, and

Rubbers, 226 Harrison Avenue, Harrison, N. J. Young and old, we are all particular about our footwear. To a certain extent, we have cause to wish to have our pedal extremities appear as nicely dressed as our other articles of dress, for bodily comfort is involved, and that's what makes the "rub" come in. A perfect fitting and easy shoe, whether it be upon the tiny foot of the rosy-cheeked baby, the boisterous school boy, the blushing maiden, the kind old man or woman, or any one else, is always a thing to be envied and admired by those who are unfortunate enough to buy where ill-fitting and uncomfortable footwear is sold. At the establishment conducted by the gentleman whose card heads this article, special attention is paid to this particular, for Mr. Bierman, who knows what a perfectly fitting shoe is, buys all his goods with a view of carrying an entire stock on the correct fit principal. Said stock is also selected by Mr. Bierman with a view of being able to offer none but strictly dependable goods to his patrons and of returning a fair equivalent for every dollar he receives. This is what we term honest business methods, and what has built up Mr. Bierman's large trade. This gentleman is a native of Newark, and has hosts of friends there, and in Harrison and Kearny. He inaugurated his enterprise in the year 1882, and it has steadily increased in patronage and in popularity ever since its inception. The store is 25x65 feet in dimensions and is admirably adapted as to location, fixtures, etc., for the boot and shoe business. Mr. B. owns the property. Two efficient and courteous assistants are employed and all patrons receive painstaking attention. We heartily endorse Mr. Bierman's store and his goods, for we believe he tries to do what is right in all his dealings with the public.

HARRIS BROS., Practical Horse Shoers.

Horses Shod on the Latest Principles, accompanied with Scientific Workmanship, No. 19 Harrison Avenue. The establishment conducted by Messrs. James and Michael Harris at No. 19 Harrison avenue, in this town, was inaugurated in the year 1865 by Mr. S. Tierney. Since its inception the stand has always been in the hands of good horse shoers, and never under better management than since the Harris Bros. took charge. Both these gentlemen are scientific, practical, theoretical, anatomical and experienced horse shoers. This takes in all the requirements to make up the necessary knowledge which a horse shoer should possess. Those owning horses may take them to this shop in perfect peace as to the work being properly executed. Lame and interfering animals are paid special attention to, and are treated humanely. Steel shoes are put on if desired, and track and road horses are shod in perfect satisfaction. The shop is 25x50 feet and accommodates many horses at once. Skilled workmen are the only ones employed, and five are kept the year round. Some of the most delicate shoes in the city are turned out from the Messrs. Harris Brothers anvils. Samples may be seen on application at the shop, and the gentlemen in question are pleased to receive visitors. We can safely recommend our readers to patronize this firm, as we rely on their superior workmanship and knowledge of their business. The prices quoted are as low as anywhere in the city, and the work executed is better. The advantages to be derived in having horses shod by the Harris Bros. are therefore obvious.

P. RIORDAN & SONS,

—— DEALERS IN ——

Choice Meats & Provisions,

No. 411 FOURTH STREET,

Cor. Latham,   Harrison, N. J.

The name of the above concern has been identified with the history of Harrison for the past thirty-two years ; and Mr. Patrick Riordan, its founder, must have seen the town in its comparative infancy, for we believe the houses were then a little more scattered than they are now. Certain it is, however, that Harrison has changed much since those days, and that it was never in a better way to prosper than at present, for a perceptible "boom" in building and business is now being enacted. Mr. Riordan is a native of Ireland, and came to this country in 1847. He was engaged in business in Milwaukee, Wis., for three years, and in Chicago two years. The greater portion of his business career has been in Harrison, however, and we deem it a pleasure to chronicle the success which has attended this gentleman's efforts in this, his adopted land. Mr. Riordan is a self-made man. What he has got he worked hard and perseveringly for. The men who have started with nothing and have succeeded in accumulating a comfortable bunch of the "wherewithal" necessary to successfully paddle through this life in ease, can be numbered. This shows that the results attained by Mr. Riordan are the fruits of his past, and even present, able business management. He began his meat business on a very small scale, but it now is one of the largest markets in Harrison, Kearny or Newark. About twelve cattle are weekly consumed, and four wagons are on the go night and day. Ten clerks are employed, and every one is served courteously and promptly. Mr. Riordan admitted his sons, David and Joseph, into partnership with him in 1884. Mr. David Riordan is a native of Milwaukee, and his brother Joseph was born in Harrison. These brothers seem to have inherited the "push" which has characterized their father, for they are business men of ability, and though yet comparatively young men, they are heavy real estate owners in this town. Mr. Joseph Riordan's residence, on Fifth street, and David Riordan's, on the corner of Third and Cross streets, are prominently fine looking dwellings in this section. Their meat market is elaborately fitted up with the costliest fixtures and a splendid ice box. The meat and vegetables handled are A1 in quality. This fact is what has built up the establishment to the good reputation it now enjoys. We advise all who do not already do so, to patronize this establishment. Economy is practiced by so doing, as the house buys in such large quantities that it can afford to sell much cheaper than smaller concerns Mr. Patrick Riordan was Alderman one term twelve years ago, and "Town Committeman" twenty-two years ago. He is a man who has traveled extensively, and recently returned from a three-months' trip to the "Old Country." We earnestly hope the success the father has attained will, in years to come, be doubly honored by his sons, for just such enterprising business men are needed to make of Harrison the important business centre it is destined to become.

JOHN J. COYLE, Carpenter and Builder, Shop, Warren Street; residence, corner Fourth and Warren Streets, Harrison, N. J. Mr. John J. Coyle is a native of Newark, N. J., and has carried on operations in Harrison for about five years. His shop is located on Warren street, and is of the dimensions of 20x50 feet, and is thoroughly equipped with all necessary facilities for carrying on carpenter work to the best possible advantage. Mr. Coyle is an experienced carpenter and builder, and devotes close and careful attention to his business, and much of the success which he has won is due to his policy of keeping thoroughly informed concerning the many details of his enterprise. He is prepared to draw plans and furnish estimates, and is constantly striving to do his best for the interests of his patrons. From fifteen to twenty-five experienced and reliable assistants are given employment, and all work is given, painstaking attention, and is executed in a thoroughly satisfactory manner, without any delays, and the terms to be made with the gentleman in question will be found to be as satisfactory as his work is reliable. Orders by mail may be directed to his residence, corner Fourth and Warren streets, and they will receive immediate attention. Mr. Coyle is known to be one of the most conscientious building contractors in this vicinity. He invariably honors every stipulation in his contracts and furnishes just what is called for in the specifications. Within three years he has erected nearly one hundred and twenty-five dwelling houses in this immediate section. His father, Mr. Michael Coyle, had been the only building contractor in Harrison and Kearny previous to eighteen years ago. A list of the fine buildings which Mr. Coyle has erected in the past five years of his business would take up more space than we have allotted; we will state, however, that it can be obtained on application, and it will be found that some of the edifices in question are architectural designs of more than ordinary merit.

THE CENTRAL HAT STORE AND Gents' Furnishing Goods, Joseph Daly, Manager, Peter J. Goodman, Proprietor, Corner Harrison Avenue and Third Street, Harrison, N. J. Also Stationery, Printing and Newspapers, 301 Harrison Avenue. The Central hat store and gents' furnishing goods house owned by Mr. Peter J. Goodman, and managed by Mr. Joseph Daly, in this town, needs no introduction to our readers, for it has now been before the public for two years, and has proven itself worthy of the large patronage it has received. Mr. Goodman inaugurated his business in 1888, as we have intimated, and as he has always carried a fine stock of hats, caps and furnishings, at prices which seemed reasonable enough to suit the most judicious buyers, the investment has been a good one. Mr. Joseph Daly, the well known genial manager of the business, deserves credit for part of the honors, for he has worked faithfully to bring about the present state of things. Every article usually carried in an establishment of this nature will be found in Mr. Goodman's stock of goods. Mr. Goodman also conducts another business at No. 301 Harrison avenue, of quite a different nature from that we have just spoken about; it is that of general newsdealer, stationer and printer. He also keeps a refreshment saloon on the second floor of this number of the street. Confectionery and ice cream are served here, and books, papers, magazines and periodicals are for sale. This is a large and pleasant apartment 25x45 feet in dimensions. Two assistants are employed at the hat store and live at the other establishment. Mr. Goodman is a native of New York city, and is the Assistant Chief of the Harrison Fire Department. He also occupies the distinguished office of Secretary of the Board of Education. We need say no more as to the esteem in which Mr. Goodman is held by his fellow towns people.

KEARNY.

Kearny township, which is another suburb of Newark, is in Hudson County, and is situated on the east bank of the Passaic river, just north of Harrison. It was included in Harrison in 1867, when it was made a separate township, and named Kearny in honor of Major General Philip Kearny, who was killed in the battle of Chantilly, Va., September 1st, 1862. General Kearny's home was in this township for many years. His homestead property is now in the possession of his son, General John Watts Kearny. It occupies a commanding hill some distance back from the river and in appearance resembles an ancient castle. It is a landmark for miles around. Kearny is fast becoming a manufacturing town of considerable importance. The Clark (O. N. T.) Thread Works have a very large series of buildings there, exceeding in size and extent their Newark plant, of which it is a part. These works give employment to over three thousand hands. At these works is the tallest factory chimney in the United States, and one of the four tallest in the world. It is three hundred and thirty feet high, is fourteen feet wide at the base and seven feet wide at the top. It required over a million bricks to construct it, and for weeks after its completion was visited by thousands of people. The Clark Thread Co. is an offshoot of the Anchor Mills at Paisley, Scotland, where the Clarks have an enormous establishment. The Kearny works were built in 1875 and have several times since been added to.

A little south of the Clark Thread Works on the river front is another vast series of brick buildings. These constitute the works of the Clark Mile End Thread Co., who also employ several thousand hands and do a very large business. A short distance to the north of the Clark (O. N. T.) Thread Works are the works of the Marshall Linen Thread Co. This Company has also a large system of buildings, and in addition to using linen thread are now engaged in spinning flax and manufacturing a number of articles from it, such as towels, napkins and other articles for household use. Indeed, it was largely owing to the efforts of this Company and the fact that they were able to demonstrate before a committee Congress that flax could be spun, bleached and woven in this country as well as in the European manufactories that Congress was induced to put a higher tariff on flax and linen goods. Still farther north on the river bank are the Nairn Linoleum Works, which also have a number of massive brick buildings and employ several hundred hands. The plant of this company is a very valuable one as it contains many large, intricate and expensive machines. This company came to Kearny a few years ago from Scotland and were induced to come here by the fact that, owing to the high tariff on imported goods of this kind, the company found it much cheaper to come to America and make their goods here.

Another point of interest in Kearny is the New Jersey Soldiers' Home, an institution supported by the State of New Jersey, for the care of sick and disabled soldiers—veterans of the late war. The main building was formerly the home of a Mr. Knapp, a wealthy New York merchant, who moved to California several years ago. The house was finished in the most elaborate style of luxury and architectural beauty in the interior, and was regarded for many years as the handsomest house in this part of New Jersey. It was purchased by the trustees of the New Jersey Home for Soldiers, some four or five years ago, after which the State expended large sums of money in altering the Knapp house, erecting additional buildings and laying out the grounds. This Home is regarded as one of the best soldiers' homes in the country. It was originally established on Seventh avenue, Newark, where it occupied a series of frame buildings, which were little more than barracks. The home is in charge of Major Peter F. Roger, who has been the Superintendent for many years, and is himself a veteran of the late war. It is under the control of a Board of Trustees, appointed by the Governor and Legislature, and is maintained by an appropriation made by the Legislature each year.

Not far from the Soldiers' Home is the Roman Catholic Protectory for boys, which is a large and flourishing institution, and is doing an excellent work in reforming unruly boys.

Leading Business Men of Kearny.

MARSHALL & CO., Manufacturers of Linen Threads, Yarns and Twines, Shrewsbury Mills, Kearny, N. J.; Mail Address, P. O. Box 256, Newark, N. J.; Shipping Address, East Newark, N. J. The Shrewsbury Mills are in all probability among the oldest of such establishments in the country. They were founded more than a century ago, in 1787, by John Marshall, in England. As is usually the case in a business of the magnitude to which this has attained, it was begun in a small way, and has gradually developed into a powerful Company. The American branch of the house was started in 1886, and incorporated with William Clark as President; R. R. Symington, Treasurer; Robert Cummings, Secretary. These gentlemen are favorably known in Newark, and the Company occupies a prominent position among the manufacturing houses in this section. They are wholesale manufacturers of linen threads, yarns and twines of every kind and variety, in which they do an enormous business, and supply wholesale and retail houses throughout the country. The main building is four stories in height and measures 500x64 feet in dimensions, besides which several other buildings are utilized. Employment is given to between eight and nine hundred skilled operatives, and the machinery, which is of the finest and most approved make, is run by an eight hundred-horse-power engine. Orders sent by mail to P. O. Box 256 Newark, N. J., will receive prompt attention, while the shipping address is Harrison, N. J. The Shrewsbury Mills are well worth a visit of inspection to those who wish to employ a few hours agreeably and profitably

THOMAS HEWITT & CO., Iron Foundry, Light and Heavy Castings Done at the Lowest Prices, Round and Square Columns of all Sizes, also Makers of the Kearny Patent Grate Bars; all Orders Promptly Attended to, Sherman Avenue, opposite Second Street, Kearny, N. J. The foundry which Mr. Thomas Hewitt & Co. conduct in this place was established by them in the year 1889. Though not yet long in existence, it has already gained its share of patronage from the numerous manufacturing establishments in this vicinity. The "Co." in the firm is Mr. James Hewitt, a native of Ireland; Mr. Thomas Hewitt is also a native of that country, and both gentlemen have long resided in the United States. They employ a dozen skilled workmen the year round, and do jobbing of all kinds. Light and heavy castings are both paid especial attention to, as well as the manufacturing of both round and square churns. The work and productions of this foundry are high in grade, and the trade has not been slow to find it out. The premises made use of are located on Sherman avenue, opposite Second street, in Kearny, and are of the dimensions of 40x75 feet. A ten-horse power engine and a fourteen-horse power boiler are features of the foundry, and the latter is fully equipped with all the necessary apparatus to successfully carry on the business, and dispatch all orders, large or small, with an accuracy and celerity worthy of commendation. Estimates cheerfully furnished in house work. Sewer rings manufactured at lowest prices

A. GREENFIELD, Grocer, Dealer in Fine Teas, Coffees and Spices, Foreign and Domestic Fruits and Nuts, Flour, Feed, Hay, Oats and Straw, Central Avenue, corner Second Street, Kearny, N. J. The purpose of this house since its inception has been to furnish reliable goods at the lowest market rates, and the enterprising efforts of the proprietor have met with hearty appreciation from his patrons. A fine stock of choice groceries, flour, feed, hay, oats and straw, together with fruits and nuts, both foreign and domestic will be found at this store, which is well fitted up and is 38x23 feet in dimensions, and there is also a large basement which is used for the storage of the stock on hand. Mr. A. Greenfield is a native of England and is very well known in this community, having served on the Board of Education for four years, 1882-1886. He began business operations here in 1880, and his success has been great and well deserved. He gives employment to two competent assistants, who attend to the filling of all orders with a care and promptness which is commendable. The goods carried in stock are all selected with great care, and with the interests of the purchasing public in view, and are sold with a guarantee to prove exactly as represented in every instance, and uniformly low rates are quoted on all commodities handled. A call at this deservedly popular store, which is located corner Second street and Central avenue, will verify the facts stated above. Orders taken for coal.

W. R. BALL, Dealer in Fine Family, Staple and Fancy Groceries, Yankee Notions, etc. Proprietor of "Union Hall" and the Elegant Restaurant in same Building, Corner of Grant and Central Avenues, Kearny, New Jersey. No one spot is better and more widely known in this town, outside of the big thread works, than that upon which stands the building known to the residents of the vicinity as "Union Hall," for it is the rendezvous of the large majority of the population of this place, both in a business and social standpoint. The well stocked grocery store of itself is a "bee-hive" for business, for hundreds of the families whose members are employed in the thread works, trade at this popular establishment. The reason of this popularity is accounted for by the fact that, since the sixteen years Mr. Ball has managed this enterprise, he has never failed to supply his patrons with any but strictly reliable and dependable goods at as low prices as can be bought anywhere in the largest retail grocery establishments in this city, or larger ones. Though doing business in a comparatively small place, the "rush from the malls" swells it largely. Mr. Ball is consequently forced to renew his stock frequently (a good thing for all concerned), and buying in such large wholesale quantities, he is enabled to share the correspondingly large rebate thereby obtained with his customers. He also conducts a spacious and elegant restaurant for the special accommodation of employees of the mills. Many of said employees have no homes and are obliged to reside in "furnished rooms" and lead a "restaurant" life. It is monotony enough, we all know, to be so situated as to be obliged to go through life thus, still, those who partake of the hospitality of Mr. Ball's restaurant do not complain, as he tries to make this portion of his business especially agreeable and homelike for one and all. A pleasant "good morning" or a kindly feeling often gladens the heart of those who have no home, and Mr. Ball seems to have a chord somewhere in "unison" susceptible of the fact, for he is a whole-handed and warm-hearted, genial gentleman, whose very presence spreads an atmosphere of content and satisfaction upon the faces of all who have dealings with him. His trade is chiefly help from the mills, but commercial travelers (the drummers) and the transients who have occasion to transact business either at Clark's O. N. T. or the Mile End Thread Works, make this popular restaurant their lunch room. Good meals are served and everybody is provided with plenty to eat, well cooked to order and substantial. People who work hard or travel all day can't live on toothpicks, nice dishes and ice-water! Nor do those who patronize this popular restaurant do so, either. In connection with this department of his business, Mr. Ball rents for concerts, dances, lectures and other purposes a large 25x56 feet hall over his restaurant. It is called Union Hall; over this are smaller halls occupied by societies, lodges, clubs, religious bodies, all among etc. Prominent among the bodies who meet in these rooms are the Knights of Honor, Knights and Ladies of the Golden Star, the Apollo Society, North Reform Mission, the O. N. T. and Mile End Spinners, Dawn

of Hope Good Templars, the First and Second District Republican Clubs, and the Methodist Sunday School and Mission. He is an old and well known resident of Kearny.

JOHN CONNOLLY, Carpenter and Builder, Jobbing Promptly Attended to, Satisfaction Guaranteed, Woodland Avenue, off Kearny Avenue, Next to Township Hall, Kearny, N. J. Mr. John Connolly has carried on business in Kearny for a number of years, and is well known and highly esteemed. He became identified with his present business here in 1883, and has gained in the time elapsed since then an enviable reputation for upright and honorable methods in all his transactions, and is known to be one of the most reliable builders to be found in Kearny. His premises are located on Woodland avenue, off Kearny Avenue, and are of the dimensions of 24x18 feet, and all necessary facilities are at hand to give prompt and skilful attention to orders for buildings of all descriptions. Six assistants is the average number employed, and this force can easily be increased at short notice when occasion requires. Jobbing orders are given prompt attention, and work is executed in a thoroughly satisfactory manner. Mr. Connolly also deals in lumber of all kinds, and can furnish it in quantities to suit purchasers at the most reasonable prices. In fact his terms in every part of his business are very moderate, and his high reputation for fair dealing has been honestly earned. Mr. Connolly buys lots, builds on them and sells. He always has several desirable houses for sale or exchange, and parties wishing to procure a house of their own can do no better than to consult him.

WM. RYAN, Dealer in Staple and Fancy Groceries, Fresh Teas, Flour, Feed, Oats, etc. 3 Kearny Avenue. Kearny, N. J. The establishment carried on by Mr. Wm. Ryan, is one of those stores which make no great pretentions, and yet could be much less easily spared than many a more imposing and more extensive place of business. Mr. Ryan occupies a store 18x37 feet in dimensions, and carries a clean and desirable stock of staple and fancy groceries, flour, feed, oats, etc. He is a native of New Jersey, and has become widely and favorably known in this vicinity, since founding his present business in 1888. The store is located at No. 3 Kearny avenue, and is supplied with all necessary facilities to enable orders to be accurately and promptly filled. The popularity of this store is due to many causes, but to none more than the uniform reliability of the goods furnished. Mr. Ryan makes it a point to obtain his supplies from entirely reputable sources, and hence is in a position to guarantee his goods to prove just as represented. Two competent assistants are employed, who render courteous and immediate attention to all callers, while Mr. Ryan gives close personal attention to his business, and sees that all his plans are strictly carried out. All prices quoted by him will bear the strictest comparison with those quoted by other dealers on similar goods, quality for quality.

THOS. SMITH, Florist; designs of every description at short notice; fine Roses and Cut Flowers; special attention to Weddings, Parties, etc.; Landscape Gardener, Nos. 54 and 56 Johnson Avenue, opposite Erie Railroad bridge, Kearny, N. J. The subject of this sketch, Mr. Thomas Smith, was born in Ireland. Coming to this country many years ago, he has, like many of his fellow countrymen, made it the country of his adoption, and is to-day one of the most esteemed citizens of this community. A proof of his having been a thrifty business man may be found in the fact that he is an extensive real estate owner in Kearny. The property on which he resides at Nos. 54 and 56 Johnson avenue, is owned by him, as well as the three spacious greenhouses in which he cultivates the beautiful flowers therein to be found; these are the dimensions of 168x8 feet each, so that 3,840 square feet of flower beds are covered by glass. Besides this, wide stretches of land extend on every side and are utilized for the growth of plants, flowers, trees, shrubbery, etc., etc. Mr. Smith has had over fifteen years experience in his chosen line of business and knows it thoroughly. He is a botanist and a deep student in everything that pertains to that science. His business was inaugurated by him four years ago, and has each day increased in growth and popularity. He is prepared to execute designs of every description at short notice. Bouquets for weddings, balls, concerts and other purposes are quoted at low prices. Fine roses and sweet scenting flowers abound on his premises, and a large stock is always on hand

WORKS OF THE NAIRN LINOLEUM COMPANY, KEARNY, N. J

THE NAIRN LINOLEUM CO. Their Works at Kearny, N. J. The growing appreciation on the part of the American public of the high value of linoleum as a floor covering, and the consequent rapid growth of the demand for this article, have, as a natural result, stimulated the competition between domestic and foreign manufacturers for an outlet in this market. In the early days of the trade, when our home manufacturing was in a crude and practically an experimental state, imported goods readily sold, owing to their superiority. But now, since our American manufacturers have built up the industry, grown skilled and powerful, foreign fabrics are at a disadvantage. The firm of M. Nairn & Co., of Kirkcaldy, Scotland, who are probably the leading manufacturers of linoleum on the other side, and who, previous to the development of our own manufacturing ability, enjoyed a large American trade, were shrewd enough to discern this fact, and recognize its full portent, at once began to consider the advisability of establishing themselves here on a permanent basis. As the result of this consideration, they associated themselves with the well known New York carpet manufacturers, W. & J. Sloane, and in the spring of 1886 the two firms organized under the laws of the State of New Jersey as the "Nairn Linoleum Company." The officers of the company are Michael B. Nairn, president; John Sloane, vice-president; Peter Campbell, treasurer and secretary. The corporation at once obtained as a site for the location of their plant suitable property in Kearny, N. J., a suburb of the city of Newark, comprising several acres of land and a valuable water front on the Passaic river. Here ground was broken for the erection of the buildings in the month of May, 1887, and in the unprecedentedly short time of a year from that date, they were completed and ready for work. The buildings, as shown in our illustration of the company's works, are six in number. Two of them are each 60x300 and two stories high; one is 130x150 and is 73 feet high, and the other three are detached buildings used for the storage of spirits, oils, etc. They are built entirely of brick, and in a manner so thorough, substantial and solid as to at once impress the beholder as being far superior to the usual methods of constructing factory buildings in this country. They are immensely strong, and apparently are intended to endure for ages. In the matter of their appointments, the same painstaking care and regardlessness of cost are to be observed, and, therefore, it can be justly said that the entire plant, buildings, equipments and all, are as complete and perfect as money and experience can make them. Motive force is supplied to the works by an immense Corliss engine of 1,000 horse power. This engine is of the most recent double compound tandem type. Steam is generated in four steel boilers, which, in the aggregate, represent the power of 7,000 horses. The value of the plant is estimated at over one-half million dollars and employment is given to 500 hands. Mr. Peter Campbell, besides being treasurer and secretary of the organization, is its efficient superintendent. Mr. Campbell, previous to assuming his present position, was connected with the parent house in Scotland, where, for over seventeen years, he had been gaining the experience and ability which now is put to such good use. Mr. Campbell states that the works at Kearny are very similar in plan to those at Kirkcaldy, Scotland, although the former are vastly superior in point of architectural design and mechanical equipment.

SHROPE & TARBOX. Fancy and family Groceries, Butter, Eggs, Vegetables, Tobacco, Cigars, Etc., Central Grocers, Corner Johnston and Kearny Avenues, Kearny, N. J. An accommodating spirit and a determination to do the fair thing in every transaction are powerful aids to success in every business enterprise, and they have not failed to exercise their usual effect in the case of Messrs. Shrope & Tarbox. The business now conducted by these gentlemen was founded in 1882 by Mr. P. W. Wolfe. In 1889, Mr. Shrope became associated with the first named gentleman, and during the current year the present firm was founded. It is composed of Mr. B. Shrope, who is a native of Hunterdon Co., (where he has been Assessor, and Overseer of the Poor), and Mr. W. A. Tarbox of Mass. The premises utilized by this firm are located corner Johnston and Kearny avenues, and comprise a store 20x50 feet in size and a basement, where a very extensive wholesale and retail trade is carried on in fancy and family groceries, butter, eggs, vegetables, etc. This stock is one of the best in Kearny, being very complete in every department. Employment is given to six thoroughly experienced assistants, and everything is so arranged as to permit of the prompt and accurate filling of all orders. A fine line of cigars of all the best brands, together with tobacco, is also carried, and the lowest terms can be made on these as on all other goods dealt in, while everything offered is guaranteed to be exactly as represented in every respect. Mr. Tarbox has recently returned from the West, where he has been engaged in the cattle and horse business. His headquarters were in Wyoming, but he also has visited Texas and California

INDEX TO BUSINESS NOTICES.

INDEX TO BUSINESS NOTICES

www.ingramcontent.com/pod-product-compliance
Lightning Source LLC
Chambersburg PA
CBHW030845270326
41928CB00007B/1218